Our Changing Rural Society:
Perspectives and Trends

Our Changing Rural Society:
Perspectives and Trends

Our Changing Rural Society: Perspectives and Trends

Published under the auspices
of the Rural Sociological Society
with the cooperation of the
Center for Agricultural and
Economic Development at
Iowa State University

James H. Copp, editor

IOWA STATE UNIVERSITY PRESS,

Ames, IOWA, U.S.A.

Other publications of the Center for Agricultural and Economic Development are available as follows.   (Work of the Center is supported in part by a grant from the W. K. Kellogg Foundation):

From the Iowa State University Press (hard-bound books):

Food—One Tool in International Economic Development, 1962.

Labor Mobility and Population in Agriculture, 1961.

Goals and Values in Agricultural Policy, 1961.

Dynamics of Land Use: Needed Adjustments, 1961.

Adjustments in U.S. Agriculture: A National Basebook, 1961.

(Problems and Policies of American Agriculture, 1959 - out of print.)

From the Center for Agricultural and Economic Development:

An Evaluation of Weather Factors in the Production of Corn, 1962.

Cold War, World Poverty and Land-Grant Colleges, 1962.

New Areas of Land-Grant Extension Education, 1962.

Bargaining Power in Agriculture, 1961.

Price and Income Policies, 1961.

How Agriculture Operates—In Production, In Marketing, 1961.

Consumer Preferences and Market Development for Farm Products, 1960.

Adjustment and Its Problems in Southern Iowa, 1959.

© 1964 The Iowa State University Press
Ames, Iowa 50010. All rights reserved

Printed in the U.S.A.

First edition, 1964
Second printing, 1965
Third printing, 1966
Fourth printing, 1971

Library of Congress Catalog Card Number: 64-13369
International Standard Book Number: 0-8138-1211-9

Facsimile Edition International Standard Book Number: 0-8138-2425-7

Preface

THIS BOOK deals with the changing rural society of the United States from a number of different points of view—population, power, community, social change. The intent of the book is to present an analysis of the contemporary context of American rural society, to closely examine changes in specific portions of that society, and to propose certain perspectives for future work. The book is a partial summarization of what rural sociologists are doing and a sign of their future contribution to the understanding of our changing society. It is presented to the public as an aid in delineating and interpreting the dramatic transformations taking place in rural life.

The chapters included were originally presented as invited papers at the 1961 annual meeting of the Rural Sociological Society at Iowa State University, Ames. Each contributor developed a major paper summarizing the state of knowledge in his field of specialization. This volume therefore surveys work in several major areas where rural sociologists are making a substantial contribution but recognizes the impossibility of covering the entire broad area.

The title, Our Changing Rural Society: Perspectives and Trends, is intended to reflect the contents of the book accurately. In a general overview of the changes in our rural society, the first chapter, by Robin Williams, is the most general—providing a broad portrait of the changes in American society. The second chapter, coauthored by Olaf Larson and Everett Rogers, continues the macroscopic approach in an analysis of the changes taking place in the rural sector of our society.

The next four chapters form the heart of the book, so far as detailed examination of trends is concerned. Donald Bogue and Calvin Beale present the major changes in the distribution and composition of the nation's population, as viewed from the perspective of rural society. Christopher Sower and Paul Miller discuss the organization and transformation of the structure of agricultural power in relation to changes in the over-all societal context. Lee Burchinal next summarizes the research

on the changing American (and rural) family. Thomas Ford and
Willis Sutton bring this second part to a close by reviewing the
findings from community research as they reflect a changing
rural society at the local level.

The next four chapters deal with social change from quite
different perspectives. The first, by George Beal, represents
his most recent conceptualization of the social action construct
for inducing change in large systems. This is followed by Joe
Bohlen's concise summarization of the empirical findings from
farm practice adoption research. This, in turn, is succeeded
by Robert Bealer and Frederick Fliegel's iconoclastic chapter
attacking the notion that "social change" should be a substantive
area of study. The section ends with Irwin Sanders' presentation of a sociological perspective for community development.
A final section discussing the future of rural sociology in
American society concludes the book.

Though the book centers on the United States case, the cosmopolitan bias of authors and editor leads them to hope that the
trends and perspectives noted herein are of more than local import or timely significance. As Sanders' paper suggests, our
orientation is outward. Most of the world's people are still
rural, and there is reason to suspect that the American case is
not an isolated instance of an industrializing and urbanizing
society.

Many others, in addition to the authors and editor, have made
this book possible: the Program Committee for the 1961 annual
meeting of the Rural Sociological Society—George M. Beal,
Emory J. Brown, Olaf F. Larson, Selz C. Mayo, Eugene A.
Wilkening, and M. E. John; the participants in the seminars at
the annual meeting; an editorial reviewing committee, composed of Thomas R. Ford, George M. Beal, and the editor; the
officers of the Rural Sociological Society by their encouragement; the Center for Agricultural and Economic Development
at Iowa State University by its generous support; and the Iowa
State University Press, through which publication has been effected. Sincere acknowledgment is hereby made to these all for
their willing cooperation and generous assistance in this undertaking.

The Contributors:

GEORGE M. BEAL--Professor of Sociology, Iowa State University.

CALVIN L. BEALE—Supervisory Statistician, Farm Population Branch, United States Department of Agriculture.

ROBERT C. BEALER—Assistant Professor of Rural Sociology, Pennsylvania State University.

DONALD J. BOGUE—Population Research and Training Center, University of Chicago.

JOE M. BOHLEN—Professor of Rural Sociology, Iowa State University.

LEE G. BURCHINAL—Welfare Administration, United States Department of Health, Education, and Welfare.

JAMES H. COPP—Associate Professor of Rural Sociology, Pennsylvania State University.

FREDERICK C. FLIEGEL--Associate Professor of Rural Sociology, Pennsylvania State University.

THOMAS R. FORD--Professor of Sociology, Rural Sociology, and Behavioral Science, University of Kentucky.

OLAF F. LARSON—Professor and Head of the Department of Rural Sociology, Cornell University.

PAUL A. MILLER--President, West Virginia University.

EVERETT M. ROGERS—Associate Professor of Rural Sociology, Ohio State University.

IRWIN T. SANDERS—Associate Director, International Training and Research Program, The Ford Foundation.

CHRISTOPHER SOWER—Professor, Department of Sociology and Anthropology, Michigan State University.

WILLIS A. SUTTON, JR.—Associate Professor of Sociology and Executive Director of the Bureau of Community Service, University of Kentucky.

ROBIN M. WILLIAMS, JR.—Professor of Sociology, Cornell University.

vii

Contents

ix

x CONTENTS

IV. THE OPPORTUNITIES

PART ONE
The Context

I

Robin M. Williams, Jr.

American Society in Transition: Trends and Emerging Developments in Social and Cultural Systems

NONE OF US NEEDS to be told that American society is changing: everyone daily experiences the impact of this transition. The problem is rather to specify how American society is changing, to discover the trends and emerging developments in its social and cultural systems. The formulation of answers to this challenge is the responsibility of every generation of sociologists, if they are to validate their claim to having unique knowledge and tools for interpreting social reality.

Although the analysis of large-scale change in complex social systems was a central preoccupation of many of the nineteenth and early twentieth century sociologists, the resulting prototheories were later subjected to justly severe criticisms which highlighted vagueness, errors, and bias. For a time in the United States, the reaction against what was regarded as wanton speculative theorizing led to rejection of any hope of systematic, empirically validated theories of change. Very recently, however, a more hopeful atmosphere has become discernible, as renewed attention is being directed to the possibilities of analysis offered by new theoretical formulations, improved research strategies, and the accumulating data. Perhaps sociology is ready to reinstate social change in a revised and tempered form, to its list of reputable topics for research.[1]

In this chapter, it would have been possible to deal primarily with problems of theory or with problems of research emphases, designs, and methods. Our choice, however, is rather to focus upon substantive topics—to describe in a general way some of the most important changes in social and cultural structures which have occurred or are now in process on a national scale. Of necessity the description is highly compressed, and many errors of omission are inevitable.

The analysis will begin with a review of well-known but basic facts concerning changes in population, technology, and economic and political organization. This will be followed by a survey of changes in the major institutional sectors: kinship, social stratification, education, economy, polity, and religion. Against this background, and still proceeding at the societal level, we will examine changes in social organization and then attempt to analyze changes in values and beliefs. Finally, we will suggest a few promising theoretic approaches for interpreting the materials reviewed.

We will begin with a few very obvious and massive facts, which may provide clues to the underlying processes. First of all, it should be recalled that the social system of the United States emerged as a product of the great period of European expansion and population growth. From 1790 to 1960 the land area of this country expanded from less than 900 thousand square miles to nearly 3 million; its population from less than 4 million to about 180 million. American society has never been a static system in a fixed equilibrium with its environment: expansion and movement have been central themes of its history.

The familiar facts of population mobility in the United States are of fundamental sociological importance. Peopled by history's greatest voluntary intercontinental migration, this country has always been a nation on the move. In modern times, industrialization, urban growth, and agricultural changes have resulted in an enormous rural-urban interchange of population.

Since 1920 some 68 million people in the United States moved from farms to nonfarm areas, and 41 million moved the other way, leaving a net migration of 27 million[2]—a number nearly equal to the entire population of the nation in 1860. The vast growth of cities and other urbanized areas is the most obvious sign of the transformation of a rural-agricultural into an urban-industrial society—a process requiring a very great amount of internal migration.

The United States has become an urban society. By 1950 two-thirds of the population lived in essentially urban settings and the three largest urbanized areas (New York, Chicago, and Los Angeles) included nearly as many people as all the "true" rural farm areas of the entire country.[3] What has happened in the United States is simply one part of the present ". . . gigantic and pervasive revolution, the urbanization of the world." The modern cities are dominant features of societies that are "mechanized, industrialized, commercialized, specialized, interdependent."[4] Technological advances and highly developed forms of economic enterprises and other social organizations have made possible the present urban agglomerations. Broadly speaking, these same developments have increased the demand for urban workers and have diminished the demand for agricultural workers. The most obvious change in the occupational structure, correspondingly, has been the sharply decreasing proportion of workers in the agricultural labor force.

It can be shown that in a dynamic economy of the kind characterizing the United States during this development, labor is unlikely to shift out of the agricultural sector of the economy rapidly enough to equalize marginal real returns to farm and nonfarm workers of comparable type and grade. A by-product of our rapid economic development is that agriculture has been chronically "overmanned."

Patterns of internal migration are primarily, although not exclusively, the consequences of differential "economic" opportunities (including nonpecuniary rewards). Over the decades for which useful data are available, general mobility shows no sign of decreasing, and may be increasing. Although each census since 1860 has shown about one-fourth of the population living outside of the state of birth, the 1950 figure of 26.5 per cent is the largest recorded. Since 1948, when data were first collected, it has been found repeatedly that about 20 per cent of the population change house of residence each year.[5] Finally, there has been a definite increase in average annual migration from farms to nonfarm areas during the last two decades; farm workers are becoming more, rather than less, responsive to nonfarm opportunities.[6]

Urbanization and population mobility thus indicate the continuation of the expansion and fluidity long noted as outstanding characteristics of American society.

But what of immigration and emigration? Is America's interdependence with other countries in world-wide political and economic affairs reflected in the permeability of her boundaries

to migration? Leaving aside the history of that immigration
which had made the United States a "nation of nations," it had
seemed in the long period of isolationism and restricted immigration following World War I that American society might become a closed system. During 1901-10 nearly 9 million
immigrants were counted; in the depression decade of the 1930's
just over one-half million. Since World War II, however, immigration has increased, exceeding 2 million in the decade
1948-57, and the symbolically important "racial" restrictions to
naturalization have been removed by the Immigration and
Naturalization Act of 1952. The number of temporary visitors,
transit aliens, and other nonimmigrants admitted to the country
increased sharply in recent years, reaching a total of over
750,000 in 1957.[7] Movement across the national boundaries thus
continues to be culturally and politically important. However, a
diminishing proportion of the population is of foreign birth and,
on the whole, the vast forces of "Americanization" are reducing
ethnic diversity.

The technological transformations which have affected the
demographic and economic trends sketched above are too familiar to require elaboration. The American social system in
the twentieth century has been continuously under pressure from
an endemic technological "revolution." Although detailed documentation here is unnecessary, the extent of technological impacts may be suggested by a casual sampling of gross facts, viz.:

. . . By 1959, television sets were in 86 per cent of the nation's homes
and each set was turned on for over five hours a day.[8]

. . . From 1930 to 1956, the combined death rate per 100,000 population
from diphtheria, whooping cough, smallpox, and typhoid and paratyphoid
dropped from 251.5 to 24.9.[9]

From 1930 to 1956, the number of motor vehicle registrations increased
from 26.7 millions to 67.1 millions.[10]

In 1860 the total horsepower of all prime movers in the nation
was just short of 14 million; by 1930 the total was over 1.6 billion; and by 1955 it had reached the incomprehensible total of
7.1 billion.[11] Productive capacities and transportation and communication facilities show similar, if less dramatic, long-term
increases.

Thus there has developed a tightly organized and elaborately
interdependent economic system accompanied by a vast increase
in total national productivity. The magnitudes of the changes are
not easy to grasp. Real gross product per man-hour in the total
economy approximately doubled from 1929 to 1955.[12] From 1939

to 1954 real national income (in constant 1954 prices) approximately doubled.[13] Although millions of people in the United States still live in what must be called actual poverty by contemporary standards, there is no doubt that on the whole we now have The Affluent Society.

Moore[14] has suggested two basic generalizations concerning long-range trends in adaptations of social systems to "external" influences. First, changes in the physical and biological environment are increasingly predictable and subject to control; in consequence, social systems have acquired increased independence of "environment." Second, however, with reference to intersystem relations ". . . the multiplication of agencies of communication serves to reduce the isolation and thus the autonomy of societies, to increase the proportion and rate of changes from external sources, and thereby to increase 'cultural' interdependence and even homogeneity." The world was once characterized by a profusion of more or less separate local histories. We have now entered into a period of planetary or "universal" history. Nations and combinations of nations are at the most only partially autonomous; all major social systems are now semi-open systems vis-a-vis others.

Whatever may be the later course of human history, within the three and a half centuries since European settlement on the North American continent there has been a continuous growth of scientific and technological knowledge, and of the artifacts and human skills necessary to use knowledge in the control of environment. Although a catastrophic interruption of this trend is quite conceivable, within the limits of historical experience to date ". . . a rational, technical orientation to the natural or social order is an essentially irreversible intellectual revolution."[15]

Against the backdrop of these changes in technology and in the economy, a certain consistency is apparent in a series of complex changes in major social institutions. Brief sketches will suggest the panorama from which we later will draw some generalized observations concerning change of the system as a whole.

KINSHIP AND THE FAMILY

The general character of social change in American family patterns over the past century is too well known to require more than a reminder. Compared with families of today, the families

of 1861 were larger, had more intensive relations with an extended group of relatives, had fewer divorces, placed more
emphasis on authority and obedience, were less likely to act on
the premise of equality of the sexes, and had a larger and more
important role for elderly parents. The family was more often
a unit of economic production and a center of religious observance. Births and deaths were more likely to occur within the
home. Although we do not have definitive proof, it is likely that
"romantic love" was stressed less and "marital duty" more.
Both birth rates and death rates were higher than now.

As the family has dropped many of its functions and activities
(which have been taken over by industry, government, church,
school, and other agencies), it has become a more specialized
social unit. It specializes in the production and maintenance of
human personalities. Typical public concerns about the family
reflect this historical shift. More is expected from the family
in terms of "happiness"—of affection and sexual adjustment, of
mutual understanding, of "good" personality development of
children.

From colonial times down to the present, the basic European
forms of the family have been retained. But extended kinship
ties have diminished, and the effective unit of the system is
being reduced to the nuclear family of husband, wife, and imma-
ture children. In general, this historical process has decreased
the continuity between generations and has resulted in a relative
lack of place or function for aged parents. A stable system of
close, reciprocal obligations between kinsmen outside the inner
circle of the nuclear family appears to be highly dependent upon
a low rate of individual social and geographic mobility.

A second major trend has been the acquisition of a large number of legal and customary rights by women, resulting in much
emphasis on equality, and in a legal individuation of the family,
and in complicated changes in sex roles. The evidence seems
quite clear that the increase in the proportion of married women
who work for pay outside the home does not mean that women
are substituting a career for family obligations. Rather, it sig-
nifies that paid employment has been added to the ". . . traditional roster of womanly duties."[16]

A rising rate of divorce is recorded in every decade from
1870 to 1950; but if divorce increased, so did marriage: decade
by decade the age at marriage has dropped and the proportion
married has increased. It does not appear that the importance
of the family to individual persons has decreased, even though
its structural place in the social system has been reduced. As

economic and social functions once incorporated in the family
have dropped away, marriage has become increasingly a matter
of individual choice, and the unit has had to depend more than in
the past upon personal satisfactions and the individual's private
sense of obligations. The relatively isolated nuclear family in a
mobile and competitive society is exposed to unusual strains. It
is also a focus of high expectations, both in terms of the ideals
of romantic love and companionship between husband and wife
and in terms of standards for child-rearing which presuppose a
high evaluation of childhood and of individual personality development. Strong needs and high expectations are thus focused
within a small human group that has through the years come to
have fewer common activities and lessened definite social
support.

Although family planning has become a widespread norm, the
"baby boom" in the years immediately following World War II
has turned out to be a continuing phenomenon. Americans are
marrying earlier and having more children than in the days
when predictions of imminent population decline were commonly
voiced. And, as urban America pours out to the new suburbs,
we are witnessing a renewed emphasis on family life. Gone is
the antifamily, anticonventional spirit of the Roaring Twenties.
Instead we have the Do-it-yourself movement, with a major advertising appeal upon family togetherness, the family outing,
and the home as haven, workshop, and recreational center.
Little systematic research exists on these matters but it is evident that earlier prophecies of the disintegration of family life
in this country are not well supported at this time.

We can understand these developments better if we recall the
twin facts of great geographic and social mobility and the ability
of other parts of the social structure to absorb functions formerly carried out, by necessity, in the family. Because of high
mobility we cannot have close-knit locality groupings of kinsmen. Because of strong political, economic, and educational
institutions the family does not have to be "government," "factory," and "school."

Noting the increased percentage of the population ever married (quite high in comparison with Great Britain and Western
Europe) and the lowered age at first marriage, it is not surprising to find that the value placed upon the surviving nuclear
unit is attested by numerous direct observations, as well as by
the indirect evidence supplied by higher birth rates and lower
divorce rates in the decade of the 1950's.

Values and practices relating to child rearing have manifested

much variability at any given point in time, and changes have
appeared as complex, short-run fluctuations, rather than as
consistent trends. Research over the past 25 years has shown
a shift in middle-class families toward greater tolerance of the
child's needs and impulses and toward freer display of parental
affection toward the child.[17] These changes do not appear to be
inconsistent with the place of the small family in an internally
peaceful, prosperous society, but there is no evidence that such
changes are irreversible.

SOCIAL STRATIFICATION

Even more directly than in the case of the kinship system,
the new urban-industrial mode of life has led to alterations in
social stratification. Since the turn of the century, the occupational structure of the nation has been transformed by (1) the
decreases in the categories of proprietors-managers-officials,
farmers, farm laborers, unskilled workers, and nonfarm
laborers; (2) the increases in all other main occupational categories, but especially in "clerks and kindred workers" and
semiskilled workers.[18] Most recently, the proportion of semiskilled workers has begun to decline.

Changes in social mobility have two main aspects. The first
consists in the movement of individual persons within a given
system of ranking, e.g., a stable occupational structure. The
second represents change in the system itself, as in the transformation of an agricultural society into a commercial and industrial society. Both types of changes have occurred on a
grand scale in American history. Much of the change in individuals' stations in life has reflected changes in the "class"
structure as such rather than movement within a fixed hierarchy
of positions. In the first instance, this meant industrialization,
drawing vast numbers from rural into urban occupations.
Secondly, it involved the creation of numerous entirely new occupations, from typist to IBM programmer to nuclear physicist.
The rise of an administrative force of clerical, supervisory,
and managerial personnel was a third important structural
change.

Further, qualitative changes have greatly altered the position
and social meaning of many occupations.[19] The individual business entrepreneur is now found in disproportionate numbers in
the relatively hazardous fields of distribution and service; even
there, he operates very often under some measure of control by

the large corporations with which he must deal.

Technological development has reduced the proportion of un-skilled workers and has brought into prominence the machine-tender and other semiskilled workers. Clerical occupations are increasingly mechanized. The salaried executive has become the prototype of the successful business man. The professional man or woman is increasingly likely to be a salaried employee of an organization, rather than the traditional "free professional" offering services to individual clients for a fee. On the whole, industrial workers in many of the major industries have ad-vanced in both relative and absolute income, in security of em-ployment, and in many so-called fringe benefits.

A recurring question in studies of the systems of social stratification in this country is whether or not classes are be-coming less "open," with social mobility slowing down and social position becoming more rigid.[20] Partly as a reaction to the Great Depression, these questions were raised with particular insistence in the twenty years following 1935. Scholars noted the diminished role of the independent entrepreneur, the virtual disappearance of the old-style Captain of Industry, the difficulty of successfully initiating small business enterprises, the mini-mal opportunity for industrial workers to advance beyond the level of first-line supervision, and the attrition of the old strata of skilled craftsmen. Studies showed the great importance of economic position in determining which of our well-qualified young people were able to secure a college education. The presence of an hereditary elite of families of great wealth and power was documented. The increasingly dominant place of the large organization in business, government, and elsewhere was seen to imply the emergence of new bureaucracies and of cor-responding elites of high officials.

The facts just cited are facts, and the total picture is impres-sive. But the evidence adduced is partial. Although compari-sons through time of social stratification are notoriously difficult, the available studies—e.g., Rogoff's research on Indianapolis—suggest that rates of occupational mobility have not changed greatly over the past fifty years. The most important changes have been the movement out of agricultural occupations; the emergence of the so-called new middle classes of salaried tech-nicians, professional persons, clerical workers, sales people, and the like; and the developing job security and quasi-professional characteristics of increasing numbers of industrial workers.[21] Against the disappearance of the independent artisan has to be set the growth of the large corps of semiprofessional workers needed by the newer techniques.

In terms of the material comforts and amenities of life, the post-depression years have brought a widespread process of "leveling up." The symbols of middle-class respectability have permeated larger and larger segments of a population, wherein the percentage of families with incomes of $4,000 or more has doubled since 1935.

Although the data are open to varying interpretations, it seems clear that income inequalities diminished during the post-depression years, even as real income increased for the great majority of the population. "Class" differentials in morbidity, mortality, and fertility appear, on the whole, to have narrowed; and the same tendency is detectable in consumption patterns and general style of life.[22] Although marked differences in certain attitudes and behavior patterns continue to characterize widely separated income and occupational strata, the over-all trend undoubtedly is toward an increasingly pervasive "middle class" society.

EDUCATION

As the occupational structure has changed, formal education has become more important, both as a mode of socialization and as a selective mechanism or channel of social mobility. This development, probably inevitable in any highly industrialized society, is emphasized in the United States by a value system which gives prominence both to "equality" and to "achievement." Given these values, an industrial society must have mass education.

American education is increasingly mass education in the sense that there are steadily growing numbers and proportions of the eligible population receiving formal instruction. In 1960, enrollment in elementary and secondary schools approached 45 million and enrollment in higher education was almost 4 million. A high school education is coming to be thought of as a democratic right; a college degree, once the rare privilege of a small elite, is on the way to being regarded as essential and taken for granted by a high proportion of the population. Two-thirds of all youth of graduating age now graduate from high school; in 1940, only one-half graduated. Of youth aged 18-22, more than one-third are attending college.

The efforts to provide equality of opportunity by various programs of scholarships, fellowships, assistantships, and

part-time employment fall short of felt needs. It is probable
that increased efforts will be made, for it is quite apparent that
the principle of equal access to educational opportunity has
strong support in our culture. Certainly, sociological research
has supported and given greater precision to the insight that
equality of educational opportunity is essential to the continued
openness of the stratification system.[23]

Formal education in America, once it shed its earlier religious and classical cast, has been pragmatic and vocationally
oriented. In spite of recent concern with "general education"
and "education for citizenship," these emphases remain prominent. Present "runaway" needs for technicians, engineers,
scientists, and mathematicians seem likely, on the whole, to increase the emphasis upon applied, vocational objectives. The
urgent demands of industry and military agencies for highly
trained specialists will not be easy to resist, and many educators will not wish to resist them.

Throughout our history and continuing today, however, a vocal
minority has opposed the relegation of humanities and theoretic
science to a secondary place in the instructional system. Sometimes the voices raise sharp questions: "Perhaps, in a mass
society, the school cannot be the transmitter of civilized values
but only a complex of training programs for various skill
groups?"[24] The ideal of "liberal" education is not likely to dis-
appear, but neither is it likely soon to win a more prominent
place.

Traditions of local support, decentralized control, national
laissez faire in educational policy, and eclecticism in content
and method of instruction are increasingly in retreat. Federal
support of education, already of great importance in the colleges
and universities, is likely to increase. National policies and
national goals are likely to have increasing influence throughout
the educational system. For a highly interdependent, economically and technologically advanced national society, in rivalry
for leadership and survival in the international arena, educational policy cannot be a matter of indifference.

THE ECONOMY

For the past hundred years or more, five trends have been
evident in all societies exposed to Western culture: (1) increased economic dependence of local areas upon a money and
market economy, with loss of self-subsistent local economies;

(2) increased reliance upon centralized political authority and decreased local autonomy; (3) complex and fluctuating movements towards secularization of many things formerly held to be "sacred" and sacralization of some formerly secular aspects of society and culture—above all in symbols of nationalism and economic enterprises; (4) increased contact between individuals and groups of differing cultures; and (5) rapid change in a wide variety of values and beliefs concerning social relationships and the basic forms of societal organization. In order to approach an understanding of these interrelated changes, let us turn to the economic sector.

Isolated local economies no longer exist. The "lessening of rural isolation," the commercialization, and the urbanization so clearly described for American rural society over a decade ago by Carl Taylor have become all-pervasive.[25] Increased specialization leads both to increased societal complexity and to increased interdependence, as two sides of the same coin.

As Clark,[26] Fisher,[27] and others have shown, the economies of industrialized countries have been marked by a movement from the primary extractive and agricultural industries to the secondary manufacturing activities and the tertiary level of exchange-facilitating activities. In recent years, the quaternary and quinary levels have greatly expanded—those occupations having to do with control and coordination and those ministering directly to the health, education, recreation, and comfort of the population. Over half of the working population is employed in pursuits other than those in "direct production" (primary and secondary industries).

The United States is an industrializing society with an expanding economy in which agriculture requires less and less of the labor force (leveling off eventually at perhaps 5-10 per cent). Capital accumulation and technological development increase industrial productivity per man-hour—as does better nutrition, health, education, and motivation of workers. High returns in urban occupations drain off rural population. Research and education contribute to greater agricultural productivity. As industry, commerce, and the city increasingly dominate the scene, the extension of transportation and communication facilities into rural areas reinforces farmers' orientation to the market, and increases receptivity to "business" methods and to newer techniques in production and marketing. A rising standard of living presses in the same direction. In short, a cumulative, self-sustaining set of specific processes continually produce further industrialization and urbanization.

Along with these transformations have gone significant alterations in the forms of economic organization and control. Over a generation ago it was already obvious that the great corporations were the primary focus of production and finance, and their importance in the whole social order continues to increase.[28] Widespread dispersion of income rights, in the form of stocks and bonds, has made the modern giant corporation possible in its present form, and this same dispersion contributes directly to the concentration of control rights in the hands of salaried management and small blocs of stockholders. With widened markets for mass production of standardized products, strong incentives were created for effective systems of central control of communication and decision making. Although such tendencies often overreached themselves and led to a measure of later decentralization, the modern corporation shows many of the characteristics of a very highly developed bureaucracy.

Large unions arose as a countervailing power to big business. Although perhaps much less powerful than the general public has been led to believe, the unions are clearly important new institutions, having become in one generation institutionalized as indispensable. However, the growth of trades and service industries relative to the extractive and manufacturing industries means that larger proportions of nonfarm workers are employed in occupations in which labor unions have attracted few members. With a total civilian nonfarm labor force of approximately 58 million as of 1956, the United States still counted only 17.5 million union members—representing a slightly smaller proportion than a decade earlier. Unionism has to contend not only with the expansion of employment in white-collar and nonindustrial occupations and with the increased employment of women, but also with the growth of various types of automation in manufacturing and mining.

On its part, the large corporation may even become a management center of a cluster of diverse industrial lines, appearing to the stockholder almost as an investment trust. As an example, consider U.S. Industries, Inc., producing items ranging "from giant presses to cookware," and proudly advertising its "Billion Dollar Board."

The institutions of property have been greatly modified during the twentieth century by the widespread distribution of corporate stocks, the concentration of corporate control, the vast growth of social insurance and pension funds, the increased role of nonindividual (and, often, "nonprofit") stockholders,[29] the separation of "ownership" from "management," the growth of labor unions, the changed scope and character of collective bargaining, and the increased role of government through taxation and regulation. With increased size of firm, imperfect competition, concentration of production, and separation of "beneficial use" from "control," relatively small, quasi-professional groupings of managers have come to direct very complex bureaucratic organizations.

The interpenetration of what were previously regarded as separate political and economic affairs is surely one of the most conspicuous trends in our national life. The interplay takes many different forms. Government sets rules for maintaining or lessening business competition; it regulates the plane or mode of competition, the conditions of employment, and the place and functioning of labor unions. Pressure groups, based on economic interests, ceaselessly attempt to influence lawmaking bodies and executive agencies. Governmental fiscal policy alone is a major factor influencing economic activity. The impact of governmental procurement and buying policies helps to shape the entire structure of the industrial system. It is perhaps a less obvious fact that as the economic role of the State expands, economic forces increasingly affect government itself. Still less easily seen is what J. M. Clark[30] calls "... the combination of political and economic characteristics in the nominally private bodies which carry on economic affairs." The reference is to the power of the large corporation, the labor union, and the trade association, and to the quasi-governmental characteristics of both their internal structures and their external relationships. As our realistic modern economists point out, the day has gone when it could be assumed that autonomous and invariant economic laws fully determined the working of the economy. The decisions of corporate and union bureaucracies are only in part "economic."[31] Their activities are increasingly freighted with a public interest. They are in part "politicized."

A crucial element in present and future social changes is the widespread expectation of and sense of legitimate claim to, high and rising levels of consumption. The development of mass claims to a higher level of "material welfare" is a worldwide phenomena, and from the time of the emergence of this development the world will not be the same again. Strong and widespread "moral expectations" concerning food, shelter, clothing, medical care, education, recreation, economic security, etc., by now have been built into the central value systems of the American population. This fact has many implications for future social changes.

As a high standard of living becomes usual, it gradually becomes a "vested interest"; in it are fused definite expectations, strong desires for gratifications, and "moral" values. Mass reduction in standard of living, then, will be greatly feared and strongly resisted. Yet, unless Adam Smith's invisible hand works more precisely and smoothly than in our past experience, periods of economic depression or recession will recur. In a political democracy, sharp reductions in real income will lead to demands for intervention by the national government. Given the conditions just mentioned, a drift toward a considerable measure of central planning and control appears inevitable, up to some limit.

With increased communication and travel, common standards of an acceptable level and style of living permeate all regions of the society. These standards apply not only to the private sector but also to the provision of public goods and services--education, highways, parks, and (increasingly) medical care. In a political democracy with a strong tradition of "equality," local and state units of government often will find it impossible to meet local demands in these areas. To the degree that smaller areas are inefficient for collection of taxes, a further pressure toward centralization will be created. Various forms of grants-in-aid already are widely utilized to redistribute revenue to provide public services and facilities. The total of Federal grants-in-aid to state and local governments has risen from about $1 billion in 1939 to $6.3 billion in the fiscal year 1959. Important future expansion of this type of social mechanism seems highly likely.

THE POLITY

The list of major changes in political institutions since the turn of the century is long and the changes themselves are complex. In the most general terms, however, such a list would have to include at least the following items:

1. Growth in the size of government operations and in the scope of the activities and issues in the "public domain."[32]
2. Increased structural complexity in governmental organization

and in the relations of governmental organization to the environing society.

3. Increased size and complexity, resulting in more intricate problems of coordination of policy and administration.

4. Partly as a result of these changes, and partly because of other pressures, domestic and international, long-term trends toward bureaucratization and centralization at all levels of government, especially in the Federal system.

5. Increased administrative autonomy through legislative delegation, growth of "independent" agencies, and de facto exercise of authority.

6. Vast growth in "administrative law" and administrative discretion. Basic policy decisions are being made outside the constitutional allocation of powers. The effective power of the executive branch has increased relative to the legislative and judicial branches, and the bureaucracy has become an increasingly important component of government.

7. Enormous expansion in size, scope, and importance of military forces and their supporting agencies. An increasing proportion of the national income goes to military use. The permanent threat of unlimited war leads to widened tasks and greater prestige for military leaders.[33] The problem of the place of a large permanent military establishment in the social system becomes conspicuous.[34]

8. The disappearance of even a limited degree of isolationalism from international politics.

9. New (at least, quantitatively) problems of "loyalty," "security," and procedural protection of rights of individuals.

10. Emergence of the "Welfare State," dedicated to maintaining certain minimal safeguards for health and economic welfare. The establishment of pervasive vested interests in certain aspects of "Welfare State" programs is best signalized by the fact that in 1958 nearly three-fifths of the total population aged 65 and over were receiving benefits from our Old-age, Survivors, and Disability Insurance program. The total monthly amount of benefits in current payment status was $850 million in 1959.[35]

11. High development of organized interest groups, which propose and "veto" nearly all important legislation. The unorganized "general public" retains only an episodic and delayed power to ratify or reject whole programs of governmental action.

12. Increased use of Federal powers in the field of political and civil rights and liberties.

13. Varied manifestations of strain and alienation in the political
    arena, ranging from antifluoridation campaigns to White
    Citizen's Councils and the John Birch Society.

As the United States has become a tightly interdependent
system, its political institutions inevitably have become more
complex, more centralized, and more pervasive. And every international involvement only accentuates these trends. A return
to the "limited government" of the eig..teenth century is not
realistically conceivable.

"Economic" and "political" aspects of our changin.z institutions converge in the modern interrelations of big government,
large unions, and giant corporations. The growth in size and
increase of complexity of organizations has resulted in new
concentrations of power. A permanent state of emergency in
international relations accelerates the tendency to concentrate
decision making. The internal pressures for coordination and
effectiveness in large organizations work toward establishment
of formal rules and hierarchical control. Relations of interdependence and conflict among such organizations simply work
in the same direction.[36]

RELIGIOUS INSTITUTIONS

The American social system is marked by a strong emphasis
upon the goal-attainment and adaptive sectors.[37] Broadly speaking, its attention to tension management, pattern maintenance,
and integration has been residual—worthy of attention only when
the primary adaptive and goal-seeking interests have had their
due. Yet the alterations in the economic and political systems
sketched above could hardly occur independently from other subsystems, and, indeed, changes in kinship, social stratification,
and education attest to the linkages among major institutional
subsystems. Therefore, the institution which classic sociological
theory has regarded as a primary locus of societal integration—
religion—is of particular interest.

The overly simple notion that the history of religious commitment and activity in the United States could be characterized
as a process of ever-increasing "secularization" gained considerable popular acceptance during the 1920's and 1930's.[38]
Since the close of World War II, belief in the reality of a mass
"return to religion" has had widespread acceptance. In both instances, the detailed evidence will not support the extreme

generalizations. Rather, there have been qualitatively complex and quantitatively varied fluctuations in religious involvement and participation. It was a great change from the theocratic society of the Plymouth Colony to the widespread deism and religious indifference of the Revolutionary decades. Subsequent periods of religious revival and decline have followed no easily discernible trend or regular cyclical pattern.

The data available to us for describing change in religious institutions and religious behavior are far from satisfactory. Based on very crude estimates, however, it seems reasonably certain that the percentage of the population holding formal membership in organized religious bodies has increased decade by decade for the past hundred years—from less than 2 of every 10 persons in 1850 to more than 6 in 10 in the late 1950's. At the present time it is likely that a larger percentage of Americans than of persons in most of northwestern Europe are effectively church affiliated. Public piety is widespread, and the militant repudiation of organized religion is extremely rare. Judged by many evidences, American society retains a strong impress of religiosity.[39]

In terms of change in belief systems no clear linear development has been demonstrated by the existing studies. On the one hand, the early colonial form of Calvinism—with its absolute and inscrutable Creator, its aristocracy of the religious elect, its emphasis on original sin, total discipline, and the terrors of damnation—clearly has gone through great transformations. Individualism, humanitarianism, and optimism emerged as hallmarks of much of popular Christianity by the close of the nineteenth century. Both "transcendental theism" and the Social Gospel were authentic outgrowths of American religious developments.

It must be noted, however, that even the apparently simple membership figures raise a number of vexing technical questions. For example: (1) Are the definitions of membership comparable from one time to another? (2) Does completeness of reporting differ from one period to another? And does completeness vary from one religious group to another at different times? (3) Do changes in rates of mobility affect the accuracy of the figures; e.g., with increasing mobility would a larger proportion of individuals and families be subject to multiple counting in the reports of denominations? (4) How have long-term estimates in membership been affected by the changing religious composition of the population? (5) Does rural-urban migration (and increasing bureaucratization of religious

organization generally) result in increasing coverage in reporting?

For example, Catholics constituted a small percentage of
religious memberships before 1850; now they account for at
least one-third of all memberships. Most Protestant churches
report only "full members," usually those aged 13 and up; the
Roman Catholic, Lutheran, and Protestant Episcopal churches
report all baptized persons, including infants. The changing
percentage of members of churches of the latter type must have
influenced the over-all membership proportions, but this factor
only rarely has been taken systematically into account in discussions of the "trend" of membership.[40]

Or to take one other case, it is known that the completeness
of reporting has varied greatly in the Census counts; e.g., the
seriously defective 1916 data versus the "good count" in 1926.
Aside from irregular fluctuations, it is plausible to suppose that
voluntary reporting by denominations may have been more complete in the period since World War II than in earlier decades.
Historical evidence also suggests that church membership is far
more easily attained and maintained now than in periods of more
exacting norms.

It is clear that intensity of religious observance may diminish
even while membership and other evidences of formal participation increase;[41] some observers think that this paradox aptly defines trends in religion in America.

But if secularization has occurred within organized religion,
there is no warrant for assuming that religious ideas and values
are merely of historical interest in the contemporary functioning of the social system. A lessening of adherence to specific
traditional, doctrinaire beliefs does not necessarily mean a
lessening of appreciation for or deference to generalized religious values. Nor does it necessarily mean that categorical
religious allegiances become any less important

The crucial sociological problems, in any case, are more
subtle. For example, over the span of national existence, the
relationships among groupings arising from dissimilar religious
affiliations have had very different characteristics in different
periods. Leo Pfeffer[42] has argued persuasively that the changing
relationships fall into three main divisions. In the earliest
period, differences of creed and theology were the focus of attention; when conflict occurred, it centered on religious differences. In the second period, beginning with the mass influx of
Irish and, later, German Catholics, the focus of antagonism was
"ethnic," i.e., not Catholicism, but "Catholic immigrants." In

the third (and present) phase, not doctrine nor ethnicity but the
public policy of organized religious bodies is the central focus
of issues, e.g., conflict of the Roman Catholic and non-Catholic
bodies over censorship, birth control, adoption, and related
matters.

As ethnic differences have faded, the internal unity of the
major faiths has increased. As the security, economic standing,
and influence of some religious groupings have increased, the
public role of religion has become more obvious. As both public
and private affairs are increasingly affected by formal organizations, religiously connected stands on social questions have a
larger impact. Interfaith organizations increase their efforts to
promote cooperation and increase understanding.

It is quite possible that in the immediate future we will see
continued consolidation of subgroupings within the main faiths,
continued tendencies toward centralization in some Protestant
denominations, and, hence, increasingly large-scale adjustments
among major groups.

SOCIAL ORGANIZATION

Crosscutting the analysis of changes in major institutional
patterns (i.e., systems of norms) is the analysis of changes in
social organization. For instance, the growing prevalence and
importance of large-scale formal organization is observable not
only in the political and economic systems but also in educational and religious fields. Obversely, the diminished stability and
functional importance of locality groupings affects all institutions.[43] In a sense, therefore, changes in social organization
summarize in tangible form many subtle changes in beliefs,
values, and norms.

At the risk of oversimplification, again, the following are
suggested as outstanding trends in social organization, characteristic of changes occurring over varying but relatively long
periods: (1) reduced autonomy and cohesion of small locality
groupings; (2) increased number and relative importance of
special-interest formal organizations; (3) diminished clarity
and exclusiveness of ethnic groupings based on national origins;
(4) increased importance of mass publics and mass communication; (5) growth in number and importance of large formal organizations, especially in the economic and political fields;
(6) centralization of control and communication within large-
scale organizations; and (7) penetration of local communities and

kinship groupings by formal, centralized agencies of control and communication.

These changes in social organization have moved the system as a whole in the direction of greater interdependence, centralization, formality, and impersonality. As we become more and more dependent upon "society in general" we are less and less dependent upon particular individual persons. In terms of Parsons' pattern variables, the main movements have been toward emphases upon universalism, neutrality, and functional specificity.[44]

As our social system has developed, and is now developing, objective interdependence continually grows—in the technological, the economic, and the political realms. Tighter and tighter causal connections create a machinelike quality in the operation of the system; failures of synchronization or coordination are not locally absorbed, but tend to be transmitted to all parts of the system. This property seems evident from all the facts at hand. Less obvious, and not as well supported by objective data, are the concurrent changes in personal-social relationships. On the whole, there seems to be a long-run tendency to reduce the area of particularistic-diffuse relations. Baldly stated, there is a growing depersonalization of social structure.[45] It is not reasonable to suppose that this trend, if it does exist, can proceed without limit. Nor is it likely that it can be adequately compensated for by the parasocial communication of the mass media and the one-way personalization of public figures in government or in the world of sports and entertainment. Future research may show that the loss of durable particularistic relations in the world of work and community is closely connected with changes in the qualities of family life and informal social relationships.

With the growth of interdependence, small communities have come increasingly under the influence of forces originating outside the local area; e.g., economic changes, mass media, migration of population, political influences, and extralocal organizations. Decreasing localism shows itself in many forms. A well-known, but striking, example is the continuous decrease in the number of public school districts from 127,000 in 1932 to 49,000 in 1958—while public school enrollment was increasing from 26.5 million to 33.8 million.[46] Never before in history have so many local areas been so permeable to external forces.

Were it possible to make a systematic comparison of all major aspects of American social life in 1900 and in the 1960's, we would probably find a consistent decrease in the sharpness of differentiation between and among major social statuses, categories, and collectivities. Rural-urban differences clearly are less. Class differentials are less obvious or sharp. Occupational status differences are blurred, especially between manual and nonmanual jobs. Ethnic distinctions, on the whole, have faded. The ways of life of Negroes and whites are increasingly similar. Regional distinctiveness, in spite of temporary resurgence in situations of conflict, gradually diminishes.

Developments in social organization in the United States suggest the possibilities that the greater the similarity of conditions in different geographic regions and the greater the sociocultural homogeneity of the population, (a) the greater the likelihood of society-wide organization, and (b) the greater the likelihood that decision making will be successfully centralized within these organizations. At the same time, the greater the perceived threat to the nation as a whole in the field of international relations, the greater the tendency to centralize decision making.[47]

Very broadly, it is probably correct to say that American culture is becoming more uniform, even though its social structure is increasingly differentiated. But the broad generalization must not obscure the numerous divergencies and discontinuities, which are both results and causes of rapid sociocultural changes; e.g., rural-urban differences in attitudes toward racial desegregation, class differences in political tolerance or in attitudes toward education. Under conditions of strain induced by rapid change, "nativistic" and "fundamentalistic" reactions are frequent—reactions ranging from local antifluoridation campaigns to McCarthyism among small businessmen.

The long-term movement toward the dominance of large-scale formal organizations is perhaps the most obvious single trend in the social structures of the twentieth century. Less than 15 per cent of American workers are self-employed. Over one-half of the labor force is employed by ultralarge organizations; by 1950, the 500 largest industrial corporations alone had about nine million employees. A so-called private utility company—American Telephone and Telegraph—counts over seven hundred thousand employees. Eighteen million workers belong to unions. Even universities have become "big business."

The pressures for discipline, coordination, and generalized conformity which are generated in large organizations, public and private, have been the objects of much discussion and analysis, most notably by David Riesman and William H. Whyte, Jr. A somewhat neglected problem, deserving much intensive research, is that of the conditions within large organizations

which permit or encourage flexibility, initiative, and freedom.
We already know that in <u>some</u> instances, as organizations become more highly differentiated and complex, organizational
controls over individuals tend to become less rigid and punitive
and to leave larger scope for self-direction and for collaborative
participation in the making of decisions. To the extent that specialized roles involve special competencies not easily reducible
to routine, the motivation and understanding of the individual
become more important, and the necessary initiative and
adaptability are not easily secured by primary reliance upon
formal rules supported by negative sanctions.[48]

It is also clear that it would not be wise for sociological
analysis to overlook the fact that the processes of differentiation
of roles, role-relationships, organizations, and collectivities
have reduced the <u>ascriptive</u> components of social structure and
have increased the potential range of choices of role-occupants.
The widening range of choice is another way of saying "increased
variety of roles"; it is, of course, also true that any <u>one</u> role may
be highly specialized and limited (e.g., machine-tender).

Along with the growth of large-scale formal organizations and
the multiplication of special-interest associations, contemporary
urban society is marked by a considerable amount of crowd behavior, mass behavior, and formation of publics and social
movements.[49] The sociological image of mass society must not
be overdrawn, for stable group structures canalize much of the
collective responses to common stimuli, and some extreme
forms of crowd behavior, e.g., lynchings, are vanishing phenomena. Nevertheless, rapidly changing collective responses
are intrinsic to the mobile, commercialized, urban social systems. Such systems also generate much highly variable and
deviant forms of behavior.[50]

It does not always or necessarily follow that extensive and
rapid change produces disintegrative effects upon culture,
society, or both.[51] Nevertheless, the generic sources of strain
internal to all societies[52] are heavily accentuated in the contemporary United States.

CHANGES IN VALUES AND BELIEFS

Implicit in the foregoing discussion is the distinction between
social and cultural systems, between actual systems of interaction and the sets of norms, values, beliefs, and knowledge which
constitute the content of the culture. It is clear that the two sets

or systems are interdependent, but not identical. Thus, systems of values may remain essentially constant even though concrete social structures have greatly changed. In a society alleged to be especially changeful, as in the United States, it is of interest to observe continuity and change in the basic standards of desirability accepted by the people, i.e., their values.

Appraisals by social scientists of changes in values continue to rest upon the disciplined judgments of perceptive and experienced observers, rather than upon systematic data designed to fit theoretically significant categories. Indeed one of the best recent analyses in this field by Clyde Kluckhohn, is an appraisal of just this kind.[53] Kluckhohn identifies, in a tentative and qualified way, the following value changes, among others:

1. Lessened emphasis on personal values, in favor of stress on the importance of group standards and welfare.
2. Increased positive evaluation of "psychological" criteria—adjustment, mental health, child training, and "self-realization."
3. Value placed on "future success" has receded in favor of "respectable and stable security" seen in shorter time span.
4. Aesthetic considerations have risen in the scale of value-standards.
5. Higher evaluation of organized religion, but largely in terms of its contributions to group affiliation and stability.
6. Greater value placed upon explicit values; more overt concern for abstract standards.

Kluckhohn's insightful but eclectic listing raises the question of where to detect important, as over against less important, changes in values. We believe that the main values of American society are of two kinds: those relatively distinctive or unique to this particular social system, and those common to at least some other societies though basic to the continued functioning of American society. Such "universals" as social conformity will be omitted in the present review, in favor of values distinctive of American society. By "main" values we mean those most directly influential in defining social statuses and systems of interaction.

Thus, Talcott Parsons has referred to <u>instrumental activism</u> as a core theme in the dominant value system of American society, and has suggested that the primary emphasis upon this theme helps to account for the widespread positive evaluation of anything which supports or increases <u>capacity to achieve</u>. For example, both public education and "health and welfare" efforts often seek support, in part, on grounds of their alleged effects in enhancing individual capacity. Even recreation is "justified" as a means to greater capacity for instrumental productivity.

From the standpoint of economic development, the value-emphasis just described must be accorded a place alongside capital accumulation as a tangible factor in economic growth. Hoselitz[54] has pointed out that in the United States between 1919 and 1957, capital increased by 1.8 per cent while income was increasing 3.1 per cent each year. A substantial part of the increase in productivity probably derives from enhanced effectiveness of the individual worker and manager resulting from improved education, increased knowledge, and improved health. Now, it is true that there is some evidence which suggests that emphasis upon achievement values—positive evaluations of competitive accomplishment against a standard of excellence—may have declined in the United States during recent years.[55] To the extent that this change actually has occurred, it would seem to be consistent with basic changes in social structure, such as those which have increased the proportion of the population dependent upon "bureaucratic" employment in large complex organizations.

Yet, present changes occur within parameters different from those of the system in earlier times, and changes of values may be of several different kinds. In the first place, values which were crystallized early in the national history have been elaborated, extended, and rationalized; thus, the basic positive evaluation of instrumental activism which was already clearly visible to de Tocqueville in the 1830's now permeates the entire social system. Of such values it is fair to say that change has meant, "the same value—only more so." It is our present hypothesis that recent indications of decreased commitment to instrumental activism reflect changes that are relatively minor in comparison with the infusion of this value complex throughout the cultural and social systems.

A second type of change relating to values consists of the situational specification of generalized values. In the American case, the implications of certain initially given values have been explored in a great variety of specific social contexts, resulting in numerous modifications and restrictions in application. Thus "freedom" is now felt to be compatible with compulsory vaccination, compulsory school attendance, and peacetime military conscription. It is now also clear that the eminently democratic "equality of opportunity" can intensify the competition for invidious distinction.

Third, the limits of certain values have been tested in relation to the demands of other values. An outstanding example is the enduring tension between "freedom" and equality"[56] or "equality" and "achievement." Thus it may be argued, as Lipset[57] has put it, that ". . . only through the efforts to maintain and extend Equality have the corrupting effects of the necessary emphasis on Achievement been prevented from dominating the society."

A fourth type of value change concerns what we can only inadequately characterize as "degree of explicitness." Many value-standards are never really "stated"; they are, rather, "assumed" or "implied." American society has long been characterized by a vast oral and written accumulation of explicit value-statements. Although it would be difficult to demonstrate a clear trend one way or the other, it seems likely that the past half century has brought increasingly explicit articulation of major values. Explicit statement of values is encouraged both by rapid changes in specific social norms and by direct challenges, including the rise and spread of totalitarian political movements.

With increased explicitness of values, especially at the highest cultural levels, and with decreased localism and decreased social segmentation generally, it seems likely that increased pressures have been created toward "consistency" in the main value systems of the society. The hypothesized enhanced "strain toward consistency" applies both to the value commitments themselves—the "content"—and to the expression or implementation of the value-standards in action.

Finally, a set of values may remain constant in all the properties thus far suggested and yet change in efficacy through increase or decrease in intensity of involvement of actors who carry the value. A vital and moot question of fact is whether or not the "strength of commitment" to various central values of American culture has been changing in recent years. The assumption that there has been a marked weakening of conviction in matters of values apparently is widely held by many intellectuals[58] as well as by a substantial proportion of the general public. The actual evidence is inadequate to convincingly demonstrate the alleged changes, in view of historical evidence of continuity, the rarity of sharp discontinuities in value transmission, and the pervasiveness of self-limiting checks on changes in values.

Knowing only that the American social system has heavily emphasized the values and norms of achievement, universalism, functional specificity, and equalitarianism, we would expect it to produce relatively rapid and extensive changes in the goal-attainment and adaptive sectors—concretely, in technology and economic practices, but also in a wide variety of other contexts. It is essential that we do not confuse the obvious changeability of specific customs, social roles, or ideologies with change in the values which undergird the major institutions. Parsons himself has recently gone on record in favor of the thesis of relative constancy rather than fundamental change in American values over a relatively long span of time.[59]

Values may be treated as dependent variables, changing with alterations in technology, modes of production, economic organization, political structures, and the like. Within limits, this is a valid mode of analysis. But values are also independent variables in social change, both as sources of innovation and as channelizing influences in reactions to innovations. Indeed, except for the crucial case of revolutionary, abrupt upheaval, the enduring nature of value systems, once institutionalized, is readily demonstrated.[60] Most of the changes in technology, population, and economic organization which we have outlined in the American case are common in considerable degree to the countries of Western Europe. Change in America has distinctive features which are direct outcomes of its peculiar arrangement and weighting of value orientations.

The directional properties of established value systems are expectable on the basis of general sociological theory. This thesis has been clearly stated by Lipset:[61]

Basic alterations of social character or values are rarely produced by change in population or in the means of production, distribution, and exchange alone. Rather, as a society becomes more complex, its institutional arrangements adjust to new conditions within the framework of a dominant value-system. In turn, the new institutional patterns may affect the continuity of the socialization processes which, from infancy up, instill the fundamental traits of personality. Through such a process, value change develops slowly, or not at all. There are constant efforts to fit the new technological world into the social patterns of the old, familiar world. Only a profound social revolution, one that destroys the mainstays of the preceding order—habitual social relations, socializing agencies, and ideas of right and wrong—can produce sudden major changes in values and social character.

Lipset presents persuasive evidence which throws serious doubt upon the hypothesis of a marked and continuing decrease in commitment to individual achievement and "inner-directed" activity.

During the past half century no major new values have appeared on the American scene, and no major old values have completely disappeared. In the midst of numerous changes in specific norms and modes of social organization, the most important value changes have been shifts of accent, emphasis, and configuration. These extraordinarily complex processes have not been adequately described, let alone understood. The analysis of value change by empirical research is a most urgent task for sociology in the immediate future.

TOWARD THE SYSTEMATIC STUDY
OF SOCIAL CHANGE

The preceding sketch of only a few features of social and cultural changes in the United States has raised, by implication, more questions than it has answered. To answer the unanswered questions, as well as to suggest new and better questions, requires more and better data, improved methods of analysis, and a more precise and powerful theoretical apparatus. In the present exploration, the technical problems of research data and methods must be left aside. It does seem essential to relate our present analysis to certain issues in theories of change.

Monofactorial determinisms have gone out of fashion, and modern sociology is not likely to revive the one-sided interpretations which sought to derive all change from a single set of geographic, or biological, or demographic, or economic factors. It is known that social and cultural changes derive from multiple causes, and that no simple a priori formula can explain the very numerous and diverse changes which are of interest to the science of sociology.[62]

At the same time, some positive theoretical conclusions have been reached, conclusions which are consistent with the data reviewed in the present discussion. Although a conception of "technological" or "economic" factors as prime movers in social change is not acceptable, a chastened notion of "instrumental action" must be given an important place in any theory of change in modern societies. Given an emphasis upon efficient means-ends adaptation, technological and economic innovations, accepted because of instrumental effectiveness, bring in their wake complex effects upon other parts of the social system. "Technology" did not cause the current development of suburban communities, but Suburbia would not have been possible without modern technology. Again, technological and economic developments have greatly enlarged the volume of business and size of market required for rural trade centers in the United States, and have made it difficult for the smaller centers to supply some of the essential services now demanded by the rural population.[63] Scientific and technological developments in medicine and nutrition are bringing worldwide demographic changes of the greatest importance. The growth of cities creates greater social mobility through development of complex division of labor, creation of new occupational opportunities, and differential birth rates. But, in addition, the urban culture and social system tend to increase knowledge of opportunities, to increase the possibilities of education, and to enhance aspirations and social skills to implement ambitions. And so on.

The point is that technological and economic developments can attain, and have actually attained, under certain social and cultural circumstances, a limited but important causal autonomy. This does not mean that "material" factors become the source of change. Modern technology derives from a vast fund of knowledge and ideas, and from a peculiar set of beliefs, interests, and values. But it is through technology, applied primarily in the service of economic and political organizations, that these cultural elements become dynamic in the social system. It is not surprising in the context of these considerations to find that Parsons[64] has gone so far, in at least one instance, as to assign the main locus of social change to the economic system (the "adaptive sector"): "Under American conditions, the main autonomous processes of social change do not operate through government but largely through the development of the economy."

Hart[65] has been willing to propose two categorical "laws" of social change which he calls the Law of Cultural Acceleration and the Law of Logistic Surges. The first essentially holds that cultural means for accomplishing purposes have increased at an accelerating rate; the second alleges that specific instances of cultural accumulation and social growth take the form of logistic curves. In more precise formulation, the principle of acceleration is stated as follows:

When research opportunities and consumer choices are kept fully free, and when makers of cultural choices are provided with available information as to the probable effects of alternative choices upon their own valued ends, the fulfillment of those ends, as measured by the most reliable measurable indexes, will progress at accelerating rates of acceleration.

Illustrations include cutting-tool efficiency, speed of travel, diffusion speeds, killing area of projectiles, expectation of life, contributions to science, education, and increase in size of governing areas. For those cases in which the generalization is applicable, the acceleration results from an increasing number of cultural elements, more powerful elements, accelerated diffusion rates, improved methods of investigation and invention, and constantly or increasingly effective motivation.[66]

Whether or not these "laws" eventually turn out to be useful formulations, they do forcefully suggest some of the elements involved in rapid innovation.[67] On the other side, the rapid acceptance of a relatively large number of innovations (including changes in social norms) is rendered likely, all other relevant conditions remaining the same, by the following: high rates of geographic mobility; high rates of occupational mobility; frequent interaction among culturally diverse population elements; a value system stressing legitimacy and desirability of a rather wide range of self-interests; and strong emphasis upon instrumental rationality in the active pursuit of goals.[68]

A somewhat neglected analytic factor in sociological studies of change is that of the risk involved in innovation and in acceptance of innovation. "Risk" is composed of uncertainty plus the importance of prospective gain or loss; maximum risk entails a high degree of uncertainty in a vital and irreversible decision. It may be supposed that technological and economic innovations are facilitated in a wealthy society because the average consequences of mistakes are less disastrous and irretrievable than in societies operating closer to the margin of physical survival.[69] Both a high level of technological advancement and the presence of stable forms of economic organization further reduce the risks of innovations by reducing uncertainty. One can glimpse in this set of considerations the possibility of a cumulative process in which, above a certain threshold, successful innovation creates conditions favorable to further innovations, up to some limits.

One important source of these limits arises from the fact that social change which is (a) rapid and (b) important will always result in some dislocation of established relationships, values, and interests. The dislocation, and accompanying psychological strain (frustration, fear, anxiety, hostility, etc.) will be minimal when the change involves new means to accepted goals within an unaltered framework of norms and beliefs; e.g., the introduction of hybrid seed corn in Iowa. Changes of this type are relatively rare. Much more common is the situation in which change results in an important degree of "maladjustment" and "disorganization."[70]

Johnson[71] has proposed that kinds of social change can be ordered from more important to less important as follows: (1) change in comprehensive social values; (2) institutional change (forms of organization, roles); (3) change in distribution of possessions and rewards; (4) change in personnel; (5) change in abilities or attitudes of personnel. The degree and kind of disturbance, and of accompanying resistances to change, presumably will vary with different types of change. If we use the Parsonian classification of "sectors" of the social system, our hypothesis would be that the likelihood of nondisruptive change would follow the order, from most to least, of (1) goal-attainment, (2) adaptive, (3) integrative, and (4) pattern maintenance and tension management (the "latency" sector, i.e., maintenance of basic cultural values).

A still more comprehensive hypothesis, suggested by the considerations just reviewed, is as follows: To the degree that the environment of a given system is heterogeneous and is rapidly changing, but within relatively narrow limits, the goal-attainment and adaptive sectors will be the locus of frequent change, with minimal and relatively nondisruptive effects in the integrative and latency sectors. As the magnitude of external system-changes increases, the adaptive and goal-attainment responses will begin to threaten integrative mechanisms and, eventually, the maintenance of the structurally central system of values. When the threatened disruption extends to the legitimacy of the authority system, either drastic repression and rigidity or revolutionary change is likely to ensue.

These approaches, then, provide some guidelines for the systematic study of social change. Although the theoretic apparatus has yet to be perfected, the supply of serviceable components is becoming more abundant. There is ample reason for the more hopeful atmosphere referred to in the introduction. In conclusion, it should be pointed out that in human affairs the future frequently "causes the past," and this process by which plans and goals shape realities antecedent to their realization, has become increasingly important in the modern world.[72] The American experiment in flexible and pluralistic goal-attainment under the conditions of the interdependent world oi the twentieth century may ultimately teach us much about the role of social knowledge in the survival of complex social systems.

FOOTNOTES

[1] Cf. Wilbert E. Moore, "A Reconsideration of Theories of Social Change," Amer. Sociol. Rev., 25:810–18, 1960. It is noteworthy that the theme of the Third World Congress of Sociology, held in 1956, was "Problems of Social Change in the 20th Century."

[2] Farm Population Estimates for 1950–59, USDA, AMS-80 (1959), Feb. 1960.

[3] Otis Dudley Duncan and Albert J. Reiss, Jr., Social Characteristics of Urban and Rural Communities—1950, Wiley & Sons, 1956.

[4] Chauncy D. Harris, "The Pressure of Residential-Industrial Land Use," in William L. Thomas, Jr., ed., Man's Role in Changing the Face of the Earth, Univ. of Chicago Press, 1956, p. 881.

[5] U.S. Bureau of the Census, Historical Statistics of the United States, Colonial Times to 1957, 1960, pp. 41-47. Also, U.S. Bureau of the Census, Current Population Reports, Series P-20, No. 104, Sept. 30, 1960.

[6] Cf. C. E. Bishop, "Economic Aspects of Changes in Farm Labor Force," in Labor Mobility and Population in Agriculture. (Center for Agricultural and Economic Development, sponsors), Iowa State Univ. Press, Ames, 1961, pp. 36-49.

[7] Figures cited are taken from Historical Statistics, op. cit., pp. 56, 63.

[8] Hans Zetterberg and Murray Gendell, Sociological Almanac of the United States, mimeo., Dept. of Sociology, Columbia Univ., 1960, p. 28.

[9] Historical Statistics, op. cit., p. 38.

[10] Ibid., p. 462.

[11] Ibid., p. 506.

[12] Ibid., p. 599.

[13] Zetterberg and Gendell, op. cit., p. 13.

[14] Moore, op. cit., pp. 812-13.

[15] Ibid., p. 813.

[16] Ruth E. Hartley, "Some Implications of Current Changes in Sex Role Patterns," Merrill-Palmer Quart. of Behavior and Development, 6:153-64, 1959-60. See also R. W. Smuts, Women and Work in America, Columbia Univ. Press, New York, 1959, p. 108.

[17] Urie Bronfenbrenner, "Socialization and Social Class Through Time and Space," in Eleanor E. Maccoby et al., eds., Readings in Social Psychology, Henry Holt, 1958, p. 425.

[18] The impact of science and technology upon occupational structure is vividly illustrated in the changing character of the military forces. Among the Union forces in the Civil War, all technical and scientific plus all administrative and clerical specialists accounted for less than one per cent of enlisted personnel, whereas these types of occupations in the Korean conflict amounted to 30.8 per cent. Historical Statistics, op. cit., p. 725. See in this connection Morris Janowitz, The Professional Soldier: A Social and Political Portrait, The Free Press, Glencoe, Ill., 1960.

[19] Here we draw upon the useful summary by Ely Chinoy, "Social Mobility Trends in the United States," Amer. Sociol. Rev., 20:180-86, 1955.

[20] The definitive review of the problem is Seymour Martin Lipset and Reinhard Bendix, Social Mobility in Industrial Society, Univ. of Calif. Press, Berkeley, 1959.

[21] The growing professionalization of the occupational system is a prominent development associated with the trend toward a "white collar society." In 1870 there were 859 professional persons per 100,000 population; in 1950, there were 3,310. Cf. William J. Goode, "Community Within a Community: The Professions," Amer. Sociol. Rev., 22:195, 1957. "The United States is probably typical of industralized societies,

in that its occupational life is coming to be characterized by professionalism, whose essence is the 'community of occupation.' "

[22] "Paradoxically, the documentation of class differences reached its peak in the post-World War II period when objective changes in the social structure had already begun to blur and attenuate many of the class differentials described and analyzed in the sociological Literature." Kurt Mayer, "Diminishing Class Differentials in the United States," Kyklos: Internat. Rev. for Soc. Sci., 12:606, 1959. Meanwhile vertical social mobility remains high; at the very least there is no evidence to justify the conclusion of lessened mobility.

[23] "In general, business success like success in public careers is coming to depend upon education to a far greater extent than formerly. Hence any selectivity in the availability of education to various population groups involves cumulatively selective opportunity for advancement in business as in other spheres of life." Gordon F. Lewis and C. Arnold Anderson, "Social Origins and Social Mobility of Businessmen in an American City," Transactions of the Third World Congress of Sociology, Internat. Sociol. Assn., London, 1956, III:265.

[24] Philip Rieff in a review of Durkheim's Education and Sociology, in the Amer. Sociol. Rev., 22:233, 1957.

[25] Carl C. Taylor et al., Rural Life in the United States, Knopf, 1949, pp. 522-33.

[26] Colin Clark, The Conditions of Economic Progress, Macmillan, London, 1940.

[27] Allan G. B. Fisher, Economic Progress and Social Security, Macmillan, London, 1945.

[28] In 1956, the 6.7 per cent of active corporations having assets of $1,000,000 or more accounted for 89.5 per cent of reported corporate assets; less than 1 per cent of the corporations owned 75 per cent of the assets. (Computed from data in U.S. Bureau of the Census, Statistical Abstract of the United States, 1959, pp. 490-91.)

[29] Cf. Paul P. Harbrecht, Pension Funds and Economic Power, Twentieth Century Fund, New York, 1959. As of December 31, 1957, 27 per cent of all stockholdings in U.S. corporations were held by "institutions," i.e., social units other than individual persons.

[30] J. M. Clark, "America's Changing Capitalism: The Interplay of Politics and Economics," in Morroe Berger, Theodore Abel, Charles H. Page, eds., Freedom and Control in Modern Society, D. Van Nostrand, 1954, p. 192.

[31] As shown, for example, in the widened scope and changing character of collective bargaining.

[32] In 1929 the budget expenditures of the Federal government were $3.1 billion, of which 49 per cent went for national security, veterans, international affairs and finance; in 1957, the corresponding figures were $69.4 billion and 72 per cent. (Historical Statistics, op. cit., p. 719.) Except for the military and quasi-military agencies, the main growth of government has come through the addition and expansion of new activities rather than through the simple growth of old ones. By 1960 about 15 per cent of the total working force were employed in government.

[33] Morris Janowitz, Sociology and the Military Establishment, Russell Sage Foundation, New York, 1959, pp. 15-17.

[34]Cf. Louis Smith, American Democracy and Military Power: A Study of Civil Control of the Military Power in the United States, Univ. of Chicago Press, 1951.

[35]U.S. Dept. of Health, Education, and Welfare, Health, Education, and Welfare Trends, 1960 ed., pp. 74-75.

[36]In a sombre vein Clark Kerr puts the argument this way: "Thus the logic of industrial society requires that there be fewer managers and more managed, and that the managed be subject to a growing burden of rules." ("Managing the Managers—The Distribution of Power in American Industrial Society," in Stephen D. Kertesz and M. A. Fitzsimons, eds., What America Stands For, Univ. of Notre Dame Press, Notre Dame, Ind., 1959, p. 91.)

[37]These distinctions, of course, have been elaborated in great detail in numerous writings of Talcott Parsons since the publication of The Social System in 1951. For extended critical commentaries on these and other aspects of the Parsonian approach see, Max Black, ed., The Social Theories of Talcott Parsons: A Critical Examination, Prentice-Hall, 1961.

[38]Nor was this acceptance contradicted by the actual evidence for the period from the turn of the century down to the early 1930's. See for example, the evaluation by Hornell Hart. Hart's data clearly showed declining emphasis on traditional religious beliefs, and he concluded: "The most fundamental change in the intellectual life of the U.S. reflected in the data covered by this study is the apparent shift from Biblical authority and religious sanctions to scientific and factual authority and sanctions." Recent Social Trends in the United States, Report of the President's Research Committee on Social Trends, McGraw-Hill, 1933, p. 390.

[39]Cf. the appraisal of the total situation in Robin M. Williams, Jr., American Society, 2nd ed., Knopf, 1960, Chap. 9.

[40]An approximate adjustment to standardize for age shows a declining percentage of members between 1916 and 1940, with a subsequent rise. See Michael Argyle, Religious Behavior, The Free Press, Glencoe, Ill., 1959, pp. 28-29.

[41]Purnell Handy Benson, Religion in Contemporary Culture: A Study of Religion Through Social Science, Harpers, 1960, pp. 563-89. See also Louis Schneider and S. M. Dornbusch, Popular Religion, Univ. of Chicago Press, 1958.

[42]Cf. Leo Pfeffer, "Changing Relationships Among Religious Groups," paper presented at Conf. of Natl. Assn. of Intergroup Relations Officials, New York, Jan. 21, 1960.

[43]"Occasional reverses notwithstanding, a powerful trend runs from homogeneous to complex, from communal to associational, from clan to city." Werner J. Cahnman, "Culture, Civilization and Social Change," paper delivered at the 55th Ann. Meet. of the Amer. Sociol. Assn., Aug. 1960, p. 13.

[44]Conflicting emphases, of course, are always present in some important degree. Space limits forbid discussion here of the very complicated shifts in the achievement-ascription and self-collectivity variables, as well as in the "adaptive structures" thereby generated.

[45]In fact, this may be only another way of stating the growth of specialized "economic" relationships in the social fabric.

[46] Health, Education, and Welfare Trends, op. cit., pp. 56, 66.

[47] Richard A. Schermerhorn, Society and Power, Random House, 1961, p. 94. "The organizational drift from local to national scope has led to increased decision-making in central headquarters; this is true of both large-scale corporations and unions. Similarly the increase of federal functions and controls in government has progressively narrowed the choices of local officials and leaders."

[48] What is very close to a crucial test case is that of military organizations. And Morris Janowitz has clearly shown how the tendencies just noted emerge in modern armed serv es. (Sociology and the Military Establishment, op. cit.)

[49] See the review of research by Herbert Blumer, "Collective Behavior," in Joseph B. Gittler, ed., Review of Sociology: Analysis of a Decade, Wiley & Sons, 1957, pp. 127-58.

[50] "A society in which there is a good deal of 'disorganization' and 'pathology' is almost certainly the necessary price of dynamic openness to progressive change. The balance between flexibility and disorganization is delicate." Talcott Parsons, The Social System, The Free Press, Glencoe, Ill., 1951, p. 309.

[51] Norman A. Chance, "Culture Change and Integration: An Eskimo Example," American Anthropologist, 62:1028-44, 1960.

[52] "There are internal sources of tension and strain in all societies. . . . The sources of strain include, at least, uncertainties in socialization from generation to generation, chance innovations, and competing role demands given scarcities of time, treasure, and energy (or affective loyalty)." Wilbert E. Moore, "Labor Attitudes Toward Industrialization in Underdeveloped Countries," Amer. Econ. Rev., 45:161, 1955.

[53] "Have There Been Discernible Shifts in American Values During the Past Generation?" in Elting E. Morison, ed., The American Style, Harpers, 1958, p. 204.

[54] Bert F. Hoselitz, "The Road to Economic Development," Commentary 27:436-42, 1959.

[55] E.g., Murray A. Straus and Lawrence J. Houghton, "Achievement, Affiliation, and Cooperation Values as Clues to Trends in American Rural Society, 1924-1958," Rural Soc., 25:394-403, 1960.

[56] George H. Sabine, "The Two Democratic Traditions," The Philosophical Rev., 61:451-74, 1952.

[57] Seymour Martin Lipset, "Equal or Better in America," Columbia Univ. Forum, 4:21, 1961.

[58] Much modern "social commentary" insists that lack of commitment, "shapelessness" and aimless eclecticism characterize the field of values in the United States; see, for example, Louis Kronenberger, Company Manners: A Cultural Inquiry into American Life, Mentor Books, 1955. Among sociologists, David Riesman and C. Wright Mills stand out as critics who suggest decreasing commitment to certain traditional values connected with "individualism" and achievement.

[59] Cf. "The Point of View of the Author," in Max Black, ed., The Social Theories of Talcott Parsons, op. cit., 346-47.

[60] This is strikingly evident in the instances of natior. or whole societies, but local value systems may also manifest great tenacity. Cf. Richard E. Du Wors, "Persistence and Change in Local Values of Two New England Communities," Rural Soc., 17:207-17, 1952.

[61] Seymour Martin Lipset, "A Changing American Character?" in Seymour Martin Lipset and Leo Lowenthal, eds., Culture and Social Character, The Free Press, Glencoe, Ill., 1961, p. 158.

[62] Cf. American Society, op. cit., pp. 568-70.

[63] Cf. Philip M. Raup, "Economic Aspects of Population Decline on Rural Communities," Labor Mobility and Population in Agriculture. (Center for Agricultural and Economic Development, sponsors), Iowa State Univ. Press, Ames, 1961, pp. 95-106.

[64] Talcott Parsons, "Voting and the Equilibrium of the American Political System," in Eugene Burdick and Arthur Brodbeck, eds., American Voting Behavior, The Free Press, Glencoe, Ill., 1959, p. 93.

[65] Hornell Hart, "Social Theory and Social Change," Llewellyn Gross, ed., Symposium on Sociological Theory, Row, Peterson, Evanston, Ill., 1959, p. 202.

[66] In spite of Hart's arguments against setting theoretic limits, it would seem that all known instances of acceleration eventually must reach thresholds at which rates cease to increase; e.g., instantaneous communication, no "premature" deaths, potentiality of total destruction of life on this planet through biological or atomic warfare.

[67] For a reminder of the rigorous, and historically rare, conditions needed for continuous innovation, see Everett E. Hagen, "How Economic Growth Begins: A General Theory Applied to Japan," Public Opinion Quart., 22:373-90, 1958.

[68] In retrospect, the widespread acceptance of technological innovation in American society may bear a misleading appearance of automatic inevitability—an appearance belied by every serious research effort to account for acceptance of or resistance to innovations. Cf. Rural Soc., 23, 1958.

[69] In the rural field, note that one of the few factors that has been found to be rather consistently and importantly related to adoption of new farm practices is the size of farm income. Cf. for example: James H. Copp, "Toward Generalization in Farm Practice Research," Rural Soc., 23:106-7, 1958; C. Paul Marsh and A. Lee Coleman, "The Relation of Farmer Characteristics to the Adoption of Recommended Farm Practices," Rural Soc., 20:289-96, 1955.

[70] For an especially informative example, see: W. F. Cottrell, "Death by Dieselization: A Case Study in the Reaction to Technological Change," Amer. Sociol. Rev., 16:358-65, 1951.

[71] "Harry M. Johnson, Sociology: A Systematic Introduction, Harcourt, Brace, 1960, pp. 627-31.

[72] In speaking of the commitment of labor to industrial employment Clark Kerr has commented: ". . . what is currently happening comes from what is to be. The future is the cause and the present is the effect." ("Changing Social Structures" in Wilbert E. Moore and Arnold S. Feldman, eds., Labor Commitment and Social Change in Developing Areas, Soc. Sci. Res. Coun., New York, 1960, p. 358.)

2

Olaf F. Larson
Everett M. Rogers

Rural Society in Transition: The American Setting

THE PURPOSE OF THIS CHAPTER is to describe the major
social changes under way in rural society in the United
States. As such, this chapter is meant to serve as a bridge
between Williams' analysis of the trends in American Society,
presented in the previous chapter, and the chapters which follow,
each dealing in detail with the sociological knowledge accumulated about some major aspect of rural society.

After a discussion of theories of social change and an ideal
typology of social systems, we will proceed to list a number of
major rural social trends. Much of what Williams stated about
the demographic and technological clues to underlying processes
of change, and much that he stated about the institutional systems,
social organization, and values, applies equally to the rural sector as well as to the larger society.

There are methodological problems in empirically testing
generalizations about social change. A panel study over time is
probably the research design best suited to the investigation of
change, but few examples of a before-after panel study with a
control can be found in the literature on change in rural society.[1]
Due to the absence of such panel studies of specific rural social
changes, we must depend almost entirely upon analyses of aggregate data from such secondary sources as the U.S. Census
(which, in one sense, is the best panel study that we have).

THEORIES OF SOCIAL CHANGE

Social change is a continuous process over a period of time
that brings about shifts in social relationships. An adequate

theory of change[2] should encompass such questions as: (1) What
is it that has changed? (2) How much has it changed (extent)?
(3) How quickly has it changed (rate)? (4) What were the conditions before and after change? (5) What occurred during the
transition? (6) What were the stimuli that induced the change?
(7) Through what mechanism(s) did change occur? (8) What
brought stabilization at a particular point in change? (9) Can
directionality be observed in the change?[3]

These questions suggest directions in which sociologists
might proceed in the development of theories of social change.
There is no present theory of social change that answers all of
these nine questions, if a theory is taken to mean the postulated
relationships among a series of general sociological concepts
that have been logically derived from observed facts. One is
faced with rather discouraging prospects if he seeks to find
generalizations or principles describing how social change
occurs. Elsewhere in this volume, Bealer and Fliegel[4] (Chapter 9) argue that a theory of change should be part of a general
theory of action and should not be viewed as a unique phenomenon.[5]

Traditional and Modern Ideal Types

One approach to the sociological analysis of social change is
the construction of ideal polar types, and the plotting of social
systems on the resulting continuum. Comparison of different
systems, and of the same system over time, is then possible.

Ideal types are conceptualizations that are based on observations of reality. The purpose of constructing ideal types is
purely methodological—to provide tools for analysis and understanding. Sociologists have conceptualized several such polar
types to analyze how social systems respond to change. These
ideal types include the Gemeinschaft and Gesellschaft of
Toennies and Loomis, Durkheim's mechanical and organic
solidarity, Weber's traditional and rational types, Sorokin's
familistic and contractual, and the sacred and secular types of
Becker.[6]

The ideal types of social systems utilized in the present
chapter, traditional and modern, are based, at least in part, on
previous ideal typologies (especially those of Lerner[7]). A number of synonyms may be used to describe the modern type:
innovative, progressive, developed, or rational. The crucial
point, in any case, is that members of modern social systems

view new ideas more favorably than do members of traditional systems.[8]

Traditional social systems are characterized by . . .

1. Less developed or complex technology
2. Low level of literacy and education
3. Localized social relationships limited mainly to the local community
4. Primary social relationships
5. Lack of economic rationality
6. Lack of empathy or open-mindedness toward new roles.

In contrast, modern social systems[9] are typified by . . .

1. Developed technology with a complex division of labor
2. High level of education
3. Cosmopolitan[10] social relationships with an accompanying breakdown of kinship relations and locality ties
4. Secondary social relationships
5. An emphasis upon economic rationality
6. Empathy[11]

In general, United States rural society is changing from a more traditional system in the direction of a more modern system. When compared to the urban sector of American society, the rural sector is probably more traditional on many measurable dimensions at the present time. The ideal type characteristics of traditional and modern systems provide a basis for analyzing the changes that have occurred and might be expected in U.S. rural society.

The Development Process

Several recent writings[12] about the development process liken developing nations to "beads being moved along a string" toward the more modern ideal type of system as previously described. In fact, the six characteristics differentiating traditional and modern systems can be regarded, from a slightly different perspective, as constituting a process that a system must pass through to become more "developed." Rostow's stages of economic growth[13] bear striking similarity to the characteristics previously listed for traditional versus modern social systems. The important point for our present concern is that the process of development from a traditional to a modern system applies as well to U.S. rural society[14] as to Tanganyika, Guatemala, or Cambodia.

RURAL SOCIAL CHANGES

There have been several attempts[15] to list the major social alterations under way in American rural society, and some agreement is apparent among these listings.[16] There are various ways in which a discussion of the major alterations in rural society might be organized;[17] we have chosen to list them on the following basis:

1. An increase in farm productivity per man has been accompanied by a decline in the number of farm people in the U.S.
2. Linkage of the farm with the nonfarm sector of American society is increasing.
3. Farm production is increasingly specialized.
4. Rural-urban differences in values are decreasing as America moves in the direction of a mass society.
5. Rural people are increasingly cosmopolitan in their social relationships, due to improved mass communications, transportation, and the realignment of locality groups.
6. There is a trend toward a centralization of decision-making in rural public policy and in agribusiness[18] firms.
7. Changes in rural social organization are in the direction of a decline in the relative importance of primary relationships (such as in locality and kinship groups) and an increase in the importance of secondary relationships (such as in special interest formal organizations, government agencies, and business firms).

1. Increased Farm Productivity and Fewer Farmers

An increase in farm productivity per man has been accompanied by a decrease in the number of farm people in the U.S. Agricultural mechanization and other technologies have allowed each farmer to increase both his per unit productivity and the size of his operation in acres. The consequence of this technological development has been a major decrease in farm population. Most analysts of American rural society perceive improved technology to be at the heart of many social changes. While we generally accept this viewpoint of technology as a basic cause of rural social changes, there is need for some caution. It is likely that improved technology and social changes often happen concurrently; for example, a small change in traditional values may lead to the limited adoption of certain

technological innovations which, in turn, leads to a further
change in values, and so on.[19]

There are, of course, other causes of rural social trends
than improved agricultural technology. For example, the nonfarm sector of U.S. society has bid the price of labor to a level
where machines must be widely substituted for agricultural
labor. The value placed on competitiveness by farmers may
also, indirectly, be a factor in rural changes by causing a rapid
adoption of technology. The innovator has a relative advantage
over the laggard because the innovator adopts innovations relatively sooner, and the laggard struggles to catch up in productive efficiency. If only the technology (and not the competitive
values) were present, fewer rural social changes would result.

Increased Productivity

In any event, there has been a tremendous increase in U.S.
farm productivity in recent decades. The production of one
farm worker in the United States in 1960 supplied the food and
fiber (and tobacco) for 26 persons at home and abroad, compared with 7.1 persons in 1910.[20] Heady estimated that if there
had not been any advance in farm productivity since 1910, an
additional 19.1 million farm workers would have been needed to
equal the farm production achieved in 1960. Had these added
millions actually been employed in farming, the total nonfarm
civilian labor force in 1960 would have been reduced by over
29 per cent; the farm labor force would have averaged out for
the year at 37 per cent of the civilian labor force rather than
10 per cent.[21]

Since 1940, efficiency in farm production has been increasing
at an accelerating rate. Actually, since about 1950, productivity
of farm workers has increased at a faster rate than that of nonfarm workers. In the 40 years from 1900 to 1940, the number of
persons fed and clothed by the production of one farm worker
increased only from 7.0 to 10.7, some 53 per cent. From 1940
to 1950, the number of persons supported per farmer increased
to 15.5, a 46 per cent increase. From 1950 to 1960, it increased
to 26 persons, or a jump of 58 per cent.[22] Real product per man-
hour had risen by 1958 to an index of 188.6 for farm workers
(from an index of 100 in 1947-49), compared with only 126.3 for
nonagricultural workers in the private economy.[23]

Fewer Farmers

Man-hours of labor in farm work reached a peak in 1918 at
24 billion. By 1959, man-hours had declined to about 11 billion,

or 46 per cent of the peak.[24] The annual average number of
farm workers, family and hired combined, peaked at 13.6 million in 1916 but was down to 7.1 million (a 48 per cent drop) by
1960.[25] The number of persons engaged in farming declined during the 1950's by about 2 to 3 per cent per year (or about 30 per
cent for the decade for a total loss of nearly 3 million). The
decline in number of farms from 1954 to 1959 occurred in all
states and in all but 42 counties of the U.S. The rate of loss was
the greatest shown for any 5-year period recorded by the Census.

The 3.7 million farms remaining include 2.4 million "commercial" farms and 1.3 million part-time, residential, and other
so-called noncommercial farms. Brewster has indicated the
conditions under which further reorganization of inadequate
family farms would reduce the number to about 1.4 million commercial farms by 1975, in addition to the noncommercial
farms.[26] The amount of manpower used per farm has remained
at about 1.8 family and hired workers per farm for the past 20
years. This is a slight decrease over the 2.0 or 2.1 for the
three preceding decades.[27] The ratio of three family workers to
one hired worker has been almost constant for years, although a
slight shift toward hired workers has appeared since 1957.[28]
These workers put in fewer hours per day or per week than even
a decade ago, but the operator still puts in a longer day than the
hired man.[29]

A reversal of the earlier long-time trend for an ever-
increasing proportion of farms to be tenant operated was first
noted in 1935, when the percentage fell slightly below the 1930
high of 42.4 per cent. The 20.5 per cent figure for tenant-
operated farms as of 1959 was the lowest since such data were
first gathered in 1880. The sharecropper form of tenure has
almost vanished. The number of croppers in the 16 Southern
states (the only states for which such information is reported)
dropped from a high of 776 thousand in 1930 to but 121 thousand
in 1959. Owner-operated farms, making up 79 per cent of the
total, are at the highest point in at least 80 years. The farmers
who are leaving farming are more likely to be tenants than
owners.

A significant new development in tenure arrangements, representing increased flexibility on the part of farm operators in
seeking the best combination of their land, labor, and capital resources, has been the steady growth for 20 years in the part-
owner category, in which the operator rents land in addition to
that which he owns. Such part-owner farms are now 22 per cent
of the total, more than double the proportion prior to World War

II. In all regions of the nation, part-owners have substantially larger acreages, larger investments, larger production expenses, and a larger scale of operations (as measured by economic class) than either full owners or tenants.[30]

Farms are increasing in acreage. The average acreage doubled in the past 35 years. The increase from 242 acres in 1954 to 302 in 1959 was the greatest in any such period recorded by the Census and greater than that of any 10-year period but one (1945-54). Since the total amount of land in farms has been relatively unchanged, the decrease in number of farms and the increase in average acreage have been achieved by the demise of smaller farms and incorporation of their land into the remaining units. Regularly, Census after Census since 1935 has recorded cuts in nearly every farm size category under 260 acres. Farms of over 260 acres have been slowly growing in number. The 336 thousand farms of 500 acres or more now make up 9 per cent of the total number.

Another measure of the movement toward larger scale operations is given by economic class of farm. Through 1954, most of the decrease in farm numbers was in commercial farms[31] with gross yearly sales of less than $2,500. Between 1939 and 1954 the number of such farms declined by almost 1.4 million, and those in the $2,500—4,999 annual sales category were cut by 200,000, while the number of farms with sales of $5,000 and over increased by 500,000.[32] During the last half of the 1950's, the same general trend continued. Percentage changes in number of farms between 1954 and 1959 (using the 1954 definition of a farm) were as follows . . .

Value of Annual Farm Sales	Change in Number of Farms
$10,000 and over	36.2 per cent gain
$5,000-9,999	7.5 per cent loss
$2,500-4,999	23.9 per cent loss
Less than $2,500	30.2 per cent loss

Despite the growing proportion of larger scale farms, low production and low income farms persist in large numbers and are a substantial proportion of the total. The situation as of 1959 was as follows . . .

Value of Annual Farm Sales	Number of Farms in Thousands	Per Cent of Farms
$10,000 and over	794	21.4
$5,000-9,999	654	17.7
$2,500-4,999	618	16.7
Less than $2,500	1,638[33]	44.2
Total	3,704	100.0

Low-income farms are to be found throughout the nation, but continue to be concentrated in the same areas where they have been most numerous for at least half a century.[34]

The farmers leaving farming tend to be tenants, operate small-sized farms (in acres), and have lower annual farm sales. The dropouts also are more likely to be younger in age and to be nonwhite (when compared to nondropouts). Improved technology probably makes it possible for farmers to have a longer active farming career. The 16.7 per cent of farm operators aged 65 and over is the largest recorded. This percentage has moved up steadily from 8.7 per cent in 1910, but changed only slightly in recent years since it has been possible for farm operators to be covered by Old Age and Survivors Insurance under the Social Security Act.[35] There has been a generally steady increase in the median age of farm operators from 1890 to the present time.

The decrease in number of farm operators has been especially rapid among nonwhite operators. Their numbers decreased 41 per cent during 1954-59, compared with 23 per cent for all farm operators. This change is mostly due to the decline in the number of Negro croppers and tenants in the South.

Dropouts From Farming

While much data is available from Census materials about trends in the farm population, adequate findings about the characteristics of individuals who enter and leave farming in an area over a period of time are more limited. Before-after studies of this type have been completed, however, in New York, Mississippi, and Ohio. These investigations show there is considerable turnover in the farm population in a relatively few years. A New York study found that within a 10-year period in one county between 30 and 35 per cent of the remaining operators were new to their farm and community, while in another area of the state between 14 and 23 per cent of the farmers were in this

classification.[36] A study of six communities in a Mississippi
county found about 8 per cent of the farmers at the end of a
three-year period were new to their farm.[37] In the Mississippi
communities 32 per cent of the farmers dropped out, and when
these were compared with those who continued, the dropouts
were more often part-time, had smaller farms, less gross farm
income, lower farm innovativeness scores, less education, and
were the very young and the very old.[38] In two Ohio panel
studies,[39] it was found that dropouts were more likely to be laggards than innovators; they were older, less educated, and had
smaller farms. In New York the "replacement" farmers were
more likely to be part-time than those who had continued for 10
years, were less likely to have livestock or poultry enterprises,
and averaged 12 to 13 years younger. Except for these characteristics, and age-related variables such as education and family
size, the replacement farmers were generally similar to the
"permanent" farmers on a series of characteristics including
levels of living and social participation.[40] These studies are
suggestive of the "upgrading" which is going on among farm
operators as a result of the selective changes accompanying the
declining number of farms.[41] As Clawson and Ackerman[42] stated,
". . . the character and quality of the human element in agriculture has improved greatly."

2. Increased Farm and Nonfarm Linkage

Linkage of the farm with the nonfarm sector of American
society is increasing. Evidence of this linkage is manifested in
several ways . . .

1. Nonfarm work by farmers
2. The trend to agribusiness
3. Contract farming and vertical integration
4. The integration of rural communities into centralized organizations
5. Increased rural-urban interaction

Heady and Ackerman[43] pointed out, "Farming is being inter-
laced tighter and tighter, in terms of interdependence, with other
sectors of the economy."

Nonfarm Work by Farmers
Disparity of farm to nonfarm incomes has become more extreme in recent years, and the trend is for the income gap to

become larger. Average income of farm people was about 43 per cent as much as average income for nonfarm people in 1959. The average purchasing power of farmers in 1959 was 2 per cent less than in 1950, while it increased about 19 per cent for nonfarmers. Not only are farm-nonfarm income differentials more pronounced, but these economic differences are more visible to rural people. As Hassinger[44] pointed out, "As long as rural society was a world apart, low farm income was not thought to be a national responsibility, but with the integration of rural and urban society, deprivation was not as acceptable."

One result of farm-nonfarm income differences is the growing proportion of farmers who engage in work off the farm and who are dependent on nonfarm sources for the major part of their income. Thus the occupational roles of farmers have been changing and their linkage with the nonfarm economy and with nonfarm-oriented social systems has been increasing. Despite the more restrictive definition of "farm" used by the Census in 1959, 44.5 per cent of the operators reported some work off the farm during the year, a proportion higher than that for any year before 1954. An all-time high of 30 per cent worked off the farm 100 days or more (an increase from 11 per cent in 1934). The increase was more marked for the last half of the 1950's than for any previous 5-year span. The most recent report shows 36 out of every 100 farm operators had nonfarm income (received by himself or family members) which exceeded the value of farm products sold; this was up from 29 per cent in 1950. Ducoff[45] has shown that on commercial farms only half the operators were completely dependent on farm sales in 1950. The larger the scale of operations, for commercial farms (except the smallest) as measured by the "economic class" used by the Census of Agriculture, the larger the proportion of operators completely dependent on farm sales, but even for the two largest scale classes of farms only 55 per cent were completely dependent on farm income.

The Trend to Agribusiness

Another linkage between the farm and nonfarm systems is the increasing dependence of farmers on agribusinessmen to supply input resources for the farm firm. Examples of the farm supplies purchased are the nearly 4.75 million farm tractors, over one million grain combines, 3/4 million corn pickers, 680 thousand pickup-balers, over 7 million tons of commercial plant nutrients and nearly 23 million tons of lime per year, and the wide adoption of hybrid seed production and artificial insemination.[46] Assets used by the average farm worker have risen steadily to the level of $21,303 in 1960, a sixfold increase since 1940 in current dollars (or a doubling in 1947-49 dollars). Heady and Ackerman[47] pointed out that assets per worker used in farm production are larger and have increased at a more rapid rate since 1910 than for the nonfarm worker. Farm production expenses have reached an annual rate of over $26 billion. Cash production expenses take an ever-larger proportion of cash farm income, increasing to 75 per cent by 1959.[48] The increasing dependence of farmers upon agribusinessmen is one index of the trend from subsistence farming to modern agriculture.

The supply side of the agricultural economy provides farmers with machinery, fertilizer, feed, seed, pesticides, and petroleum products. It includes services of the veterinarian and the repairman and credit through public and private channels. The adoption of many technological innovations by farmers is facilitated by suppliers' activities. Technical advice and even on-the-farm operations sometimes accompany sales.

Some parts of the supply side are under farmer control; most parts are not. Close to 1,000 electric power cooperatives, with more than 4 million members, and about 7,400 farmer cooperatives handling production supplies, suggest the growth of cooperatives.[49] While farmer cooperatives do not have the strength on the supply side which they manifest in marketing, about 20 per cent of total sales to farmers for feed, seed, fertilizers and lime, and petroleum are handled cooperatively, and the proportion has been increasing.[50] Farmer cooperatives are an extension of the farm firm into nonfarm business functions, and, as such, constitute yet another illustration of interdependence between these two sectors of the U.S. economy.

The farm, at the center of the agricultural economy, is increasingly linked with other economic systems through the use of purchased inputs, as has just been shown, and with nonfarm marketing services. This trend reflects the increased specialization in function of the farm firm and specialization of the role of the farm operator. In fact, the trend to agribusiness is but an illustration of the more complex division of labor that occurs as societies change from traditional to modern. While the farm labor force has decreased, the nonfarm agricultural labor force has grown. Estimates place about 6 million workers on the agricultural supply side and 10 million on the marketing side. When combined with farm workers these supply and marketing agribusinessmen constitute 23 million workers in the total agricultural economy.[51]

The market for most farm products is nationwide, rather than local or regional.[52] This vast distribution network involves co-ordinated and often large-scale economic organization, and is made possible by modern transportation facilities[53] and food processing technology.[54] The specialization of farm production and the urban concentration of the population make longer hauls of produce necessary. The nineteenth century trend for the marketing channels between farmer and consumer to become more complex has now been reversed. While the distance that the farm product travels has increased greatly, the number of changes in ownership between farmer and consumer has been reduced. This change has resulted from the growth of direct buying from farmers, which is increasingly on a specification basis, by large-scale processors and retailers. Vertical inte-gration contributes to shortening market channels. So does the decline in the number of such assemblers as country store-keepers and the changes in conducting wholesale functions. The importance of central markets for livestock, terminal market auctions for fruit and vegetables, and produce exchanges for eggs and butter has decreased greatly.

Contract Farming and Vertical Integration

Yet another economic interrelationship between farm and non-farm sectors is the recent increase in contract farming. Con-tract farming, a form of vertical integration of the farm with nonfarm business, has been the practice in several farm enter-prises for many years, but a rapid increase in additional enter-prises has been recently noted, and often with concern. Contract farming involves the farmer's sharing some of his managerial decisions and production and marketing risks with others. Shar-ing may be with a corporate or privately owned nonfarm supplier, processor, or distributor; or integration may be accomplished through a farmer-owned cooperative, representing an extension of the farm firm. The functions covered by vertical integration vary widely, and farmer concern about nonfarmer-controlled integration is a function of the degree to which the management role is shifted from the farmer to others. Contract farming has been in effect for decades in the production of fruits, nuts, vege-tables for canning and freezing, sugar beets, and in beef cattle feeding, among other enterprises. Recently, an estimated 95 per cent of the commercial production of broilers has come under some type of integrated arrangement, as has half the turkey pro-duction. Types of vertical integration are being tried for dairy cattle and milk production, hogs, and market eggs, but currently cover only small percentages of the total.[55] There is evidence that farm areas most receptive to adoption of contract farming are those where both farm and nonfarm economic opportunities were most restricted.

The Community and Centralized Organizations

Local rural communities have become linked to the wider society in yet another way. An increasing number of centralized organizations have local professional representatives (or local levels of their hierarchy) in the rural community. As Hassinger[56] pointed out, the ASCS, Extension Service, SCS, FHA, and other government agencies use local committees as linking devices between the centralized organization and the small community. Many decisions once reached solely within the boundaries of the locality system are now made in the county seat, the state capital, Washington, D.C., or the central office of large-scale organizations. The integration of local units of organization into hierarchies of centralized authority external to the community is illustrated in a New York community by Vidick and Bensman,[57] and in a Missouri community by Gallaher.[58] Gallaher stated:

Under the impact of rapid culture change and accelerated contact with the mass society, Plainvillers are confronted with many problems too complex to be resolved by customary internal adjustments. This causes them to surrender, sometimes happily, sometimes not, local authority and responsibility in many decision-making processes to sources outside the community. This, in itself, is a major culture change for Plainvillers, perhaps the major culture change, and is a logical consequence of their greater involvement with and dependency upon the wider urban world about them.

Increased Rural-Urban Interaction

Yet a final type of interdependence is that due to increased interaction of rural and urban people as a result of the growing proportion that live under the immediate influence of large urban centers. In 1960, 113 million people, or 63 per cent of the total, lived in the 212 "standard metropolitan statistical areas," counties centered about a city of 50,000 or more inhabitants.[59] In 1950 less than 85 million, 57 per cent of the total, lived in 168 such areas. Williams stressed the enormous magnitude of interchange of people between residence areas in the previous chapter. The cumulative figures for annual movement amount to 68 million moving from farm to nonfarm residences since 1920; 41 million moved the other way, making a net off-the-farm migration of 27 million. From 1950 to 1959, net migration from farms is estimated to have made up over a fourth of the nonfarm growth.[60]

In contrast with the rural-farm, the rural-nonfarm population has continued to grow in numbers, now totaling 38.4 million (under the old Census definition, this would have been 46.5 million). While the rural-farm population lost 7.4 million in the decade of the 1950's, including losses by change of definition, the rural-nonfarm portion gained 7.2 million despite definition changes. The rural-nonfarm people, who increasingly make up a larger portion of the total rural population, may serve to link farm people with metropolitan centers more closely. Suburban commuting may act as a type of rural-urban personal communication, just as does part-time farming.

3. Specialization

Farm production is increasingly specialized. Farmers are increasingly putting "all their eggs in one basket." Of 20 major enterprises, the average farm had 5.4 in 1940 and 4.7 in 1954. Enterprise specialization grew faster during the 5 years between 1954 and 1959 than it did during any previous 10-year period of Census records.

One example of farm specialization is dairying. Each year about 4 or 5 per cent of the U.S. farmers with dairy enterprises quit keeping milk cows. As the total number of milk cows remains about the same, this means there are larger dairy herds on fewer farms. One reason for specialization is technological developments. The average dairyman cannot afford to purchase large machinery and equipment unless he has a large enterprise. Bulk milk handling, for example, has speeded the process of dairy specialization. Farms with milk cows were but 48 per cent of the total number of farms in 1959, compared with 76 per cent in 1940. Sales of milk and cream were reported in the 1959 Census by 27.5 per cent, compared with 42 per cent in 1944; farms with chickens are now 59 per cent of the total number, compared with 90.5 per cent in 1920; sales of eggs were reported by 29 per cent, compared with 63 per cent in 1919; and the harvesting of Irish potatoes declined from 47 per cent of all farms in 1929 to 18.5 per cent in 1959.

While farmers have increasingly specialized in what they produce, there have been some changes in area specialization as well.[61] Production areas have shifted; more diversity has

been introduced within areas; and there have been small areas
of increased specialization, usually with a new enterprise. To
generalize broadly, cotton has moved from the old Cotton Belt
east of the Mississippi to Texas, New Mexico, Arizona, and
California, where it is relatively less dominant;[62] soybeans have
been added to the Corn Belt;[63] the Corn Belt has moved outward;[64] and the old Cotton Belt area has diversified and shifted
more to livestock. Specialization in a new enterprise in a new
area is illustrated by broiler production; in 1939, 8 counties in
6 states sold as many as 2 million chickens each; in 1954, 88
counties in 21 states sold that many.[65]

Reasons for the trend to specialization lie in farm mechanization, possible gains in efficiency, and the difficulty in keeping
up to date with farm innovations unless one specializes. Farm
specialization is one illustration of the general trend toward a
more complex division of labor in a more modern system.

In summary, it is plain that the general farmer of yesterday
is being replaced by the dairy "producer" (who may resent being
called a dairy "farmer"), the broiler grower, and the orchardist.
As farm specialization increases, there is less need for economic services from a local community center. More cosmopolitan
social relationships are likely to result as the specialized
farmer purchases his farm supplies from sources many miles
distant, seeks new farm ideas directly from agricultural scientists, and maintains friendships with geographically distant
farmers in his specialty.

4. Rural-Urban Value Differences

Rural-urban differences in values are decreasing as America
moves in the direction of a mass society. The many linkages
between farm and nonfarm sectors of American society described previously result in an interchange of values between
rural and urban people. The breakdown of isolation, once characteristic of rural life, aids the trend toward a mass society in
which (1) mass communications pass the same ideas along to
everyone in a society at about the same time, and (2) the population displays more standardized values.

While the U.S. is moving in the direction of a mass society,[66]
there are still important rural-urban value differences that stem
from historical, occupational, and ecological differentials.
Actually, much of what can be stated about rural-urban value
differences must be accepted in a rather cautious way due to the

lack of adequate research findings on this topic. As Larson[67] stated, "... there is currently a paucity of data, on a national or representative basis, to portray in any scientifically adequate way the values currently held by the farm people of the nation."

Beers[68] analyzed data from public opinion polls to indicate rural-urban value differences in regard to values on education, abstinence from drinking alcohol, personal freedom and independence from government intervention, and on the value of rural life.

In addition to this rather scattered evidence on rural-urban value differences, behavioral differences such as in fertility and occupation between rural and urban America may be noted. However, the lack of a uniform, sharp break in population characteristics between urban and rural on a size-of-place scale was documented on a national basis by Duncan and Reiss as of 1950.[69] Their work raised doubts as to the unidimensionality of a rural-urban continuum. Yet their findings, and the earlier work of Kolb and Brunner,[70] who studied tiers of counties around middle-sized cities, showed the persistence of a gradient pattern as one moves out from the urban centers for a series of characteristics such as fertility, educational attainment, and labor force participation by rural-farm females. Tang's study[71] of the impact on agriculture of industrial-urban development over nearly a century in 16 Piedmont counties of Georgia and South Carolina clearly shows such development to be associated with larger farms, more part-time farms, farm enterprise shifts, and higher incomes for farmers.

The growing number of metropolitan centers, together with the growing number of ways in which urban-centered influences are exercised, may facilitate the interchange of rural and urban values. The spatial proximity of the rural population to metropolitan centers should not, however, be overestimated. In 1960, 11.8 per cent of the rural-farm population resided within standard metropolitan area counties, as compared to the 11.6 per cent of 1950.[72] The percentage of the population in close proximity to metropolitan influences is largest in the New England, Middle Atlantic, and Pacific Census areas.

The present significance of rural-urban value differences is summarized by Slocum,[73] who stated, "The modern American farm population resembles the urban population more than it does the farm population of 1900."

5. Cosmopolitanism

Rural people are increasingly cosmopolitan in their social
relationships, due to improved mass communications, transportation, and the realignment of locality groups. Cosmopolitanism
is defined as the degree to which an individual's orientation is
external to a particular social system.[74] At one time, almost
all of a rural person's social relationships were limited to the
boundaries of his community. The increased separation of place
of residence and place of work, symbolized by the part-time
farmer and the rural-nonfarm commuter, leads to more cosmopolitan relationships.

Improved transportation methods make it less difficult to
have friendships and memberships in organizations outside of
the area of residence. However, some of the technological developments have a reverse twist for some communities. There
are instances in which physical isolation is clearly increased as
a result of transportation changes, as in the case where rail
service is dropped, bus service is reduced, or automobile traffic
is switched to limited access highways.

As in the case of value differences, there is little empirical
evidence from research studies that cosmopolitanism is increasing, but there is no reason to doubt this trend. Investigations of agricultural innovators, who in a sense are probably
symbolic of the farmer of the future, indicate that they are much
more cosmopolitan than the average farmer. Rogers[75] found, for
example, that most innovators in Ohio traveled outside of their
county each year to seek new ideas and many ventured to other
states.

Gallaher[76] concluded that the major change taking place in
Plainville, a Missouri rural community studied in 1940 and 1955,
was the entrance of Plainvillers into "ever-widening circles of
awareness of, participation in, and dependency upon the surrounding urban world." Perhaps it is significant that Sears
Roebuck and Montgomery Ward catalogues now offer assorted
travel packages, ranging from "Two glamorous weeks in Las
Vegas," to an "Exciting four-month trip around the world."

6. Centralization

There is a trend toward a centralization of decision making
in rural public policy and in agribusiness firms. Williams
pointed out in the previous chapter that a general trend toward

centralization exists in American society today. This same alteration is apparent in rural life. The tendency for policy decisions once made within the rural community to be now reached in complex governmental or business organizations external to the local community has already been pointed out.

Both centralizing and decentralizing trends are under way in farm marketing, but the trend toward centralization is probably predominant. The trend toward fewer and larger-scale buyers, operating on a regional or national basis, and the shift from central and local markets to direct buying raise questions about how prices are being set for farm products and about the farmer's bargaining power in the market place. Farmers' marketing cooperatives handle, in one way or another, about one-third of the total volume of products marketed by farmers, with the percentage being much higher for some commodities such as citrus fruits. The number of marketing cooperatives, about double the number of purchasing cooperatives,[77] has shown a tendency to decline as the pressures for large-scale operation bring consolidation and merger.

Government at the local, state, and federal levels affects marketing in many ways. A number of regulatory measures protect the farmer's local, regional, or national markets while at the same time other measures protect the consumer. The federal government serves as a third market for farm products (the other two are the domestic and foreign markets). One response to changes in the market structure is the use and rapid expansion of federal and state market orders and agreements.[78]

Where there were more than 18,000 gins in the cotton states in 1921, there are now fewer than 6,000, as trucks have replaced draft animals in moving cotton from the farm and as gins have become larger and more efficient. Food processing is being centralized in fewer plants located in larger centers, a trend noted a decade ago. In dairy areas, changes in the handling of fluid milk associated with bulk tank pickup at the farm have increased the dairy producer's dependence on centralized authority.

The self-employed segment of the U.S. labor force has decreased from 40 per cent to 13 per cent since 1870 while the proportion that is salaried has increased from 7 per cent to 31 per cent. Williams indicated that over half of the labor force is employed by really large organizations (by 1950 the number of employees in the 500 largest industrial corporations exceeded the entire farm labor force in size). He shows the concentration of corporate control, the separation of ownership from management, and the imperfect competition which characterize the changing U.S. economy. Farming continues as the only major exception to this characterization. In 1959, despite farm enlargement, there were only 1,200 units with sales exceeding $500,000. Farming is also the major instance in which place of work, place of residence, occupation, and family continue to be so tightly wrapped together. Furthermore, farming continues as a conspicuous example of an "open" occupation, with neither legal nor organized barriers to entry.

Nevertheless, there is a general trend throughout most of rural society toward the centralization of both economic and political power. It is likely that the political power relationships of the rural and urban sectors in the U.S. are due for transition. Political scientists have shown that rural areas are overrepresented, in relation to their share of the total population, in nearly all legislative bodies. Urban public opinion and the recent judicial decisions on reapportionment will be strong pressures for less rural political power in the future. One result may be a still greater centralization of authority in rural America.

7. Primary to Secondary Relationships

Changes in rural social organization are in the direction of a decline in the relative importance of primary relationships (such as in locality and kinship groups) and an increase in the importance of secondary relationships (such as in special interest formal organizations, government agencies, and business firms). There are many indirect indications, but few adequate research findings, that the social relationships of rural people are becoming more formal, impersonal, and bureaucratized.

By prescription, prohibition, and reward, the federal, state, and local governmental agencies are increasingly influencing decisions and practices at the farm level, and not only through the federal farm program. There is a whole host of new partners in the farmer's decision-making process—the technical agricultural specialists, such as Extension agents and private professional farm management consultants, and the representatives of government agencies such as those dealing with credit and land use.

Part-time farming has consequences for the personality and family behavior of household heads with a nonfarm job. The primary relationships of the small community are partially replaced by the bureaucratized nature of factory life. As the economic firms with which rural people deal become larger and more complex, a depersonalization of social relationships is likely to occur.

Density of population is one of the basic factors affecting social organization and, particularly, the primary-secondary nature of relationships. Changes in the number of people within a given geographic area affect services and facilities such as retail trade, schools, churches, and health care resources, for which "volume of business" is vital. Changes in occupational and age composition have an important bearing upon a wide range of community services and organizations.

The fact that between 1950 and 1960 about half the U.S. counties (1,536) lost in population while the other half (1,574) gained is another indication of a rural society in transition. These variations in population change are felt keenly at the community level. Considering the centers only, it is quite clear that the population changes vary greatly by size of center and by region. During the decade of the 1950's for incorporated centers in Iowa, growth was positively associated with size of center.[79] Only in that class of centers with 5,000 or more population did a majority of the centers grow; one-third of the centers with less than 500 population at the beginning of the decade had declined 10 per cent or more by 1960.[80] In Mississippi, growth was characteristic of centers of 1,000 and over, while 51 per cent of those under 500 declined.[81]

Rural communities are growing larger in size, in part, because of a need to increase their required population and geographic base. As Kolb[82] pointed out for Wisconsin (also supported by research elsewhere), multiple community patterns are emerging. There is an over-all trend toward mutual interdependence among locality groups, with different functions localized among different centers. Rural families typically use a number of centers for different services. In the multiple pattern, each type of social and economic service tends to have its own unique service area. Further, there is little similarity between the areas served by community facilities and the areas encompassed by local governmental units. In this process, community boundaries in the conventional town-country community sense become blurred. Locality groupings have significance in the daily lives of a great many rural people, but the ties that bind are more voluntary and psychological than in the past. The decline of the rural neighborhood and a shift from group relationships based upon territoriality and proximity to relationships based upon common interests (whether they be kinship, flying airplanes, or feeding cattle) was documented in a research series on rural social organization.[83]

Kinship and family relationships probably are less primary and more secondary in nature among contemporary rural residents than was the case decades ago. We have seen earlier in this chapter that as a society becomes less traditional it usually features an attenuation of kinship relations. With modernization, individuals in a society have less need for interaction with their kin in the face of increasing geographical and social mobility. This tendency for the breakdown of primary kin relationships in the face of the development of modern society is generally supported by observation and analysis, but has recently been challenged by Greenfield.[84]

Some recent research in urban settings indicates a persistence of certain primary group relationships (such as kinship and locality). Perhaps, for many individuals, primary relationships are not "dropped off," secondary relationships are merely "added on." Primary relationships may be important in a modern system, but they are likely to operate within the framework of secondary relationships. Nevertheless, we conclude that a major change in rural social organization is from primary to secondary relationships.

CONCLUSIONS

One of the themes of the present chapter is that many aspects of rural society are changing and that there is a need for adjustment to these changes. It is pertinent at this point to ask what contributions rural sociologists have made to investigating the problem of agricultural maladjustment. Evidently both the public and government officials see this problem as almost entirely economic in nature. This is in spite of the fact that agricultural adjustment is largely concerned with changing values that are not economic, at least in a strict sense. The attention given to sociological discussions of the adjustment problem in recent publications on this topic is negligible when compared to the length of discourse by agricultural economists. Perhaps rural sociologists might accept the invitation of Heady and Ackerman[85] to concentrate more of their attention on agricultural adjustment.

The changes in social organization which Williams finds for the American system as a whole apply equally well to rural society; these changes are in the direction of greater interdependence, centralization, formality, and impersonality. There is little doubt that further changes in rural society in these directions must be anticipated, with the usual proviso for the unanticipated consequences of episodic events.

It was pointed out that as any society develops from traditional to modern, six major changes occur:

1. A more developed technology with a more complex division of labor.
2. Higher levels of literacy and education.
3. Cosmopolitan rather than localistic social relationships, with a breakdown of kinship relations and locality ties.
4. Less primary and more secondary social relationships.
5. A greater emphasis upon economic rationality.
6. An increase in empathy or open-mindedness toward new roles.

An application of these six steps in the development process to U.S. rural society leads to the following major alterations in rural society, each of which were described in this chapter.

1. An increase in farm productivity per man has been accompanied by a decline in the number of farm people in the U.S.
2. Linkage of the farm with the nonfarm sector of American society is increasing.
3. Farm production is increasingly specialized.
4. Rural-urban differences in values are decreasing as America moves in the direction of a mass society.
5. Rural people are increasingly cosmopolitan in their social relationships due to improved mass communications, transportation, and the realignment of locality groups.
6. There is a trend toward a centralization of decision making in rural public policy and in agribusiness firms.
7. Changes in rural social organization are in the direction of a decline in the importance of primary relationships (such as in locality and kinship groups) and an increase in the importance of secondary relationships (such as in special interest formal organizations, government agencies, and business firms).

In spite of the significance of these seven rural social changes, there are also stabilities in rural society that prevent complete social disorganization from occurring. Another caution against overgeneralization about the present seven rural changes is that important diversities remain between rural and urban styles of life in the U.S. As Williams stated in the previous chapter, "The sociological image of mass society must not be overdrawn." American rural society in transition presents basic persistencies and stabilities, along with great and rapid changes.

FOOTNOTES

[1] Examples of the before-after panel study with a control sample are Wade H. Andrews et al., "Benchmarks for Industrialization: A Study of Rural Development in Monroe County, Ohio," Ohio Agr. Exp. Sta. Res. Bul. 870, 1960 (although the study is not yet fully completed); and a New York study-restudy design reported in William A. Foster, "Rural Resident Community Identification and Community Change over a Ten-Year Period: A Study of a South Central New York Rural Community, 1947-1957," Ph.D. thesis, Cornell Univ., Ithaca, N.Y., 1958; and in Olaf F. Larson, "Research for Experimental Community Projects in New York," Rural Soc., 15:67-69, 1950. A study-restudy design (with no control) for the investigation of change in one rural community is illustrated by Art Gallaher, Jr., Plainville Fifteen Years Later, Columbia Univ. Press, New York, 1961.

[2] Roscoe C. Hinkle, "Howard Becker's Approach to the Study of Social Change," Sociol. Quart., 2:155-80, 1961. Most of the descriptive material about rural social changes presented later in this chapter seeks to answer questions 1, 2, 3, and, to a lesser extent, question 6.

[3] Ibid., p. 177

[4] Robert C. Bealer and Frederick C. Fliegel, "A Reconsideration of Social Change in Rural Sociology," Chapter 9 in this book. The same point is made by Wilbert E. Moore, "A Reconsideration of Theories of Social Change," Amer. Sociol. Rev., 25:810-18, 1960.

[5] Bealer and Fliegel, op. cit., trace a convergence of two research traditions in rural sociology, the diffusion of farm innovations and rural youth migration. A similar convergence is needed between discussion of change in social systems and the diffusion of innovations within (or between) social systems. Diffusion research essentially seeks to determine behavioral changes in response to new ideas, yet few of 503 publications on the diffusion of innovations make even a passing mention of social change (see Everett M. Rogers, Diffusion of Innovations, The Free Press, Glencoe, Ill., 1962). Efforts are needed to develop theoretical statements about social change from diffusion research findings, as well as the reverse process of deriving testable hypotheses for diffusion studies from a general theory of action.

[6] A discussion of the common grounds in these various ideal typologies may be found in Charles P. Loomis, Social Systems: Essays on Their Persistence and Change, D. Van Nostrand, 1960, pp. 57-63.

[7] Daniel Lerner, The Passing of Traditional Society: Modernizing the Middle East, The Free Press, Glencoe, Ill., 1958.

[8] This point was particularly emphasized by Becker, who essentially defined his sacred type as characterized by an intense opposition to change. Howard Becker and Alvin Boskoff, Modern Sociological Theory in Continuity and Change, Dryden, 1957, p. 142.

[9]The present list of characteristics of traditional and modern systems follows closely Becker's descriptions of sacred and secular societies, except that Becker also included (1) a high prestige of science and (2) advanced communication as descriptive of the secular type. Howard Becker, Through Values to Social Interpretation, Duke Univ. Press, Durham, N.C., 1950, especially pp. 68-72. Characteristics of traditional and modern systems similar to the present six are described by Max F. Millikan and Donald L. M. Blackmer, The Emerging Nations: Their Growth and United States Policy, Little, Brown, 1961, pp. 3-6; and Everett E. Hagen, On the Theory of Social Change: How Economic Growth Begins, Dorsey Press, Homewood, Ill., 1962, p. 56. Hagen states, "A traditional society, in short, tends to be custom-bound, hierarchial, ascriptive, and unproductive."

[10]Cosmopolitanism is defined as the degree to which an individual's orientation is external to a particular social system.

[11]Both Lerner, op. cit., and Bruno Benvenuti, Farming in Cultural Change, van Gorkum, Assen, Netherlands, 1961, have constructed "modernism" scales composed of empathy-type items in order to place individuals on the traditional-modern continuum. Empathy is defined as the degree to which an individual is able to place himself in others' roles.

[12]Examples are W. W. Rostow, The Stages of Economic Growth: A Non-Communist Manifesto, Cambridge Univ. Press, New York, 1961; John Kenneth Galbraith, Economic Development in Perspective, Harvard Univ. Press, Cambridge, Mass., 1962; Lerner, op. cit.; and Hagen, op. cit.

[13]Rostow, op. cit., specifies five stages in the development process: (1) tradition, (2) preconditions for take-off, (3) take-off, (4) drive to maturity, and (5) high mass-consumption. At each stage, certain actions must occur for the development process to continue. For instance, at the take-off stage, emergence of a new leadership, the rise of values similar to the Protestant Ethic, and a lifting of social and economic expectations must occur (p. 26).

[14]In fact, an important intellectual task would be to apply theoretical notions about the development process (written in reference to underdeveloped nations) to U.S. rural development programs such as the current Rural Areas Development Program being conducted by the USDA and the U.S. Department of Commerce.

[15]For example, Edmund deS. Brunner and J. H. Kolb, Rural Social Trends, McGraw-Hill, 1933; Carl C. Taylor et al., Rural Life in the United States, Knopf, 1949, pp. 522-33; Robin M. Williams, Jr., "Rural Sociology in a Changing Society: Future Problems and Prospects," in North Central Regional Rural Sociology Committee, Rural Sociology in a Changing Society, Ohio Agr. Ext. Serv., mimeo., 1959; and Everett M. Rogers, Social Change in Rural Society, Appleton-Century-Crofts, 1960, pp. 3-19. It is interesting to note that Thomas C. McCormick, "Major Trends in Rural Life in the United States," Amer. Jour. Soc., 36:721-34, 1931, foresaw most of the major rural social trends under way today.

[16]Actually, many of the rural social changes listed in this chapter are closely interrelated, and can be viewed separately only in an analytical sense.

[17]For example, these changes might be listed under a farm versus rural-nonfarm breakdown. The general lack of research findings about

the rural-nonfarm population segment, making up about two-thirds of the U.S. rural population, suggests a needed emphasis in rural sociology if our field is to be more than the sociology of farm life.

[18] Agribusiness is defined as the manufacture and distribution of farm supplies plus the processing, handling, merchandising, and marketing of food and agricultural products plus farming itself. The term has become quite popular (which is, in itself, quite significant) since being coined by John H. Davis, "From Agriculture to Agribusiness," Harvard Bus. Rev., 34:107-15, 1956.

[19] This concurrent interaction between two variables is widely encountered in many types of human behavior. Symbolically, the process may be written as $\Delta X \rightleftharpoons \Delta Y$, where ΔX represents a very small increment in variable X and ΔY represents a corresponding small increment in variable Y. A large increment of either X or Y may cancel the mutual relationship. Zetterberg refers to this $\Delta X \rightleftharpoons \Delta Y$ interaction as an "interdependent relationship," and likens it to a flirtation between individuals X and Y. Hans L. Zetterberg, "Notes on Theory Construction and Verification in Sociology," paper presented at the North Central Rural Sociology Committee, Chicago, 1961.

[20] Earl O. Heady, "Nature of the Farm Problem," in Mervin G. Smith and Carlton F. Christian, eds., Adjustments in Agriculture: A National Basebook, Iowa State Univ. Press, Ames, 1961, pp. 55-84. For the basis of this index see "Changes in Farm Production and Efficiency: A Summary Report," USDA Stat. Bul. 233, 1961, p. 43.

[21] Percentage estimates were derived from Heady, op. cit., and from averages for 1960 in Monthly Report on the Labor Force; Dec. 1960, U.S. Dept. of Labor, 1961, Table 14.

[22] Heady, op. cit., p. 73.

[23] Based on the BLS index in "Trends in Output per Man-Hour in the Private Economy, 1909-1958," U.S. Dept. of Labor Bul. 1249, 1960.

[24] Changes in Farm Production and Efficiency, op. cit., Table 15.

[25] The 1960 figure was given in Heady, op. cit. See also "Farm Employment; Monthly by States, 1950-57; United States, by Years, 1910-57, by Months, 1940-57," USDA, Stat. Bul. 236, 1958.

[26] John M. Brewster, "The Changing Organization of American Agriculture," paper presented at meeting of the Agricultural Committee of the National Planning Association, Washington, D.C., 1961. Clawson and Ackerman have predicted a decrease to about 2 million in the total number of farms by the end of this century; Marion Clawson and Edward A. Ackerman, "Toward a Permanent Farm Policy," paper presented at the Second National Congress on Environmental Health, Ann Arbor, Michigan, 1961.

[27] Orlin J. Scoville, "Machines and Farm Organization," in Power To Produce, The 1960 Yearbook of Agriculture, USDA, pp. 389-95.

[28] Agricultural Outlook Charts, 1956, and Farm Labor, USDA Crop Reporting Board, 1960.

[29] Reuben W. Hecht and Eugene G. McKibben, "Efficiency of Labor," in The 1960 Yearbook of Agriculture, op. cit., pp. 317-31. On September 1, 1959, farm operators averaged 9.8 hours of work a day, hired workers averaged 8.9 hours; 10 years earlier these averages were 11.1 and 9.5 hours, respectively.

[30]"A Statistical Summary of Farm Tenure, 1954," USDA Inf. Bul. 200, 1958.

[31]Commercial farms exclude (1) those with under $250 annual sales and (2) those with sales of under $2,500 with the operator working off-farm 100 days or more or with other income of family members exceeding farm sales.

[32]Heady, op. cit. The 1939 yearly sales figures were calculated in 1954 dollars.

[33]Of the farms with under $2,500 sales, 404 thousand had operators aged 65 and over, 882 thousand were part-time, and 348 thousand had operators under 65 and were not part-time. Also included were 3,099 "abnormal" farms.

[34]Olaf F. Larson, "Sociological Aspects of the Low-Income Farm Problem," Jour. of Farm Econ., 37:1417-27, 1955.

[35]Frank H. Maier et al., "The Tenure Status of Farmworkers in the United States," USDA Tech. Bul. 1217, 1960.

[36]Unpublished data from current rural sociology research projects in community development at Cornell University.

[37]Andrew W. Baird and Wilfrid C. Bailey, "Farmers Moving Out of Agriculture," Miss. Agr. Exp. Sta. Bul. 568, 1958.

[38]The sample included only operators who made their own decisions, owned work power, worked on the farm at least one-third of the time during the year, and had at least five acres of cropland. The dropout category in both the Mississippi and New York studies included operators who died, retired from farming, and who moved to another community to farm; 15 per cent of the Mississippi "dropouts" were of this latter type. The two New York studies are in general agreement on the selective characteristics of the "dropouts."

[39]Data (1) from one Ohio county gathered in 1958 and 1960, and (2) from a statewide sample gathered in 1957 and 1959 as part of rural sociology research projects at Ohio State Univ., reported in Everett M. Rogers, Diffusion of Innovations, The Free Press, Glencoe, Ill., 1962.

[40]A part of this study is reported in A. S. Lackey and O. F. Larson, "Turnover and Changing Characteristics of the Farm Operator Population," Canad. Jour. of Agr. Econ., 7, No. 2:70-85, 1959.

[41]Another study with a different design but with generally supportive findings is J. R. Bowring and O. B. Durgin, "The Population of New Hampshire: Factors Influencing the Attitudes of Farmers Toward Migration Off Farms," N. H. Agr. Exp. Sta. Bul. 458 (no date, c. 1959).

[42]Clawson and Ackerman, op. cit.

[43]Earl O. Heady and Joseph Ackerman, "Farm Adjustment Problems: Their Cause and Nature and Their Importance to Sociologists," in North Central Rural Sociology Committee, Rural Sociology in a Changing Economy, Univ. of Illinois College of Agr., mimeo., 1958.

[44]Edward Hassinger, "Social Relations Between Centralized and Local Social Systems," Rural Soc., 26:354-64, 1961.

[45]Louis J. Ducoff, "Classification of the Agricultural Population in the United States," Jour. of Farm Econ., 37:511-23, 1955. Of farms other than "commercial," only 8 per cent of the operators were completely dependent upon sales of farm products, and 80 per cent had non-farm sources as the major source of income.

[46]These data are from a preliminary report on the 1959 Census of

Agriculture (Series AC59-1, Summary for the 48 States) and Changes in Farm Production and Efficiency, op. cit.

[47]Heady and Ackerman, op. cit.

[48]Asset and expense data are from USDA Agricultural Outlook Charts, 1961, Tables 10, 19, and 26. See also Kenneth E. Ogren and Orlin J. Scoville, "Farm Supply and Marketing Activities in Relation to Agricultural Adjustment," in Smith and Christian, op. cit., pp. 229-59.

[49]Ogren and Scoville, op. cit., Table 9.5.

[50]As an illustration of the advantages to farmers of technology and large-scale operations through cooperatives, one cooperative reported to its members that weekly cost figures for 44 possible ingredients of dairy feed with 27 specifications were fed into a data processing machine to determine the least-cost acceptable quality feed formula.

[51]Ogren and Scoville, op. cit.

[52]This section on marketing is drawn largely from the analysis by Ogren and Scoville, op. cit.

[53]The influence of technological changes in truck, railroad, water, and air transportation on market facilities and processors and on the location of farm enterprises is discussed by John C. Winter, "Railroads, Trucks and Ships," in The 1960 Yearbook of Agriculture, op. cit., pp. 297-307.

[54]Technological developments on the farm also influence marketing, as illustrated by the bulk milk tank.

[55]For a summary of current data and an analysis, see "Contract Farming and Vertical Integration in Agriculture," USDA Inf. Bul. 198, 1958; and "Contract Farming and Vertical Integration: A Selected List of References," USDA Library List 64, 1958.

[56]Hassinger, op. cit.

[57]Arthur J. Vidich and Joseph Bensman, Small Town in Mass Society, Princeton Univ. Press, Princeton, N.J., 1958.

[58]Gallaher, op. cit., p. 242.

[59]Philip M. Hauser, "The Census of 1960," Scientific American, 205:39-45, 1961.

[60]Calvin L. Beale and Karl G. Shoemaker, "Adjustments in Rural Human Resources," in Smith and Christian, op. cit., pp. 260-84.

[61]A good indication of changes on a state basis is given in Margaret F. Cannon, "Cash Receipts from Major Farm Commodities by States as Percentage of State Totals, 1924-57," USDA Stat. Bul. 246, 1959.

[62]For changes in cotton production see W. B. Andrews, Cotton Production, Marketing and Utilization, published by the author, State College, Miss., 1950; John L. Fulmer, Agricultural Progress in the Cotton Belt Since 1920, Univ. of North Carolina Press, Chapel Hill, 1950; and James H. Street, The New Revolution in the Cotton Economy, Univ. of North Carolina Press, Chapel Hill, 1957. The number of farms growing cotton in 1959 was 509,404, as compared with 1,986,726 at the 1929 peak; the percentage growing cotton fell to 13.8 from the 31.6 per cent of 1929. A part of this change is accounted for by changes in tenure arrangements in cotton-growing areas.

[63]Ray A. Goldberg, The Soybean Industry, Univ. of Minn. Press, Minneapolis, 1952, pp. 14-17.

[64]Howard G. Roepke, "Changes in Corn Production on the Northern Margin of the Corn Belt," Agricultural History, 33:126-32, 1959.

[65]Ogren and Scoville, op. cit., Figure 9.4. Irish potatoes also are an example of growth in area concentration as well as farm specialization, accompanied by a shift in the areas of major production; see Roger W. Gray and others, "An Economic Analysis of the Impact of Government Programs on the Potato Industry of the United States," Minn. Agr. Exp. Sta. Tech. Bul. 211, 1954.

[66]There is probably not only a decline in rural-urban value differences, but also a decrease in regional differences in the United States.

[67]Olaf F. Larson, "Basic Goals and Values of Farm People," in Goals and Values in Agricultural Policy, Iowa State Univ. Press, Ames, 1961, p. 146.

[68]Howard W. Beers, "Rural-Urban Differences: Some Evidence from Public Opinion Polls," Rural Soc., 18:1-11, 1953.

[69]Otis Dudley Duncan and Albert J. Reiss, Jr., Social Characteristics of Urban and Rural Communities, 1950, Wiley & Sons, 1956.

[70]Kolb and Brunner, op. cit.

[71]Anthony M. Tang, Economic Development in the Southern Piedmont, 1860-1950: Its Impact on Agriculture, Univ. of North Carolina Press, Chapel Hill, 1958.

[72]For 1950 data, see Duncan and Reiss, op. cit., p. 154; for 1960 data, see Series Census AMS (P-27), No. 28, Table D.

[73]Walter L. Slocum, Agricultural Sociology: A Study of Sociological Aspects of American Farm Life, Harpers, 1962, p. 22.

[74]Rogers, Diffusion of Innovations, op. cit.

[75]Everett M. Rogers, "Characteristics of Agricultural Innovators and Other Adopter Categories," Ohio Agr. Exp. Sta. Res. Bul. 882, 1961.

[76]Gallaher, op. cit., p. 226.

[77]On the basis of major function, there were 6,503 farmers' marketing cooperatives, compared with 3,373 purchasing cooperatives, in 1956. See U.S. Bureau of the Census, Historical Statistics of the United States, Colonial Times to 1957, 1960, p. 288.

[78]Although marketing orders were introduced in the 1935 amendment to the Agricultural Adjustment Act of 1933, the major permissive legislation has been the Agricultural Marketing Agreement Act of 1937, as amended. By 1960, close to 190,000 producers delivered milk to over 2,000 handlers regulated under federal milk orders in about 80 markets throughout the United States. "Supplement for 1959 to Federal Milk Order Market Statistics," USDA Stat. Bul. 248, 1960.

[79]Using 10 per cent or more gain as a measure of "growth," 10 per cent or more loss as a measure of "decline," and a gain of less than 10 per cent or loss of less than 10 per cent as a measure of stability.

[80]Percentages for 1950-60 for Iowa were strikingly like those for 1940-50; see Olaf F. Larson and E. A. Lutz, "Adjustments in Community Facilities Taking Place and Needed," in Smith and Christian, op. cit., pp. 285-336.

[81]George L. Wilber and Ellen Bryant, "Growth of Mississippi Counties and Cities, 1950 to 1960," Miss. Agr. Exp. Sta. Bul. 608, 1960. In New York, a state characterized both as more urban and with a faster rate of population growth than Iowa or Mississippi, the smaller the center, the more likely it was to be in the "growing" category. This trend, which is opposite to that found in Iowa and Mississippi, may be more common in more highly urbanized states. Larson and Lutz, op. cit.

[82] J. H. Kolb, Emerging Rural Communities, Univ. of Wis. Press, Madison, 1959.

[83] Examples of this series are Paul J. Jehlik and J. Edwin Losey, "Rural Social Organization in Henry County, Indiana," Purdue Univ. Agr. Exp. Sta. Bul. 568, 1951; Paul J. Jehlik and Ray E. Wakeley, "Rural Organization in Process: A Case Study of Hamilton County, Iowa," Iowa Agr. Exp. Sta. Res. Bul. 365, 1949; Donald G. Hay and Robert A. Polson, "Rural Organizations in Oneida County, New York," Cornell Univ. Agr.Exp. Sta. Bul. 871, 1951; Frank D. Alexander and Lowry Nelson, "Rural Social Organization in Goodhue County, Minnesota," Minn. Agr. Exp. Sta. Bul. 401, 1949; and Selz C. Mayo and Robert McD. Bobbitt, "Rural Organizations: A Restudy of Locality Groups in Wake County, North Carolina," N.C. Agr. Exp. Sta. Tech. Bul. 95, 1951.

[84] Cross-cultural and historical evidence was utilized by Greenfield to challenge the hypothesis that the nuclear family is a consequence of the urban-industrial revolution. The Japanese, French-Canadians in Montreal, and Brazilians are cited as examples where industrialization occurred but not nuclear families. Barbados has nuclear families but no industrialization. Perhaps nuclear family types occurred concurrently with industrialization in Western Europe and the United States because of the existence of the nuclear family prior to industrialization in these countries. Sidney M. Greenfield, "Industrialization and the Family in Sociological Theory," Amer. Jour. of Soc., 67:312-22, 1961.

[85] Earl O. Heady and Joseph Ackerman, "Farm Adjustment Problems and Their Importance to Sociologists," Rural Soc., 24:315-25, 1959.

PART TWO

The Particulars

3

Donald J. Bogue
Calvin L. Beale

Recent Population Trends in the United States and Their Causes*

I

REVIEW OF POPULATION TRENDS

IN THE YEAR 1962, the population of the United States increased in size by 2.8 million persons and grew at the rate of 1.5 per cent. This was only a typical year of the type experienced since World War II when the famed "baby boom" reversed the historic downward trend of the birth rate. Never before in the history of the nation have so many human beings been added to the population by natural increase in one decade as in the last 10 years. By January 1963, we had passed the 188 million population mark. Unless some drastic and unexpected downturn in birth rate occurs soon, the Census of 1970 will exceed the 210 million mark.

Such phenomenal growth is forcing analysts in many fields to re-evaluate their expectations of future developments. Continued population increases of this magnitude will be certain to alter almost every phase of economic, social, and political life. They raise fundamental questions: For example, do they threaten to lower the real per capita income of the nation, or are they a

*A substantial part of the statistical work required for this report was supported from a grant to the Population Research and Training Center, University of Chicago, given by the Rockefeller Foundation. This chapter, with minor editorial changes, has also been published under the title, Recent Population Trends in the United States with Emphasis on Rural Areas, USDA, Agr. Econ. Rept. No. 23, 1963.

Underscored figures in parentheses refer to references listed at the end of this chapter.

precondition of even higher levels of living? Is our supply of national resources adequate to withstand this development, or will we soon follow the course of many nations of Europe and incur a net domestic deficit of basic industrial materials? Such questions are now being studied more seriously than ever before.

Dramatic as it is, change in population size is only a part of a complex set of population trends. There are changes underway in population distribution and in population composition that are equally impressive and that have economic, social, and political implications equally as fundamental. It is the purpose of this chapter to review some of the most outstanding of these changes and to describe their underlying causes. Special attention is given to trends having particular significance for rural areas.

A. Distributional Trends

Between 1950 and 1960, the population shifted significantly in its distributional pattern in the following ways:

1. There was a very strong interregional movement toward the Pacific Coast and the Gulf Coast (including the Atlantic side of Florida).
2. There was a heavy movement toward metropolitan areas, both intraregional and interregional.
3. The growth of metropolitan areas, however, was concentrated largely in suburban metropolitan "rings" outside the central cities, rather than within the central cities themselves.
4. In nonmetropolitan areas there was a very strong urbanization movement; on the average, cities in the more remote hinterland grew quite rapidly.
5. Suburbanization assumed extreme dimensions, with suburban fringes springing up around the peripheries of small cities and even villages.
6. The rural population outside metropolitan areas, and especially the rural-farm population, suffered very substantial losses through outmigration.
7. The rural nonmetropolitan parts of the interior portions of the nation suffered especially severe losses of population; the peripheries of the nation facing the Atlantic, Pacific, and Gulf sections tended to have less severe drains, or even gains, in rural population.
8. The Negro population has made a dramatic rural-to-urban shift as well as a South-to-North (and West) shift. Moreover, it has begun what promises to be a major suburbanward movement.

Each of these distributional shifts is described and documented briefly in this section; an interpretation of their causes is undertaken in Section II. None of these shifts is new; each represents a continuation of changes underway since 1930 or even earlier. Their effect upon the national social life should be viewed as the cumulative effect of several decades of change.

1. Regional Distribution. Between 1950 and 1960, there were very substantial regional differences in the intercensal rate of population growth. The system of Economic Regions delimits the regions of rapid growth from those of slow growth more effectively than do the traditional nine geographic divisions, and shows the changes noted in Table 3.1. Two regions grew at extraordinarily rapid rates in comparison with the national intercensal rate of 18.5 per cent:

	Per Cent Increase
Region IX. Atlantic Flatwoods and Gulf Coast Region	48.1
Region XIII. Pacific Southwest Region	50.1

In contrast, four interior regions (three of them in the South) grew slowly:

Region II. Eastern Great Lakes and Northeastern Upland Region	9.7
Region VII. Central and Eastern Upland Region .	5.1
Region VIII. Southeast Coastal Plain and Piedmont Region	9.6
Region X. South Center and Southwest Plains Region	8.3

The remaining six regions grew at nearly the national rate, except that Region XI, the Rocky Mountain and Intermountain Region, increased at the moderately-above-average rate of 26.7 per cent.

Despite the substantial differences in rate of growth, the total redistributive effect for the single decade 1950-60 was not great. As Table 3.1 makes clear, the rapid gains of Regions IX and XIII resulted in a net addition to their combined population of the equivalent of 3.3 per cent of the national population, and the slow growth of Regions II, VII, VIII, and X caused all four combined to suffer a net redistributive loss equivalent to only 2.9 per cent of the national population. However, the prolonged operation of these trends over several decades is building up a dense

Table 3.1. Per Cent Distribution of Population by Economic Provinces and Economic Regions, 1950 and 1960; With Measures of Distributional Change, 1950–1960

Province and Region	Region Number	Per Cent of Total Population		Percentage Point Change	Per Cent of Population Increase 1950–60
		1960	1950		
Total	....	100.0	100.0	0.0	18.5
A. Atlantic Metropolitan Belt Province	....	20.3	20.5	-0.2	17.5
Atlantic Metropolitan Belt Region	I	20.3	20.5	-0.2	17.5
B. The Great Lakes and Northeastern Province	....	22.9	23.5	-0.6	15.7
Eastern Great Lakes and Northeastern Upland Region	II	5.6	6.1	-0.5	9.7
Lower Great Lakes Region	III	14.1	14.0	+0.1	18.6
Upper Great Lakes Region	IV	3.2	3.3	-0.1	14.5
C. The Midwestern Province	....	13.0	13.5	-0.5	13.6
North Center (Corn Belt) Region	V	9.6	10.1	-0.5	12.6
Central Plains Region	VI	3.4	3.4	0.0	16.4
D. The Southern Province	....	29.0	30.0	-1.0	14.7
Central and Eastern Upland Region	VII	8.3	9.4	-1.1	5.1
Southeast Coastal Plain and Piedmont Region	VIII	9.1	9.9	-0.8	9.6
Atlantic Flatwoods and Gulf Coast Region	IX	6.6	5.3	+1.3	48.1
South Center and Southwest Plains Region	X	5.0	5.5	-0.5	8.3
E. The Western Province	....	14.8	12.5	+2.3	39.6
Rocky Mountain and Intermountain Region	XI	2.6	2.4	+0.2	26.7
Pacific Northwest Region	XII	2.7	2.7	0.0	21.7
Pacific Southwest Region	XIII	9.5	7.5	+2.0	50.1

Source: Bogue and Beale, Economic Areas of the United States, Table A (1).

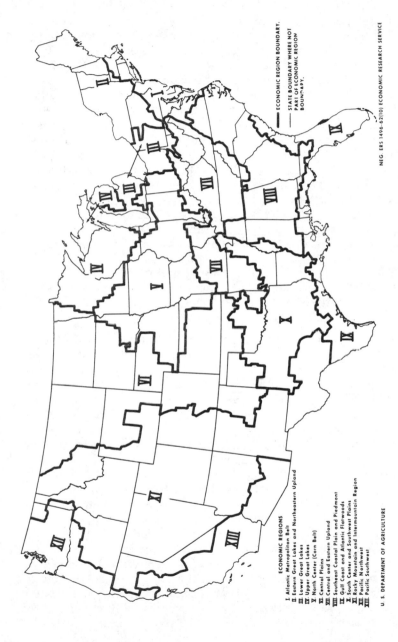

ECONOMIC REGIONS

I Atlantic Metropolitan Belt
II Eastern Great Lakes and Northeastern Upland
III Lower Great Lakes
IV Upper Great Lakes
V North Center (Corn Belt)
VI Central Plains
VII Central and Eastern Upland
VIII Southeast Coastal Plain and Piedmont
IX Gulf Coast and Atlantic Flatwoods
X South Center and Southwest Plains
XI Rocky Mountain and Intermountain Region
XII Pacific Northwest
XIII Pacific Southwest

U S DEPARTMENT OF AGRICULTURE

——— ECONOMIC REGION BOUNDARY.

⎯⎯ STATE BOUNDARY WHERE NOT
PART OF ECONOMIC REGION
BOUNDARY.

NEG ERS 1496-62(10) ECONOMIC RESEARCH SERVICE

Fig. 3.1. Economic regions of the United States.

population along the southern and Pacific coastal fringes of the country and giving the interior sections of the South a slowly diminishing share of the national total.

Within each of the economic regions there are substantial growth variations which are revealed by the economic subregions and the individual state economic areas. Of the 121 economic subregions into which the economic regions are divided, 19 lost population, and an additional 38 increased by less than 10 per cent. At the other extreme, five subregions increased by 50 per cent or more, and an additional 17 increased by 25-49 per cent. Figure 3.2 shows the subregions of above-average and below-average growth. Table 3.2 lists the subregions of exceptional population gain and actual population loss.[1] The subregions where population declined are concentrated in the hilly or mountainous portion of the Appalachians and Ozark-Ouachita Highlands, depressed coal-mining areas, agricultural sections of the Old South Coastal Plain, rural sections of the Northern Central Plains, and marginal portions of the Corn Belt.

Thus despite a fairly rapid rate of national growth, much of this growth accrued only to a comparatively few subregions while a majority of regions and subregions grew moderately slowly, and some actually lost population.

2. Metropolitan and Nonmetropolitan Distribution. Between 1950 and 1960, the long-term drift toward the metropolitan centers of the nation continued unabated. The 1960 Census recognized 212 "standard metropolitan statistical areas" (hereafter referred to as SMSA's).[2] Together, these major population clusters contained a total of 112-plus million persons, or 63 per cent of the total population. Between 1950 and 1960, these areas grew by 26.4 per cent and managed to capture 84 per cent of the increase in the total population of the nation. The vast nonmetropolitan territory grew only at the rate of 7.5 per cent, or only about 28 per cent as fast as the SMSA's. This was merely a replication of the 1940-50 experience which saw about 80 per cent of the total national increase absorbed by even fewer metropolitan areas and during which the nonmetropolitan areas grew only 27 per cent as fast as the metropolitan areas.

Inasmuch as the Economic Areas system distinguishes between metropolitan and nonmetropolitan areas, it is possible to measure the extent of population concentration and comparative rates of growth in metropolitan and nonmetropolitan portions of each economic province and region. Table 3.3 presents this

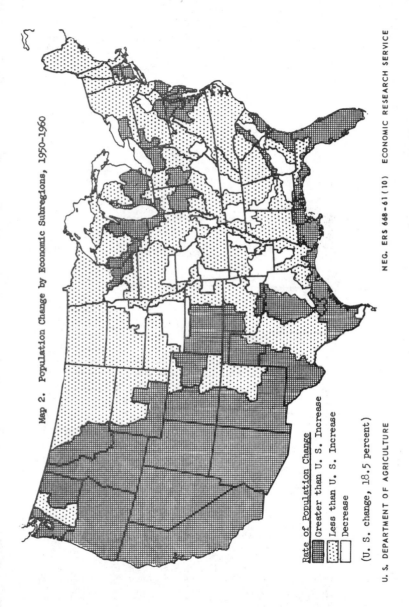

Map 2. Population Change by Economic Subregions, 1950–1960

Rate of Population Change
Greater than U. S. Increase
Less than U. S. Increase
Decrease

(U. S. change, 18.5 percent)

U. S. DEPARTMENT OF AGRICULTURE

NEG. ERS 668–61 (10)   ECONOMIC RESEARCH SERVICE

Fig. 3.2. Population changes by economic subregions, 1950–60.

Table 3.2. Economic Subregions That Experienced an Intercensal Population
Growth of 25 Per Cent or More, or a Population Loss,
1950–60

Region	Subregion Number	Name of Economic Subregion	Per Cent Change 1950–60
		Subregions increasing 25.0 per cent or more, 1950–60	
I	14	Philadelphia Subregion (Part in New Jersey)	42.2
I	15	South Jersey Coast, Delmarva and Virginia Peninsulas Subregion	29.3
I	19	Northern Piedmont Subregion	29.8
VIII	35	South Carolina-Georgia Fall Line Sand Hills Subregion.	25.6
IX	39	Florida Peninsula Subregion	101.0
IX	40	Florida Flatwoods Subregion	46.3
V	47	West Central Ohio-Central Indiana Subregion	26.1
IX	58	Central Gulf Coast Subregion	29.6
IX	77	Louisiana Sugarcane Subregion.................	26.0
IX	78	Louisiana-Texas Coast Prairies Subregion	41.1
IX	98	Corpus Christi-San Antonio Subregion	26.8
X	102	Southern High Plains Subregion	55.4
VI	103	South Central Plains Subregion	31.7
XI	108	Trans Pecos and Southern New Mexico Subregion	45.0
XI	112	Snake River Valley, Wasatch Front, and Utah Valleys Subregion..................................	26.3
XI	113	Western Desert, Semi-Desert, and Mountain Subregion.	27.3
XIII	114	Southern Arizona Subregion...................	84.9
XIII	115	Southern California Subregion	59.7
XIII	116	California Central Valley Subregion	35.4
XIII	117	Central Pacific Coast and San Francisco Bay Subregion.................................	36.5
XII	120	Alaska Subregion............................	150.3
XII	121	Hawaii Subregion............................	26.6
		Subregions losing population, 1950–60	
II	11	Pennsylvania Anthracite Subregion	-9.3
VII	31	Southern Appalachian Coal Mining Subregion	-13.5
VIII	36	South Carolina-Georgia Upper Coastal Plain Subregion.................................	-1.4
VIII	41	Georgia-Alabama Central Coastal Plain Subregion....	-0.8
VII	44	Eastern and Western Highland Rim Subregion	-7.7
VIII	56	Alabama Upper Coastal Plain Subregion	-4.2
VIII	60	Tennessee-Mississippi Fall Line Slopes and Pine Hills Subregion	-9.5
VII	62	Southern Illinois Subregion	-10.3
V	71	Southern Iowa-Northern Missouri-West Central Illinois Subregion	-4.3
X	75	Crowley's Ridge and Arkansas Prairies Subregion ...	-14.6
X	80	Arkansas-Louisiana-Texas Coastal Plain Subregion...	-6.6
VII	81	Ouachita Mountains Subregion	-11.7
VII	82	Springfield Upland Subregion	-1.4
V	84	Kansas-Missouri Corn Belt Border Subregion	-0.5
V	87	Minnesota-South Dakota Corn Belt Margin Subregion ..	-2.4
V	88	Minnesota Forest Margin Subregion	-0.9
VI	91	Black Prairies Subregion (Southern Part)	-2.5
V	92	Nebraska-South Dakota Corn Belt Margin Subregion...	-3.1
V	93	Kansas-Nebraska Corn Belt Winter Wheat Transition Subregion	-9.4

Source: 1960 Census of Population, Table 38 (10).

Table 3.3. Percentage Change in Total Population of Metropolitan and Nonmetropolitan Portions of Economic Regions, by Urban-Rural Residence, 1950-60

Province and Region	Region Number	All Areas			Metropolitan Areas			Nonmetropolitan Areas			Per Cent Metropolitan, 1960
		Total	Urban	Rural	Total	Urban	Rural	Total	Urban	Rural	
Total..........	...	18.5	29.3	-0.8	26.4	30.6	1.8	7.5	24.9	-1.6	62.1
A. Atlantic Metropolitan Belt Province	...	17.5	18.6	10.8	16.2	17.5	4.8	32.1	44.9	22.7	90.6
Atlantic Metropolitan Belt Region	I	17.5	18.6	10.8	16.2	17.5	4.8	32.1	44.9	22.7	90.6
B. The Great Lakes and Northeastern Province..	...	15.7	19.6	6.5	19.4	22.1	3.5	8.9	10.1	8.0	67.4
Eastern Great Lakes and Northeastern Upland Region	II	9.7	8.4	11.8	12.2	10.8	18.0	7.5	4.4	9.9	48.2
Lower Great Lakes Region	III	18.6	22.1	5.8	20.3	23.2	0.5	11.7	12.9	10.8	82.0
Upper Great Lakes Region....	IV	14.5	27.9	-0.1	28.9	39.1	-15.1	7.4	16.0	2.2	37.2
C. The Midwestern Province	...	13.6	28.0	-2.0	30.1	35.6	4.4	5.2	19.3	-2.9	38.3
North Center (Corn Belt) Region....	V	12.6	23.7	0.2	25.2	29.3	6.1	5.6	16.6	-0.7	39.6
Central Plains Region....	VI	16.4	41.6	-8.1	49.5	59.5	-2.9	4.1	26.3	-8.6	34.7
D. The Southern Province	...	14.7	38.3	-6.3	35.0	43.5	1.6	2.7	29.4	-7.6	43.7
Central and Eastern Upland Region ...	VII	5.1	20.2	-6.6	18.2	22.2	1.7	-2.6	15.9	-7.8	41.7
Southeast Coastal Plain and Piedmont Region	VIII	9.6	32.3	-5.1	28.8	37.7	5.2	2.1	26.4	-6.6	33.3
Atlantic Flatwoods and Gulf Coast Region........	IX	43.1	63.2	14.7	56.7	63.4	16.7	33.8	62.5	13.9	66.1
South Center and Southwest Plains Region.........	X	3.3	40.8	-19.9	37.8	55.2	-28.3	-3.8	26.6	-18.8	37.1
E. The Western Province	...	33.6	55.7	1.9	48.5	58.8	-7.0	21.4	42.9	6.6	71.4
Rocky Mountain and Intermountain Region	XI	25.7	54.2	0.3	60.2	79.4	-15.7	18.0	41.4	1.7	26.2
Pacific Northwest Region	XII	21.7	34.2	4.3	23.9	33.7	-5.7	19.2	35.1	9.0	54.7
Pacific Southwest Region	XIII	50.1	61.6	1.4	53.0	62.1	-6.5	30.8	54.3	13.2	88.4

Source: Bogue and Beale, op. cit., Table A (1).

information. The extreme right-hand column of this table presents data which show the per cent of each economic region's population residing in metropolitan areas in 1960.

Five of the regions are predominantly metropolitan, and eight are predominantly nonmetropolitan in composition. Region I (Atlantic Metropolitan Belt), Region XIII (Pacific Southwest), and Region III (Lower Great Lakes) are especially heavily metropolitanized. The eight least metropolitanized regions are:

	Population Per Cent Metropolitan, 1960
Region XI. Rocky Mountain and Intermountain Region	26.2
Region VIII. Southeast Coastal Plain Region .	33.3
Region VI. Central Plains Region.	34.7
Region IV. Upper Great Lakes Region.	37.2
Region X. South Center and Southwest Plains Region	37.4
Region V. North Center (Corn Belt) Region . .	39.6
Region VII. Central and Eastern Upland Region	41.7
Region II. Eastern Great Lakes and Northeastern Upland Region	48.2

There is almost no correlation between degree of metropolitanization and rate of growth. While it is true that both of the fastest growing economic regions are highly metropolitanized, two other highly metropolitanized regions (Regions I and III) grew only at an average rate. Moreover, the least metropolitanized region of all (Region XI) grew faster than all but two of the more metropolitanized regions. Thus, despite the fact that metropolitan areas were growing much faster than nonmetropolitan areas, the over-all regional rate of growth was only mildly influenced by the proportion of the population residing in metropolitan areas. This apparent inconsistency is explained by the fact that there are great regional differences in the rates of metropolitan growth. In three regions (Regions I, II, and VII), the metropolitan areas grew more slowly than the average growth rate for the nation while in Regions VI, IX, XI, and XIII metropolitan growth was almost explosive. In other words, there is a genuine regional differential in metropolitan growth.

In the more densely settled regions, nonmetropolitan areas tended to grow some as a result of the spill-over from metropolitan areas; Region I was especially noteworthy in this respect for the nonmetropolitan areas grew faster than the metropolitan areas.

Although metropolitan areas grew more rapidly than nonmetropolitan areas, there was wide variation in this. Perhaps the most extraordinary metropolitanization development occurred in Regions VI, X, and XI where metropolitan areas grew moderately rapidly despite the fact that the nonmetropolitan portions grew very slowly and even lost population over much of their territory.

Table 3.8 reveals the somewhat surprising fact that the size of the SMSA had almost nothing to do with its rate of growth. SMSA's of one million or more grew at nearly the same rate as SMSA's of less than 100,000. The variations in growth between places of different size are associated primarily with regional location of such places rather than with size as such.

3. Rural-Urban. In considering changes in the population by urban-rural status, one must distinguish clearly between changes in comparable areas over time and changes that reflect reclassification of the status of areas as a result of the trends occurring within them. The census results show only the latter type of data. On this basis the urban population of the nation gained by 29.3 per cent from 1950-60 while the rural population declined by 0.8 per cent. On current boundaries, urban people numbered 125,269,000 in 1960, or nearly 70 per cent of the total population, whereas rural people numbered 54,054,000. The fact that in 1960 the Current Population Survey of the Bureau of the Census was still being conducted on the urban-rural boundaries of 1950 enables us to estimate how many persons live in territory that was rural in 1950 but that was reclassified as urban in 1960. The CPS for April, 1960, showed 69,964,000 rural people, or nearly 16,000,000 more than the decennial census. Some of this difference could be attributed to sampling variation in the CPS. Some of it stems from the fact that the concept of urban residence was broadened somewhat from previous usage by changes introduced into the 1960 Census. But, the overwhelming part of the 16,000,000 reclassified population results from growth of suburban districts or former small towns that changed the character of the areas concerned from rural to urban.

The total territory of the nation that was rural in 1950

experienced a net inmovement of population in the decade, despite the heavy losses from the farm population. This net inmovement was probably on the order of 10 per cent of the 1950 base population. (The amount cannot be measured precisely.) However, if one considers the rural population as currently defined in each decade, then rural people remained almost stationary in numbers and lost an amount equivalent to their natural increase from outmovement and the change in the character of communities from rural to urban.

One phenomenon which may not be widely appreciated is that within the slow-growing nonmetropolitan territory of the nation, the urban population is growing at an above-average rate. In fact, its 25 per cent rate of increase from 1950-60 almost equals the rate of growth of all SMSA's. Even in regions where the rural parts of nonmetropolitan areas were declining, the urban population increased substantially. Most of this growth is real, rather than the fruit of ambitious annexation policies.

Of the 13 economic regions, in only two did rural people still comprise a majority of the population in 1960 (see Table 3.4). These were the Central and Eastern Upland (which includes the Appalachians), and the Southeast Coastal Plains and Piedmont. The rural proportions in these most rural regions were 50.1 and 52.5, and will surely decline below 50.0 in the very near future. The most urban region is no longer the Atlantic Metropolitan Belt which has been regarded as the epitome of urbanism for so long. As a result of the tremendous growth of the Pacific Southwest since 1950—plus the existence of rather liberal annexation policies—that region has become the most urban (87.1 per cent). With the notable exception of the Pacific Southwest, where the rural population was nearly stationary, one finds that the rural population has grown where the urban population is relatively most numerous, but has declined in the least urban areas. The existence of a large, dense, and growing urban population in a region tends to create conditions of population growth in rural counties of the same region. This is true not only because an ever-larger number of the rural counties are within commuting range of urban centers, but also because more distant counties are affected by the accession of businesses or residents who do not need frequent commutation to the city but whose work or choice of residence is related to the city— especially the large metropolitan city. These are counties beyond "exurbia" which the geographer Wilbur Zelinsky has referred to as the "urban penumbra."

Table 3.4. Population by Economic Provinces and Regions, by Urban-Rural Residence, 1960

Name of Region	Region Number	Population, 1960			Per Cent Urban	Per Cent Rural
		Total	Urban	Rural		
Total	. . . . .	179,323,175	125,270,616	54,052,559	69.9	30.1
A. Atlantic Metropolitan Belt Province . . .	. . . . .	36,500,804	31,603,170	4,897,634	86.6	13.4
Atlantic Metropolitan Belt Region	I	36,500,804	31,603,170	4,897,634	86.6	13.4
B. The Great Lakes and Northeastern Province .	. . . . .	41,079,517	29,798,281	11,281,236	72.5	27.5
Eastern Great Lakes and Northeastern Upland Region	II	10,116,810	6,087,691	4,029,119	60.2	39.8
Lower Great Lakes Region	III	25,212,494	20,358,868	4,853,626	80.7	19.3
Upper Great Lakes Region	IV	5,750,213	3,351,722	2,398,491	58.3	41.7
C. The Midwestern Province	. . . . .	23,183,783	13,550,952	9,632,831	58.5	41.5
North Center (Corn Belt) Region	V	17,169,930	9,942,641	7,227,289	57.9	42.1
Central Plains Region	VI	6,013,853	3,608,311	2,405,542	60.0	40.0
D. The Southern Province	. . . . .	52,079,103	29,616,166	22,462,937	56.9	43.1
Central and Eastern Upland Region	VII	14,882,135	7,421,755	7,460,380	49.9	50.1
Southeast Coastal Plain and Piedmont Region	VIII	16,391,896	7,788,643	8,603,253	47.5	52.5
Atlantic Flatwoods and Gulf Coast Region . .	IX	11,812,018	8,971,391	2,840,627	76.0	24.0
South Center and Southwest Plains Region .	X	8,993,054	5,434,377	3,558,677	60.4	39.6
E. The Western Province	. . . . .	26,479,968	20,702,047	5,777,921	78.2	21.8
Rocky Mountain and Intermountain Region . .	XI	4,568,878	2,727,282	1,841,596	59.7	40.3
Pacific Northwest Region	XII	4,918,314	3,169,316	1,748,998	64.4	35.6
Pacific Southwest Region	XIII	16,992,776	14,805,449	2,187,327	87.1	12.9

Source: Bogue and Beale, op. cit., Table A (1).

4. <u>Farm-Nonfarm</u>. The rural-farm population, as counted in
the 1960 Census, numbered 13,445,000, or just 7.5 per cent of
the total population. The count in 1950 was 23,048,000. A heavy
decline in farm population has assuredly occurred, but unfortunately, a major change in definition makes direct comparison
of the 1950 and 1960 figures impossible. (17) The authors estimate that roughly two-fifths of the change shown between the
two censuses is caused by use of a more restrictive definition
of farm residence in 1960. (The Current Population Survey
showed a higher count of farm people than did the decennial
census in both 1960 and 1950, but the absolute amount of change
over the 10 years was about the same as in the census.)

The South and the Northeast show the greatest rates of farm
population loss. Heavy declines in the South have stemmed especially from (1) the wide-spread abandonment of tenant farming
in cotton and tobacco areas and the consolidation of land by landlords into larger operating units, (2) the rapid conversion of
certain upland areas to forestry, and (3) the reclassification as
nonfarm of many residential-type operations, especially in the
Appalachian areas. In the overwhelmingly nonagricultural
Northeast, the increased conversion of farmland to urban and
other nonfarm uses and the reclassification in the census of
many areas from rural to urban have added to the long-time
decline of agriculture in that region to produce large farm population losses.

There are some scattered areas where farm population increased, but only in Texas can one find a sizeable number of
them. Texas had 16 counties showing such increases. Irrigation developments—mostly in the High Plains—were generally
responsible for these exceptions to the over-all pattern.

There has been a tendency for an increasing proportion of
farm operators to live off-farm, but in absolute terms the number of farmers doing so has not increased since 1950. The
group still accounts for only 7.6 per cent of all farmers, according to the Census of Agriculture. Thus, although one finds this
trend commented upon in various parts of the country, it has not
as yet resulted in any general relocation of farm operators in
towns.

5. <u>Size-of-place Distribution</u>. The growth of population settlements induced the incorporation of nearly 1,000 additional
communities in the 1950's, raising the total number of incorporated places to 18,088. Three-fourths of the new incorpora-
tions are found in urbanized areas, for there, after all, is where

much of the creation of new communities in the form of suburbs
has taken place. The most notable trend in the distribution of
population by size of place was the declining population within
the limits of the largest cities. In 1950, there were 18 cities in
the country of 500,000 or more residents and every one of them
had grown during the 1940's. In a marked reversal of trend, 14
of these 18 cities declined in population during the 1950's—some
rather sharply—and the four that grew did so only through huge
annexations of territory or by having an abnormally large land
area at the beginning of the decade. In every instance the declining size of the largest cities reflects only a redistribution
of population within the metropolitan area rather than a mori-
bund state in the metropolitan area as a whole.

Three size classes of cities have absorbed most of the
growth of population (Table 3.5). They are the groups 10,000 to
25,000, 25,000 to 50,000, and 50,000 to 100,000. In each of these
classes, most of the places already in the group in 1950 grew,
additional cities were added as a result of the growth of smaller
places, and completely new cities—usually suburban—were
created by incorporation. Together, these size classes contained 19.5 per cent of the nation's population in 1950, but had
25.8 per cent by 1960. Towns of 5,000 to 10,000 size held their
own in retaining their share of the total population during the
decade. Towns of 2,000 to 5,000 people experienced some absolute growth of population as a group but declined relatively.
The population in places of less than 2,000 population dropped
slightly (even when urban suburbs are included) and the proportionate importance of such communities fell sharply. Thus, the
nation has had a rapid development of its medium-sized munici-
palities, a rather average growth of places just above or below
medium size, and a stationary condition or decline of population
in the largest and smallest places. A decline in the number and
population of small places had been evident since 1950. However, although the loss of population in the large cities was not
surprising to demographers who had followed the trends in
demolition of housing units in cities and in changing size of
urban households, it came as a shock to incredulous mayors
and chambers of commerce to whom population growth was the
sine qua non of civic pride.

6. County Distribution by Population Size. Of the 3,134 counties and equivalent units in the United States, 361 are entirely
or partly included in metropolitan areas. The metropolitan
counties number less than 12 per cent of all counties, yet 84 per

Table 3.5. Population in Groups of Places Classified
According to Size: 1960 and 1950

| Size of Place | Population | | Percentage Distribution | | Per Cent Change in Population |
	1960	1950	1960	1950	1950–60
Total U.S. population	179,323,175	151,325,798	100.0	100.0	18.5
Total, all places	125,802,087	100,049,413	70.2	66.1	25.7
1,000,000 or more	17,484,059	17,404,450	9.8	11.5	0.5
100,000–1,000,000	33,529,298	27,155,201	18.7	17.9	23.5
50,000–100,000	13,835,902	8,930,823	7.7	5.9	54.9
25,000–50,000	14,950,612	8,834,919	8.3	5.8	69.2
10,000–25,000	17,568,286	11,877,759	9.8	7.8	47.9
5,000–10,000	9,779,714	8,192,636	5.5	5.4	19.4
2,000–5,000	9,577,903	8,403,563	5.3	5.6	14.0
Under 2,000	9,076,313	9,250,062	5.1	6.1	-1.9

Source: 1960 Census of Population, Tables 5, 7, and 8 (10).

cent of the nation's total population growth in the 1950's occurred within them. In view of this concentration of growth it is
not surprising to note that almost half of all counties (49 per
cent) actually declined in population. The same type of phenomenon took place in the 1940's, but since the over-all amount of
population growth was much lower in that decade the anomaly
between the rapid growth of metropolitan areas and the decline
or near-stationary trend of most other counties was more impressive in the 1950's.

For many years the modal-sized counties have been those
having between 10,000 to 50,000 people. However, in contrast to
so many other aspects of American life in which the tendency
has been towards an increased clustering trend around the mode
or average and a reduction of extremes, the modal-sized county
has been declining in frequency.

Table 3.6. Distribution of Counties by Population Size, 1960,
1950, and 1940   (Includes independent cities
and other county equivalents)

Population Size of County	Number			Per Cent Distribution			Per Cent Change in Number of Counties Since 1940
	1960	1950	1940	1960	1950	1940	
Total	3,134	3,112	3,100	100.0	100.0	100.0	1.1
50,000 or more . .	596	501	442	19.0	16.1	14.3	34.8
10,000 to 50,000 . .	1,683	1,833	1,940	53.7	58.9	62.6	-13.2
Under 10,000	855	778	718	27.3	25.0	23.2	19.1

Source: 1960 Census of Population, Table H (10), and 1950 Census of
Population, Table H (6).

It can be seen from Table 3.6 that there were 257 fewer
counties having between 10,000 and 50,000 people in 1960 than
there were in 1940, and that such counties now comprise barely
more than one-half of all counties. By contrast, both extremes—
the very populous counties and the very small counties—became
more numerous. It is obvious from these data that the nation is
experiencing an increasing divergence in the density of land

settlement in its basic political unit—the county.

Of the counties that have been losing population or that have less than 10,000 people, the great majority are agricultural. It is not the purpose of this report to deal with the implications of current trends, but it is obvious that declining population and the accompanying problems of very low density of settlement and low absolute population levels per county are exceptionally widespread in rural areas. It would be unfortunate if the attention being focused on the rapid growth of metropolitan areas and suburbs were to obscure the antithetical trend which affects so much of the rest of the nation.

7. Type-of-place Distribution. As yet the authors have made only a few tentative analyses of population trends with communities classified according to type. Exploratory work indicates that on a nationwide basis a community's regional or subregional location is more significant than its economic type in influencing its growth rate. Some significant exceptions to this are (1) the educational centers, (2) the medical centers, and (3) the recreational centers; these tend to be growing more rapidly than the communities of corresponding size in the region in which they are located. We also hypothesized that governmental centers (such as county seats) would grow more rapidly than other nearby towns, but exploratory tabulations did not support the idea very consistently.

SMSA's of a type where manufacturing is a dominating element of the basic economy grew more slowly, on the average, than other types of SMSA's. This may be demonstrated by classifying SMSA's according to the classification of metropolitan areas of 300,000 or more (see Table 3.7) recently developed by O. Dudley Duncan and his associates (3).

This slower growth of manufacturing S̄MSA's was also characteristic both of their central cities and their metropolitan rings. It is not clear, however, whether this is due uniquely to their economic classification or to the fact that all are located in regions where over-all growth was low. The very rapidly growing "special cases" are primarily developing centers along the southern border of the nation, which many persons still mistakenly regard merely as winter vacation spas or retirement communities (Miami, Tampa, San Diego, San Antonio, Phoenix, etc.)

8. Central Cities and Metropolitan Rings. In each decade since 1920, the "metropolitan ring," or the part of the SMSA lying outside the central city, has grown more rapidly than the

Table 3.7. Population Growth Rates in Metropolitan Areas
of 300,000 Persons or More, by Type of Metropolis,
1950-60

Type of Metropolis	Average of Per Cent Change for Individual Places, 1950-60		
	Total	Central Cities	Metropolitan Rings
1. National metropolis (5 largest) . . .	25.9	2.2	70.9
2. Diversified manufacturing with metropolitan functions	16.2	-8.2	41.4
3. Diversified manufacturing with few metropolitan functions	20.9	0.4	49.4
4. Specialized manufacturing	15.5	2.1	34.4
5. Regional metropolis	33.2	17.0	62.0
6. Regional capital submetropolitan . .	31.7	16.4	68.5
7. Special cases	51.6	62.5	49.5

Source: Duncan, et al. (3).

central city itself, and the 1950-60 decade continued this trend.
Whereas the central cities had an average growth of only 10.7
per cent between 1950 and 1960, the metropolitan rings increased at a rate of 48.6 per cent. This large differential between central cities and suburbs was characteristic of all
regions (see Table 3.8). In fact, almost all of the modest net
increases in the population of central cities were due to annexation. Table 3.8 shows population growth rates for the central
cities and metropolitan rings according to their 1950 boundaries.
With population gain from annexation thus controlled, central
city growth was almost zero (1.5 per cent) while suburban
growth was 61.7 per cent. Thus, as a group, central cities were
among the demographically stagnant parts of the nation. Since
their birth rates were well above replacement, this could mean
only that they were losing population in substantial amounts
through outmigration.

Table 3.9 shows that this tendency toward slow central city
growth and rapid suburban growth was characteristic of both
small and large SMSA's. This suggests that most central cities
in the nation, irrespective of size, have largely filled up their
space with settlement, and that henceforth they can grow only
by annexation or by increasing average density.

Table 3.8. Per Cent Increase in Population Within Central
Cities and Metropolitan Rings of Standard Metropolitan
Statistical Areas, Holding City Boundaries Constant,
1950-60, by Region and Size of SMSA

Census Region and Size of SMSA in 1960	SMSA Total	Central Cities	Metropolitan Rings
United States, total.....	26.4	1.5	61.7
Regions:			
Northeast...........	13.0	-3.3	35.0
North Central	23.5	-1.6	66.5
South	36.2	5.3	83.3
West	48.5	14.5	84.1
SMSA population in 1960:			
3,000,000 or more	23.2	0.6	72.2
1,000,000 to 3,000,000...	25.0	-2.2	52.7
500,000 to 1,000,000	36.0	4.8	81.1
250,000 to 500,000	25.6	2.2	51.9
100,000 to 250,000	25.8	4.6	54.5
Under 100,000	24.4	8.6	69.9

Source: 1960 Census of Population (11).

9. Urbanization and Suburbanization of Negroes. In 1960,
73.2 per cent of the Negro population was residing in urban
areas. Consequently, it was somewhat more urban than the
white population. Only two decades ago, less than one-half of
the Negro population was living in urban areas and Negroes
were considerably more rural in their distribution than were
whites. This change represents the climax of a process that
has been underway for more than a century; since 1850, the
Negro population has been urbanizing at an accelerating pace.
Inasmuch as the remaining rural Negro population still has
many landless tenant farmers and farm laborers, it may be expected that the urbanward movement of Negroes will continue.
This flow is not only toward Northern industrial centers, but
toward cities in the South and West as well.

Until World War II, Negroes migrating to the city usually
settled in deteriorating areas adjoining central business districts. As a result, they tended to be almost entirely central
city residents. During the 1940-50 decade, small evidences of

Table 3.9. Metropolitan Central Cities That Lost Population From 1950-60
(Boundaries not held constant where annexations occurred)

City and State	Per Cent Change, 1950-60	
	SMSA	Central City
Albany-Schenectady-Troy, N.Y.	11.6	- 6.8
Altoona, Pa.	- 1.6	-10.1
Atlantic City, N.J.	21.5	- 3.4
Augusta, Ga.*	33.7	- 1.2
Baltimore, Md.	22.9	- 1.1
Binghamton, N.Y.	15.1	- 5.9
Boston, Mass.	7.4	-13.0
Bridgeport, Conn.	22.2	- 1.2
Buffalo, N.Y.	20.0	- 8.2
Canton, Ohio	20.2	- 2.8
Charleston, S.C.	31.3	- 6.1
Chattanooga, Tenn.-Ga.*	14.9	- 0.8
Chicago, Ill.*	20.1	- 1.9
Cincinnati, Ohio-Ky.*	18.5	- 0.3
Cleveland, Ohio	22.6	- 4.2
Detroit, Mich.	24.7	- 9.7
Fall River, Mass.-R.I.	0.6	-10.7
Harrisburg, Pa.	18.1	-11.0
Hartford, Conn.	29.2	- 8.6
Huntington-Ashland, W.Va.-Ky.	3.7	- 2.2
Jackson, Mich.	22.3	- 0.7
Jacksonville, Fla.	49.8	- 1.7
Jersey City, N.J.	- 5.7	- 7.7
Johnstown, Pa.	- 3.6	-14.7
Knoxville, Tenn.	9.2	-10.4
Lancaster, Pa.*	18.6	- 4.3
Lawrence-Haverhill, Mass.-N.H.	2.8	- 8.2
Lowell, Mass.	16.2	- 5.3
Macon, Ga.*	33.6	- 0.7
Minneapolis-St. Paul, Minn.	28.8	- 4.4
Muskegon-Muskegon Heights, Mich.	23.4	- 1.8
Nashville, Tenn.*	24.2	- 2.0
New Bedford, Mass.	0.8	- 6.1
New Haven, Conn.	15.6	- 7.5
New York, N.Y.	11.9	- 1.4
Newark, N.J.	15.0	- 7.6
Peoria, Ill.*	15.3	- 7.8
Philadelphia, Pa.-N.J.	18.3	- 3.3
Pittsburgh, Pa.	8.7	-10.7
Portland, Me.	0.6	- 6.5
Portland, Oreg.-Wash.	16.6	- 0.3
Providence-Pawtucket, R.I.-Mass.	7.4	-12.6
Reading, Pa.	7.7	-10.2
Richmond, Va.	24.5	- 4.5
Rochester, N.Y.	20.3	- 4.2
St. Louis, Mo.-Ill.	19.8	-17.4
San Francisco-Oakland, Calif.	24.2	- 4.5
Scranton, Pa.	- 8.9	-11.2
Syracuse, N.Y.	21.2	- 2.1
Trenton, N.J.	15.9	-10.8
Washington, D.C.	36.7	- 4.8
Wheeling, W. Va.	- 3.0	- 9.3
Wilkes Barre-Hazelton, Pa.	-11.5	-14.9
Wilmington, Del.	36.4	-13.2
Worcester, Mass.	6.7	- 8.3
York, Pa.*	17.6	- 9.1

*Denotes central cities declining in total population despite annexation of at least 1,000 people during the decade.
Source: 1960 Census of Population (10).

a suburbanward movement of Negroes appeared. During the
1950-60 decade this movement became a noticeable flow. Since
the pattern of entrance into a new neighborhood by any ethnic
group is typically one of rapid acceleration after an initial penetration, it may be expected that during the 1960-70 decade this
comparatively new development will become a trend and pick up
speed.

Table 3.10. Change in Negro Population of the Five Largest
Standard Metropolitan Statistical Areas, 1950-60

SMSA	Increase 1950-60 (number)		Per Cent Increase 1950-60	
	Central cities	Metropolitan rings	Central cities	Metropolitan rings
New York	340,323	67,075	45.5	92.4
Chicago	320,372	33,867	65.0	77.6
Los Angeles . .	168,971	76,976	96.3	177.8
Philadelphia . .	153,199	38,030	40.7	36.6
Detroit	181,717	19,353	60.5	33.8

Source: 1960 Census of Population (12).

A ten-year flow of 20,000 to 75,000 Negroes into the suburbs
of each of the five largest SMSA's is indeed a new development
(see Table 3.10). That this is not just an isolated event of these
very largest places may be seen from Table 3.11 which reports
the number of Negroes living in metropolitan rings of the 15
largest SMSA's and the per cent of the ring population which now
is Negro. In 11 of the 15 the number exceeds 50,000, but the
proportion Negro is still low, not exceeding 7 per cent.

B. Composition Trends

In addition to distributional shifts, the population experienced
significant compositional changes between 1950 and 1960. As
with distribution, most of these changes were continuations of
trends already underway in the 1940-50 decade or earlier.

1. Age Composition. The age composition of a population is
closely tied to its fertility rate. Low fertility brings an older

Table 3.11. Negro Population of the Metropolitan Rings
of the 15 Largest Standard Metropolitan Statistical
Areas, 1960

SMSA	Metropolitan Ring, Negro Population 1960	Per Cent Negro 1960
New York, N.Y.	139,694	4.8
Los Angeles–Long Beach, Calif. . . .	120,270	3.1
Chicago, Ill.	77,517	2.9
Philadelphia, Pa.	142,064	6.1
Detroit, Mich.	76,647	3.7
San Francisco–Oakland, Calif.	80,753	4.8
Boston, Mass.	14,616	0.8
Pittsburgh, Pa.	60,807	3.4
St. Louis, Mo.-Ill.	80,496	6.1
Washington, D.C.-Md.-Va.	75,446	6.1
Cleveland, Ohio	6,455	0.7
Baltimore, Md.	51,986	6.6
Newark, N.J.	86,049	6.7
Minneapolis–St. Paul, Minn.	677	0.1
Buffalo, N.Y.	12,006	1.6

Source: 1960 Census of Population (12).

age composition while high fertility brings a younger age composition. During the long decline in fertility from 1820 to 1940,
the median age of the population rose steadily from census to
census until, in 1950, it attained 30.2 years. Because of the
cumulative effect of the baby boom, this trend was reversed
during the 1950-60 decade, and for the first time the median age
declined, to 29.5 in 1960. The effect upon the age structure of
this fertility upsurge is summarized in Table 3.12.

Between 1950 and 1960, the proportion of elderly persons increased, mostly as a result of the aging of population associated
with fertility decline before 1940. Thus, between 1950 and 1960,
there was a simultaneous increase in the proportion of young-
sters and oldsters, with a compensating decline in the proportion of adults.

As noted in the discussion of distributional trends, the population of nearly half the counties in the country dropped both in
the 1950's and the 1940's. These losses of population have been
produced by heavy outmigration of people. Such migration is
selective of age groups and where it has been sudden or prolonged

Table 3.12. Distribution of U.S. Population by Stages of the
Life Cycle, 1960, 1950, 1880

Stage of the Life Cycle	Percentage Distribution of Population		
	1960	1950	1880
Childhood (0-8 years)	19.9	18.0	24.4
Youth (9-17 years)	16.4	13.2	19.4
Adulthood (18-64 years)	55.0	60.6	52.8
Old age (65 and older)	8.7	8.2	3.4

Source: 1960 Census of Population, Table 46 (15).

has resulted in severe distortion of the age structure of many
affected counties. The highest rates of outmigration occur
among people between 18 and 30 years of age. If a county is exposed to such outmigration over a period of time it becomes
heavily weighted with middle-aged or elderly persons. The
median age of the population rises and, with the departure of so
many young parents and potential parents, the number of very
young children declines. This phenomenon has occurred in
hundreds of small and medium-sized counties. No summary
data have yet been compiled on the subject but an example will
illustrate the point.

In Mills County, Texas, a completely agricultural county, the
median age of the population in 1940 was lower than the median
for the United States as a whole (27.7 years compared with
29.0). Between 1940 and 1960 the population of Mills County declined by 44 per cent as the result of heavy outmigration stemming from extensive adjustments in the organization of farming.
In consequence, the median age in the county soared to 44.6
years by 1960 and was 15 years higher than the U.S. average,
which rose only to 29.5 years. The number of young adults in
the county who are 20-29 years old is now less than half as
large as the number of persons 50-59 years and is even considerably smaller than the number of elderly people 70-79
years old. Needless to say, such a relationship in the size of
the different age groups of the population is strikingly different
from that which prevails in almost any urban or growing area.
With the loss of potential or actual young parents, the number
of children under 5 years old in Mills County is now smaller
than the group 5-9 years old which in turn is smaller than the

number 10-14. This is a new situation for this county and for the many similar counties that exist.

In the most advanced cases of prolonged or severe outmigration, the distortion of the age structure has increased the proportion of older persons and decreased the proportion of young married couples to the point where deaths now exceed births. A sprinkling of such counties began to appear in the mid and late 1950's in states like Missouri, Kansas, Kentucky, Oklahoma, and Texas. That the abnormal excess of deaths over births is caused by the odd age structure of the counties rather than by low fertility or high mortality can readily be demonstrated by applying the age-by-age birth and death rates of the United States to the population of such a county. In 1959, in the nation as a whole, the crude birth rate per 1,000 total population was 24.1 and the crude death rate 9.4. Thus there were more than two and one-half times more births than deaths nationally. However, in Daviess County, Missouri, which is a Corn Belt area with a long history of outmovement, the same age-by-age birth and death rates applied to the 1960 county population would produce a crude birth rate of only 16.6 and a crude death rate of 18.6. Deaths would exceed births by about one-eighth even though family size and health conditions were normal. Under these conditions it is not surprising that there actually are more deaths now in this county than there are births.

It should be emphasized that the great majority of counties that declined in population in the 1950's are rural and predominantly agricultural. The rapid agricultural adjustments that are taking place are by no means completed. The number of counties losing some population through outmigration because of agricultural changes is not likely to increase much, if any, over the present high levels. But, counties in which outmigration becomes so pronounced as to create a condition producing more deaths than births are likely to increase substantially in the coming decade.

2. Color Composition. Between 1950 and 1960, the Negro population increased from 15.0 to 18.9 million, a gain of 25 per cent compared with an increase of 18 per cent for the entire population. The larger rate of Negro growth resulted from a marked decrease in Negro death rates accompanied by continued high birth rates.

Migration as well as rapid natural increase caused particular parts of the nation to gain large increments of Negro population, especially industrial centers in the Northeast, Midwest, and California, as shown in Table 3.13.

Table 3.13. Increase in the Negro Population
in Selected Large States, 1950-60

State	Amount of Negro Population Increase	Per Cent Increase 1950-60
New York	499,320	54
California	421,689	91
Illinois	391,490	61
Michigan	275,285	62
Ohio	273,025	53
Pennsylvania	214,265	34
New Jersey	196,310	62
Indiana	95,107	55

Source: 1960 Census of Population (12).

In sharp contrast, three states in the South experienced substantial Negro population decline, and most of the others had
slow rates of growth (Table 3.14). Florida, Texas, and
Louisiana, where substantial metropolitanization of Negroes
occurred, are exceptions, as were Delaware and Maryland,
which are as much northern as southern in character.

Most of the growth of Negro population in metropolitan areas
accrued to the central cities. Since central cities were almost
stationary in their total growth, this meant that there was a
very sharp rise in the proportion of the population of these central cities that is nonwhite. For example, the following central
cities had more than 20 per cent of their population nonwhite in
1960:

Per cent nonwhite
1960

Washington	53.9
Atlanta	38.3
New Orleans	37.2
Memphis	37.0
Baltimore	34.8
Detroit	28.9
Cleveland	28.6
St. Louis	28.6
Philadelphia	26.4
Chicago	22.9
Houston	22.9
Cincinnati	21.6

Table 3.14. Negro Population and Per Cent Negro, 1960,
and Per Cent Change in Negro Population, 1950-60

Geographic Division and State	Negro Population 1960	Per Cent Negro	Per Cent Change 1950-60
U.S. total	18,871,831	10.5	25.5
New England	243,363	2.3	70.3
Middle Atlantic	2,785,136	8.2	48.5
New York	1,417,511	8.4	54.4
New Jersey.	514,875	8.5	61.6
Pennsylvania.	852,750	7.5	33.6
East North Central	2,884,969	8.0	59.9
Ohio	786,097	8.1	53.2
Indiana	269,275	5.8	54.6
Illinois	1,037,470	10.3	60.6
Michigan	717,581	9.2	62.2
Wisconsin	74,546	1.9	164.5
West North Central	561,068	3.6	32.2
South Atlantic	5,844,565	22.5	14.7
Delaware	60,688	13.6	39.2
Maryland	518,410	16.7	34.3
District of Columbia . .	411,737	53.9	46.6
Virginia	816,258	20.6	11.2
West Virginia	89,378	4.8	-22.2
North Carolina	1,116,021	24.5	6.6
South Carolina	829,291	34.8	0.9
Georgia	1,122,596	28.5	5.6
Florida	880,186	17.8	45.9
East South Central	2,698,839	22.4	.01
Kentucky	215,949	7.1	6.9
Tennessee	586,876	16.5	10.6
Alabama	980,271	30.0	0.1
Mississippi	915,743	42.0	-7.2
West South Central	2,768,203	16.3	13.8
Arkansas	388,787	21.8	-8.9
Louisiana	1,039,207	31.9	17.8
Oklahoma	153,084	6.6	5.2
Texas	1,187,125	12.4	21.5
Mountain	123,242	1.8	85.5
Pacific	962,446	4.5	88.5*
Washington	48,738	1.7	58.8
Oregon	18,133	1.0	57.3
California	883,861	5.6	91.2
Alaska	6,771	3.0	(NA)
Hawaii	4,943	0.8	(NA)

*Excluding Alaska and Hawaii.

Source: 1960 Census of Population (12).

It is not unlikely that within 15 years the nonwhite population will be in a majority in many of these cities, unless there is a substantial change (1) in the differential rates of reproduction of white and nonwhite populations, (2) in the tendency for nonwhite population to be segregated within the central city, or (3) in city boundaries.

Nonwhite groups in the United States other than Negroes are as yet a small fraction of the total population—less than one per cent—but are increasing at very high rates (Table 3.15).

Table 3.15. Change in Population of Nonwhite Population Groups, Other Than Negro, 1950-60

Group*	1960	1950	Per Cent Change
Indian	508,675	370,788	37.2
Japanese	260,059	141,768	83.4
Chinese	198,958	117,629	69.1
Filipino	106,426	61,636	72.7
All other	75,045	21,226	253.6

*48 states only. 1950 data for Indian and "All Other" adjusted to be comparable with 1960.

Source: 1960 Census of Population, Table 44 (15).

The American Indian population now numbers more than one-half million, the highest number ever counted. It is thought that the identification of Indians in the 1960 Census was improved by the self-enumeration features of that census. The Japanese and Chinese groups have grown in part from the immigration of brides, many of them married to American soldiers. Data for Hawaii are not shown here, but Hawaii ranks as the only state in which the white population is a minority group.

3. Sex Composition. Between 1950 and 1960 the sex ratio (males per 100 females) declined from 98.6 to 97.1 or by 1.5 ratio points. This is the second decade during which women have outnumbered men; all censuses before 1950 had shown a predominance of males. This change is associated principally with differential mortality. At all ages women enjoy lower mortality rates than men. Other factors are a declining sex ratio in the composition of immigrants, an increase in the proportion of

the population at older ages, and the dying out of older generations of foreign born in which males were a substantial majority.
The trend toward lower sex ratios has been under way since
1910. If the current level of fertility persists, the sex ratio decline will tend to level off in the next 10-20 years unless the sex
differential in mortality widens. However, a decline in the birth
rate could depress the sex ratio further, because of the greater
number of males than females among newborn infants.

Until recently, the predominance of females in the population
was an urban phenomenon confined largely to the more industrial
and commercial regions of the nation. By 1960, however, it had
spread to such an extent that now only a few western and plains
states with large ranching, mining, Indian, or military population have a majority of males. These states are:

State	Sex ratio, 1960
Alaska	132.3
Hawaii	114.8
Nevada	107.1
Wyoming	104.9
North Dakota	104.5
Montana	103.8
Idaho	102.9
South Dakota	102.4
New Mexico	101.8
Arizona	101.2
Washington	101.2

4. Marital Status. Between 1950 and 1960 there was a leveling off of the tendency toward earlier marriage, which was such
a dramatic change between 1940 and 1950. Although the median
age at marriage drifted downward slightly after 1950, the change
was not great and toward the end of the decade appeared to be
reversing itself and rising a little. The "marriage boom" appeared to have reached its peak about 1955-57, and since that
date the further tendency toward teen-age marriage has been
halted (Table 3.16). As a result, the percentage increase in the
number of married couples was almost identical with the percentage increase in the population 14 years and over.

However, there has been a continuation of the tendency for
widowed, divorced, and single older persons to marry. For
example, the proportion of males 45-64 years of age who are
married increased from 1950 to 1960 by a greater number of

Table 3.16. Median Age at First Marriage, 1940-60

Year	Male	Female
1960	22.8	20.3
1955	22.6	20.2
1950	22.8	20.3
1940	24.3	21.5

Source: Current Population Reports, Table D (9).

points than during the 60 years from 1890 to 1950.

The tendency for a higher proportion of the Negro population to have broken marriages by separation or divorce persists, but the differential seems to have diminished by a significant amount since 1950.

5. Education. The already favorable rates of school attendance among the population under 25 years of age improved substantially in the last decade. Between ages 6 and 15, school attendance now is almost 100 per cent. Most of the gain came in attendance rates for ages 16 to 21, and reflects a greatly heightened interest in completing high school and attending college. Table 3.17 summarizes attendance rates for the older age groups and shows the change that has taken place.

Table 3.17. Per Cent of the Population 16-24 Years Old
Enrolled in School, 1957-59 and 1950-52

Age	1957-59	1950-52	Percentage-point Change
16 years	88.4	80.6	7.8
17 years	73.5	65.2	8.3
18 years	42.8	35.8	7.0
19 years	29.3	20.6	8.7
20 years	23.0	16.8	6.2
21 years	16.6	12.1	4.5
22 years	10.5	7.4	3.1
23 years	8.4	6.4	2.0
24 years	7.6	4.7	2.9

Source: Current Population Reports, Table A (8).

Despite the fact that there have been substantial improvements in the school attendance rates of the nonwhite population, the proportion of nonwhite children and youth attending high school and college still is below that for the white population. This color differential has shrunk most dramatically during the past decade, especially for ages 14-19 years. It is still large for the years of college enrollment (Table 3.18).

Table 3.18. Per Cent of Youth 14 to 21 Years Old Enrolled in School, by Color, 1957-59

Age	Nonwhite	White
14-15 years	93.9	97.9
16-17 years	76.3	83.8
18-19 years	33.6	37.3
20-21 years	11.6	19.9

Source: Current Population Reports, Table 3 (8).

As a result of improved school attendance over many decades, the general level of education of the adult population is rising steadily. The median years of school completed by persons 25 years of age or over for the last three decades is as follows:

1960 . . . . 10.6   1950 . . . . 9.3   1940 . . . . 8.6

It is expected that by 1970 the median will be 12.0 years of education. The proportion of adults with a 4-year college education now is about 8 per cent. The nation is passing an educational landmark, in that persons who held the bachelor's degree (8 per cent), in 1962 slightly outnumbered the "functional illiterates" (persons with 0-4 years of schooling).

The regional difference in educational attainment between the South and the rest of the nation has not been narrowed. Data from the 1960 Census indicate that the median years of school completed by adults in the South had risen only 1.0 years since 1950, whereas the median of the nation as a whole rose 1.3 years (Table 3.19). The North Central Region in particular, and the Northeastern Region, moved up closer to the level of the Western Region, where educational attainment is highest, but in the process they pulled further away from similarity with the South. Attainment levels in the South have failed to keep pace with the nation as a whole despite the heavy movement of Negroes of low average education out of the South and into the North and West. Because these statistics represent the entire adult population of 25 years or over, they still partly reflect old differences in educational opportunities and attitudes.

Table 3.19. Median Years of School Completed for Persons
25 and Over, by Regions, 1950-60

Area	1960	1950	Increase
United States	10.6	9.3	1.3
Northeast	10.7	9.6	1.1
North Central	10.7	9.4	1.3
South	9.6	8.6	1.0
West	12.0	11.3	.7

Source: 1960 Census of Population, Table 105 (16), and 1950 Census of
Population, Table 67 (7).

Among the major residence groups, urban people are the best educated. This is a traditional and widely observed fact. Urban adults averaged 11.1 years of school in 1960 compared with 9.5 for rural nonfarm and 8.8 for rural farm. Less widely appreciated, however, is the fact that the lead of urban people over rural people in average educational attainment has widened rather than narrowed. The median years of school completed by urban adults (25 years old and over) was .9 year higher in 1960 than in 1950, whereas the median for the rural-nonfarm population rose by .7 year and that of rural-farm people by only .4 year (Table 3.20). The rate of improvement in the farm population has lagged despite the large-scale exodus of Negroes from the farms to nonfarm areas. Negro farm people average three years less schooling than white farm people. Therefore, other things being equal, their heavy outmigration should have raised the average of education among farm people and retarded it among nonfarm people.

However, the continued low level of formal education among farm adults is partly the result of the heavy outmigration of young people from the farm population—both white and nonwhite alike—and of the unique age distribution that the outmigration

Table 3.20. Median Years of School Completed for Persons
25 and Over, by Residence, 1950-60

Residence	1960	1950	Increase
Urban	11.1	10.2	.9
Rural nonfarm	9.5	8.8	.7
Rural farm	8.8	8.4	.4

Source: 1960 Census of Population, Table 76 (16) and 1950 Census of
Population, Table 44 (7).

has produced. Figures on school enrollment show that at the
typical high school ages of 16 and 17 years, the proportion of
farm children in school (81.8 per cent) is now just as high as
the proportion of urban children enrolled (82.0 per cent). The
difficulty is that the majority of well-educated farm youth leave
the farm by the time they are 20 years old. Thus, the adult
farm population is heavily weighted with middle-aged and older
people who in their day received less education than does the
younger generation. This partly accounts for the depressed
average level of education of the farm population as compared
with that of urban people. Furthermore, during the 1950's the
rate of early outmigration by farm youth increased. This had
the effect of raising the already high average age of the adult
farm population and partly explains the pronounced lag in improvement of the average level of education of farm people at a
time when enrollment rates of high school age farm children
have caught up with the rest of the country.

6. Family and Household. At the 1960 Census the comparability of family and household statistics with those of previous
years was impaired by changing the unit of study from the
"dwelling unit" to the "housing unit," but in general it can be
said that the number of households and families is now rising
moderately rapidly because of renewed population growth. Even
larger increases are in prospect due to the fact that the children
born during the first years of the "baby boom" are now beginning
to marry in substantial numbers. Soon the pace of family formation will reach unprecedented dimensions. High levels of prosperity and the large volume of new home construction have had
the effect of causing fewer families to live in shared quarters,
or to be cramped into inadequate space. Greater security in
older age is permitting a larger share of elderly couples to

retain their households, and widows or widowers commonly occupy an apartment alone rather than living with a child.

The average size of family in 1960 (3.68 persons) was slightly higher than in 1950 (3.54). This resulted from continued high
fertility levels, which offset the growth in the number of single,
widowed, or divorced persons who live alone or with friends,
rather than with relatives.

7. Economic Characteristics. Since 1950 there has been a
slight lowering of the labor force participation rate for males
14 years of age and over (from 78.7 per cent to 77.4) due primarily to greater college attendance and earlier retirement.
This has been offset by a greater participation rate for females
(from 28.9 to 34.5), so that the rate for both sexes combined did
not change much between 1950 and 1960. Increased employment
by women is not usually related to hardship. There is now a
general trend for women to return to work in early middle age
after bearing children and rearing them to a responsible age.

During the past decade a series of economic recessions has
gradually accumulated a sizable body of unemployed persons.
This has been aggravated since 1959 by the annual entry of an
unusually large number of young people into the labor force
from school. Between April 1959 and April 1962, the number of
youth 18 and 19 years old in the labor force grew by half a million. Hereafter, almost every passing June will witness an
ever-increasing number of new entrants. The extent to which
these will be absorbed is one of the major questions which the
events of the next two decades will answer.

In the last 10 years the occupational composition has shifted
steadily in the direction of reducing unskilled labor to a minor
part of the work force, and enlarging white collar work—especially professional and clerical employment. The percentage
of workers doing white collar work rose from 37 in 1950 to 45
in 1962. One of the most dramatic changes has been the great
improvement of the occupational position of Negroes. Between
1950 and 1962 the number of Negro men employed in all white
collar occupations doubled and the number of Negro women
working in clerical and sales jobs tripled. Simultaneously, the
number of Negroes working as laborers declined.

Average family income levels rose by 84 per cent over-all
between 1949 and 1959, and by about 50 per cent taking into account the changing purchasing power of the dollar. There has
been a substantial shrinkage in the proportion of families that
live at the poverty line or below, and an increase in "middle

class" families that can live comfortably. For example, in 1949, 29 per cent of all families had less than $2,000 of money income and only 17 per cent received from $5,000 to $10,000. By 1959, these percentages were more than reversed; only 13 per cent of the families had incomes of less than $2,000 and 43 per cent received from $5,000 to $10,000. Income gains have been made by all population groups but families receiving low incomes are still heavily concentrated among farm families and nonwhite families. Families headed by farm operators or farm laborers made up only 8 per cent of all families having employed heads in 1960, but such farm-employed families comprise 39 per cent of all families with employed heads in which total income is less than $2,000. Only 9 per cent of all families are nonwhite, yet these families make up 25 per cent of all families receiving less than $2,000 income. There is some overlap between the two groups mentioned in that some families are both farm employed and nonwhite. However, it can be said with confidence that farm employed and/or nonwhite families, which together make up not more than 15 per cent of all families, comprise at least one-half of the families whose income is less than $2,000 annually.

The median income of all families in 1959 was $5,660. In terms of constant (1959) dollars, this represented an increase of $1,899 in the decade. Because of fluctuations in business conditions, the trend has been irregularly upward, with most of the improvement coming in the early and late years of the decade. The nonwhite population gained in income at about the same rate as the white and at the end of the decade median nonwhite family income was still little more than half that for white families (13).

Comparison of 1959 regional income data with those of 1949 provides an interesting contrast with regional trends for education (Table 3.21). In both characteristics—income and education—the West is the highest and the South lowest. However, whereas the non-West as a whole was narrowing its education differential with the West during the decade, this was not true of income. The skilled nature of typical jobs in the West, coupled with high wage and salary levels, has provided an economic climate in which absolute dollar gains in family income continue to outstrip the rest of the country. Furthermore, the percentage increases in median family income in the West have also exceeded those in the North. In the South, the relative growth of family incomes has been somewhat faster (99 per cent from 1949-59 compared with 85 per cent in the West). However, average money income levels in the South were so far behind in

Table 3.21. Median Family Income (dollars),
by Regions, 1959 and 1949

Area	1959	1949	Increase	Per Cent Change
United States	5,660	3,073	2,587	84
Northeast	6,191	3,365	2,826	84
North Central	5,892	3,277	2,615	80
South	4,465	2,248	2,217	99
West	6,348	3,430	2,918	85

Source: 1960 Census of Population, Table 106 (16), and 1950 Census of
Population, Table 85 (7).

1949 that absolute gains from Southern families remain behind
those for other regions.

II

CAUSES OF BASIC POPULATION TRENDS

A. Natality and Mortality

In November, 1945, a group of competent, well-known
demographers gathered in Washington to forecast the number of
births that would occur in the United States in postwar years.
After a discussion of all the evidence and speculation available
relating to age groups, marriage rates, the current distribution
of women by number of children, and other factors affecting
birth rates, it was agreed that not even under the highest fertility assumptions would the number of births in the postwar
period reach 3,000,000 in any year. Fortunately for the reputa-
tions of the committee members the forecasts were not published, for in no year since World War II has the number of
births proven to be as low as 3,000,000. This story illustrates
how completely unexpected, indeed astonishing, was the postwar
baby boom which continues unabated today.

Nearly 41,000,000 children have been born during the 1950's.
This is about 8,750,000 more children than were born in the
1940's. By contrast, the number of deaths in the 1950's
(15,650,000) was only 1,000,000 higher than the number in the

1940's. The absolute increase in the population has been so great from the combination of increased birth rate and decreasing death rate that one can safely say that at least 40 per cent of all the people who have ever lived in the United States since its colonial settlement are alive today.

Until recently the tendency of many demographers has been to attribute the increase of births to a making up of births deferred during past years, to an increase in the proportion of the population that marries, to a decrease in age of marriage, and to a borrowing of births from the future. There seemed to be a reluctance to admit the possibility that an increase in the average completed size of family might be occurring. All of the factors mentioned above that were used to explain away the increase in births without an increase in family size are valid to some extent. But the birth boom has now continued so long—20 years—that we need no longer speculate about whether an increase in completed fertility of women will result. The data are available and they show clearly that the cohorts of women now approaching the end of the childbearing years have borne substantially more children than those who completed their childbearing 5 to 10 years ago (14). The principal mechanism of this change has been a marked rise in the proportion of women having 3 and 4 children and a striking decline of the number having none or one. But there is also evidence that the women passing through the peak of their childbearing period during the 1950's will show a rise in the proportion having 5, 6, 7, or more children, as compared with those who bore children in the 1930's and 1940's. To this extent, a partial return to the large family system has occurred—and voluntarily, considering the widespread knowledge of family limitation practices.

The decrease in age at marriage has been accompanied by a shortened length of generation which has served to stimulate population growth. It is not simply the completed size of family that determines ultimate population growth but rather at what age parents bear their children. Thus, for example, a society in which mothers averaged their bearing of children at age 25 would produce 4 generations in a century whereas one in which children were born at an average maternal age of 30 would produce only three and one-third generations per century. Among white women born between 1930 and 1934, the average age at which they bore their third child (including a liberal allowance for those yet to be born) was about 26.0 years. By contrast, women born between 1910 and 1919 and having 3 or more children bore their third child at an average age of 29.8 years.

Thus the 3-child family of today, while regarded as a modest-sized family, has a measurably greater impact on population growth than did the average 3-child family of 20 to 30 years ago. The reduction in the median age of mothers at births of all children (regardless of birth order) is less than that for mothers of third or other order children because of the fact that the average number of children born per mother has been increasing. However, women born from 1930 to 1934 will show a median age at birth of all children nearly two years younger than that observed among women born from 1910 to 1919, even if the 1930-34 cohort bears 50 per cent more children per woman than did the 1910-19 cohort.

As has been noted often, the increased childbearing has been most marked among urban couples, where it had been very low in the prewar years. The narrowing of urban and farm fertility differentials continued during the 1950's, but the gap between them has by no means been closed. In August 1959, the number of children ever born per 1,000 women then in the childbearing period (aged 15 to 44 years) was 1,629 for urban women and 2,298 for rural-farm women.[3] This represented an increase of 36 per cent since 1950 in the rate for urban women but only 11 per cent for rural-farm women (see Table 3.22).

The role that health factors have played in the birth boom is not unimportant. In particular, the reduction by half of the formerly high rate of childless marriage is thought to be due principally to reduction of involuntary sterility rather than reduction of voluntary childlessness. But for the basic causes of the birth boom one must look to sociological answers. Much research has been undertaken, but the answers thus far tend not to be much different from those based on common sense reasoning. It has been verified that a complex of factors is operating, involving both a major change to an economic climate permissive of childbearing and a reorientation of cultural values which has encouraged it. The increase has taken place despite the concurrent presence of three trends thought to be clearly inimical to fertility, namely, the rise in educational attainment, the large-scale entry of married women into the labor force, and the increase in urbanization.

Changes in mortality levels have been less unexpected or newsworthy than those in natality. Nonetheless, they have been important. In general, over-all mortality rates have decreased steadily except for the interruption caused by the effects of the so-called "Asian flu" epidemics in the late 1950's, and improvements have been observed in all age groups. If the age-specific

Table 3.22. Women by Number of Children Ever Born, United States, 1959 and 1950

| Year and Age of Women | Women Ever Married | | | | | | | | Children Ever Born Per 1,000 Women |
| | Total | Per cent by number of children ever born | | | | | | | |
		None	1	2	3	4	5 and 6	7 or more	
1959									
15-44 years	100.0	14.8	19.7	27.0	18.8	9.9	7.0	2.7	1,762
30-34 years	100.0	9.8	14.6	28.6	22.7	12.9	8.6	2.9	2,447
45-49 years	100.0	18.1	20.6	24.5	15.9	8.9	6.9	5.2	2,214
1950									
15-44 years	100.0	22.8	26.6	24.7	12.5	6.1	4.7	2.7	1,395
30-34 years	100.0	17.3	23.4	28.6	15.5	7.4	5.4	2.4	1,871
45-49 years	100.0	20.4	19.8	21.7	13.8	8.7	8.4	7.2	2,292

Source: Current Population Reports, Table 1 (14).

death rates of 1950 had prevailed all through the following decade, approximately 1,000,000 more deaths would have occurred
in the period than actually took place.

Between 1950 and 1959 the average expectation of life at birth
rose from 68.4 years to 69.7. Typically, mortality rates have
improved most among classes of the population where they were
worst; for example, the expectation of life for nonwhite population groups has been rising more rapidly than that of the white
population. However, a notable and somewhat perplexing exception to this trend is the widening difference in the expectation of
life for males and females. Under 1940 conditions, expectation
of life at birth for females was 4.4 years longer than for males
(65.2 years vs. 60.8), but by 1959 this difference had grown to
6.5 years (73.0 years vs. 66.5). The principal cause of this effect is the worsening position of males to females in respect to
heart disease and cancer.

Although it is seldom used, the median expectation of life at
birth is probably superior to the traditional mean expectation as
an expression of the life probabilities inherent in current mortality conditions. Because the age at which a person dies is
weighted in the mean calculation, the high mortality for infants
greatly affects the mean, causing it to be lower than the median.
Under 1959 mortality rates, the mean expectation of life in the
United States at birth was 69.7 years, but the median expectation—to which half of the children born might expect to live—was
about 74 years, or 4 years longer than the mean. For white females the median was 78 years. At the pace at which mortality
rates are declining it seems eminently safe to say that there are
already cohorts of white women of adult age in which half of the
original cohort will survive to 80 years of age.

B. Immigration and Migration

Immigration in the United States has never reassumed the
magnitude—either proportionate or absolute—that it had in the
pre-World War I era. Its importance is still substantial, however, and should not be overlooked in evaluating the sources of
growth of the nation. From July 1, 1950, to July 1, 1960, a net
of 3,000,000 civilians entered the country. They accounted directly for about 10 per cent of the nation's population increase.
However, their impact on population growth does not cease with
their immigration, for the great majority of immigrants are
young adults or children who contribute to further growth by

bearing children in later years. Net immigration in the 1950's
was nearly 50 per cent greater than the figure of 2,020,000 during the previous decade. The war years of the 1940's cut greatly
into the levels of immigration during that decade but created the
conditions for a steady flow of refugees and military brides to
augment the more normal flow of immigrants in the 1950's. The
rise of net immigration in the 1950's was just as important a
source of increase in national population growth as was the decline in mortality rates. Net immigration tends to vary more
from year to year than do births and deaths because of changes
in legislation or in the state of world affairs (such as the Hun-
garian and Cuban revolutions). On the average, it is likely to
retain its relative importance among the components of U.S.
population growth in the present decade.

All but a minor fraction of the distributional changes noted
above are created by migration streams. Fertility and mortality
rates determine the over-all growth, but interregional differences
in rates of natural increase have now shrunk to a fraction of their
former size. For this reason, they could not possibly account for
the shifts of population toward the West, the Gulf Coast, the
metropolitan centers, the nonmetropolitan urban places, the suburbs, and into communities of particular types. Moreover, birth
rates in these rapidly growing places sometimes are no higher
than in the areas where population growth is slow (farm areas,
rural South, etc.). Hence, if any two communities, A and B, are
growing at differential rates, the researcher should look first
for a migration differential rather than a natural increase differential, between them. In interpreting the trends of Section I,
therefore, it should be presupposed that there is a net flow of
outmigration from most places that did not grow at the rate of
18.5 per cent or more between 1950 and 1960 and a net flow of
inmigration to most places that grew faster than 18.5 per cent.
The extent of deviation from the average rate of growth may be
taken as a crude indication of the probable extent of net inmigration or outmigration.

C. Patterns of Regional Economic Growth

The population flows that have been described above are not
arbitrary movements unrelated to trends in economic growth.
All regions and metropolises where growth has been extraordinarily rapid have simultaneously undergone industrial and commercial expansion. The Gulf Coast, Florida, southern Arizona,

and California's coast and valley are outstanding examples. Areas of shrinking economy have been areas of population stagnation or decline. The decline in employment in the coal industry, the mechanization of farms, the elimination of submarginal farms, and the shift of industries out of old industrial centers (such as the southward movement of the textile and paper industries) are examples. The process is more than a simple cause-and-effect one, however, because the loss of units of "basic" industry has a disproportionate effect due to the lowered demand for local services, and because some new industries and new commercial activities are entering the same communities where old ones are dying or moving. Population growth brings with it demands for additional service, and this stimulates economic growth. Hence, although it is difficult to disentangle the "cause-or-effect" aspect of population and economic trends, there is a high and persistent correlation between them, both spatially and temporally.

To support this general assertion, the rate of change in manufacturing employment, 1954-58, was correlated with the rate of population change, 1950-60, for those SMSA's for which data are available, by economic regions. This was done in two ways, once as a simple correlation between per cent change in population 1950-60 (variable x) and per cent change in manufacturing employment (variable y), and once as a "partial" correlation, holding constant the degree of industrialization already attained, expressed as per cent of the labor force employed in manufacturing in 1950 (variable z). The results are as follows:

	r_{xy}	$r_{xy \cdot z}$
Total 135 SMSA's	.70	.63
Region I	.64	.29
Region II	-.38	-.58
Region III	-.60	-.18
Region V	.47	.49
Region VII	.60	.63
Region VIII	.13	.08
Region IX	.89	.86
Region X, XI, XII	.60	.47
Region XIII	.85	.86

In the United States as a whole, there was a moderately close relationship between the rate of industrial employment and the rate of population change. In the faster growing regions the tendency for the places that experienced a substantial growth in manufacturing employment to experience a rapid population growth also was especially strong. In all regions except three, the correlation is high and positive. Only in the heavily indus- trialized areas of the Lower Great Lakes and the interior North- east (Regions II and III), and in the Old South (where all SMSA's grew rapidly regardless of character) was the correlation nega- tive or low.

D. Patterns of Urban-Rural Economic Equilibrium

In addition to the specific decline in the number of farms and farm people, there have been other economic changes that have affected the balance between urban and rural settlement. One that is visibly obvious in many sections of the country is the decline in the vitality of small rural trading centers. This has been undoubtedly fostered by the decline in retail business from farmers and by the growing concentration of processing, mar- keting, and service facilities for agriculture in larger centers of urban size.[4] The rural-urban balance has also been affected by the fact that both mining and lumber operations—the two princi- pal rural industries other than farming—have been declining in over-all manpower needs. Changes in these activities are often sudden and produce some of the most vivid examples of stranded communities.

On the other side of the coin, certain industries of a more traditionally urban character have been decentralizing into rural areas or into small cities accessible to rural people. For ex- ample, the garment industry has migrated to a substantial de- gree from the larger cities of the North to more rural districts of the South. Rural areas have also furnished the sites for many military installations (discussed separately below) and research facilities, both of which are increasingly prominent features of our economy. Some of these facilities require rural, thinly settled surroundings because of the noxious, dangerous, or secretive aspects of their work.

Recreation industries are also steadily altering the charac- ter of the rural economy. One particular feature of the current great expansion in businesses based on use of leisure time is the rapid increase in, and dispersion of, dams. Dams are usually built for an avowed purpose other than recreation—such as flood control, reclamation, navigation, or power—but almost without exception they soon become important as recreational

centers. Some of the most traditionally landlocked states now
have large expanses of reservoir water surface and an ardent
clientele of water sportsmen and vacationists. Dams, state
parks, and other recreational facilities provide many new opportunities for employment, and especially for the founding of small
trade and service businesses. They tend to attract urban people
to rural areas to run such businesses and thus diversify both
the rural economy and the rural population. Such areas, if sufficiently large and attractive, also become centers for retirement of older people. Perhaps the best example of the transformation of an interior rural county through the building of a dam
is Camden County, Missouri, where the population grew by 16
per cent during the 1950's as the result of businesses and
retirement homes fostered by the Bagnell Dam and its reservoir,
the Lake of the Ozarks. The rural economy and population had
declined in this county for 50 years before the recent reversal.

In summary, the rural population has fallen as a proportion
of the total population, due to the overriding effects of the decline in agriculture employment and, to a lesser extent, mining
and lumbering. However, other activities of a nonagricultural
nature are on the increase in many rural districts and tend
either to increase the similarity to urban activities of the work
performed by rural people or to draw urban people into rural
communities.

E. Metropolitan Decentralization

From studies of the 1940-50 decade, we know that metropolitan growth patterns included a dramatic flowing into the suburban ring of economic activities of a great variety (shopping
centers, factories, service establishments, and even administrative, research, and record-keeping activities). The census
data are too new to have been analyzed yet, but one takes no
great risk in stating that this peripheral drift of economic
activity has been accelerated during the 1950-60 decade. Also,
although the data are not yet at hand to test the proposition, it
seems quite plausible from the 1940-50 trends to expect that
the characteristics of the suburban population are more nearly
like the national average for all urban population than previously. One should expect the suburbs of today to have a larger
proportion of lower and lower-middle socioeconomic groups,
more Negroes, and more blue-collar workers than previously.
This arises from the diversification of the economic base of

suburbs and from the transition of suburbanization from an esoteric to a mass residential adjustment. Nevertheless, in comparison with suburbs, many central cities will look like major "social problem" populations or "depressed areas" in the nation. In addition to being demographically stagnant, they have a disproportionate concentration of poor, less educated, lower-occupation people because they are ports of entry for low income migrants. They have lost and are losing better educated and higher income citizens through flight to the suburbs. Many a central city tends to see its inflowing population as an increased burden on its welfare, police, educational, and judicial systems, and its outflowing population as a large net financial loss in tax-paying power.

F. Military Installations and Defense Activity

Among the forces producing widespread change in the distribution of the American population, one that is sometimes overlooked or else underrated is the tremendous growth in the number and size of military installations. The reference is to military bases per se rather than to private manufacturing and research complexes working on military projects. Military population growth is especially important in any consideration of rural growth because of the tendency for military populations to be located disproportionately in rural territory. Furthermore, because military bases often require substantial amounts of land, they are frequently located on land that previously was not thickly settled. The introduction of military personnel and associated civilian employees greatly increases population density, and military bases are thus commonly associated with the most spectacular examples of rapid population growth.

Between 1950 and 1960 the number of military personnel stationed within the United States rose by more than 750,000, or by 76 per cent. Of the Armed Forces, the proportion living in rural territory was 44 per cent compared with only 30 per cent of the civilian population. Under current practices many military personnel have wives and children who follow them about. This amplifies the demographic effect of a military base on a locality, especially where large numbers of the families must live off base.

In addition to the Armed Forces themselves, many military installations employ large numbers of civilians, and this is particularly true of certain installations common to rural areas,

such as storage and maintenance depots, and testing grounds.
Military bases typically induce commuting from long distances,
perhaps because of publicity, good wages, the number of jobs
available, and relative lack of discriminatory practices. As a
result, some of them form the major payroll for sizeable numbers of surrounding rural counties. The number of civilians
employed directly by the Department of Defense in the United
States increased by more than 300,000, or by 40 per cent, from
1950 to 1960. During the 1950-60 decade there were about 60
nonmetropolitan rural counties in the nation that experienced
high rates of population increase due substantially, or even entirely, to military developments. (All data derived from published sources.)

Military bases have varied effects on the areas in which they
are located. Those employing numbers of highly trained professional people, civilian or military, may greatly upgrade the
level of services and the general attractiveness of an area.
Some, such as ammunition depots, employ relatively few military or professional level civilians and thus simply provide
more unskilled and semiskilled jobs for local residents. Other
types of bases and camps having large numbers of young, un-
married, transient personnel may create many social problems
for the community.

The action taken by the government in the fall of 1961 to enlarge the military establishment indicates that during the intermediate future, military location decisions will continue to have
significant effects on population distribution.

G. The Continuing Agricultural Revolution[5]

The decline in the number of farms and the number of farm
people has received much publicity in recent years, particularly
during periods when agricultural policy has been a prominent
political issue. Behind the rapid decline in the number of people
engaged directly in farming looms the effect of the tremendous
revolution in the methods and economics of agriculture—a revolution that has by no means been completed. The following list
summarizes those aspects of recent trends within and outside
of agriculture, that have resulted in a loss of farm population.

1. The difficulties faced by young men in getting started in farming today, in view of the decline in number of farms available
   because of consolidation trends, and in the light of the high

capital resources required for an adequate acreage and equipment to operate it.
2. The low income received from many farm units, especially in comparison with the wages and salaries available from nonfarm jobs.
3. The attraction of city life and nonfarm occupations to younger farm people, associated with higher educational attainment, compulsory military service, short work hours, increased exposure to nonfarm life, and the aspirations of minority racial groups for a better life.
4. A decline in the amount of manpower needed in farming caused by mechanization and by withdrawal of land from production through participation in various Government programs.
5. A decline in the specific need for tenant farmers and full-time, resident hired hands brought about by changing technology and other factors.
6. The take-over or use-conversion of farm land by suburbanization, highways, reservoirs, industrial facilities, military bases, recreational facilities, sustained-yield forestry, and other nonfarm uses.
7. Discouragement of older or small-to-medium scale farmers by inability to obtain labor of the number and kind desired or at feasible wages.
8. The increasing burden of real estate taxation.
9. Persistence in some areas of such older rural disadvantages as the lack of good roads, adequate schools, and other community facilities.

The effect of this imposing combination of negative factors is so strong that only in a few scattered areas has the farm population increased or remained stationary. Where reclamation projects or well-water irrigation have permitted a rapid intensification of land use—as in the Columbia Basin of Washington or the High Plains of Texas—there has been no shortage of aspiring younger farmers to compete for the land. This would seem to indicate that although farming has lost prestige for some as an occupation, there are still many people who would like to go into it where the conditions are promising.

One of the most dramatic changes in the farm population for which some form of measure is already available is the change by race. Using the data on color of farm operators obtained in the 1959 Census of Agriculture, one finds that the number of nonwhite farmers (97 per cent of whom are Negroes) fell from

581,000 in 1950 to 315,000 in 1959, a drop of nearly one-half.[6]
The pace of this loss accelerated during the course of the
decade, with the rate of decline rising from 18 per cent in the
years 1950-54 to 35 per cent in the years 1955-59. The rate and
amount of loss were especially severe in the intensive tenant-
organized farming of the Mississippi Delta. Here, in the counties comprising Subregion 76, Negro farmers dropped from
73,000 to 31,000 in the 5 years from the autumn of 1954 to the
autumn of 1959. In this area, the loss of Negro farmers is in-
separably linked with the fact that the overwhelming majority of
them have been cotton-share tenants. The rapid shift to completely mechanized cotton operations has permitted the abandonment by landlords of the tenant system in favor of a unified
operation employing hired farm workers. This is corroborated
by the rapid increase in regular hired workers shown in the 1959
Cens (employed at least 150 days). In the Subregion 76 they
rose from 26,000 in 1954 to 41,000 in 1959. Many of these
workers are undoubtedly the former tenants in a new job relationship to the landlords. However, the increased labor efficiency
of the new system is so great that for every three or four tenant
farmers dropped in the subregion as a whole, only one additional
wage worker has been hired. Some of the wage workers continue
to live on the plantation and continue to be counted as farm residents, but many others are reported to have severed their housing relationships with employers and to be commuting to work
from town or other nonfarm places.

H. The Structure of Business

The structure of American business has been shifting rapidly
during the past decade, with strong emphasis upon mergers and
centralization of business control into fewer but larger and more
complex units. There is no evidence that this trend will not continue in the near future. It is too early yet to undertake the research necessary to study the effect this has had upon population
trends; all of the data are not available. However, it appears to
be a plausible hypothesis that American business is focused
more and more on the metropolitan centers, with the result that
opportunities and growth are channelled there. Many corporations are known to advertise only in the newspapers of cities
recognized as metropolitan by the Bureau of Budget and to concentrate their purchasing in such places.

I. Expansion of Higher Education

The provision of college and professional postgraduate training to the oncoming waves of youth is causing a rapid expansion
in the physical plant and staff size in colleges and universities
all over the nation. In 1950 an estimated 2.2 million persons
were enrolled in colleges and professional schools. By 1960
this had risen to 3.6 million. An increase of 65 per cent in 10
years is a most substantial gain. It can only have the effect of
causing "college towns" and the college community in large
cities to grow rapidly. But the end is not yet in sight. A revised set of projections released by the U.S. Census Bureau
shows another doubling within the 1960-70 decade, so that there
will be a grand total of 7.1 million college and professional
students at the time the 1970 Census is taken. For a decade or
so thereafter, however, the rate of growth will be much slower
because the period of most rapid increase in the birthrate will
already have been reflected during the 1960's.

J. Drift Toward Warmer Climates

With few exceptions, those portions of the nation which have
severe winters are experiencing below-average growth, and almost the entire zone of the country that is blessed with mild
winters is growing rapidly. For example, those economic subregions which have an average January minimum temperature
of less than 10 degrees showed an over-all population increase
of 10 per cent from 1950-60, whereas the subregions having an
average January minimum of 40 degrees or more had a population growth of 45 per cent. In part, this development is being
created by the building of "retirement colonies" by elderly people moving to Florida, the entire Gulf of Mexico coast, and into
Arizona and California. The Social Security program first made
a mass move of this type possible two decades ago, and it is
swelling steadily into a major social movement. Canadians as
well as U.S. citizens join in it. Probably the movement will
double and redouble in volume in the next two decades. Even
inland places, such as the Sandhills of Carolina and Georgia
(which are dry as well as mild), the Ozarks, and the Appalachian
Uplands are attracting people entering retirement and desiring
or needing a change of climate.

But this drift toward warmer climates appears to be more
than just a retirement phenomenon. Winter brings hazards and

and inconveniences which many people of all ages now seek to
avoid, and which the heightened national prosperity makes it
possible to avoid. Whether the population is leading business
or following it is not certain. Yet it is clear that much light industry, such as electronics, missiles, research, and appliance
fabrication and assembly is moving into these southern zones
also. Air conditioning is making it easier for the newcomers to
have the equivalent of a cool summer and a warm winter. Also,
certain costs of living are lower. As employers become more
congestion-conscious and more aware of the desires and values
of their employees, it may be expected that more industry than
ever before will be located with climate as one of the variables
given serious consideration.

K. Mining

One of the most common economic causes of population
change, especially of decrease, is change in mining activity.
Considerable attention has been focused on the problems of
eastern areas suffering from unemployment and partial depopulation due to declines in coal mining. However, in other parts
of the nation, especially the Great Plains and the West, developments in mineral industry are often associated with rapid population growth rather than decline. One may generalize that
developments in mining, as with military activities, are likely
to be rather sudden and far reaching, whether they produce
population growth or decline.

In the Eastern States alone, about 80 counties suffered absolute losses of population from 1950-60, stemming primarily
from the decline in coal mining employment. This has resulted
both from mechanization of mines and from falling production
caused by competition of other fuels or exhaustion of workable
reserves. These absolute population losses frequently amounted
to 15 to 20 per cent, despite the high rates of natural increase
traditional among coal miners. The bulk of such counties are
concentrated in a belt extending southwestward from west
central Pennsylvania to northeastern Tennessee. Elsewhere
east of the Mississippi, about 30 other counties declined in
population size from difficulties affecting other mineral industries, especially metals and oil and gas.

Declines in mining activity contributed greatly to population
loss in about 45 counties west of the Mississippi. On the other
hand, in the Great Plains and Mountain States, there were about

60 counties that experienced net inmigration of people because
of discoveries or development of mineral resources. Oil and
uranium account for a majority of these cases. Such counties
are often not far distant from those where mining is in decline,
and there are no large blocks of counties suffering unrelieved
distress from mining unemployment such as that of the East.
The demographic effects of mining trends are of particular
reference to rural interests because mining is the most rural of
all nonagricultural industries, aside from the logging and milling
of wood. (At the 1950 Census, 64 per cent of all mining workers
were rural residents.) Thus it is rural communities that are
most typically affected by the volatile conditions of both growth
and decline that currently prevail in mineral industries.

L. Styles and Levels of Living

In a discussion of the causes of population trends there would
seem to be a legitimate place for a paragraph on styles and
levels of living. Styles may be partially subject to manipulation
and levels may, to a great extent, be dependent on the economy,
but they appear also to exert an independent influence of their
own.

Living in the suburbs is unquestionably a necessity for many
young metropolitan families simply because of the lack of sufficient older housing or space for housing within the city. But the
fight to the suburbs probably has in it a component of style or
desire not related solely to need. The post-World War II marriage and birth boom came after more than 15 years of low volume of housing construction. Millions of people were living in
houses or apartments which were far behind the newest buildings
in style, variety, setting, and modernity of equipment. Surely
this factor alone, combined with a high level of earning, stimu-
lated in part the exodus from the city proper.

The greatly increased prevalence of retirement plans and the
increased adequacy of such plans, coupled with the rapidly growing number of elderly people, has caused the movement of
hundreds of thousands of persons to new homes. In Florida, the
most notable example of growth from retirement, there were
roughly 300,000 more persons aged 65 and over in 1960 than
would have been expected from the population 55 and over in
1950, making allowance for death. The movement of older persons is often related to the drift to warmer climates, but it is
the rising, assured income of such persons that makes the move
possible.

In addition to improved ability to retire, there has been a general improvement in the amount of vacation time available to the labor force and a decline in the proportion of jobs at which a long work week is required. Those circumstances, reinforced by the generally high level of wages and employment have provided the means for the great expansion of recreation businesses everywhere and of specialized resort areas. Many counties can be identified in which recreation businesses have been a major source of population growth. Recreation and retirement areas often develop in the same locations and both show the demographic consequences of rising levels of living.

Another type of population movement that is partially rooted in changes in style and levels of living is the movement of young people from rural areas. Quite aside from considerations of economic necessity, there are large numbers of rural youth who have a preference to live in urban environment. This seems to be especially true of girls and of village residents. For example, a study recently conducted by Michigan State University and the USDA showed that 40 per cent of the girl high school seniors in four rural counties preferred an urban place to live, and that 63 per cent of the village girls had such a preference. Corresponding figures for boys were 27 per cent and 50 per cent (2).

M. Changes in the Social and Economic Status of Negroes

The public notice that has attended the efforts of the Negro population towards improved social and economic status has been so widespread and of such central political importance that there is no need to elaborate this point. Demographically, these efforts have resulted in a heavy migration of Negroes to cities in all regions, and a migration into the Northern and Western States. Within the Census South region, the Negro population increased by only 11 per cent, with much of the increase taking place in peripheral areas of only a quasi-Southern character, such as the District of Columbia, the Florida Peninsula, Maryland, and Delaware (see Table 3.14). In strong contrast, the Negro population in the rest of the United States grew by 55 per cent. The non-Southern portion of the Negro population now amounts to 40 per cent of the whole, as compared to 32 per cent in 1950. The heavy migration has produced some extraordinarily distorted age distributions in the sending and receiving populations. The areas of outmigration show very small proportions of Negroes in the ages 20 to 39, except in the cities, but the very high fertility of the population has maintained a disproportionately large number of young children in the population. Movement out of rural areas to cities has been so great that in hardly more than a generation the Negro population has been transformed from the most agricultural group in the American population to one of the most urban.

Aside from factors affecting the residential distribution of Negroes, the efforts being made to raise the educational and occupational levels and opportunities of this part of the population are being reflected in the rapidly changing educational, occupational, and income characteristics of the group.

III

CONCLUSION

A judgment of the principal conclusions to be drawn from the trends reported in this study inevitably depends upon one's interests and point of view. To the person concerned with metropolitan developments, the most important trend may be the rapid concentration of the majority of the nation's people into the metropolitan areas. In the decade of the 1950's, the percentage of people living in metropolitan territory rose from 56 to 63, as 84 per cent of all population growth took place in the less than 9 per cent of our land area that lies within the standard metropolitan areas. Ample national physical space and the existence of strategic and moral imperatives which assert the desirability of decentralization have not been sufficient factors to overcome other economic and social forces that foster metropolitan concentration.

On the other hand, within the metropolitan areas a substantial dispersal or decentralization of settlement has been the salient feature to students of urban society. The growth of suburbs has not only been rapid, it has usually been accomplished in part at the expense of the central city. Few metropolitan central cities have been able to increase or even retain their population size without annexations of territory. (Indeed, this is also true of scores of nonmetropolitan places.) Despite the huge growth of suburban population, the density of settlement per square mile in the urban fringes of metropolitan cities decreased, because the new suburbs have been built at a lower density than the old ones. Of equal importance to the redistribution of population within the metropolitan areas has been the continued rapid increase of the Negro population within large central cities. This increase, when accompanied by a loss to the suburbs of white population, has substantially altered the income, educational, and occupational structure of the population of numerous central cities.

To the person with rural interests, the greatest impression from current trends may be the conclusion that demographic changes in rural communities have never been more radically different from those in urban communities—metropolitan or nonmetropolitan—than they are today. This is not to contradict the fact that in many material aspects of life, rural and urban communities are more similar than they were a decade ago. For example, rural areas are closing the gap in availability or possession of electricity and electrical appliances, telephones, indoor water and bathroom facilities, automobiles, and hard-surfaced roads. However, never before have there been so many rural areas declining in population at a time when most urban areas are growing so rapidly. Never before have there been such differences in the age distribution of farm and nonfarm population as there are now, nor such disparities in the directions in which the age distributions are changing. Never has the number of deaths approached or exceeded the number of births in rural counties as it is beginning to do in some areas today, in contrast to the large natural increase of population being recorded in the cities. The difference between rural and urban population trends is such that in many rural areas the problem is to find economic uses for land that will retard depopulation, whereas in urban areas the problem is often how to choose between competing demands for land use, caused by high population growth.

If one's interest is focused on national growth or on manpower potentials, the most significant trend of recent years may be the maintenance of a relatively high fertility rate which has been the principal source of rapid population growth. About 73,000,000 children were born from 1940 to 1960. As these children, themselves, grow up, the number of potential parents will increase to the point that in 1975 there should be about 50 per cent more women in the peak of the childbearing years than there are today. Thus, unless the rate of fertility should soon decline substantially, the number of children to be born in the late 1960's and the 1970's, and the amount of further population increase resulting will greatly overshadow the births and increase of the last two decades.

In addition to the trends in distribution, composition, and growth of population summarized above, changes are evident in the characteristics of population such as education, income, and occupation. In some instances they have operated to homogenize the population and lessen the social and economic disparities between groups. In others they have served to widen differences. In either case, the changes in the basic demography of the population have been and continue to be exceptionally rapid. Their implications are far reaching, and are not to be ignored.

FOOTNOTES

[1] Rates of growth, 1950-60, are reported for the total urban and rural portions of each economic region, economic subregion, and state economic area, separately for metropolitan and nonmetropolitan parts, in Table A of Bogue and Beale, Economic Areas of the United States (1).

[2] Except in New England a standard metropolitan statistical area (SMSA) is a county or group of contiguous counties which contains at least one city of 50,000 inhabitants or more or "twin cities" with a combined population of at least 50,000. In addition to the county or counties containing such a city or cities, contiguous counties are included in an SMSA if, according to certain criteria, they are essentially metropolitan in character and are socially and economically integrated with the central city.

[3] Standardized for age.

[4] Two large-scale studies of factors associated with population change in small population centers are now being undertaken by rural sociologists, James Tarver of Oklahoma and Glenn Fuguitt of Wisconsin.

[5] For a fuller discussion of recent adjustments in the farm and other rural population see Chapter 10 of Smith, Adjustments in Agriculture (5).

[6] Number based on old, comparable definition. There were 286,000 nonwhite farmers in 1959 on the new definition.

LITERATURE CITED

(1) Bogue, D. J., and Beale, C. L.: Economic Areas of the United States, The Free Press, Glencoe, Ill., 1961. (Studies in Population Distribution, No. 15)

(2) Cowhig, J. D., Artis, J. W., Beegle, J. A., and Goldsmith, H.: "Orientations Toward Occupation and Residence," Mich. Exp. Sta. Spec. Bul. 428, 1960.

(3) Duncan, O. D., et al.: Metropolis and Region, Johns Hopkins Press, Baltimore, 1960.

(4) Eldridge, H. T.: "The Process of Urbanization." Social Forces, 20:311, 1942.

(5) Smith, M. G., and Christian, C. F., eds.: Adjustments in Agriculture—A National Basebook (the Farm Foundation and Center for Agricultural and Economic Development, sponsors), Iowa State Univ. Press, Ames, 1961.

(6) United States Bureau of the Census: 1950 Census of Population, Vol. I, "Number of Inhabitants." 1952.

(7) —: 1950 Census of Population, Vol. II, "Characteristics of the Population." Part 1, Chap. B, 1952.

(8) —: Current Population Reports, "Population Characteristics." Ser. P-20, No. 101, 1960.

(9) —: Current Population Reports, "Population Characteristics." Ser. P-20, No. 105, 1960.

(10) —: 1960 Census of Population, "Number of Inhabitants." Final Rept. PC(1)-1A, 1961.

(11) —: 1960 Census of Population, "Supplementary Reports." PC (S1)-1, 1961.

(12) —: 1960 Census of Population, news release. March 7, 1961.

(13) —: Current Population Reports, "Consumer Income." Ser. P-60, No. 35, 1961.

(14) —: Current Population Reports, "Population Characteristics." Ser. P-20, No. 108, 1961.

(15) —: 1960 Census of Population, "General Population Characteristics." Final Rept. PC (1)-1B, 1961.

(16) —: 1960 Census of Population, "General Social and Economic Characteristics." Final Rept. PC (1)-1C, 1962.

(17) —, and Agricultural Marketing Service: "Farm Population." Ser. P-27. (Census-AMS), No. 28, 1961.

4

Christopher Sower
Paul A. Miller

The Changing Power Structure in Agriculture: An Analysis of Negative Versus Positive Organization Power

THE PURPOSE of this chapter is to relate how a system of agricultural power, responsive to national goals, developed in the United States and how it later declined, as organizational contests reduced its responsiveness to newly emerging national purposes. We hope to suggest the major elements of agricultural power, the factors which led to organizational contests, the implications of the agricultural case for a sociological understanding of power in American society, and the alternatives which agricultural power now confronts.

I. ON THE THEORY OF SOCIAL POWER

A. Power as a Component of Organization Behavior

The literature of contemporary social science advances two models for interpreting the exercise of social power in issue resolution within American society. Both models, the negative and the positive, stress the importance of large-scale organizations.[1] Though there are a few instances of individuals having unusual influence, most studies of power—for the community, state, region, or the nation—indicate that the roles of organizations are crucial in resolving issues.[2]

In turning to an interpretation of the role of organizations in affecting decision making, it is necessary to start with the unique character of any formal organization. As distinguished from a community, family, or other types of social organization units, a formal organization is a social system with specific and limited goals. While it may be possible to conceive of an organization whose goals are related only to its members, most organizations dealing with public issues envisage the provision of some service or goods for other persons or groups. As stated by Parsons:[3]

An organization is a system which, as the attainment of its goal, "produces" an identifiable something which can be utilized in some way by another system; that is, the output of an organization is, for some other system, an input.

This general model indicates "three anchor points of legitimation" for an organization: (1) the systems from which it receives its inputs of resources; (2) the values, structure, and norms which compose the organization as a system; and (3) those systems which use the output of the organization as an input. In some respects, an organization is only a collectivity of positions from which a certain specific goal achievement is expected. The positions are occupied by "position incumbents" to which specific behavior expectations are directed, both from "relevant others" (at all three anchor points of legitimation) as well as from the "self-expectations" of the incumbent.

Though large-scale organizations present certain complications for society as well as for their position incumbents, they are unique social inventions. They appear to be the only social structures capable of achieving the vast and complex goals of modern society. Yet, the problem for any society is that of planning its organizations so that desired goals are achieved, while minimizing the detrimental consequences of their functions to either the total society (such as the undue exercise of power), or to organization personnel (such as the destruction of initiative which results in the negative component of the "organization man").

B. A Negative Model of Power

In assuming the negative model of power in American society, most writers have limited the scope of the concept to the

problems of controlling issue resolution in the legislative process and of manipulating the market to the advantage of particular
groups. Organizational contest is the most frequent means used
in wielding such power. The literature about what is called
agricultural or farm power is of particular interest not only because it too is so narrowly defined, but also because most of the
work has been done by scholars who are not employed by the
Departments of Agriculture, the farm organizations, or the
agricultural colleges.[4]

Yet, as the social scientists and other observers from positions external to agricultural organizations write about the agricultural system, they seem to maintain a particularly narrow
focus on agricultural power. They seem to observe only the
organizational manipulations of the last four decades when organized agricultural power has been in a stage of serious and
extensive readjustment. For instance, in contrast to the viewpoint stated by Eddy[5] that the American system of land-grant
colleges is unique and gaining world-wide attention, Selznick[6]
viewed the local actions of the land-grant college extension
county agent system as behavior preventing the TVA from
carrying out policies for the national welfare. He describes in
some detail how the "agriculturalists" attempted to "co-opt"
the power of decision making within TVA, tried to use this
power to prevent the inauguration of a fertilizer program directed toward soil conservation, and at the same time en-
deavored to favor the larger farmer, prevent equality of
advantage for the Negro farmers and the Negro land-grant colleges, and block such federal agencies as the Soil Conservation
Service. He concluded that the land-grant extension system was
more interested in protecting organization prerogatives and enhancing the interests of the more prosperous farmers than in
the area-wide planning goals of the TVA, which in turn he saw
as synonymous with the national welfare. Hardin[7] also is basically critical of the land-grant colleges as he describes the
arena of organizational relationships which brought state and
federal agencies and farm associations into patterns of deep and
pervasive contest.

While these and other observers[8] of the agricultural system
appear to be basically accurate in describing segments of the
total American agricultural establishment which they observed,
it is both justifiable and important to examine the theoretical
constructs and methodological tools which have been utilized by
social scientists in conducting studies of the exercise of power.
No scholar can justify either supporting or not criticizing

selfish and manipulative actions of agricultural organizations or those of any other sector of American society. It is suggested, however, that many of these writers have theoretically circumscribed their observations about the nature of power and that there is another model of power in American agriculture which has provided dynamic arrangements for achieving outstanding and highly positive contributions for the United States as well as other countries.[9]

C. A Positive Model of Power

What is it that observers of the agricultural system have overlooked as they have analyzed agricultural power? They do not seem to have observed the organizational interplay which has succeeded in producing one of the most "powerful" achievements in human history: the transformation of the American farmer to a scientific and technically competent producer of commodities. To have designed the organizational structure necessary to produce the knowledge and technology, and to have affected the behavior of so many millions of people, represents the exercise of real "power" over the decision making of human behavior. Also, while the public press exhibits great concern over the so-called "farm scandal" of managing food surpluses, the fact seems to have been forgotten that for the first time in human history a society not only has freed itself from food scarcity, but that this American agricultural system has produced the food required by millions of people in other countries.

The problem is that much discussion of agriculture as well as other types of national power is viewed in negative terms. Parsons[10] describes these in his criticisms of the assumptions implicit in C. Wright Mills' book The Power Elite:

Unfortunately, the concept of power is not a settled one in the social sciences, either in political science or in sociology. Mills, however, adopts one main version of the concept without attempting to justify it. This is what may be called the "zero-sum" concept; power, that is to say, is power over others. The power A has in a system is, necessarily and by definition, at the expense of B. This conception of power then is generalized to the whole conception of the political process when Mills says that "Politics is a struggle for power." . . . The essential point, at present is that, to Mills, power is not a facility for the performance of function in, and on behalf of, the society as a system, but is interpreted exclusively as a facility for getting what one group, the holders of power, wants by preventing another group, the "outs" from getting what it wants.

Parsons proceeds to present two criticisms of Mills' conception of power: (1) it tends to exaggerate the empirical importance of power by alleging that it is only power which "really" determines what happens to society, and (2) it tends to think of power as presumptively illegitimate. ". . . if people exercise considerable power, it must be because they have somehow usurped it where they had no right, and they intend to use it to the detriment of others."

Though Parsons' discussion concentrates upon the three main versions of individualistic utopianism—the liberal, the capitalist, and the socialist—he concludes by presenting another approach to defining the role of power in modern society. He states:[11]

If the individualistic assumptions are modified in favor of a set which not only admit the necessity but assert the desirability of positive social organization, much of the ideological conflict between the three positions as "total systems" evaporates. Above all, it can be positively asserted that power, while of course subject to abuses and in need of many controls, is an essential and desirable component of a highly organized society.

As the theory of positive organizational power is related to the achievements of the agricultural organizational enterprise, it is necessary to describe this case before dealing further with the theory. Hence, the case will be presented in Part II. The concept will be given further elaboration in Part III.

II. ON THE NATURE OF AGRICULTURAL POWER

A. Foundations of Agricultural Power

The system of organized agricultural power in the United States grew from a heritage idealizing rural life and the common man. The ideal was reenforced by a commonality of interest in the rural family and in family economic enterprise, in kinship groups, in closely knit neighborhoods, communities, and in the primary associations of rural institutions.[12] The majority of the population was characterized by this homogeneity and they were isolated from the few centers of industrialism and capitalistic enterprise. The separation, together with the ideal of rural society and the rural majority of the population, conspired to generate the agrarian movements of the late Nineteenth Century and to lay the foundation of agricultural power.

The agrarian movements from 1850 to 1896, and the era of

reconsideration which continued to the agricultural depression following World War I, had several characteristics which facilitate an understanding of the foundation of agricultural power. They consisted of an undifferentiated mass as an organization, the national aim of development as a goal, and a strategy of attacking the special interests of others rather than pursuing their own. Following the defeat of the Populist Party in 1896, agricultural power was left with only a series of outlooks: the glorification of farming as a way of life; a belief in the curtailment of the exercise of power by the few; a dedication to an equality of economic opportunity for the farmer.[13]

The agricultural prosperity of the early Twentieth Century, the conciliatory hopes of the industrial community to quiet the agrarians, and the increasingly visible edifice of a differentiated economy—all converged in the twenty years following to translate the outlooks of agriculture into institutional and organizational forms and to change its strategy from protesting the special interests of others to the setting forth of its own.[14]

B. Structure of Agricultural Power

From the debates over McNary-Hauganism and the Federal Farm Board in the 1920's to perhaps the close of the Korean War we have seen a viable, organized, focused, and goal-oriented system of agricultural power in the United States. Its effectiveness demands that such a model of organized power be described.

Organized agricultural power in the United States has possessed certain basic elements to influence the resolution of issues. The first is technical knowledge and expertise in its dissemination—institutionalized in the national system of land-grant colleges, the USDA, and the county agent system in local counties. The second is the ability to consistently influence and sometimes "co-opt" the appropriation process within county governing bodies, state legislatures, and Congress—frequently made possible by the disproportionate political representation of rural people. The third is facile access to all levels and types of institutions in American society—made possible by systematic organizational linkages and the ability to form coalitions of groups devoted normally to advancing their own special interests. The fourth is serving as the standard-bearer for the belief that the grass-roots ideology was a prime necessity for the functioning of political democracy—made possible by direct ties (largely unidentified) at the community level with the political party as a chief locus of power.[15] Such are the elements of power in the agricultural system. How they have been distributed, mobilized, and focused leads to the elaborate structure of the system.

Organized agricultural power has formed at four levels of American society—the national government, the major regions of the United States, the states (the state legislatures in particular), and the local units of communities and counties. At each of these levels three major types of organizations were perfected—agricultural administrative agencies, general farm organizations (especially the Farm Bureau), and legislative bodies. The elements of power were distributed with reference to these organizational types. The technical expertise was possessed by the administrative agencies—the organizational complex represented by the land-grant colleges, the Extension Service, and the USDA. The appropriation process was institutionalized in the legislative bodies, and the general farm organizations—the Farm Bureau, the Grange, and the Farmers Union—which possessed the element of access and the ability to influence large numbers of communities and voters by invoking the grass-roots ideology. Moreover, several hierarchical articulations were possible: local farm bureaus, state farm bureaus, and the American Farm Bureau Federation; the National Grange and the National Farmers Union and their state and local chapters; state legislatures, local county governing boards, and the Congress; and, by reason of formally constituted memoranda of agreement, the land-grant colleges, the extension services, and the USDA.

This deployment of the elements of power provided for coalition-formation at each of the levels between members of the three types of organizations: between the Extension Service and the Farm Bureau; between the farm organizations and the rural component of state legislatures; between the farm organizations and the rural component of the Congress, notably the House of Representatives; and between the regions of the United States as embodied in the earlier farm bloc.[16]

Such was the nature of agricultural power as the United States moved on from World War II. That such a system could develop is due to the following reasons. First, it was not enmeshed in the political party machinery: the system moved horizontally to the party system with a real or imagined majority of votes and functioned with strategies and tactics which assumed a majority position. Second, though locally based agricultural power could still be watchful over the execution of

power by the few, organized agriculture had defined its own
goals. Third, such goals of development and parity were clearly
in the national interest: the industrial society was insatiable in
its demand for a transfer of resources from agricultural to industrial development, and the increase in farming efficiency was
a major strategy. Fourth, advancing the national product was at
perhaps its highest emphasis; national deference to agriculture's
goal of parity was little enough in exchange for the accelerating
productivity of agriculture. Fifth, the centers of political power
were responsive to the high rank of domestic issues, and, within
them, those of food production and such agrarian ideals as the
family farm.[17] Sixth, the depression and war emergencies of the
United States from 1934 to 1952 were such as to make food production of unusual importance.

   Yet, the vast alliance of organized agricultural power had
within itself a natural condition for tension and instability. In
recent years this condition, surrounded by the changes of an industrializing society, forced increasing attention to organizational maintenance duties in order to prevent the bifurcation of
loyalty. This condition resulted from the difference in orientation between the chief administrative agencies and the farm organizations and legislative bodies. The administrative agencies
—as they became structured as large-scale bureaucratic organizations—desired as their goal the development and dissemination of technical expertise. They were bureaucratically oriented
to the rational planning of objectives, and to the impersonal
specification of roles, incumbents, performance, and rewards.
Accordingly, they preferred to withdraw from conflict and out-
right contest. But at the same time, their detachment from the
very coalitions upon which they had come to depend made them
vulnerable. On the other hand, the farm organizations and
legislative bodies—designed to mobilize, distribute, and employ
the elements of power which the system possessed—responded
more to idiosyncratic roles, personal and erratic assignment
and evaluation of incumbents, performance, and rewards.
Theirs was a natural orientation to conflict.[18] Two important
examples of this contrast in orientation are the contests over
the administration of the A.A.A. and Land-Use Planning.[19]

   This disparity in orientations within organized agriculture
frequently generated differential expectations of the Extension
Service role by the farm organizations. Later moves by the
Extension Service to mediate these expectations—between a
subject-matter role and an organizational role—were strategic
in opening up the structure of organized agriculture to new

organizations brought about by the changes in agriculture and in the society at large.

C. Decline of Agricultural Power

As a result, in the past decade the system of organized agricultural power has declined in its effectiveness in advancing and reaching its goals and it is more frequently involved in charges of self-interest. Agricultural power grew from a tradition of insistence that the special interests of others must be kept within the national purpose; today it is being attacked with the same indictment. The nature of this reversal may be suggested to social scientists as a major case for understanding the natural history of power in a changing society undergoing the transfer from agrarian to industrial life.

Change in the Total Society Which Affected Agriculture

Our central hypothesis with reference to this reversal is that the differentiation of industrial society at all its levels opened up the structure of organized agricultural power, bifurcated the loyalties and reduced the goal-dedication of its members, increased the maintenance functions to preserve coalitions, and reduced the system's ability to reconcile its specific goals with newly emerging national purposes.

The first change was as wide as American society. During and following World War II, the entire industrial establishment of the United States moved into a new maturity of corporate group activity, extreme specialization in the production, marketing, and distribution processes, and an increased visibility of the business and industrial sector in relation to the political party processes. Simultaneously, the sector of organized labor, with a similar visibility, joined with business and government as a major locus of power.[20] With such compartments in the national arena of power, and with a new national sophistication in relating to political parties, organized agriculture has increasingly encountered the dilemma of participation in power contexts without the political party connections and the sophistication possessed by business and labor. Closely related to this phenomenon is the persistent shift in orientation of the political institution to large urban centers, not only for votes but because the centers of party power are increasingly found there. The strategies of recent national elections are a case in point. In addition, the large urban centers of the country finally have found their own theme of protest—not unlike that of the agrarians a hundred years before—that their massive populations are trapped between an unimaginative national government and rural-dominated state legislatures.

A second national phenomenon was generated by the paradox entailed in the goals of organized agricultural power to gain economic parity. The paradox was that the massive technological revolution, expedited at the level of individual farmers, was an economic gain for the individual farmer; but, due to the inelasticity of demand for agricultural products, resulted in permanently troublesome imbalances in aggregate supply and demand.[21] In spite of the grass-roots creed of organized agricultural power, the paradox forced the stronger and stronger mediation of government and implied to the society at large that agriculture seemed to be increasingly interested only in itself. This revelation was made all the more acute when dislocations occurred from time to time in the automated and mechanized processes of the larger industrial complex—labor unemployment and the demise of thousands of small privately owned businesses. In short, organized agriculture seemed to be insisting upon a national stance with reference to agricultural stability that was not being achieved by individual workers and small businesses.

A third national trend, accelerating in the decade of the fifties, was the emergence of a new national purpose with reference to the world community. It led to a process which is still under way—a reordering of national values. Inevitably a new sophistication was required which would enable the continuous reconciliation between domestic and foreign policies. Domestic issues had to give way, and with them the domestic paradox of surplus agricultural production. Simultaneously, and again, the goals of organized agriculture seemed to be at variance with the national good; for in such areas as international trade, agricultural policies seemed based on advantage for domestic agriculture and inconsistent, if not contradictory, with foreign policy.[22]

Such impacts at the national level of American society found organized agriculture with defined special interests for domestic agriculture at a time when a growing interdependence of national issues was occurring. During this same period other sectors of power such as business and labor were developing new identifications with and sophistication about the chief locus of political power, the party. The result has been that the national apex of agricultural power is confronted with halfway interests, the tactics of delay, and uncertainty upon the part of its members.

State and Regional Adjustments to National Change

Change and enlarged differentiation also developed at state and regional levels. First, and of unusual importance to the present analysis, was the redistribution of one element of agricultural power—that of technical expertise. The depression years of the thirties produced a proliferation of new technical agencies, each and all of them the focus of contest with organized agriculture at their inception. World War II provided a kind of moratorium for the contest, but at its close such new administrative agencies as the Soil Conservation Service, the Farm Security Administration, the Agricultural Adjustment Administration—although changed in title and sometimes in purpose—were permanently entrenched. At the same time, the commercialization of agriculture, and the attending connections with the industrial sector, produced a great number of private firms rendering services.[23] Feed and fertilizer companies, commercial spray firms, private consulting offices, and such innovations as vertical integration in the poultry industry have added massively to the available number of technical experts. Organized agricultural power, as it was first envisaged and constructed, is no longer the sole owner of one of its elements of power.

A second trend since World War II is the change in the organization and administration of the land-grant colleges and their schools of agriculture by reason of accommodation to different social, economic, and political contexts at state and regional levels.[24] The emergence of regional universities, state colleges, and community colleges has reorganized the structure of higher education in many of the states, distributed more widely the centers of technical competence related to agriculture, and reduced the priority of claims from agriculture on the traditional land-grant college. The result has been a growth in schools of business with interests in agricultural business; more college presidents with professional preparation in fields other than agriculture; and intracollege conflicts between the liberal and professional disciplines.

With such changes underway in the parent land-grant colleges, the Extension Service at state-national levels, observing its place in organized agricultural power, has become more active in its own response. It has penetrated the business sector under such new program rubrics as marketing research and education. New types of clientele have been added, but they have produced such dilemmas as the dissemination of technical expertise for economic advantage to both sellers and buyers.

Further, the Extension Service has moved successively and sometimes nervously to maintain historic coalitions and their support in gaining access to the appropriation process.

Moreover, in less than five years in the late fifties, such new movements as Farm and Home Development,[25] Program Projection, and Rural Development have been promoted. This succession, though in response to a growing ineffectiveness of the old coalitions, seemed to arouse only passive and passing interest on the part of the organizations in organized agriculture. Also, the additional program formats produced some tension at state levels: they sharpened the old issue of whether the county agent should play the role of organizer or of technical expert.[26] The issue was deepened by changing community structure which produced problems less amenable to direct applications of technology in the planning and coordinating process. In the 1957-58 period the Extension Service responded once again by a national planning effort to determine its appropriate goals and produced the Report on the Scope and Responsibility of the Extension Service. The Report stressed agricultural production and marketing problems, but moved the definition of extension work into the broader realms of adult education and development planning, and reduced the stress on service to rural people.

Such changes in the administrative sector of organized agriculture at state level, and the attending responses, suggest that the older administrative-organization-legislative coalitions are less dependable and, therefore, less useful in accommodating to new issues.[27] Accordingly, the administrative sector, although inherently its place in organized agriculture precluded it, has been and is continuing to assume the risk of seeking new areas of service, new clienteles, and new coalitions. Here and there, for example, informal alliances with the labor movement are under way in connection with food surplus disposal programs, workers' education, and 4-H Club work. Also the extension marketing program is developing working relationships with processing and distributing organizations.

A third trend which continues to open up and reduce the closely articulated organization of agricultural power at state level is the agricultural commodity association. The commercialization of agriculture increased specialization along single commodity lines, increased the size of farm and firm, increased the number and variety of factors to be managed, elaborated production schedules, and refined the functions of storage, processing, distribution, and transportation. Efficient production for profit depends more and more upon the purchase of supplies from the business community and has more clearly distinguished between labor as a factor of production and entrepreneurial ability.[28] The commodity association is a vehicle of expression for a new class of entrepreneurs engaged in the risks of investment, credit, and narrow profit margins. It has carried its members into association with other representatives of the business community, searched for goals related to a particular agricultural commodity, and has looked to the centers of technical expertise for support of a highly specialized type. In so doing, the commodity association has disrupted the normal functioning of organized agriculture in the following ways: it has overlooked the grass-roots creed in by-passing the local centers of technical expertise at state, regional, and national levels; it has challenged such administrative and program units as the county on the assumption that commodity areas do not correspond to jurisdictional units; it has offered political support for programs of narrow commodity interest; it has negotiated new legislative liaisons with such agencies as state departments of agriculture to secure specific appropriations for promoting consumer demand and securing specialized research facilities.

Though the agricultural commodity association suggests itself to organized agriculture as a happy new form of alliance, the difficulties are considerable: it calls for specialization in agriculture at a time when other forces call for such emphases as community and area development; it is oriented to profit making and not to the distinctiveness of rural society, the family farm, and the grass-roots creed; it is more prone, as all business, to identify and employ the political processes to achieve limited goals. A new redistribution of power—expertise, the appropriation process, the ability to influence the members of farm organizations by a shared ideology—is underway as the economically paradoxical phenomenon of a commercial agriculture moves into the sixties.

A fourth trend at state level is the emergence of new ententes of power in the larger metropolitan centers. The critical needs of these areas—problems of administration, taxation, and urban renewal—have encouraged special alliances between business and labor for purposes of urban development.[29] The recent histories of Pittsburgh, Milwaukee, St. Louis, and Detroit are cases in point. These ententes are significant to agricultural power in that they intensify the conflicts between urban and "upstate" legislators, sharpen the issue of disproportionate representation, and call for a reordering of intrastate values not unlike the domestic-foreign reconciliations at the national level.

Among several specific consequences, such ententes have produced uncertainty in the administrative agencies of organized
agriculture about their role in metropolitan development.

Local Adjustments to National Change

There remains the local level. Rural sociologists have
scored many insights with reference to the impact of the urbanizing society at the community level. Only the barest of essentials concerning the opening up of agricultural power need be
cited here. However, it must be said that the very shift in terms
employed by the rural sociologists is indicative of the shift in
both the nature of the countryside and in the roots of organized
agricultural power: from the rural and urban community, to the
"rurban" community, to "suburbia," to the "metropolis," to the
emerging industrial-agricultural region.[30] The changes in man-
land relationships, in community services, and in interpersonal
relationships—each and all have produced a spectacular growth
of interdependence of the rural sector with the urban.

In the relationships of man to land, the number of farms has
declined, land has been diverted from farm production and used
for the new satellite communities surrounding metropolitan
centers, highways and industrial installations, recreational
areas, shopping centers, and drive-in movies. Communities
and counties have formed into new ecological arrangements by
the extension of communication and transportation. In-migrants
have swept into cities and then out along the highways into the
countryside. Simultaneously, rural families have moved city-
ward in order to consume more of the goods and services of the
industrial society. Such shifts in man-land relationships have
rendered increasingly obsolete those local political and administrative units which were formed in earlier and more simple
days.

With reference to community services, the rural family has
ranged wider and wider as it changed its orientation from family
production to family consumption. The newer requirements of
family living were purchased in a fashion not unlike the purchase of supplies for modern farming. Interest grew in the collective provision of services through group and governmental
action and heavy pressures came to be placed upon community
standards, boundaries, and taxes. New techniques of planning
for expanded services were called for, since new people were
showing up in rural communities with more luxurious and sometimes different standards. In short, for the provision of community services, the rural family was no longer dependent upon

itself or others like it: more and more the rural family has come to have the same wants and to confront the same means as the urban family—depending upon others for obtaining them.

At the point of interpersonal relationships, interdependence and integration were also moving rapidly. An earlier rural view at local level—an application of the ideal which rural life offered—led to a belief in the wholesomeness and integrity of a rural life in intimate connection with the mystery of nature, in a sureness of the difference between rural and urban living, in the strength of rural family life, in the relation of its personal and moral qualities to community responsibility. But the technological emphasis in modern rural life has reduced the mystery of nature, just as the diffusion of conveniences in the industrial society has eroded the rural-urban contrasts in personal and family life. The proliferation of special interest associations have tied city and country together with a myriad of overlapping memberships and communications. The suburbanization of rural areas has been paralleled by the disintegration of the old rural-urban stereotypes; the city dweller grew less "depraved" and the rural resident grew less "noble." Both have come to confront the multiplying volume and variety of goods and services and a more uniform set of standards in taste, conduct, and the use of leisure.

Such rhetorical comment, calculated only to capture the mood of local community change and for which substantial evidence and observations exist, implies a dissolution of the distinct creeds and of the singular structures upon which the foundation of agricultural power was built. The following consequences are briefly cited.

First, the undivided loyalty of organizational membership is less amenable to being sustained and influenced. This consequence affects both the farm organizations and the Extension Service. Part-time farmers may belong to labor unions and full-time specialty farmers may extend their membership in the Rotary Club and the local Chamber of Commerce.[31] As the mutual self-help associations of rural neighborhoods have dissolved, one hypothesis is that formal farm organizations take on more aspects of social class and rank.[32] Though the Farm Bureau has nominally secured the more commercial class of farmers as its members, it is this very class which has penetrated the specialized industrial sector and, as it appears, distributed its portfolio of associational membership, and perhaps loyalty, more widely. The commercial and specialty farmer is also involved in the rise of the commodity association.

Second, the Extension Service, embodied in the county agent at local level, competes daily with specialists from other public agencies and the private sector for the attention of his once dependable clientele. Currently the commercial farmer obtains technical expertise wherever he can get it—the feed dealer, the spray company, the state experiment station, frequently bypassing the county agent altogether. In short, the county agent system, basic to the structure of agricultural power, is no longer unique and distinctive as a purveyor of technical expertise. Every community need has come to be matched with a service and every service with an agency. Each such agency requires its own clientele as well as the means to create the demand for still more service, while communities have become joined with countless others into local and national networks of particular agencies engaged in promoting and dispensing particular services.

Then, too, the new community problems are not easily attacked by the free-lancer. They have moved from the private realm of decision in family, church, and store to the public realm in government, the planning commission, and new forms of intercommunity and intercounty agreements. The problem of the county agent is how to invade the newer arrangements, to understand, to persist, and, with his particular role identification, to participate. The dilemma of the modern county agent is knowing what role to choose and what organization(s) will support his system: to limit himself to the new production-marketing complex of the commercial-specialty farmer and thereby regain a further distinctiveness; or expand to adult education and coordination of other specialties with an orientation to issues of public responsibility and leadership.[33] And the major question he faces is: What organizations can he count on, as he could his coalitions with the farm organizations, for support in the appropriation process?

Third, though local legislative bodies have remained the most consistent members of coalitions with farm organizations and the Extension Service, the interdependence of the modern community has produced changes in them of both structure and outlook. In the more preponderantly urban regions the cities have demanded a larger representation on such legislative groups. The pressures and complexities of taxation, annexation, and zoning—with attendant problems of policy administration— have required more time on the part of county legislators.

While county legislators have been forced to new levels of abstraction in the conduct of their duties, their loyalties to one agency engaged in disseminating technical knowledge to what is now a minority of the voters can scarcely be expected to remain constant. One needs only to review the activities and programs of county agent conclaves to all levels to sense the concern for improved relationships with the controllers of the appropriation process.

In summarizing this analysis of changes and dissolution at the various levels of organized agricultural power, the new issues and purposes at every level of American society call for alliances, in and out of the party system, which go beyond the singular distribution of the elements of power which has characterized the agricultural system. The farm organizations still are attempting to hold and influence members, with goals which are scarcely new, with members who can obtain technical expertise almost anywhere. New groups such as the commodity associations move into the arena of power with functionally specific goals of advantage and special interest; they are in the minority but they know it. The Extension Services, confronted as a national system with a range of impact due to industrialism, are attempting successively different formats in the hope of strengthening the old and discovering new centers of support. And with the absence of definitive alternatives to the economic paradox of domestic agriculture, together with the orientation of American society to internationalism, the structure of agricultural power is perfused with agricultural problems rather than with opportunities. Hence, there rise occasional interorganizational contests, a mood of watchfulness about old alliances, and trial and error in keeping viable a system of agricultural power.

III. IMPLICATIONS AND ALTERNATIVES IN AGRICULTURAL POWER

Having stated the empirical case of agriculture, it now is possible to delimit four major hypotheses and related implications and alternatives about the nature and component parts of positive organizational power.

A. Power as the Ability of an Organization or Group of Organizations To Affect Issue Resolution at the Different Levels of Governmental Decision Making (National, State, County, or City)

We suggest that organized agriculture will continue to exercise influence over the resolution of issues if the society at large perceives that it is achieving goals which are important to national, state, and local decision making. The major problem for agriculture is that major change has taken place in the whole society. The earlier tasks of internal development in the United States, for instance, were possible with a minimum of involvement with other nations. The great tasks ahead, however, are related to our ability to stabilize areas of the world which are not under communist rule, and to help other nations develop abilities to achieve their own national development goals. Since the achievement of these goals is related directly to keeping to the forefront in the development of new knowledge, and in maintaining high American economic production and productivity in the basic commodities, it seems certain that agriculture will have important roles to perform. The following are specific functions which agricultural organizations can assume with reference to the national welfare:

1. The continued production of large amounts of food, even in surplus quantities, is a necessity for American society, at least until other nations can learn the technology of producing sufficient food for themselves.

2. Only a large, complex system of highly specialized and organized technology such as characterizes American agriculture is capable of providing the technical personnel necessary to help other countries do the basic and applied research, and to teach their food producers, processors, and distributors how to provide adequate food supplies for the masses of people of the world.[34] (In this respect, it is of particular importance to social planning to note that even though the Soviet Union, using communist theoretical guidelines, appears to have been able to develop much of the necessary social organization for achieving industrial productivity comparable to the parliamentary nations, the evidence seems clear that they have not been able to duplicate the social organization which is capable of achieving the "incentive to produce" which has resulted from the American system of agriculture.)

3. It is certain that the achievement of such important national goals as those described above will be dependent upon the continued development of new knowledge and new ways of using knowledge. Even if our own food production system failed to require such emphasis, the vast problems of applying knowledge to meet the needs of underdeveloped countries will alone necessitate the continuation of basic and applied research. Indeed, the nation which has the knowledge to produce is allocated high prestige in the world struggle to determine which system is going to be most able to win the allegiance of the "developing" nations.

4. Another set of national goals to which organized agriculture may contribute is in helping to develop a broadly defined conception of area, economic, and human resources and manpower development. There are serious area development problems in this country, such as in the depressed areas of low agricultural productivity, the heavily populated agricultural production areas which comprise the "daily commuting to work" zones surrounding urban centers, and the inner sections of large cities. Sound national development planning must assess the relationship of food production and distribution planning to all other facets of such an effort.

B. Power as the Ability of an Organization To Affect Legislative or Other Decision Making so as To Provide the "Inputs" Needed To Maintain Its Existence

While this second type of organizational power in the long run is a consequence of the ability of the various organizations to fulfill the urgent national and state needs described above, it also is a consequence of the types to follow, namely, the ability to provide outputs which can be used by food and fiber producers and others who are the basic users of their services. This essentially represents one end point of the output-input cycle. It is an important focal point between organized agriculture and the total society.

Organized agriculture desires that legislative decision makers appropriate funds to the agricultural establishment. The problem is how the decision makers for the total society can justify the allocation of societal resources to a minority sector. This raises the question of how a society grants any of its individuals or sectors the right to exercise either authority or influence, or how it justifies taxing the total in order to allocate disproportionate resources to a minority. The rural population was once the majority. Accordingly, the whole was taxed to facilitate the majority to perform services which were for the benefit of the whole. Currently, the agricultural sector of American society is not only a minority, but it is performing only one of the basic services vital to an industrial society.

One of the major problems in relating to society is the cost of agriculture: especially that dealing with the attempt to control and manage food surpluses. Yet organized agriculture has permitted a "food surplus" label to be placed on the fruits of its achievement, even though much of such product has been used to help stabilize the economies of other countries, one of our important national goals. In addition, the process has been confounded by interorganizational, interregional, and political party contests.

There obviously are many problems involved in a reconsideration of the relation of any sector to society, especially during periods of basic social change. There is also the problem of defining what is meant by agriculture. Is it primarily food production, or does it include processing and distribution? Does it any longer include all of the geographic areas which are not definable as urban? If so, what is rural society? Does it any longer exist? If so, how is it delimited and distinguished from urban society? Such are the challenges of organized agriculture.[35] While power relates to the appropriation process, it would seem important for all sectors of the society to give "agonizing reappraisals" to their rationales for requesting total societal resources from either national, state, or local legislative decision makers.

C. Power as the Ability of an Organization To Affect the Behavior of Its Clientele (the Recipients of Its Output)

The third observation about the achievements and role of organized agricultural power in American society is that history will likely show that it made one of the unique social inventions in human history. It appears that the social organization and technology which transformed the American farmer is very likely the most effective known method available to any government to bring about basic changes in the performance of its population. In fact, the basic components of the method are being used in other sectors of our own society, such as in health and urban redevelopment programs, as well as in related types of programs in underdeveloped countries.

There appear to be two main characteristics of the social invention which American agricultural leaders designed to achieve the goals of maximizing food production.[36] The first is an assumption about the nature of the ability of the common man. Unique to early American thought was the radical idea that the range of intelligence is about the same for the masses as for the elite of the society; that the masses can learn and can rule themselves if provided the opportunity of education and the means of making their own decisions. The lack of belief in this assumption presents a major problem in transplanting this social invention to other populations. For example, there is considerable difficulty in persuading the leaders and decision makers of American cities that this assumption also applies to the multi-racial mass population of the inner city. Likewise, many leaders and decision makers in underdeveloped countries have difficulty in believing this basically American creed which implies that their village and urban mass populations have the same range of intelligence and ability as those who occupy positions of privilege and power.

The second characteristic of this social invention is what can be labeled the "development organization." It has different characteristics from the usual governmental bureaucracy. Its operation must have a linkage based on cooperation and influence with the recipients of the program.[37] In order to do this, many of its goals must be set at the level where the bureaucratic organization establishes its linkage with its clientele. Otherwise, it merely attempts to force central government goals upon local groups. When this occurs, the local recipients of the output of the organization do not respond by granting the representatives of the organization the right to "influence" their behavior in the directions desired by the central organization. Yet, if the "natural history" of organized agricultural power in the United States is an example, development organizations would appear to have built into them the inherent tendency to bureaucratize and grow less responsive to the always new issues and goals which they themselves are partly responsible for generating.

D. Power as the Ability of an Organization To Set and
Achieve Either Intraorganizational Goals or Group
Goals With Other Organizations at Coordinate Levels

It appears that internal organizational variables are important in determining the extent to which a "development organization" has the ability to focus interest and an orientation of
achievement toward common goals on the part of its members.
It is suggested that the more agricultural organizations achieve
goals which are useful inputs to their clientele, the more power
they will have in the various arenas of power. Important hypotheses can be derived at this point from organization theory,
namely, that there are several variables which are related to
predicting organizational goal achievement. In fact, there appears to be a relationship between goal achievement and the extent to which the position incumbents of the organization are
personally interested or dedicated in achieving the goals. (Here
there is a linkage between personal interests and organization
goals.) In turn, there would appear to be a relationship between
the interest of the position incumbents in achieving the goals of
the organization, and the extent to which an organization is able
to achieve consistency in behavior expectations (from the different anchor points of legitimation) as they are directed to the
different position incumbents.[38] Finally, there would appear to
be a consistency in relationship between the extent to which an
organization is able to define consensus in role definitions for
its members, and the extent to which it is able to define its
goals in a consistent and clear manner. Figure 4.1 presents a
diagram of the possible hypothetical relationships between
(a) internal organizational variables of goal clarity and consistency, (b) role consensus, (c) the extent to which the incumbents of 'locality linkage' positions are basically interested in
achieving the goals of the organization, and (d) the actual extent
of achievement of the different types of organization goals. It
presents also a possible hypothetical relationship between organization variables and those pertaining to the development of
emotional tension from performing organizational tasks.

With this very hasty overview of how organizational variables
may be related to goal achievement and the exercise of power,
it is possible to apply certain principles to the formulation of a
set of questions about agricultural organizations.[39]

As illustrated by the total agricultural establishment today,
there appears to be serious disagreement or "lack of consensus"
between the different "anchor points of legitimation." There are

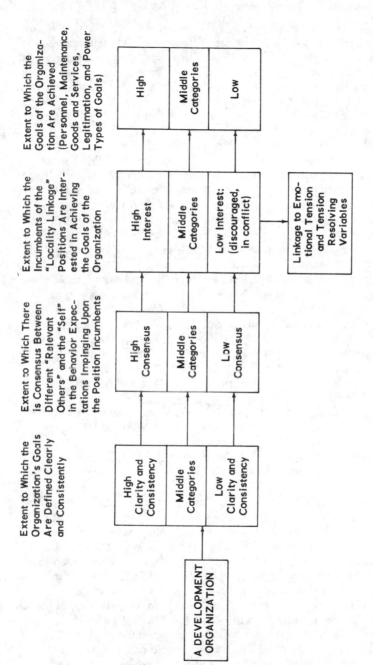

Fig. 4.1. Model for explaining and predicting the relationships between internal organizational variables and the extent of goal achievement for a development organization. (Source: Christopher Sower et al., "Highway Change and Locality Change: Base Line Studies," Part IV, (mimeo.), Mich. State Univ., East Lansing, Mar. 1961, p. 110.

the differences between entrepreneurial producers and the commercial farmers, and still other differences between these two and the traditional general farmer, the subsistence farmer, and the part-time farmer. There are the differences between those who think that the agricultural establishment should concentrate upon food and fiber commodities versus those who think that it should be concerned with the problems of the whole of the "non-urban" society.

There are differences in the behavior expectations between the different levels of national, state, and local governments. The whole agricultural establishment is caught uniquely within the multiplicity of conflicting behavior expectations from its different traditionally legitimate but also traditionally consistent sources of expectation and support. Furthermore, it increasingly appears that each major sector is organized into "special interest" organizations, each of which seems more interested in exerting organized pressure to achieve its own particular goals than in maintaining the effectiveness and strength of the total agricultural establishment. Hence, the whole system seems caught within interlocking webs of organized interest groups with increasingly divergent grounds for agreement. In this situation, as no sizeable body of influential members appears concerned about the welfare of the whole, the total establishment seems to suffer from either indecision or from having its decision making captured by the machinations of interorganization contest and coalitions.

Other elements of any organizational analysis are the consequences of its actions (both manifest and latent) to its maintenance over time, its goal achievement, or to its position incumbents (whether this be discouragement, role conflict, lethargy, or dedication to the goal achievement of the organization).

The importance of these hypotheses is that the ability of the organization to achieve its goals—whether it be to affect the legislative process or to affect the behavior of farmers and other recipients—seems directly related to the ability of the organization to set clearly definable goals and to maintain itself with minimal internal and external conflict. Also, it seems that any organization is more likely to have dedicated members if its goals are accepted by the rest of the society as for the public good. The constant criticism about the "farm scandal" and the interorganizational contests within the agricultural establishment appears to have had detrimental consequences upon the extent to which members of agricultural organizations are dedicated to achieving the goals of their organizations. It seems predictable that confusion, discouragement, contest, and conflict will characterize agricultural organization until the total establishment can again be brought into line with perceiving itself and being perceived as making a vital contribution to the needs of a troubled society.

Hence, a final hypothesis is that organizational establishments which are in basic contest and conflict, those which receive constant public criticism, those which are charged with using manipulations to self-advantage, and those whose goals have not kept up with a changing society—that these organizations lose their dynamics of personal dedication. In turn they become subject to capture by still more self-interested subgroups. Under these conditions, increasingly larger portions of the total available human energy go into maintenance functions, organizational contest, and the pursuit of personal and subgroup advantage. These processes leave an ever-decreasing amount of human dedication and energy for the task of organization goal achievement.[40] Finally, the goal-setting and decision-making process becomes enmeshed in intergroup contest, and there is the problem of older generations retaining the decision-making command posts to the point that young men go elsewhere for the great causes to which they might ordinarily dedicate their lives.

In assuming a final value stance, we would suggest to both the students and leaders of organized agriculture that the development organization which it represents is still a remarkable and uniquely American phenomenon. It may yet face its most essential chapter. But the next chapter will be intellectually encircled by national and international needs, not predominantly by the boundaries of states and counties, nor the contests of narrowing and divergent interests. The value question which confronts organized agricultural power is not the question of whether it is right or wrong or necessary or unnecessary. It, from the developmental challenges at the intersection of national and international purposes, is both right and necessary. The essential question is: Will it be sufficient? Is the present agricultural organizational structure a dependable arrangement for achieving urgent future national goals?[41]

A final comment may help to delimit some of the problems in defining the terms under which the present agricultural establishment can become "sufficient" to the task of meeting present and future national needs.[42] One of the greatest myths in American agricultural organizations appears to be the belief that somehow or other there are basic differences in the scope of the problem between the approaches of the two major political parties in dealing with agriculture; that one or the other has the solution—largely based on ideology. The primary premise of this paper is that the problems are primarily organizational and not ideological. In fact, any government, whether totalitarian or democratic, is faced with essentially the same problem of how to organize to achieve the consequence of maximizing the incentive of its citizens to produce goods and services. Hence, the primary issue facing American agriculture as well as the development program of any modern nation is that of how to gain access to the interest and incentive involved at state and local levels of voluntary citizen action while at the same time designing the organizational structure of over-all planning to achieve the necessary degree of central government control and decision making to achieve urgent national goals. It seems an obvious conclusion that national planning cannot be achieved in many areas merely by grants of national funds to state agencies, even to universities, unless these are sufficiently responsive to the national government to assure the achievement of the goals for which the national funds were appropriated.

FOOTNOTES

[1] Floyd Hunter's work is of particular interest in this respect. While his carefully documented studies on the exercise of power at community, state, and national levels show that most persons who exercise power are incumbents of positions in organizations, his analysis seems to concentrate upon "individuals of power." The analysis does not deal systematically with the roles of the organizations. He describes one of the characteristic features of the American national power structure as follows: "While it is not a single pyramid of influence and authority, it is a kind of informal circuit (not circle; not group) of representatives of many of the major influence groups." Floyd Hunter, Top Leadership, U.S.A., Univ. North Carolina Press, Chapel Hill, 1959, p. 8. Note too that in the top 20 of 106 national organizations potentially influential in nation policy development in 1953, The American Farm Bureau Federation is listed in 7th position and the National Grange in 10th position. See also, Floyd Hunter, Community Power Structure, Univ. of North Carolina Press, Chapel Hill, 1953.

[2] The following studies used a "relevant organizational relationships" model designed by Delbert C. Miller and W. H. Form instead of the customary public opinion polling to predict the outcomes of public elections over controversial issues: Delbert C. Miller, "The Prediction of Issue Outcome in Community Decision Making," Research Studies of the State College of Wash. 25:137-47, 1957. Also, Robert C. Hanson, "Predicting a Community Decision: A Test of the Miller-Form Theory," Amer. Sociol. Rev., 24:662-71, 1959.

[3]Talcott Parsons, "Suggestions for a Sociological Approach to the Theory of Organizations," Administrative Science Quart., 1:63-85, and 225-39, 1956. Reproduced in Talcott Parsons, Structure and Process in Modern Societies, The Free Press, Glencoe, Ill., 1960, Chaps. 1 and 2.

[4]Philip Selznick, TVA and the Grass Roots, Univ. of Calif. Press, Berkeley, 1953; Charles M. Hardin, The Politics of Agriculture: Soil Conservation and the Struggle for Power in Rural America, The Free Press, Glencoe, Ill., 1952; also, "The Bureau of Agricultural Economics Under Fire," Jour. Farm Econ., 28:635-68, 1946; also, "Farm Political Power and the U.S. Governmental Crisis," Jour. Farm Econ., 40:1646-59, 1958; William J. Block, The Separation of the Farm Bureau and the Extension Service: Political Issue in a Federal System, Univ. of Ill. Press, Urbana, 1960; Grant McConnell, The Decline of Agrarian Democracy, Univ. of Calif. Press, Berkeley, 1953; Ross B. Talbot, "Farm Organizations and the National Interest," The Annals, 331:110-15, 1960; Kenneth E. Boulding, The Organizational Revolution, Harpers, 1953.

[5]Edward Danforth Eddy, Jr., Colleges for Our Land and Time, Harpers, 1957.

[6]Selznick, op. cit.

[7]Hardin, Politics of Agriculture, op. cit., p. 19.

[8]While C. Arnold Anderson charges that scholars within the agricultural organizations have exhibited certain limiting characteristics because of undue influence from the organizational bureaucracies which employ them, still a careful search of their literature reveals other possible reasons. For instance, the history of the journal, Rural Sociology, shows a heavy preponderance of interest upon achieving certain desired goals for rural society, including the community, family, etc. Until the recent interest in the adoption of approved agricultural practices, rural sociologists gave relatively little attention to the social organization of purely agricultural production problems. With a few exceptions, they have shown little systematic interest in social movements, large-scale organizations (even though they have been very much a part of them), or the exercise of power over issue resolution. See C. Arnold Anderson, "Trends in Rural Sociology," in, Robert K. Merton, et al., eds., Sociology Today: Problems and Prospects, Basic Books, 1959, Chap. 16.

[9]Paul H. Appleby, Policy and Administration, Univ. of Ala. Press, University, Ala., 1949.

[10]Talcott Parsons, "The Distribution of Power in American Society," Structure and Process in Modern Societies, The Free Press, Glencoe, Ill., 1960, Chap. 6, pp. 219-20.

[11]Ibid., p. 224.

[12]For the roots of the rural heritage, see A. Whitney Griswold, Farming and Democracy, Harcourt, Brace, 1948; for analyses of the rural ideal, see Ibn-Khaldun, "Comparison of Rural and Urban People," in, P. A. Sorokin, C. C. Zimmerman, and C. J. Galpin, A Systematic Source Book in Rural Sociology, Univ. of Minn. Press, Minneapolis, 1:55-61, 1930; Carl C. Taylor, The Farmers' Movement—1620-1920, Amer. Book Company, 1953; such writings as Richard Hofstadter, The American Political Tradition, Knopf, 1948; A. C. True, A History of Agricultural Education in the United States—1785-1925, USDA Misc. Publ. No. 36, 1929; and for a more recent work, Grant McConnell, The

Decline of Agrarian Democracy, Univ. of Calif. Press, Berkeley, 1953, initial chapters.

[13]See Paul H. Johnstone, "On the Identification of the Farmer," Rural Soc., 5:32-45, 1940; L. H. Bailey, The Holy Earth, Scribners, 1915; and What Is Democracy, Comstock Publishing Co., Ithaca, N.Y., 1918; also, Carl C. Taylor, op. cit.

[14]See the significant statement of this shift in J. K. Galbraith, American Capitalism, Houghton Mifflin, 1952, Chap. 11; for a useful summary of the immediate post-World War I period, see McConnell, op. cit., Chaps. 2, 3, 4, and 5.

[15]For the ad hoc arrangement of agricultural power with reference to the party mechanism, see E. A. Engelbert, "The Political Strategy of Agriculture," Jour. Farm Econ., 36:375-86, 1954.

[16]See Wesley McCune, The Farm Bloc, Doubleday, Doran, 1943.

[17] National political centers had come to support the Resettlement Administration and the Farm Security Administration; both were attempts to recognize the importance of families upon the land. Note Griswold, op. cit., pp. 205-10; Leonard A. Salter, Jr., "Farm Property and Agricultural Policy," Jour. Pol. Econ., 51:13-22, 1943.

[18] Our insight into this stress and orientation is due basically to J. J. Preiss, "The Functions of Relevant Power and Authority Groups in the Evaluation of County Agent Performance," unpublished Doctoral dissertation, Michigan State Univ., East Lansing, 1954. Preiss develops a model about the constructs of authority and power, and applies it to a detailed analysis of organizational alliances and overlapping directorates in four Michigan counties. For the interlocking structure of organized agricultural power, see J. B. McKee, "An Analysis of the Power Structure of Organized Agriculture in Michigan," unpublished M. A. thesis, Wayne State Univ., Detroit, 1948.

[19]McConnell, op. cit., pp. 67-83; O. M. Kile, The Farm Bureau Through Three Decades, Waverly Press, Baltimore, Md., 1948; D. C. Blaisdell, Government and Agriculture, Farrar and Rinehart, 1940; Speech of the President of the American Farm Bureau Federation, Edward O'Neal, to the Association of Land-Grant Colleges and State Universities, Proceedings, (1933), pp. 87-91. For the detailed Mt. Weather Agreement, see J. M. Gaus and L. O. Wolcott, "Public Administration and the United States Department of Agriculture," Public Administration Service, Chicago, 1940. See also Neal C. Gross, "A Post Mortem on County Planning," Jour. Farm Econ., 25:644-61, 1943; and Hardin, "Bureau of Agricultural Economics Under Fire," op. cit., pp. 643-45.

[20]See Edward S. Mason, ed., The Corporation in Modern Society, Harvard Univ. Press, Cambridge, Mass., 1960, especially, Chap. 5, by Carl Kaysen, "The Corporation: How Much Power? What Scope?" pp. 85-105; W. H. Form and D. C. Miller, Industry, Labor, and Community, Harpers, 1960, pp. 440-44, 461-71, 477-82; and P. H. Odegard and E. A. Helms, American Politics, Harpers, 1938, Chaps. 8 and 9.

[21]D. Gale Johnson, "The Dimensions of the Farm Problem," Problems and Policies of American Agriculture, (Center for Agricultural and Economic Development, sponsor), Iowa State Univ. Press, Ames, 1959, pp. 47-62; E. O. Heady, "Nature of the Farm Problem," Adjustments in Agriculture—A National Basebook, (Center for Agricultural and Economic Development, sponsor), Iowa State Univ. Press, Ames, 1961, pp. 55-84.

[22]Note the following from Lawrence Witt, "Trade and Agricultural Policy," The Annals, 331:6, 1960: "During the five-year period between 1952-1953 and 1957-1958, total exports, in quantity, increased by 18 per cent while agricultural trade increased by 55 per cent. Thus, most of the increase was agricultural. On the import side during the same period total imports rose by 20 per cent and agricultural imports remained constant. Agriculture is out of step both in policy and with actual market trends." Also, D. Gale Johnson, "A Sound Trade Policy and Its Implications for Agriculture," op. cit., p. 8: "A move toward freer trade, involving reducing tariffs and export subsidies and eliminating import quotas, simplification of customs, and consistent maintenance of these changes, is the national interest." (Underline ours.) See also C. C. Zimmerman, "Pathological Economics and Agriculture," Rural Soc., 21:126-34, 1956; also, Kenneth Boulding, op. cit., Chap. 7.

[23]See the impressive compendium on the structure of such services in J. H. Davis and R. A. Goldberg, A Concept of Agribusiness, Graduate School of Business Administration, Harvard Univ., Boston, 1957, especially Chap. 3; also the excellent article by Lowry Nelson, "Rural Life in a Mass-Industrial Society," Rural Soc., 22:20-30, 1957; O. J. Scoville, "Where to in Agriculture-Business Integration?" AES, USDA, mimeo., Feb. 1958.

[24]Cf. Roland R. Renne, "Land-Grant Institutions, the Public, and the Public Interest," The Annals, 331:46-51, 1960; and B. Sexton, "A Responsibility Forgotten: A Relationship Between the Land-Grant Colleges and the Labor Movement," American Association of Land-Grant Colleges and State Universities, Proceedings, 1955, pp. 89-94; also, Paul A. Miller, "Adjustment Needed in Extension Thinking and Organization," Jour. Farm Econ., 41:1435-45, 1959.

[25]See, for example, Murray A. Straus, "Managerial Selectivity of Intensive Extension Work," Rural Soc., 24:150-61, 1959.

[26]With reference to the paradoxical role conflicts of extension workers, see E. A. Wilkening, "The County Agent in Wisconsin," Wis. Agr. Exp. Sta. Res. Bul. 203, 1957; E. A. Wilkening, "Consensus in Role Definition of County Extension Agents Between the Agents and Local Sponsoring Committee Members," Rural Soc., 23:184-97, 1958.

[27]For a helpful background analysis, see C. A. Anderson, "The Need for a Functional Theory of Social Class," Rural Soc., 19:152-60, 1954; also, Lowry Nelson, op. cit.; also, R. B. Talbot, op. cit., p. 110, "One major difficulty . . . is the inability of American farm organizations to see the central issue of our times and to concentrate their unified efforts upon this objective."

[28]See Karl Brandt, "Total Economic Growth and Agriculture," Adjustments in Agriculture—A National Basebook, Iowa State Univ. Press, Ames, 1961, pp. 22-54: "This improvement in productivity depends increasingly on the purchase of farm supplies. Farms become more and more tied into the commercial economy and subject to the dictate of market prices. The obligation to pay taxes and the use of credit ties the farmer more closely to the commercial economy." (P. 24.)

[29]Cf. C. R. Adrian, State and Local Governments, McGraw-Hill, 1960, especially Chap. 12; also, A. W. Bromage, "Political Representation in Metropolitan Areas," Amer. Pol. Sci. Rev., 52:406-18, 1958; also, Robert C. Wood, 1400 Governments, Harvard Univ. Press, Cambridge, Mass., 1961.

[30] Edmund deS. Brunner, The Growth of a Science: A Half-Century of Rural Sociological Research in the United States, Harpers, 1957; also, A. J. Reiss, Jr., "The Sociological Study of Communities," Rural Soc., 24:118-30, 1959; G. A. Hillery, Jr., "Definitions of Community: Areas of Agreement," Rural Soc., 20:111-23, 1955.

[31] G. McBride and G. L. Taggart, "Michigan Milk Producers' Association: An Analysis of MMPA-Member Relations, Attitudes, and Characteristics," Quart. Bul. of the Mich. Agr. Exp. Sta., 39:382-92, 1957. These authors found that eight per cent of the members of this organization belonged to a labor union (p. 391).

[32] S. T. Kimball, "Rural Social Organization and Co-operative Labor," Amer. Jour. of Soc., 55:38-49, 1949: ". . . farmers are freeing themselves from one another. Scientific agriculture and mechanization make this possible. But as he is freed from one type of social system based upon the technological process, the individual finds himself caught up in another system—the equally significant system of social class. The new relationships which are forged in associations, churches, and informal groups become related to the manner in which one consumes the products of his own efforts and the efforts of others. . . ." (P. 48.)

[33] Note the recent extension project in some seven states, sponsored by the Fund for Adult Education under the title, "Leadership for Public Responsibility." This project rests upon the assumption that the extension worker should develop new ways to involve local leaders in confronting public issues and policies.

[34] For instance, Paul Appleby describes the technical system of American agriculture, even in 1933, as follows: "It was the largest research organization in the world. It had the most extensive organization for disseminating to farmers and to the public the fruits of that research. The issuance of crop reports, crop estimates, statistical analyses, and research findings through thousands of press releases and thousands of formal bulletins, and the distribution of this information through agricultural colleges and county agents, tied in with related work done at state experiment stations—these things alone made a great and complex administrative task." Paul H. Appleby, Big Democracy, Knopf, 1945, p. 12.

[35] Kenneth Boulding, op. cit., see especially Chap. 6, "The Labor Movement," Chap. 7, "The Farm Organization Movement," and Chap. 8, "Business Organizations."

[36] Precedents for certain ideas can be found in earlier developments, such as in the work of Christian missions, or even in the reign of India's King Asoka, (269 B.C.). See Charles W. Ranson, That the World May Know, Friendship Press, 1953; also, A. L. Basham, The Wonder That Was India, Sidgwick and Jackson, London, 1954.

[37] While there is considerable theoretical complexity to the task of explaining such "linkage" relationships, several scholars have dealt with various facets of it. C. P. Loomis uses the term "systemic linkage," and has analyzed its implications in many cases of technological change: C. P. Loomis, Social Systems, D. Van Nostrand, 1960; C. P. Loomis and J. A. Beegle, Rural Social Systems, Prentice-Hall, 1950. Edward Spicer labels them "cultural linkages": Edward H. Spicer, Human Problems in Technological Change, Russell Sage Foundation, New York, 1952, p. 290. Philip Selznick uses the term "organizational

links" in describing a related process, that of how communist organizations gain access to target groups: Philip Selznick, The Organizational
Weapon, McGraw-Hill, 1952. For an analysis of the organizational
phases of development organizations, see Christopher Sower, "External
Development Organizations and the Locality," Mich. State Univ., East
Lansing, mimeo., 1959; Christopher Sower, "The Roles of Organizations
in Achieving National Development Goals: The Case of Ceylon," papers
prepared while serving as a member of a United Nations Technical
Assistance Mission in Ceylon, Mich. State Univ., 1962.

[38] See two studies of consensus in role definition concerning Coopera-
tive Extension positions: Eugene A. Wilkening, op. cit.; also, Bond L.
Bible, et al., "Consensus on Role Definition of the County Extension
Executive Committee Member," Rural Soc., 26:146-56, 1961. For a
more extensive analysis of role consensus, see Neal Gross, et al.,
Explorations in Role Analysis, Wiley & Sons, 1958.

[39] For further references on organization goal achievement, see
Paul A. Miller, Community Health Action, Mich. State Univ. Press,
East Lansing, 1953; Christopher Sower, John Holland, Kenneth Tiedke,
and Walter Freeman, Community Involvement, The Free Press, Glencoe,
Ill., 1957; James G. March and Herbert A. Simon, Organizations, Wiley
& Sons, 1958; R. N. Adams and J. J. Preiss, eds., Human Organization
Research, Dorsey Press, Homewood, Ill., 1960; Ralph M.Stogdill,
Individual Behavior and Group Achievement, Oxford Univ. Press, New
York, 1959; Mason Haire, ed., Modern Organization Theory, Wiley &
Sons, 1959; Alvin W. Gouldner, "Organizational Analysis," Chap. 18, in
Robert K. Merton, Leonard Broom, and Leonard S. Cottrell, Jr.,
Sociology Today: Problems and Prospects, Basic Books, 1959; Amitai
Etzioni, Complex Organizations: A Sociological Reader, Holt, Rinehart
& Winston, 1961.

[40] See Amitai Etzioni, "Two Approaches to Organizational Analysis:
A Critique and a Suggestion," Administrative Sci. Quart., 5:257-78,
1960. Etzioni suggests two models for measuring organizational effectiveness: a system model and a goal model. He states at one point,
"The unit's activity can be assured only by concessions, including such
concessions as might reduce the effectiveness and scope of goal activities (but not necessarily the effectiveness of the whole unit)." (P. 276.)

[41] An initial attempt to delimit certain "change models" for the system is made in the following paper by Christopher Sower: "The Land-
Grant University 'Development Organization' in Transition: The Case
of the Cooperative Extension Service," in Robert C. Clark and Noel P.
Ralston, eds., Directing the Cooperative Extension Service, Nat. Agr.
Ext. Center for Advanced Study, Univ. of Wis., Madison, 1962. The
appendix section states selected principles of interorganizational involvement.

[42] Paul Appleby wrote a most insightful book about many of these
issues, after he had served as Assistant Secretary and Under Secretary
of the U.S. Department of Agriculture and in other high governmental
positions from 1933 to 1947. In Big Democracy, op. cit., he makes several significant statements which may represent basic principles of
large-scale organizational planning:

"The first principle in achieving administrative unity—where there
is already an established government unity—is not to farm out essential

functions to unintegrated agencies, but to organize all responsibilities in unified but decentralized hierarchies." (P. 88.)

"No Secretary of Agriculture will ever use, willingly and continuously in direct administration, organizations and personnel not really responsible to him. And Congresses and Presidents may come and go, but in their case, too, none will be really satisfied with an arrangement that would deprive a Secretary of essential authority in fields over which they hold him responsible." (P. 87.)

"The fifth most essential qualification for top administration in a Department is the ability to provide that which otherwise tends to be pushed out by the process of getting an organized product—dynamics. If an agency is to succeed significantly, it must organize against the tendency of all organizations to petrify." (P. 46.)

5

Lee G. Burchinal

The Rural Family
of the Future

WHILE VALUE-STATEMENTS and idealized descriptions of the rural family—particularly of the farm family—abound, until recently there has been a dearth of research studies on rural or farm family patterns. The rudiments of a body of research data on rural and farm family relationships is represented by the recent reports by Brown (11, 12),* Bauder (1), Wilkening (89-91), Straus (79-81), and Blood and Wolfe (8). However, data from these and a few additional studies provide only meager information on rural family structure and processes. The most systematic and comprehensive data related to family patterns in the United States are derived from studies of white, urban, middle-class, Protestant couples. In the absence of comparable data for rural family patterns, descriptive data from this urban category of American families may be useful in predicting and understanding changes in rural family organization. Detailed consideration of this premise led to the development of ten interrelated propositions which form the framework of this chapter.

1. In the past century, the foundation of American society has shifted from relatively isolated, self-sufficient rural communities with an agricultural economy to metropolitan complexes with an industrial economy.
2. The American family system, originating in the frontier era, was shaped by and adapted to the rural environment. As a pattern maintenance system, it has been continuously adjusting to the demands of urban ways of life, which are largely a

---

*Numbers underlined within parentheses refer to literature cited at the end of this chapter. No attempt has been made to provide an exhaustive reference list; rather, the most significant or typical references pertaining to a given point are cited.

function of the scientific, technological, and industrial developments in our society.

3. In this process of change, the family system has most frequently been required to adapt to extrafamily requirements of change rather than to prompt extrafamily system changes. The family system is taken as a set of dependent variables whereas economic and other nonfamily social organization changes are taken as the independent variables in the change model.

4. A prototype of the emerging family system can be discerned in urban society. This family type, which has its modal representation among the college educated, professionally employed urban couples, is probably the best gauge of the direction of future change in the American family system.

5. Functionally important linkages connect rural society and the larger society. These linkages provide the bases for diffusion of knowledge, values, and behavioral patterns from one sector of society to another or from one region of the country to another.

6. It is assumed that most changes in the American family system have been developing in urban communities and have been diffusing to rural communities by means of the institutionalized and informal linkages between the rural and urban populations.

7. The six preceding propositions suggest that important data for understanding changes and for predicting future developments in rural family systems may be obtained by studying changes which have been occurring in the urban family system, especially those observable in the prototypal professional families.

8. The above premises are not meant to imply that changes in rural family patterns occur only through the diffusion of urban family patterns to the rural population. Endogenous changes in rural community organization and family patterns are associated with the continuing technological changes in American agriculture. The effects of agricultural technology are reflected in the higher levels of living and education for rural persons and in the specialization and professionalization of rural and farm occupational roles. In turn, these developments generally reinforce changes in rural family patterns induced by the diffusion of the developing urban family patterns.

9. Yet, changes in any system introduced by elements outside that system are selective. Simple analogies from urban to

rural family systems with appropriate time lapse estimates are likely to be deceptive. The intrinsic relationship between the farm family and the farm firm conditions the nature of farm family patterns. Moreover, differences in rural and urban levels of living or in aspects of community organization such as education, health, and welfare facilities may differentially affect the functioning of families.

10. Therefore, some important differences may still exist between rural and urban family systems. It is important to assess available data to determine in what ways rural and urban family systems are most similar and in what ways they are most different. These data will be useful in predicting future directions of change in rural family systems and in assessing potential strengths and weaknesses of the rural family system for adapting to an urban, industrial, bureaucratic society.

The foregoing ten propositions provide an overview of this chapter. First, attention will be given to general changes in urban family patterns. Then, on the basis of these changes, an attempt will be made to characterize the prototype of the emerging urban family. Next, some inferences will be drawn regarding the present status of rural-urban differences in family patterns. Finally, the preceding data will serve as the basis for pointing out some problems and potentialities of the rural family system.

EMERGING PATTERNS IN THE AMERICAN FAMILY SYSTEM

In comparing early with contemporary American family relationships, a great number of transitions are apparent. In the following section, some of the most significant emerging patterns in the organization of American family life will be briefly deliniated under ten headings. The presentation should be regarded as suggestive rather than exhaustive.[1]

1. Enhanced Status of Women

One of the most far-reaching social changes related to family organization in the United States has been the comparatively recent elevation in the status of women. Equal education for men and women, expansion in the frequency and range of employment opportunities for women, the decline of segregation of sexes in work roles, adoption of masculine dress by women, and a wider range of social contacts for women before and after marriage are just a few of the unmistakable signs of increasingly equal status for women and men. Furthermore, there is now a formidable basis for male-female equality under the law.

The results of this transition toward equality in male-female status include a trend away from the semipatriarchial authority patterns of the last century, the emergence of equalitarian dating and courtship patterns, and a consequent shift toward equalitarian and personality-centered marital relationships.

A powerful combination of factors operate to maintain equal status relations between the sexes, both before and after marriage. It is clear that the long-term increase in the status of women to approximate equality with men will be a prominent feature of American family organization in the foreseeable future.

2. Less Stereotyped Division of Tasks

A favorite generalization of family sociologists is the change from sex-linked division of labor in home and family activities to shared activities performed freely by either or both spouses. Some research (45) strongly supports these generalizations. Middle-class husbands have most freely accepted responsibility for family tasks. Also, middle-class spouses perceive more tasks as joint responsibilities than their lower status counterparts.

A different conclusion is reported by Blood and Wolfe (8). The division of labor in their sample of Detroit families coincided with the division of labor in the traditional rural family. The authors report, however, that the sexually differentiated roles of Detroit couples were not rooted in the "dead hand" of culture, but were a reflection of equity: roles were assigned on the basis of the amount of time, energy, and skill which each family member could contribute to the common family tasks.

Both studies agree in reporting that household division of labor is more likely to be based upon the interpersonal relationships of the couple than upon widely accepted cultural norms. General societal trends support the movement toward informality in household division of labor and spousal decision-making processes.

3. Changed Definition of Children

Children were an economic asset in the earlier, fertile, relatively self-sufficient rural family, but they occupied an inferior status position in their parent-oriented or father-centered family. A lowered birth rate was one of the adjustments of the family system to urbanization (52, p. 198). Reductions in fertility have been accompanied by an increased status for children vis-a-vis their parents and by dedication to corresponding modes of child rearing.

Changes in child-rearing techniques reflect the movement from formal parent-child relationships based upon differential status positions with clearly defined roles toward the informal, varied, and person-centered relations in the modern family. These changes are manifested in the greater use by both parents of "psychological" or "symbolic" techniques of discipline, greater permissiveness for child behavior, freer expression of affection, greater participation by children in family decision making, and more conscious attempts by parents to help children develop their intellectual, social, and emotional potentialities (10). These changes in family socialization patterns actively promoted by family life educators, also receive increasing societal support.

4. Increased Use of Person-centered Criteria in Mate Selection

The improvements in the level of living freed adolescents from the labor market, provided them with leisure time and, with the relatively equal sex standards which have been developing, created the conditions for contemporary dating and courtship patterns. One result has been an increase in the spatial mobility of youth and, with this, an opportunity for a wider choice among dating and potential marriage partners (20, 25). In this context of wider choice in prospective mates, mate selection standards based on love and companionate interests appear to be overcoming institutionalized endogamous norms such as those forbidding interfaith marriages (19, 20, 43, 84). It appears that norms of class endogamy have remained unchanged or, given the wider territorial range in mate selection, may even have become stronger (25).

5. Increasing Permissiveness of Sex Norms

A revolution in American sexual norms has occurred in the last half-century. There has been a socially sanctioned change in attitudes toward the rights of both men and women to attain enjoyable and satisfactory marital sex relations. Expectations for enjoyable sex relations at varying levels of involvement have carried over into dating and courtship relations. Premarital coital relations are still condemned, and the double sex standard is still openly tolerated, but all available data point to increases in nonmarital sexual activity. Given the emphasis on free selection of dating and courtship partners, affectionate and companionate personal relations, individualism, equality of male and female status, secularization of values, earlier ages for initial dating, and more serious emotional involvements at younger ages, the double sex standard has become less tenable and there are fewer societal supports for continence.

The Kinsey studies and other data indicate that the increase in premarital coital activity occurred during World War I and shortly thereafter. The change in female behavior was more marked than in male behavior. Present evidence suggests that the prevalence of premarital coital activity has remained relatively stable during the past several decades. However, rates of petting have increased notably since the 1920's (26, 55, 56, 73). This increase in petting may lead, in time, to an increase in the number of couples who will accept premarital coitus (73). The prediction that premarital coital rates will increase is based on the probable diffusion of the single standard, permissive-with-affection sex code evolving in American society. This code permits greater freedom, ultimately leading to nonmarital coitus, in person-centered relationships where a high degree of affection is present. Reiss argues that such a sex code is associated with the emerging male-female equality and the emerging individuated, companionate, affectional marriage system (73).

6. Differentiation and Specialization in Family Functions

Industrialization and consequent urbanization, plus geographical mobility, have decreased the importance of the extended family and have increased the significance of the nuclear family in the provision of services for its members. This movement from an extended family system to a nuclear family system and the resulting specialization of functions within the nuclear family

system has led to the familiar portrayal of the "loss of functions" in the nuclear family organization. While it is true that
the American family no longer represents a "little society" to
its members, there are still certain generalized functions which
the family system, now in its nuclear form, continues to provide
for society in general. These include the reproduction of new
members, child care, and important contributions to the
socialization of children. The family also continues to provide
tension management for its members, including the regulation
of sexual behavior and the provision of affectional-companionate
relations. Beyond these sexual, socializing, and maintenance
functions, the family system retains the function of initial status
ascription and provides a basis for the transfer of property.

Williams (92) and Bell and Vogel (7) approach the subject of
specialization of functions within the family system by focusing
on the interchanges between the family system and the other
social systems. In this context, lists of functions which the
nuclear family system is expected to fulfill become less relevant. The important foci become the nature of the systemic
linkages between the family system and other social systems
(including the roles, status, norms, and values involved), and
the associations between intrafamily activities which are related to the systemic linkage roles and the activities performed
in the systemic linkage roles. Of particular importance, are
the systemic linkages between the family system and the
economic or occupational systems.

General changes in society, previously cited in this book by
Williams and Larson as well as in this chapter, require specialization in the family system and at the same time increase
the importance of the nuclear family in providing adequate
socialization, personality development, and tension-management
experiences for its members. The importance of these functions
of the family will likely increase, not diminish, as marital roles
will likely be increasingly based on personally perceived satisfactions arising from interpersonal relations.

7. Reassertion of Kinship Ties and Family
Continuity Patterns

Another widely accepted generalization in the family literature is that industrialization and urbanization are antithetical to
close and continuous relationships among kin. Until recently
sociologists have described the American family as primarily a

simple conjugal system with no important kinship connections. Litwak (61, 62) has carefully analyzed several of the assumptions of the Parsonion model and has suggested an ideal type, the "modified extended" family, as appropriate for describing contemporary kinship patterns among urban nuclear families. The "modified extended" family differs from the "classical extended" family in that it does not demand territorial propinquity, occupational involvement, or nepotism, nor does it have a hierarchical authoritarian pattern. On the other hand, it differs from the isolated, nuclear family structure in that it does provide significant and continuing aid to the nuclear family.

Research in various metropolitan areas of the United States and England support the validity of the modified extended family system in urban social structures. These studies reveal a kin family system involving a network of mutual assistance, visiting, and socio-emotional support encompassing several generations.[2]

8. Professionalization of Marital and Parental Roles

Specialization in family functions has led to professionalization of parental and marital roles for both partners, but especially for the wife. Wives cannot rely upon their informally acquired "folk knowledge" as a basis for performing their roles. The knowledge necessary for performance of contemporary marital and parental roles must be rationalized and kept up to date. Coeducational classes on preparation for marriage and family life, in-service training as provided by the women's magazines, study, and discussion groups, and consultation with specialists at the medical clinic, nursery school, PTA meeting, or in the counseling office reflect the desire to prepare for, or seek help in, performing marital and parental roles.

9. Development of Programs To Increase the Well-being of the American Family

At the turn of the century, most people had great respect for the institution called the family, yet they were reluctant to learn much about it. The family was taken for granted and was expected to cope automatically with whatever internal or external crises occurred (45). As the ban on discussion of family matters has been lifted and as the results of research and reflection

have permeated the society, a wide variety of educational,
counseling, judicial, and governmental programs have evolved
to ameliorate problems associated with American family life.
These programs will probably receive increased support and be
staffed by increasingly competent persons in the future.

10. Interpersonal Criteria of Success
and Stability of Marriage

The emerging norms for evaluating marriage and family relationships are based on the interpersonal needs and relationships of all family members. These norms impose far greater
demands on family members than criteria based on economic
interdependence or on legal and social obligations. The long-
term increase in divorce rates represents a shift from the
criterion of relative permanence, come what may, to the
criteria of interpersonal relations, which permit divorce if the
relationship between the spouses becomes intolerable.

Contrary to the beliefs of traditionalists, there are indications that the interpersonal criteria for evaluating marital and
family relations are associated with increased stability in marriage. Marriage and remarriage arc at the height of their
respective popularities. Divorce is not a rejection of marriage;
rather it apparently represents an attempt to improve marital
experiences. Divorce rates have declined from an all-time
high in the late 1940's, are now fluctuating in a narrow range,
and may be expected to remain at their present levels or to
show a long-term, gradual decline, although they will probably
never reach the low level of the late 1880's (34, 51).

Reasons for expecting a decline in divorce rates would include
the emergence of socialization patterns which are oriented to the
acquisition of interpersonal competence skills, opportunities for
greater freedom in mate selection, the relative equality between
men and women, greater flexibility in male and female roles,
increased emphasis on sex satisfaction for both spouses, the
desire for and satisfactions gained from child rearing, less
puritanical attitudes toward deviations from chastity, increased
levels of living, additional support for nuclear families through
the revitalization of the kinship system, and the professionalization of marital and family roles—all of which are buttressed by
private and public family service programs.

Another way of supporting the prediction of increased marital
stability in the United States is to compare divorce rates among

different segments of the population. As Foote (29) has pointed out, the standard assertion that urbanization and industrialization are inexorably destructive of family stability and solidarity is contradicted by the fact that the families of college educated, salaried, professional couples have a low divorce rate. Yet these families are the fullest beneficiaries of such aspects of industrialization and urbanization as the reliance upon science, spatial and social mobility, and emphasis on the welfare and freedom of the individual. The professional group is most liberal in its attitude toward divorce, is most equalitarian in its views on the employment of married women, and strongest in espousing equality of status and flexibility of roles between husbands and wives. And this group appears to be most cosmopolitan in its selection of marriage partners, least affected by propinquity, and closest in age at marriage.

At present, it seems that the voluntary commitment to marriage based upon companionship and mutual development, as found among the professional groups, is a stronger bond for marriage than functional economic interdependence and the social and legal sanctions which held traditional families together.

THE EMERGING URBAN PROTOTYPE

Precise empirical data for documenting the characteristics of an emerging urban family organization are lacking. The currently offered typologies—traditional, companionate or colleague, for example—appear to be inadequate for conceptualizing urban family organization (35). For this reason, a neat typology cannot be used to summarize the current pattern of urban family organization or that of the urban professional class. Yet a prototype of urban family organization may be inferred from projections of past changes. This prototype is most clearly represented among families in the urban professional class and, in varying degrees, reflects the following characteristics: enhancement of the welfare, freedom, and personality of individual family members by means of family relationships; development of nuclear and extended family bonds based upon loyalty, affection, and companionship; maintenance of equalitarian relationships and a flexible family division of labor; differentiation in family and occupational roles resembling the colleague conceptualization of Miller and Swanson (68) or the mutually contingent careers idea of Foote (29); desire for children based on the opportunities for providing for the personality development of the children and the enrichment which the children bring to the couple; active pursuit and implementation of knowledge (professionalization) related to marital and family roles; use of person-centered criteria in dating, courtship, mate selection, and marriage; and tolerant views toward nonmarital sexual experiences.

It cannot be established when these prototypal patterns will become modal characteristics of urban families.[3] It is even less clear when and in what ways rural family organization will reflect these prototypal patterns. However, in terms of long-run developments, these prototypal patterns may be used as a point of departure for assessing circumstances which rural families will probably encounter as they continue to change under the joint impact of specialization through social and technological developments in the rural scene and of "modernization" of family patterns spreading from urban to rural communities.[4]

CHANGES IN THE RURAL FAMILY SYSTEM

How have the changes described for the urban family system, and now emerging in a prototypal urban pattern, affected rural family organization? Adequate research data are not available to answer this question, but some tentative inferences, suggested as hypotheses, may be drawn from the available data. In the discussion which follows, overgeneralization and oversimplification cannot be avoided unless the results of available research were rigidly limited to the particular state, county, or community from which the samples were drawn. A broader canvass than this is needed for the presentation of tentative assessments of the relationships between rurality and family patterns. Therefore, in the present discussion, speculation has been granted a freer hand and careful limitations have not been placed on generalizations.

All empirical data consistently support the generalization that changes in rural family organization have followed those described for the urban family system. While this statement is hardly startling, the generalization is valuable as a perspective for predicting changes in rural family patterns. For instance, Brown's observations of changes in the organization of Kentucky mountain families (11, 12) indicate that changes in the family patterns of these relatively isolated people parallel, but lag

about 50 years behind, those in the general society. If the relatively isolated, strongly kinship-oriented family of Beech Creek
is undergoing many of the same changes as the family system
in the wider society, but not as quickly, it is likely that family
systems in less isolated rural areas will display even less difference from the emerging urban family patterns (1, 32, 54).
Unfortunately, data are not available for systematic analysis of
this proposition. But some indication of the narrowing gap in
the family-related values and attitudes may be gleaned from a
number of investigations.

Twenty-five years ago Beers observed that the patterns of
New York farm families which he studied were becoming more
like those of urban families. These farm families were smaller,
less familistic, and the roles of parents and children were becoming more flexible, with a definite democratization in family
status positions. The latter was best evidenced by the shared
executive roles of the fathers and mothers, although these joint
decision-making patterns appeared to be a function of the economic scale of the farm enterprise rather than the result of a
democratic normative pattern (5).

The generalization of declining familism in the rural family
system is supported by additional research (24). Several investigations of differences in opinions between rural and urban
wives on problems related to marriage failed to reveal many
striking differences (57, 76).

While the foregoing data and portions of additional data which
follow indicate that changes in rural family organization are
following changes in urban family patterns, some differences
may still exist between rural and urban family systems. Available descriptive data for comparable rural and urban family
patterns may be organized under the following eight headings.

RURAL-URBAN DIFFERENCES IN FAMILY PATTERNS

1. Family Decision-making Patterns

Only small or nonsignificant differences in family decision-
making patterns have been reported by two studies, each of
which employed a different dichotomy for studying the relationship between rural-urbanism and family decision-making patterns. Blood and Wolfe compared farm and Detroit, Michigan,
couples (8); Bock and Burchinal employed a farm-nonfarm

distinction for Greene county, Iowa, families and applied controls for age and educational levels (9). The absence of uncompromising paternal dominance patterns and evidence for husband-wife sharing of the executive role in farm families have also been reported in earlier research (5, 27).

The decision-making items in all of the preceding studies pertain to family interaction patterns which did not directly involve work or occupational roles. Research by Wilkening and Straus can be used to test the validity of the companionate model for farm operations decisions. This model is implied in most of the thinking and the action programs related to farm family and farm firm interrelationships. Husband-wife interaction in relation to decisions about farm operations is not a simple function of the status of either spouse or the complexity of the farming enterprise. Rather, the joint decision-making pattern appears to be a function of the extent to which farm family and farm firm decisions are viewed as having joint consequences for both the farming enterprise and the household (91). Wilkening further suggests that the roles played by husbands and wives in decision making are determined more by their perceptions of farm and household needs than by culturally determined patterns of interaction.

Under these conditions, wide variations in husbands' and wives' roles in decision making should be observed. The needs perceived by the couple may vary over time and interact in numerous ways with the degree of commercialization of the farm and the levels of aspiration of the farm operator and his wife. For instance, contrary to what might have been assumed to be the dominant interests of farm wives, Wilkening found that more farm wives than farm operators in one sample preferred purchases of farm items over purchases of household equipment (89).

Wilkening's social psychological frame of reference, including perceived needs and consequent interaction patterns of husbands and wives, is congruent with the general thesis emerging from Straus' investigations of farm family role differentiation. In his investigation of the wives' contributions to success in settlement in the Columbia Basin Project (80, 81), Straus found that wives in the high success group and wives in the low success group of settlers were not appreciably different in background characteristics or in their direct economic contributions to their respective families. Instead, the qualities which differentiated the two groups of wives were certain attitudes, values, and personality characteristics.

The wives in the high success group more frequently accepted the traditional pattern of male dominance in the economic area. They were more active in food preparation, less active in farm work roles (further evidence for a traditional sex-linked division of labor), were better adjusted psychologically, were more optimistic, and were more persevering than were the wives of the low success settlers. Straus draws an analogy between the wives of the high success group and the image of the successful corporation wife, suggesting that the differentiating factors between the wives in high and low success categories are those which "enable the wife to play a supportive and complimentary role in helping her husband meet the many decisions, difficulties, and frustrations which arise in developing a new farm" (81, p. 64).

In later research, Straus tested the relationship between the integrative, supportive wife role and the technological competence of her husband. The existence of the "wife role factor" in understanding the adoption of farm practices by the husband was demonstrated, but no causal relationship was implied (79).

Wilkening also studied relationships between adoption of farm practices and family-related variables (89, 90). No consistent relationship was found between the authoritarian role of the husband-father or between measures of familism or family integration and the farm operator's acceptance of changes in farm technology. Instead, roles and values of family organization centering around acquiring a good living, education for the children, security, recreation, and health were related to the acceptance of changes in farm technology.

2. Household Division of Labor

Blood and Wolfe found that farm and Detroit wives reported the same median number of sex-stereotyped household task allocations, five out of eight tasks (8). However, farm wives performed a consistently greater share of household roles than city wives and helped their husbands more frequently with their work. In the aggregate, about 70 per cent of the farm wives did more than half of the eight tasks all by themselves while only 39 per cent of the city wives handled as many tasks on their own.

Data related to husband-wife role differentiation for samples of farm and nonfarm families are also available for Greene County, Iowa. Age and educational level controls were used in all comparisons of items related to household tasks, child care

tasks, and management of money tasks. In general, the farm
and nonfarm wives described similar patterns of husband-wife
role differentiation in the three areas tested (9).

3. Employment of Wives Outside the Home

Aside from the several comparisons already cited, farm and
nonfarm or city wives appear to contribute to the economic welfare of their families in distinctively different ways. The comparison of economic functions of wives showed that farm wives
more frequently made most of their dresses, prepared more
baked goods, more frequently raised summer vegetables, and
canned or froze more foods. The Detroit wife apparently looked
more frequently to paid employment as her means of contributing
to the family income and gaining whatever satisfactions work
meant to her. Twenty-four per cent of the sample of the Detroit
wives were employed compared with only nine per cent of the
farm wives (8).

Comparisons of employment rates of farm and nonfarm wives
in Greene County, Iowa, have the advantage of controlling for
employment opportunities for the two populations of women living in the same county (17). In this county, approximately eight
per cent of the farm wives included in a probability sample were
employed off the farm in contrast to approximately 26 per cent
of the nonfarm wives who were employed outside their homes.
In each of three farm-nonfarm comparisons using controls for
the educational level of the wives, a greater proportion of nonfarm wives were employed. Also, significantly greater proportions of the nonfarm wives were employed before their marriages
and continued to work after marriage than the farm wives.

Data available from another survey in Cass County, Iowa,
agreed with the Greene County results (17). Only about nine per
cent of the wives in a random sample of Cass County farm
families with children in school were employed, in comparison
with 31 per cent of the nonfarm wives with children in school.

A general premise of this chapter, the diffusion and acceptance of urban-developed values by rural persons, points to
greater participation of farm wives in the nonfarm labor force.
Questions frequently arise as to the "effects" of employment of
married women on family variables. Because of the recent and
expected long-term increases in employment of married women,
a brief and highly generalized summary of research on relationships between maternal employment and family variables appears
warranted.

A growing body of research based mainly on urban families, though including some studies based on farm families (2, 3, 17, 70, 74), indicates that family task patterns and spousal decision-making patterns are related to the employment status of the wife.[5] Among families where the wives are employed, husbands generally are more active in household task roles, but the data are not as clear in regard to alterations in the spousal balance of power which may be associated with the employment of wives. Some studies report that wives enhance their power vis-a-vis their husbands when they are employed, but Hoffman questions this conclusion. Her results led her to suggest that employment of wives does not affect family power relations directly, but only in interaction with the existing ideology and personality of the actors. Power relationships, unlike division of labor, are either too deeply interrelated with psychological components of the husband-wife relationship to respond readily to the impact of the wife's employment, or employment per se is too weak a variable to accomplish this change (48).

The most extensive data on employment of farm wives and associated patterns of spousal relationships are those reported by Bauder (2, 3).[6] Bauder found that employment of farm wives was associated with increased household task performance by farm husbands. Nonfarm employment of farm husbands had no apparent effect on the spousal division of labor. The most pronounced effects on the spousal division of labor occurred among farm families where both husband and wife were employed off the farm. For these families, household tasks were performed more frequently by the children or adults other than the parents, and when they were performed by one spouse, they were done by the person who had the most time or who happened to be available.

The same pattern was observed in relation to husband-wife decision-making patterns, although it was less marked than for the division of labor patterns. For instance, major punishment of children was typically a joint decision role between farm parents when neither was employed off the farm. It generally remained so when either the husband or wife worked, but when both were employed major punishment of children was less frequently reported as a joint decision responsibility. Instead, it was decided more frequently by either the father or mother, generally on the basis of who was available at the time.

A modest body of research pertaining to relations between employment of mothers and developmental characteristics of children has appeared in recent years. The usual assumption about the detrimental influence of employment of mothers on their children has not been supported by most of this research. In the most carefully designed studies, generally small, nonsignificant, or inconsistent differences in personality and social characteristics have been found between children and youth whose mothers have been employed and those whose mothers have not been employed: see the summaries by Burchinal (18) or Herzog (44).

Exceptions to these null differences between children whose mothers have been and have not been employed come from two studies based on samples of rural families. In these studies the results suggest that employment of rural mothers is associated with positive child development and family relations results. In three of five comparisons between younger children of employed and nonemployed mothers and in all five comparisons between similar groups of older children, Nolan and Tuttle (70) found differences favoring the children whose mothers had been employed. The comparisons were based on teachers' ratings on children's academic achievement, relations between ability and achievement, acceptance by peers, acceptance of the teacher's supervision, and evidence of home training.

In a study of rural and town families living in Washington, Roy found that "rural families in general benefited from the employment of the mother, in that the girls, and, in part, the boys, showed less delinquency, more affection, more fairness of discipline, more democracy and more cooperation in their families." (74, p. 349).

4. Satisfaction With Marriage and Family Relations

Some data show no differences between marital satisfaction levels of farm and nonfarm couples; other data suggest higher satisfaction levels among nonfarm couples; and with only relatively minor exceptions, no data of which the writer is aware suggest higher satisfaction levels among farm couples. In the aggregate, however, the data suggest that farm family living may produce lower levels of marital and personal satisfaction than nonfarm family living.

Null differences in marital satisfaction or happiness scores between farm and city wives were reported by Blood and Wolfe (8) and among farm, rural nonfarm, and small-town couples studied by Burchinal (15). Other data indicate that people living in metropolitan areas express greater marital happiness and less feelings of inadequacy than other persons, particularly rural persons (38, p. 229). Blood and Wolfe observed that the pattern of disagreement or complaints regarding marriage was similar for the farm and city families. Both samples of wives reported that companionship in doing things with their husbands was the most valuable aspect of marriage to them.

Blood and Wolfe found several differences related to marital relations between the samples of farm and Detroit families. Husbands' responses to their wives' troubles was one of these. Farm-reared husbands tended to be passive listeners, whether they still lived on farms or had moved to Detroit. Men still engaged in farming were more likely than city husbands to dismiss their wives' troubles. Their failure to help the wife in her crisis seems to correspond with their slight participation in household tasks (8, p. 209).

Another farm-Detroit marital relationship difference centered on satisfaction-with-love scores. Satisfaction with love was the only aspect of marriage in which Blood and Wolfe found a significant difference between farm and city wives. Farm wives were less satisfied in their love relationships with their husbands than city wives (8, p. 223). Further analysis of the wives' satisfaction-with-love scores, based on the sizes of communities in which the wives had spent most of their lives, suggested that family expressions of love and affection are most widely encouraged and practiced by persons with urban socialization experiences.

Other data suggest less satisfaction in marital and personal relations in farm families as compared with nonfarm families. In 1940, McVoy and Nelson found that farm women were more dissatisfied than village women in regard to a number of categories of family living, had lower social participation scores, displayed poorer general adjustment, and had poorer self-happiness ratings. When the samples of farm and village women were matched on several variables, the farm women still had significantly lower satisfaction scores, poorer general adjustment, and lower happiness scores (66). In a restudy of the farm and nonfarm populations in the same county ten years later, Taves found that although living conditions had improved markedly for both populations, and more so for the farm families, farm women still had lower family living satisfaction scores than village women (83).

Thorpe's investigation of farm and town family interaction patterns suggest that there was greater spousal companionship among the town couples than among the farm couples who were included in her Michigan samples (85). Town husbands and wives, in comparison with farm couples, spent more time together exclusive of other family members.

Results of two other studies suggest that interpersonal relations in farm or rural families are less often marked by affection than those in the urban families. Beers observed that the shared activities and group rituals of the New York farm families he studied were not ordinarily accompanied by overt demonstrations of affection. Traditions of restraint and habits of emotional control may have been vestiges of the earlier pioneer attitude of inner control (5, p. 596).

Indirect support for the view of less affectionate or companionate relations between farm husbands and wives comes from the study of rural-urban differences between young married women in Washington. The most striking rural-urban differences between the young married women with rural and urban socialization background was the much higher proportion of rural than urban women who considered sexual adjustment a major problem in marital happiness or unhappiness (57). The greater perception of sexual difficulties among the rural-reared married women may reflect less satisfactory spousal relations, which, in turn, may be based on socialization experiences which make it more difficult for rural-reared spouses than urban-reared spouses to develop satisfactory sex and love relationships. Otherwise, the Kinsey data suggest that only minor differences exist in the variety and frequency of sexual outlets among rural- and urban-reared males and females, although urban-reared persons were generally more active in most outlets (55, 56).

5. Divorce Proneness

All available data support the generalization that marital stability is higher among farm or rural couples than among urban couples (51, 52, 60, 64). All of the foregoing studies, though, suffer from a common limitation—the analyses were based upon current residence at the time of divorce. Information is not available regarding what proportion of urban divorces include persons who had a rural residence immediately prior to divorce. Undoubtedly, some relationship exists between divorce and migration from farm to urban areas. On the other hand, it is easy to overgeneralize the frequency of migration-linked divorces and, consequently, to underestimate the true magnitude of rural-urban differences in divorce rates. Some Iowa data suggest that the observed differences in rural and urban divorce rates are not spurious, even though urban divorce rates may be inflated as a consequence of separation, migration, and subsequent divorce (69).

Divorced farm men are not under the same necessity to migrate from the farm as divorced farm wives. Therefore, divorce ratios based upon men's occupational roles should provide a better estimate of rural-urban differences in divorce rates than those based on residence at the time of divorce. Monahan has provided divorce ratio data by occupational categories for Iowa males in 1953. The ratio of divorces per 1,000 employed farm laborers was 0.9 against 26.9 for other laborers; the divorce ratio for farm operators was 1.7 against 2.9 for owners and officials engaged in nonfarm occupations (69). Clearly, some combination of circumstances associated with farm socialization and farm living, especially for the lowest occupational status comparison, are reflected in these farm-nonfarm divorce ratio differences.

Goode has provided data which support the view of greater reluctance of persons with rural backgrounds to seek divorce. Respondents with rural backgrounds had the longest median duration of marriage, the longest period of serious consideration of divorce before filing and, when the divorces occurred, most frequently reported trauma associated with their divorces. Urban-reared wives were most different from rural-reared wives while the wives from small towns were intermediate in these respects (36).

6. Social Relationship Patterns

Numerous studies support the generalization that farm husbands and wives are less active in social organizations than nonfarm couples who live in the same areas served by the organizations. This generalization appears to have been true for at least three decades: see Leevy, data from 1935 to 1938 (58); McVoy and Nelson, 1940 (66); and Bock and Burchinal, 1958 (9). If farm couples do not participate as actively in social organizations as neighboring nonfarm couples, it could be hypothesized that farm couples have more active informal social relationship patterns, including visiting with relatives, than the nonfarm couples.

Two recent studies, conducted in the Midwest, provided tests of differences in kinship-related visiting and nonkinship-related visiting by farm and nonfarm couples. In Greene County, Iowa, farm and nonfarm families appeared equal in the total number of families or individuals with whom they regularly visited. But the farm families reported that a larger proportion of the families they visited were related to them while the nonfarm families reported that a larger porportion of the families they visited were unrelated to them. However, there appeared to be little difference between the farm and nonfarm families in the frequency of visiting related families. A large difference between farm and nonfarm families in the total frequency of visiting was observed because nonfarm families reported a greater frequency of visiting with nonrelated persons or families (9).

Key (53) failed to find a linear relationship between residence position along a rural-urban continuum and the degree of social participation of men and women in either their nuclear or extended families. Instead, he observed a U-shaped curve, with the low point at the village or small urban category and with the high points at the extremes—the rural sample, on the one hand, and the middle-sized city or metropolitan sample on the other hand.

To a limited degree, the results of these studies suggest that visiting patterns based on extended family relationships were stronger among rural than among the nonfarm or urban family members, but that the nonfarm or urban families visited nonrelated families more frequently. However, no controls were used for the presence of related families.

7. Child-bearing and Child-rearing Patterns

Historically, the farm family has been more fertile than the urban family, but the size of rural-urban difference in fertility rates has varied with general socioeconomic conditions in the United States. The effect in recent years has been toward a narrowing, but not a vanishing, fertility differential between rural and urban women (52, 63).[7]

Some fragmentary data from Blood and Wolfe (8) suggest a future similarity in farm and urban birth rates. They found that both farm and city wives wanted approximately four children and that two to four children was considered as the ideal family size.

What children mean to parents appears to have somewhat different meanings for the farm and city mothers in the Detroit area study. The ranking of criteria for defining what was good

about having children was the same for the farm and city
mothers, but the two groups of mothers gave differential emphasis to some of the good things about having children. For instance, city wives mentioned emotional satisfaction more often
than farm wives. Farm wives were more apt to mention the
companionship of the child, the belief that the presence of the
child strengthened the home, and that children helped parents
and provided security.

The meager data that are available on parent-child relationships in rural and urban families support the generalization that
parent-child relationships are less satisfactory in rural and
farm homes than in urban homes. In the early 1930's Burgess
reported that parent-adolescent relationships were less satisfactory in rural than in city families (88). Researchers in
Washington found that both urban-reared mothers and daughters
more frequently rated their parental homes as very happy than
did rural-reared mothers and daughters. The urban daughters
more frequently than any other group came from very happy
parental homes (76). The foregoing data from different time
periods and from different parts of the country are buttressed
by the results of a careful study by Nye. Nye found that children
from Michigan city families enjoyed better parent-adolescent
relationships than other children, and that parent-adolescent adjustment declined with increasing rurality. When family socioeconomic status was held constant, the differences were absent
at the high socioeconomic level and, though diminished, were
still evident in the medium and low levels (71).

8. Rural-Urban Differences in Preparation for Adult Roles

Recognition of the increased similarity in rural and urban
socialization systems has led to the generalization that personality or value-related characteristics of rural and urban children
or youth are not very different; or if differences currently exist,
they will become smaller and even negligible in the future. A
considerable body of data points to the opposite conclusion—that
there are significant differences in the socialization experiences
of rural and urban youth. These differences are shown in school
achievement levels, occupational aspiration and achievement
levels, value-orientations, and personality-related characteristics of rural and urban youth.[8]

Historically, rural males have had lower educational levels
than urban males. This is still true for rural and urban

populations in general and for current populations of rural and urban youth. Among persons 16 to 24 who were not enrolled in regular or special schools in October, 1959, the farm population showed the highest proportion who lacked a high school education, as well as the lowest proportion with some college (86). Furthermore, reports from farm, rural nonfarm, and urban high school seniors about their college plans and the degree to which they realized their plans one year later point to the maintenance of a better educated urban-reared than rural-reared population. In the national sample of youth surveyed in 1959, the smallest proportion of high school seniors who planned to go to college came from farm homes, rural nonfarm youth were intermediate, and urban youth most frequently planned to go to college. Rates of college attendance one year later were highest for urban youth and lowest for farm youth (87).

Controls for intelligence levels, grade in school, socio-economic status of family, and sex of child, tend to diminish rural-urban differences in educational aspiration, but do not entirely remove the differences (37, 67, 75). For instance, Sewell found that Wisconsin farm children, regardless of their sex, levels of intellectual ability, or family status levels, generally had lower educational aspirations than similar children from village homes and almost always had lower levels than comparable urban children (75). An intriguing result of this study was that the differences in the proportions of farm, village, and urban youth who reported college plans were greatest for the comparisons where least differences might have been expected, among high intelligence high socioeconomic status groups. It is these groups which should provide the greatest proportions of college students. Results from an investigation in Florida agree with those from Wisconsin. High school seniors from rural and urban communities were matched on intelligence levels. Larger proportions of urban white males than rural white males, at each of several intelligence levels, reported plans to attend college (67).

The fact that sizable differences existed among the educational aspirations of farm, rural nonfarm, and urban youth after controls for intelligence and status were applied indicates that these variables do not explain why rural youth lag behind urban youth in educational aspirations. Differences in the value given education by rural and urban persons probably provides a more adequate explanation of the educational aspiration and achievement differences between rural and urban youth. Results from some markedly different studies support this view.

First, the lack of emphasis on advanced education for rural youth relative to urban youth, as reflected in their educational aspiration or achievement levels, may be a vestige of the view that advanced education is unnecessary, even a luxury, for youth who plan to enter farming. Research in a number of states indicates that this view still persists (21). Generally, farm youth who plan to farm are less likely than any other category of youth to consider education beyond high school. The norm of lower educational attainment for farm youth planning to farm may also influence educational norms for rural nonfarm students in rural communities, thus lowering educational aspiration norms for rural youth as a whole in contrast to urban youth.

Second, in the October 1959 survey of rural and urban youth, there was evidence that attitudinal differences outweighed economic differences in the formation of the educational plans of rural and urban youth. The most important difference in reasons for not attending college given by farm and nonfarm persons was the higher proportion of farm males (45 per cent) than nonfarm males (30 per cent) who reported "no desire" to attend college. Smaller and generally negligible differences were found for other reasons, such as finances, marriage, military service, or employment (87).

Finally, parental encouragement of male high school seniors to attend college was reported considerably more frequently by a sample of urban than by a sample of rural nonfarm or farm boys in Iowa. Whether they planned to farm or to enter nonfarm careers, the farm boys least frequently reported definite parental encouragement to attend college, and urban boys most frequently reported definite parental encouragement to attend college (16). In all three residence samples (farm, rural nonfarm-small town, and urban) mothers were reported to have more frequently provided definite encouragement to attend college than were fathers.

Most studies agree in finding lower occupational aspiration levels, probably related to lower educational aspiration levels, among rural youth as compared with urban youth. The differences in occupational aspirations of rural-urban or farm-urban high school boys persist when intellectual levels or family socioeconomic levels have been controlled (37, 67). Among boys living in a highly industrialized area of Michigan, Haller found that the difference in occupational aspiration between farm and nonfarm youth was principally due to farm-reared boys who planned to farm (41). When the occupational aspiration levels of only the farm boys who planned nonfarm careers were compared

with those of the nonfarm boys, nonsignificant differences in occupational aspirations were observed between the two groups of
boys. Different results were found in an Iowa investigation (16).
When the Iowa farm-reared boys who planned to enter the nonfarm jobs were compared with small-town and city boys, the
occupational aspirational levels of the nonfarm-oriented farm-
reared boys approximated those of the nonfarm and small-town
boys, but both were lower than the occupational aspiration levels
of the city boys.

Compared with the urban boys, the Iowa rural or small-town
boys less frequently reported that their parents discussed the
boys' occupational plans with them or were involved in the boys'
occupational decision-making processes (16). Other data suggest high school boys planning to farm were less well informed
about nonfarm job opportunities and training requirements, were
more satisfied with their present sources and levels of occupational information, and were less actively seeking information
about nonfarm job opportunities (39, 40).

Rural-urban differences in adolescent personality characteristics are another reflection of rural-urban differences in
socialization experiences. Results of various studies of rural-
urban differences in personality characteristics have presented
all three possible conclusions: (a) better adjustment characteristics among rural as contrasted with urban youth (65, 78);
(b) better personality adjustment characteristics among urban
as contrasted with rural youth (42, 93); and (c) no difference
between personality characteristics of rural and urban youth (14).
The two most recent and probably most powerful studies support
the second generalization.

The Minnesota study, based on more adequate samples than
have been used previously and the use of more powerful personality diagnostic instruments, reported that farm and rural
youth more frequently than urban youth expressed feelings of
shyness, self-deprecation, and suspicion or distrust of others.
Urban youth were more likely to rebel against authority, be less
self-critical, and be less suspicious of the motives of others
than rural adolescents (42).

Results of research in Michigan generally confirm those derived from the Minnesota comparisons. Wolff and Haller found
that in comparison with village and rural nonfarm boys or urban
boys, farm boys had the greatest indications of submissiveness,
shyness, or withdrawal tendencies. The farm boys tended to be
less willing to move away from their home communities and
were less likely to believe that man has much control over

events which influence his life. Urban boys scored highest on dominance, aggressiveness, self-confidence, and independent self-sufficiency. The urban boys took a more positive attitude toward moving and tended to believe man can have control of events which influence his life (93).

Other data from several studies indicate that important differences in general value-orientations exist between boys who planned to farm and those who planned to enter nonfarm careers. The boys who preferred to farm were more localistic in their orientations, had greater interest in physical or mechanical work, and had less interest in work requiring use or development of social relations (21).

Haller also has reported personality-related differences between farm youth who plan to farm and those who do not plan to farm. These differences followed the farm-nonfarm comparisons just presented. In comparison with boys who planned to farm, farm boys who did not plan to farm had greater emotional stability, greater independence and self-sufficiency, and a greater interest in people, or at least were less afraid of social relationships. The youth intending to enter nonfarm roles were more confident of themselves and their relations with others (39, 40). Additional differences between farm youth who plan to farm and those who plan nonfarm careers are discussed by Burchinal (21).

Evidence of possible differences in rural and urban socialization patterns is reflected in the comparisons of occupational achievement levels of farm-to-urban migrants and urban-reared males. Rural-reared persons who migrate to urban areas are generally found disproportionately in lower income or lower prestige occupations. For instance, in a recent study in Cedar Rapids, Iowa, farm-urban migrant males were underrepresented in the high status occupations and overrepresented in the low status occupations, as compared with two urban-reared control groups (22). Similar results were still observed after controls for age and education level were applied. The discovery that greater proportions of similarly aged and educated urban-reared men than farm-reared men were in middle or high status occupations was interpreted as indicating that factors other than years of formal education contributed to the greater occupational achievement among the urban-reared males. The "other factors" would very likely include differences in value-orientation and personality characteristics between the farm-reared and urban-reared men, such as those previously reviewed, as well as possible differences in the quality of the educational experiences of the rural-reared and urban-reared men who had equal years of formal education.

When the Cedar Rapids study was repeated in Des Moines, Iowa, less consistent results emerged (4). In the Des Moines study, the usual differences in occupational achievement of farm-to-urban migrant men as against urban-reared migrant men or men who were natives of Des Moines were found for the total samples. However, when the age and educational controls were applied to these samples, nonsignificant differences in occupational achievement levels were obtained among the three samples for all but the lowest level of education. For males having less than 12 years of education, the occupational achievement of farm-reared males was only slightly lower than that of urban natives, but both were lower than that of urban migrants.

The partially conflicting results of the two Iowa studies may be the result of numerous factors. First, there is the possibility that sampling error in each of the studies may account for the differences in the results between the two studies, but this is probably less important than other factors. More likely, the occupational structures of the two metropolitan areas serve to attract and retain workers having different levels of education and skills. Cedar Rapids has a wider diversification of light and heavy industry while Des Moines, being the state capital and an insurance office center, has a greater portion of its labor force in clerical and white collar employment.

Other studies of the occupational achievement of farm or rural-reared versus urban-reared men are limited in their information value because controls for age and education were not used (6, 31, 94).

Other data related to comparisons of social participation patterns of farm-urban migrants and other urban inhabitants suggest that farm- or rural-reared persons are less able to cope with the complexities and formal characteristics of urban life than urban-reared persons (6, 31, 94). Rural migrants belonged to fewer formal organizations and participated less in the organizations to which they belonged. Farm migrants had the slowest rate of entry into the formal social structure of the city. The rural migrants, especially the wives, took part in fewer informal activities and tended to be less active politically than the urban migrants or the natives of the city. However, Zimmer found that given time, all migrant groups, including those having farm origins, eventually become similar to the natives in their social activity patterns (94).

IMPLICATIONS OF RURAL-URBAN DIFFERENCES AND CHANGES IN RURAL FAMILY PATTERNS

Consideration of the rural family, apart from comparisons of rural-urban differences in family patterns, requires a high and somewhat spurious level of generalization. Each population, rural and urban alike, involves great heterogeneity in racial, ethnic, and status characteristics. Most of the available research, however, is based on white, predominately Protestant, middle status families. If our interest is restricted to rural and urban populations from white, predominately Protestant, and middle status families, the foregoing data point to many implications for persons interested in rural family life, only a few of which can be handled in the present section. Partly for similar and partly for different reasons, rural and urban family organizations are becoming more alike.

Rising levels of education in the rural population will continue to contribute to the convergence of rural and urban family patterns. One of the conclusions of a recent national study of the mental health of the American people offers additional support for the view of rural-urban convergence in family patterns and personality characteristics. The researchers found that a "young, educated, male farmer is more like a young, educated, male New Yorker than either of these people is like his own father" (38, p. 230). This conclusion is based on young farm or rural and urban males having approximately equal levels of education and, consequently, approximately equal status. Some similarities in rural and urban family patterns apparently exist today despite educational and status differences between the two populations. Rural-urban differences in other family patterns are at least partly a reflection of variables associated with educational and status differences between the two populations. Brief examination of present similarities and differences in rural and urban family patterns, against the backdrop of rising educational levels in rural areas and the diffusion of urban norms, suggests some critical areas of change in rural family relationships.

Family and household decision-making patterns and role performances do not appear to be very different between the two populations. The revitalization of kinship ties among urban families, if the decay of this network of relationships ever occurred to the extent that some social theorists maintained, suggests that urban families are becoming more like the traditional rural families in this respect.

However, the rural family reflects some vestigial elements which still differentiate it from the urban family. The fact that the rural family is still more fertile than the urban family is not of pressing importance at the moment. Rural and urban family size will probably move toward the moderately sized family. This trend may be desirable. Some family sociologists believe the moderately sized family provides the best structure for meeting interpersonal needs and for contributing to the development of all family members.

The lower divorce rates among farm and rural couples is evidence for the greater retention among rural than urban persons of the value of marriage permanence despite personal evaluations of the marital relationship. The rural-urban divorce rate differential remains despite the fact that the rural population has a lower educational level, lower income, and a lower level of living than the urban population—conditions which should, if operating by themselves, produce higher divorce rates among rural couples than among urban couples. Also, the rural-urban divorce rate differential exists even though some data suggest less satisfactory family relationships among the farm and nonfarm families as compared with city families.

It is difficult to say whether the rural-urban differential in divorce rates will continue as the companionate, mutual development, and personal-centered norms for evaluating marital relations diffuse more widely in rural areas. It could be hypothesized that at present more rural and farm couples are willing to tolerate less satisfactory interpersonal relations in marriage than urban couples, but that rural wives, in particular, may be less willing to do so in the future. Continuing this conjectural mood, future farm wives may expect their husbands to be more responsive to their emotional needs and to be more companionate than currently. Rural and farm males will probably have to become more attentive to and skillful in the nuances of interpersonal relations and especially heterosexual relations, if they are to meet the expectations of their wives.

The possibility of changes in rural divorce rates or other family patterns, raises a number of theoretical questions. For example, by what mechanisms and through what channels do urban norms of marital stability or other family patterns diffuse to rural areas? By what mechanisms and through what roles will the processes continue? Is it through the occupationally-linked roles of her husband? Or by means of the roles of the wife, her reading of the mass media, her awareness of the family educators' opinions, or perhaps through her employment

and other extrafamily experiences? Do the children provide the
basis for changes in parent-child relationships and perhaps even
marital relationships as a result of their school and community
experiences? The effects on rural family life may be very different depending on the status and role positions of the family
members who introduce the ideas of change and how these interact with the particular status and role systems in the family.
These are difficult and important research questions which need
to be examined.

Consideration of alternative norms for evaluating marital relationships leads to what appear to be the most significant differences in rural and urban family patterns. These differences
concern the role of companionate or affectionate relationships
in family relationships, the importance of attempting to meet
interpersonal needs of family members, and the emphasis put
upon developing interpersonal competence skills among family
members. The present ways in which urban families are struc-
turing their marital relationships do not represent perfect
models. However, the meager data which are available suggest
that greater emphasis is being given to these matters among
urban families, and apparently more satisfactory results are
being attained by urban than by rural families.

The prototypal urban family patterns discussed earlier represent the development of family patterns which currently permit
the greatest expression of companionship and affection in the
family, recognize and attempt to meet interpersonal needs of
family members, and attempt to enhance development of interpersonal competence skills. Family relationship patterns based
on these norms reflect adjustments to the newly emerging and
varied sex roles of American men and women. The decline in
the segregation of sexes and in sex-stereotyped roles need not
lead to reductions in masculinity or femininity. Instead, the potential satisfactions which may be achieved from heterosexual
relationships have been conspicuously heightened. As Nelson
Foote has put it: "The repertoire of masculine and feminine
sexual roles has widened among most segments of our society.
Many now enjoy experiences that once were the possession or
prerogative of a few" (30, p. 329).

Present research suggests that the socialization experiences
of urban youth as compared with those of rural youth are more
likely to help the urban youth realize their potential heterosexual
satisfactions. Now and in the future, success in marriage and
family relationships will be related less to propinquity and
homogamy patterns and will be increasingly related to the

interpersonal competency of the spouses. The association between successful family relationships and the ability to develop companionate or colleague roles based on mutually enhancing love will increase in the future. Present social organization apparently gives an advantage to urban youth in preparing them for adult family roles based on these emerging norms. Consider, for instance, the following quote from Blood and Wolfe:

Farmers and immigrants come from environments which give low priority to the expression of love and higher priority to the economic and other functional interdependencies of husband and wife. Love is an artistic creation which reaches its widest perfection in the sophisticated upper reaches of American society. It is a boon which a more leisurely, better-educated society has conferred upon its members. The progressive urbanization, acculturation, and education of the oncoming generation suggests there is likely to be correspondingly more expression of love in the future. (8, pp. 234-35).

The social organization of both rural and urban segments of our populations can be changed to provide greater support for enhancing expressions of love and for contributing to human development. Present information indicates that the rural family will have to undergo more radical changes than urban families. Furthermore, the demands for adequate socialization of youth may be more exacting for rural than for urban families. Families in both populations have responsibilities for the personality development and tension management of family members. The greater demands placed on the rural family lie in the fact that rural families must prepare their children and youth for adult experiences in either the rapidly changing rural social systems, of which the parents and young people have considerable awareness, or in urban social systems, of which they are less well aware. And the preparation must not be for the family, occupational, and community systems as they are known today, but for the requirements of these systems 20 years or more from now.

Adaptation to the new interpersonal demands will not be easy. Also, rural families face certain handicaps as they attempt to cope with present changes and to reintegrate behavior around interpersonal norms. How can rural families and communities compensate for their present low level of education? The arts of human relationships and family living are probably best, though far from perfectly, practiced in what has been called the urban professional class. Yet the demands for successful functioning will increasingly require that these arts be practiced at all social levels in rural as well as urban society. In moving toward the prototypal norm, families in urban communities have the advantages of higher levels of education, assumed to be a rough index of general personal resources, and greater opportunities for help and support of all kinds than rural families. In general, rural communities have fewer educational and ameliorative agencies and specialists whose services can help prepare persons for professionalization in marriage and family roles and support them in these roles.[9]

On the other hand, rural and farm families have certain structural and functional strengths which can be used in meeting changes. For the farm family, there are certain stable, integrative factors built around attachment to the land and family development of resources through shared tasks and common enterprise. These factors do not insure family solidarity, nor by themselves do they automatically contribute to the development and maintenance of interpersonal relationships built upon affection, companionship, or mutual respect. However, these characteristics provide mechanisms for doing so, provided the parents perceive the value and importance of developing family and work interaction patterns which contribute to integrated personality development and enhancement of personal identity and interpersonal competence.

American families, rural and urban alike, have shown great ability to adjust to drastic changes in societal organization. Today, the family is in a better position than ever before to adjust to the amazing technological developments predicted for this particular age. This optimism is based upon the universality of the family, the past record of American society and American family organization in meeting changes and crises, and the development of a body of research about family functioning serving as the basis for educational and ameliorative programs designed to integrate and strengthen family life.

FOOTNOTES

[1] Descriptions of the Colonial or pre-Civil War northern rural family systems are taken as the base points for descriptions of changes in American family patterns: see Sirjamaki (77) or Cavan (23). In his discussion of the changing rural family, Hill distinguishes among several types of rural southern family patterns of which the yeoman-farmer pattern was dominant (46). Data for these ten points are drawn mainly from Foote (28), Hill (45), Ogburn and Nimkoff (72), and Sirjamaki (77).

[2] For an extensive review of the literature on the isolated, nuclear American family and a theoretical critique, see Marvin B. Sussman and Lee G. Burchinal (82).

[3] There may be alternate and competing patterns of family organization emerging among different social groupings in the United States. Only one set of patterns, assumed to be the most general, has been identified. Differences associated with racial and status characteristics are known to exist. Also, Lenski organizes a considerable body of data to suggest that differences in family organization patterns exist among socioreligious groupings, and that differences between white Protestants and Catholics may be increasing, not decreasing as generally assumed ([59]).

[4] Olaf Larson uses "modernization" in place of the impact of "urbanization" to describe changes in rural family patterns which are probably related to urban value systems and the use of urban reference groups by rural persons.

[5] Several reviews of the literature on relationships between maternal employment variables and child development and family relationship variables are available: see Herzog ([44]), Burchinal ([18]), and Hoffman ([48], [49]). The most recent significant research on the employed mother, motivations for work, development of children, marital relations, and other characteristics of the employed mothers are reported in a forthcoming book edited by Hoffman and Nye ([50]). See also the November, 1961, issue of Marriage and Family Living, Vol. 23, which contains eleven articles on "Women and Work."

[6] See also Nolan and Tuttle ([70]), and for a report of the attitudes of rural homemakers toward employment of married women, see Glenn ([33]).

[7] Loomis and Beegle also present some data on demographic differences between rural and urban families which are not treated in this paper ([63], pp. 69-81).

[8] For a more extensive discussion and summery of studies related to the occupational decision-making process of rural youth and rural-urban differences related to educational and occupational aspiration and achievement levels, see Burchinal, Haller, and Taves ([21]).

[9] See ([13]) for the differences in medical facilities in rural and urban communities. It is assumed that these differentials also carry over in most educational, religious, and welfare agencies.

LITERATURE CITED

(1) Bauder, W. W.: "Characteristics of Families on Small Farms," Ky. Agr. Exp. Sta. Bul. 644, 1956.

(2) ———: "Effect of Nonfarm Employment of Farm Wives on Farm Family Living," paper given at the Rural Sociological Society meeting, Pa. State Univ., Aug., 1960.

(3) ———: "Impact of Wife's Employment on Family Organization in Farm and Urban Families," paper given at the National Council of Family Relations meeting, Salt Lake City, Aug. 1961.

(4) ———, and Burchinal, L. G.: "Occupational Achievement of

Rural-to-Urban Migrant Males in Comparison With Two Urban Control Groups," paper given at the American Sociological Association meeting, St. Louis, Sept. 1961.

(5) Beers, H. W.: "A Portrait of the Farm Family in Central New York State," Amer. Sociol. Rev., 2:591-600, 1937.

(6) ———, and Heflin, C.: "Rural People in the City," Ky. Agr. Exp. Sta. Bul. 478, 1945.

(7) Bell, N. W., and Vogel, E. F.: "Toward a Framework for Functional Analysis of Family Behavior," in Bell, N. W., and Vogel, E. F., eds., A Modern Introduction to the Family, The Free Press, Glencoe, Ill., 1960, pp. 1-33.

(8) Blood, R. O., and Wolfe, D. M.: Husbands and Wives, The Free Press, Glencoe, Ill., 1960.

(9) Bock, E. W., and Burchinal, L. G.: "Comparisons of Spousal Relations, Community Participation and Kinship Relation Patterns Between Farm and Nonfarm Families," paper given at the Midwest Sociological Society meeting, Omaha, Apr. 1961.

(10) Bronfenbrenner, U.: "The Changing American Child," Reference Papers on Children and Youth, prepared for the 1960 White House Conference on Children and Youth, 1960, pp. 1-8.

(11) Brown, J. S.: "The Family Group in a Kentucky Mountain Farming Community," Ky. Agr. Exp. Sta. Bul. 588, 1952.

(12) ———: "The Farm Family in a Kentucky Mountain Neighborhood," Ky. Agr. Exp. Sta. Bul. 587, 1952.

(13) "Building America's Health," a report to the President by the President's Commission on the Health Needs of the Nation, Washington, D.C., 1952.

(14) Burchinal, L. G., Hawkes, H. R., and Gardner, B.: "Adjustment Characteristics of Rural and Urban Children," Amer. Sociol. Rev., 22:81-87, 1957.

(15) Burchinal, L. G.: "Correlates of Marital Satisfaction for Rural Married Couples," Rural Soc., 26:282-89, 1961.

(16) ———: "Differences in Educational and Occupational Aspirations of Farm, Small-town, and City Boys," Rural Soc., 26:107-21, 1961.

(17) ———: "Factors Related to Employment of Wives in a Rural Iowa County," Iowa Agr. and Home Econ. Exp. Sta. Bul. 509, 1962.

(18) ———: "Maternal Employment, Family Relations and Selected Personality, School-related and Social Development Characteristics of Children," Iowa Agr. and Home Econ. Exp. Sta. Res. Bul. 497, 1961.

(19) ———, and Chancellor, L.: "Ages at Marriage, Occupations of Grooms and Interreligious Marriages," Social Forces, 40:348-54, 1962.

(20) ———, and ———: "What About School-age Marriages?" Iowa Farm Science, 12:12-14, 1958.

(21) ———, in collaboration with Haller, A. O., and Taves, M., for the subcommittee on family and youth of the North Central States Rural Sociology Committee: "Career Choices Among Rural Youth in a Changing Society," Minn. Agr. Exp. Sta. Bul. 458, 1962.

(22) ———, and Jacobson, P.: "Occupational Achievement Differentials Among Farm-Urban, Other Urban Migrant and Native Males," paper given at the Midwest Sociological Society meeting, St. Louis, Apr., 1960.

(23) Cavan, R.: The American Family, Crowell, 1953.

(24) Cleland, C. B.: "Familism in Rural Saskatchewan," Rural Soc., 20:249-57, 1955.

(25) Dinitz, S., Banks, F., and Pasamanick, B.: "Mate Selection and Social Class: Changes During the Past Quarter Century," Marriage and Family Living, 22:348-51, 1960.

(26) Ehrmann, W.: Premarital Dating Behavior, Holt, 1959.

(27) Fitzsimmons, C., and Perkins, N. L.: "Patterns of Family Relationships in Fifty Farm Families," Rural Soc., 12:300-303, 1947.

(28) Foote, N. N.: "Changes in American Marriage Patterns and the Role of Women," Eugenics Quart., 1:254-60, 1954.

(29) ———: "Matching of Husband and Wife in Phases of Development," Transactions of the Third World Congress of Sociology, Internat. Sociol. Assn., London, 1956, 4:24-34.

(30) ———: "New Roles for Men and Women," Marriage and Family Living, 23:325-29, 1961.

(31) Freedman, R., and Freedman, D.: "Farm-reared Elements in the Nonfarm Population," Rural Soc., 21:50-61, 1956.

(32) Gladden, J. W., and Christiansen, J. R.: "Emergence of Urban Values in Mining Families in Eastern Kentucky," Rural Soc., 21:135-39, 1956.

(33) Glenn, H. M.: "Attitudes of Women Regarding Gainful Employment of Married Women," Jour. Home Econ., 51:247-52, 1959.

(34) Glick, P. C.: American Families, Wiley & Sons, 1957.

(35) Gold, M., and Slater, C.: "Office, Factory, Store and Family: A Study of Integration Setting," Amer. Sociol. Rev., 23:64-74, 1958.

(36) Goode, W. J.: After Divorce, The Free Press, Glencoe, Ill., 1956.

(37) Grigg, C. M., and Middleton, R.: "Community of Orientation and Occupational Aspirations of Ninth Grade Students," Social Forces, 38:303-8, 1960.

(38) Gurin, G., Veroff, J., and Feld, S.: Americans View Their Mental Health, Basic Books, 1960.

(39) Haller, A. O.: "Planning To Farm: A Social Psychological Interpretation," Social Forces, 37:263-68, 1959.

(40) ———: "The Occupational Achievement Process of Farm-reared Youth in Urban-Industrial Society," Rural Soc., 25: 321-33, 1960.

(41) ———: "Research Problems on the Occupational Achievement Levels of Farm-reared People," Rural Soc., 23:355-62, 1958.

(42) Hathaway, S. R., Monachesi, E. D., and Young, L. A.: "Rural-Urban Adolescent Personality," Rural Soc., 24:331-46, 1959.

(43) Heer, D. M.: "The Trend of Interfaith Marriages in Canada: 1922-1957," Amer. Sociol. Rev., 27:245-50, 1962.

(44) Herzog, E.: "Children of Working Mothers," Children's Bureau Publ. No. 382-1960, Washington, D.C., 1960.

(45) Hill, R.: "The American Family Today," in Ginzberg, E., ed., The Nation's Children. Part I: The Family and Social Change, Columbia Univ. Press, New York, 1960, pp. 76-104.

(46) ———: "Family Patterns in the Changing South," Transactions of the Third World Congress of Sociology, Internat. Sociol. Assn., London, 1956, 4:127-45.

(47) ———: A revision of Waller, W. The Family, Holt, Rinehart and Winston, 1951.

(48) Hoffman, L. W.: "Effects of the Employment of Mothers on Parental Power Relations and the Division of Household Tasks," Marriage and Family Living, 22:27-35, 1960.

(49) ———: "Effects of Maternal Employment on the Child," Child Development, 32:187-97, 1961.

(50) ———, and Nye, I.: The Employed Mother, Rand McNally, 1963.

(51) Jacobson, P. H., and Jacobson, P. F.: American Marriage and Divorce, Rinehart, 1959.

(52) Kenkel, W. F.: The Family in Perspective, Appleton-Century-Croft, 1960.

(53) Key, W. H.: "Rural-Urban Differences and the Family," Sociol. Quart., 2:49-56, 1961.

(54) Keyfitz, N.: "A Factorial Arrangement of Comparisons of

Family Size," Amer. Jour. of Soc., 58:470-80, 1953.

(55) Kinsey, A. C., Pomeroy, W. B., and Martin, C. E.: Sexual Behavior in the Human Male, W. B. Saunders, 1948.

(56) Kinsey, A. C., et al.: Sexual Behavior in the Human Female, W. B. Saunders, 1953.

(57) Landis, P. H.: "Two Generations of Rural and Urban Women Appraise Marital Happiness," Wash. Agr. Exp. Sta. Bul. 524, 1951.

(58) Leevy, J. R.: "Contrasts in Urban and Rural Family Life," Amer. Sociol. Rev., 5:948-53, 1940.

(59) Lenski, G.: The Religious Factor, Doubleday, 1961.

(60) Lillywhite, J. D.: "Rural-Urban Differentials in Divorce," Rural Soc., 17:348-55, 1952.

(61) Litwak, E.: "Geographic Mobility and Extended Family Cohesion," Amer. Sociol. Rev., 25:385-94, 1960.

(62) ———: "Occupational Mobility and Extended Family Cohesion," Amer. Sociol. Rev., 25:9-21, 1960.

(63) Loomis, C. P., and Beegle, J. A.: Rural Sociology: The Strategy of Change, Prentice-Hall, 1957.

(64) Mangus, A. R.: "Marriage and Divorce in Ohio," Rural Soc., 14:128-37, 1949.

(65) ———: "Personality Adjustment of Rural and Urban Children," Amer. Sociol. Rev., 13:566-75, 1948.

(66) McVoy, E. C., and Nelson, L.: "Satisfaction in Living: Farm Versus Village," Minn. Agr. Exp. Sta. Bul. 370, 1943.

(67) Middleton, R., and Grigg, C. M.: "Rural-Urban Differences in Aspirations," Rural Soc., 24:347-54, 1959.

(68) Miller, D. R., and Swanson, G. E.: The Changing American Parent, Wiley & Sons, 1958.

(69) Monahan, T. P.: "Divorce by Occupational Level," Marriage and Family Living, 17:322-24, 1955.

(70) Nolan, F. L., and Tuttle, D. H.: "Certain Practices, Satisfactions, and Difficulties in Families with Employed Homemakers," Pa. Agr. Exp. Sta. Bul. 655, 1959.

(71) Nye, I.: "Adolescent-Parent Adjustment—Rurality as a Variable," Rural Soc., 15:334-39, 1950.

(72) Ogburn, W. F., and Nimkoff, M. F.: Technology and the Changing Family, Houghton-Mifflin, 1955.

(73) Reiss, I. L.: Premarital Sexual Standards in America, The Free Press, Glencoe, Ill., 1960.

(74) Roy, P.: "Maternal Employment and Adolescent Roles: Rural-Urban Differentials," Marriage and Family Living, 23:340-49, 1961.

(75) Sewell, W. H.: "Rural-Urban Differences in Educational

Aspirations," paper given at the Amer. Sociol. Assn. meeting, New York, Aug., 1960.

(76) Sheeley, A., Landis, P. H., and Davies, V.: "Marital and Family Adjustment in Rural and Urban Families of Two Generations," Wash. Agr. Exp. Sta. Bul. 506, 1949.

(77) Sirjamaki, J.: The American Family in the Twentieth Century, Harvard Univ. Press, Cambridge, Mass., 1953.

(78) Stott, L. H.: "Some Environmental Factors in Relation to the Personality Adjustments of Rural Children," Rural Soc., 10:394-403, 1945.

(79) Straus, M. A.: "Family Role Differentiation and Technological Change in Farming," Rural Soc., 25:219-28, 1960.

(80) ———: "Matching Farms and Families in the Columbia Basin Project," Wash. Agr. Exp. Sta. Bul. 588, 1958.

(81) ———: "The Role of the Wife in the Settlement of the Columbia Basin Project," Marriage and Family Living, 20:59-64, 1958.

(82) Sussman, M. B., and Burchinal, L. G.: "Kin-Family Network; Unheralded Structure in Current Conceptionalizations of Family Functioning," Marriage and Family Living, 14: 231-40, 1962; "Parental Aid to Married Children: Implications for Family Functioning," Marriage and Family Living, 14:320-32, 1962.

(83) Taves, M. J.: "Farm Versus Village Living: A Decade of Change," Rural Soc., 17:47-55, 1952.

(84) Thomas, J. L.: "The Factor of Religion in the Selection of Marriage Mates," Amer. Sociol. Rev., 16:487-91, 1951.

(85) Thorpe, A. C.: "Patterns of Family Interaction in Farm and Town Homes," Mich. Agr. Exp. Sta. Tech. Bul. 260, 1957.

(86) U.S. Bureau of the Census, Farm Population, P-27, No. 27, 1960.

(87) U.S. Bureau of the Census, "Educational Status, College Plans, and Occupational Status of Farm and Nonfarm Youths: Oct., 1959." Farm Population. P-27, No. 30, 1961.

(88) White House Conference on Child Health and Protection: "The Adolescent in the Family." Report of the sub-committee on the function of house activities in the education of the child. E. W. Burgess, chairman. Appleton-Century-Croft, 1934.

(89) Wilkening, E. A.: "Adoption of Improved Farm Practices as Related to Family Factors," Wis. Agr. Exp. Sta. Res. Bul. 183, 1953.

(90) ——: "Change in Farm Technology as Related to Familism, Family Decision-making, and Family Integration,"
Amer. Sociol. Rev., 19:29-37, 1954.

(91) ——: "Joint Decision-making in Farm Families as a
Function of Status and Role," Amer. Sociol. Rev., 23:187-
92, 1958.

(92) Williams, R.: American Society, 2nd ed., Knopf, 1960, pp.
39-86, 113-14, 520-27.

(93) Wolff, C. E., and Haller, A. O.: "Farm, Village, Rural
Nonfarm, and Small Urban Differences in Selected Per-
sonality Orientations of 17-Year-Old Boys in Lenawee
County, Michigan," paper given at the Rural Sociological
Society meeting, Pa. State Univ., University Park, Aug.
1960. Later published as Haller, A. O., and Wolff, C. E.:
"Personality Orientations of Farm, Village, and Urban
Boys," Rural Soc., 27:275-93, 1962.

(94) Zimmer, B. G.: "Participation of Migrants in Urban Structures," Amer. Sociol. Rev., 20:218-24, 1955.

6

Thomas R. Ford
Willis A. Sutton, Jr.

The Impact of Change on Rural Communities and Fringe Areas: Review of a Decade's Research

FOURTEEN YEARS AGO a reviewer of community research put forth the mordant judgment that "if the maturity of a scientific discipline is measured by the clarity of its terminology, the precision of its concepts, the articulation of hypotheses and constructs with general theory, and the congruity of theoretical generalizations with empirical observations, then the field of community, within the larger sociological domain, lies on a very low level of scientific development."[1] A judgment of such severity demands periodic reconsideration as new evidence accumulates in the form of subsequent research studies. Accordingly, a selection of twenty-six recent studies of rural communities and twelve recent studies of rural-urban fringe areas has been reviewed to ascertain the current status of the field.[2] In the process of review it became apparent that, whatever the over-all scientific quality of the studies, they indicated significant changes taking place in rural community organization.

The review will proceed by examining the thirty-eight studies under the following rubrics:

1. The concept of community or fringe employed
2. The statement of the research problem
3. The identification of independent, dependent, and mediating variables
4. The aspects of change focused upon
5. The substantive contributions to sociological knowledge

6. The substantive contributions toward solutions of community adjustment problems.

Anyone familiar with the nature of the community research of the past few decades—involving tremendous variations in theoretical orientations, methodology, and focus of interest—will recognize the formidable difficulties of the reviewing task. We hope that the strengths of this review will facilitate more systematic community research and that the inadequacies will stimulate improved codifications.

CURRENT STATUS OF THE CONCEPTS "COMMUNITY" AND "FRINGE"

The ambiguous and varied meanings attached to the concept "community" by sociologists have been thoroughly documented and condemned in numerous papers over the past two decades. As Hillery has noted,[3] the only qualities of "community" upon which a substantial number of sociologists have been able to agree are (a) that it consists of people (b) in a specified area (c) who interact and (d) have a common tie or ties. Most sociologists would also agree, however, that these qualities do not uniquely define "community." Indeed, as Reiss has pointed out,[4] nearly all social groups possess these characteristics. Consequently, each researcher tends to add other qualities, conditions, or attributes to the definition and many of these, being arbitrary, are controversial. Since these additional qualifications often exclude certain territorial groups commonly considered communities and these groups continue to be referred to as communities by many, confusion is further compounded. The dilemma in applying the concept is that one must either resort to the lowest common denominator and thus embrace a wide variety of disparate social groups or else adopt a more restricted definition and thereby exclude some groups "conventionally" considered communities. There is no necessity, of course, to adhere to old conventions, but at least some conventions must be established if a concept is to have scientific utility.

Even a cursory examination of recent studies is sufficient to confirm that little progress has been made toward a common definition of "community." In a detailed examination of the twenty-six community studies, we recorded each explicit and implicit definition used in the studies surveyed and separately classified its areal and social aspects. Considering first the

areal component, eight of the "community" studies dealt with a
small town or village, eleven with a larger political subdivision
such as a township or county, five with a trade or service area,
and the remainder with some other type of area delineated for
the special purposes of the study. However, not all of the
authors claimed to be dealing with a "community"; some referred to "localities" or "locality groups" and others to "neighborhoods" in an unspecified community. We included such
studies for two reasons: (a) other investigators dealt with substantially similar areas as "communities"; (b) they were classified as community studies in standard bibliographical
sources.[5]

Social aspects of the community concept were equally varied.
The one most commonly employed—a territorial group bound by
social ties and possessing sentiments of group identity—was
used in nine studies, particularly those of villages and trade or
service areas. In six studies community was defined in terms
of a specific locality and the sharing of institutions, but with no
mention of sentiments of group unity or identification. Six other
studies failed to specify the social components beyond that of a
population residing in a particular area, and in many such cases
it was obvious that the residents shared few local institutions.
In the remaining studies the community was conceptualized implicitly as either a congeries of social systems or as a type of
social system, although none explicitly projected the community
as a unitary system.

The use of the concept "fringe" in the twelve studies reviewed
was somewhat more consistent, probably because it has been defined primarily in terms of location and land use rather than
social relationships. Most researchers were in agreement that
the fringe lies just outside the limits of corporate cities and
recognized suburbs, and embraces an area of mixed urban
(mostly residential) and rural (mostly agricultural) land use.
But if there was general consensus on what the fringe is, there
was considerable variation in the methods used to delineate its
boundaries, as Kurtz and Eicher have recently documented.[6]
Five researchers, including Martin (26),* Anderson (7), and
Blizzard (10) employed an inspection technique; three, like
Queen and Carpenter (34) used the nonurbanized portions of
census metropolitan areas; and five others followed the boundaries of entire townships or counties that met, at least in part,

---

*Underlined numerals within parentheses refer to literature cited at
the end of this chapter.

the criteria of mixed land use and proximity to major urban areas.

Since the fringe was delineated primarily on the basis of location and land use, social qualities were rarely employed as criteria.[7] This is not surprising since the social structure of the fringe is so amorphous. Indeed, the nature of the fringe as a social system is yet to be established. It may be merely a metamorphic stage. Until its qualities as a social form are better delineated, we cannot speak with validity of the fringe as a social entity; we can only deal with people and social systems in fringe areas.

RESEARCH PROBLEMS AND VARIABLES

The abstraction of problem statements from the studies revealed, as expected, a tremendous range and variety. The topics treated were classified according to the types of variables involved and, in addition, a rough classification was made of the analytical level of each study. Four analytic categories were defined as follows:

1. Descriptive—studies primarily concerned with the description of conditions, characteristics, or situations with little effort made to relate changes to other general or specific factors.
2. General analytic—studies in which changes in phenomena under observation were explicitly related to general conditions (such as technological change) either within or outside the study area.
3. Specific analytic—studies in which changes in phenomena under observation were related to other specific factors such as migration or the location of an industry in the community.
4. Formal analytic—studies in which formal hypotheses were stated and tested.

The allocation of studies to each of these categories is shown in the following tabulation:

	Community Studies	Fringe Area Studies
Descriptive	11	4
General Analytic	8	3
Specific Analytic	7	3
Formal Analytic	0	2

Even allowing for some unreliability in the above classification, the failure of many studies to proceed beyond the descriptive level poses serious problems for the cumulative development of knowledge in the field. More will be said about this later.

It is a reasonable supposition that most sociologists view changes in one set of community phenomena as the consequences of prior changes in some other set of phenomena to which they are related. Operating on this premise, we hoped that by identifying specific variables or sets of variables dealt with in studies of roughly comparable situations and by recording the nature and direction of the relationship, we could both identify common problems and arrive at some substantial generalizations. For example, a number of studies of social organization in counties with decreasing populations should provide a basis for some general conclusions concerning the adjustment of various types of community organizations to population decline.

Of approximately 250 sets of relationships identified in the community and fringe studies, approximately a fourth involved, on one side of the relational equation, "general changes" either in the local or nearby environmental situation or in the national or "mass" society. Most of the relatively specific independent variables or sets of such variables could be broadly classified in order of frequency as (a) sustenance methods involving either the economic base or technology; (b) population; (c) transportation and communication; and (d) social organization and relationships. In fringe area studies population was the most common independent variable, occurring in about half of the relationships identified.

Of the dependent variables identified in the community studies about a third dealt with some aspect of "social organization." Approximately a fourth of these involved social structures or relationships extending beyond the bounds of the defined community. Specific economic institutions figured as dependent variables next most frequently, followed by population, and the general sustenance base of the community. In the fringe area studies the most common dependent variables were population, land use, and economic institutions.

Probably as significant as the classes of variables studied were those that received little attention. Social control was rarely treated as a dependent variable, a neglect earlier noted by Reiss in his evaluation of community studies.[8] Economic, educational, and governmental institutions were involved relatively frequently, but the family, health and medicine, recreation, and social welfare were not often treated. Systems of values and beliefs were generally neglected, at least as specific objects of study. An important exception to this generalization is Vogt's <u>Modern Homesteaders</u> (37), in which the effects of major value-orientations on community settlement and development were explored. As might perhaps be expected, greater attention to values was accorded by anthropologists (20, 31, 36) than by sociologists.

Sociologists more commonly focussed on various aspects of social structure, but the relatively great attention paid to social organization reflected more than a coincidence of interest. Five of the county studies (1, 2, 3, 17, 21) were part of the series of studies of major farming areas initiated by the old Division of Farm Population and Rural Life in the Bureau of Agricultural Economics, USDA, under the leadership of Carl C. Taylor. The purposes of these studies conducted in counties representing major types of farming areas in the United States were, in part, "to analyze the types of groups in which rural people are organized and the patterns of group relationships through which they participate in local and nonlocal programs and services" and "to show pertinent changes in different types of organization."[9]

ASPECTS OF CHANGE STUDIED

In the study of social change, one may focus on any of a variety of aspects--the preconditions for change to take place, the process of a change action, the effects of the introduction or alteration of a particular variable or set of variables, the responses or adjustments of selected variables to the introduction of change-producing elements, or the influence of specific mediating variables on the change process. Any one study may, of course, deal with several of these aspects, and they are not entirely mutually exclusive.

Most of the reviewed studies were primarily concerned with the responses of selected community phenomena to change-producing agents, although the particular agents were not always identified. Only one study (20) concentrated on the necessary conditions for change to occur. Half a dozen community studies --but, strangely, no fringe area study--dealt primarily with the process of change. Six community studies and three fringe studies dealt with the social effects of a particular variable or set of variables (usually population size and composition). A few studies of each type were concerned with the effects of particular mediating variables; e.g., length of residence on attitudes regarding the desirability of the fringe as a place to live, or place of residence as a factor influencing participation in social organizations.

SUBSTANTIVE CONTRIBUTIONS TO SOCIOLOGICAL UNDERSTANDING

What then, does the research of the past decade on the impact of change on rural and fringe communities give us in the form of generalizations, propositions, or conclusions? In the absence of any generally accepted systematic body of theory, the answer to this question can be framed only through some ad hoc ordering of phenomena.

The method of ordering adopted was to classify propositions and conclusions according to their relevance to certain elements or aspects of the sociocultural structure of communities or locality groups. This was felt to provide a sufficient variety of categories into which the highly differentiated data could be fitted without procrustean violence or indiscriminate lumping. Such categorization also seemed to be of greater relevance to sociological theory than other methods considered. In addition, this framework offered the advantage of corresponding fairly closely to categories of data rather frequently used in community studies. Three major divisions were adopted, as follows: internal organization; internal-external relationships; and leadership and decision making. By far the largest segment of data pertained to the first of these categories. Hence, a further subdivision of internal structure into five components was developed: (a) population; (b) social organization; (c) values, beliefs, and attitudes; (d) institutions; and (e) technology and economic base.

Obviously it was often difficult to specify the particular category of structure under which a given proposition or conclusion should be classified, interrelationships between structural elements being manifold. However, because of the necessity of some ordering, our attention has focussed on the primary directions or emphases of the various conclusions. Some treatment of their interrelationships will be given in the final section of this chapter, which deals with a more general evaluation.

Propositions re Internal Organization

Population. Although population variables received some attention in nearly all of the studies, only seven offered major conclusions or principles concerning population. Four of these dealt with fringe areas; two with total counties and one with particular rural communities. The only finding reported in all areas was that occupational structure had become more diverse. Agreement on general trends in other aspects of population structure throughout the range of area types was not otherwise apparent, probably because of the relatively slight overlap in foci of interest.

The following conclusions were derived from the pertinent county studies. Part-time farming opportunities have made the population more heterogeneous (17). Similarly, it was reported that in Price County, Wisconsin (12), few open-country people were employed exclusively in a single occupation. Partly because of age selectivity in the migration process, migration from Price County reportedly had not raised the level of living. As economic conditions worsened, more persons in the productive ages departed and their departure served further to depress the level of living. Quite different findings were reported from a study of four North Dakota counties (4) in that level of living in low income rural areas rose as farm population declined.

Fringe residents vary widely in their socioeconomic status (10). While most persons moving into the fringe come from urban areas, relatively more fringe than central city residents were born in a rural area (8). All four studies of fringe area population reported similarities and differences of fringe residents compared with those of rural and urban areas. In some ways the fringe is more similar to the urban and in other ways more similar to the rural population (34). Fringe residents differ significantly from those of both urban and rural areas (10), but farm and nonfarm "fringers" are themselves becoming more homogeneous (33). They resemble the city least with regard to fertility and the gainful employment of women (34), but also differ significantly with respect to occupation, industry, income, educational attainment, age of household head, and ownership of dwelling (8). North Lansing fringe areas were reported to have more laborers, fewer professionals, relatively more people in manufacturing, and a greater variation in educational levels than the central city (8). On the other hand, Queen and Carpenter's study (34) of seven fringe areas found that the

industrial employment pattern of fringe residents clearly re-
sembled that of the city residents. They concluded, however,
that their data fail to support the idea that the fringe is closer
to urban than to rural characteristics and emphasized that this
marginal population, like the marginal, second-generation off-
spring of immigrants, is pulled in two directions—both toward
the city and toward the rural pattern.

Social Organization. Classified under the heading of social
organization were conclusions or principles having to do with a
number of aspects of the internal organization of the areas
studied. Relatively few fringe studies considered whether the
total pattern of life in the fringe areas tended toward a rural or
an urban model. One study (33) concluded that the urban type of
life dominates the rural. On the other hand, with regard to acceptance of local norms, to land use, socioeconomic status, and
a number of other characteristics, Queen and Carpenter (34)
indicated fringe area residents are in an intermediate position
between urban and rural populations.

A somewhat greater amount of attention was shown aspects
of internal organization involving stability, continuity, integration, and cohesion. With regard to the general question of
whether local cohesion is maintained in the face of considerable
change in the number and quality of social contacts in the locality, the slender evidence points in both directions.

Kolb and Day (22) found in their restudy of Walworth County,
Wisconsin, that "no vehicle, personnel, or even symbol" for
total group action had emerged during a period in which general
social contacts had multiplied and intensified. In a "near-fringe"
area of North Carolina, however, Schaffer (35) found that patterns of locality cohesion and integration had emerged and developed in a situation of organizational and interactional change
somewhat comparable in scope and intensity to that of Walworth
County. Such differences clearly point to the need for studies to
determine the conditions under which collective action, structures, and symbols do develop in the wake of forces and events
that bring about radical social modifications.

In the North Carolina community, serious strains were imposed by adjacent urban growth and the increasing employment
of residents outside the locality. The adaptive change of the
community took the form of "urbanizing" its own patterns of
family, church, and voluntary group organization to a competitive
level, thus maintaining if not strengthening the continuity and
stability of the community system. This suggests that the rural

community in modern society which does not change invites dis-equilibrium, increased internal tension, and eventual disintegration. Depending upon its nature, change may preserve system continuity as well as destroy it.

This thesis is also evident in Vogt's conclusions from his study of values in Homestead (37). Here the failure of values to change in the face of shifting economic and ecological conditions posed a threat to the ultimate survival of the community. Nevertheless, the fact of Homestead's continued existence in spite of the stresses and strains between different components of its structure, demonstrates the considerable flexibility of community systems, and it casts some doubt upon any categorical insistence that in the midst of change, continuity can be insured only by a restructuring and reorientation of the local sociocultural system. The findings of Vidich and Bensman (36) also testify to the resiliency of community systems under severe stress. They concluded that in spite of basic contradictions between values and reality in Springdale, the community continued to function in an integrated manner.

Considerable theoretical importance must be attached to the fact that relatively few studies lend strong support to the widely held view that change in one part of a community system in-evitably affects all other parts. On the contrary, more studies document the alternative thesis that change in any one component of a social structure does not automatically produce changes in other components, even when the derivative changes would seem to be functionally implied. Despite the increasingly difficult economic problems faced by individual farmers in the arid Homestead area in western New Mexico (37), rugged individualism, mastery of nature, and an optimistic faith in the future remained major value-orientations. Similarly in the up-state New York community of Springdale (36), radical changes in the diffuse collective life seemed to have little effect on the structure of organizational and political control. And though social contacts intensified among the people of a Wisconsin county, techniques of collective action and a feeling of identity failed to emerge (22).

The effects of in- and out-migration on community cohesion and stability also engaged the attention of researchers. Two fringe studies (8, 38) documented the looseness of cohesion and social organization, presumably in part a consequence of in-migration. In spite of large proportions of old-timers, Beegle and Schroeder (8) reported that in the North Lansing fringe there was little solidarity and a somewhat diffuse social organization.

Whitney (38) concluded that in an increasingly urban fringe, the larger and more homogeneous the group of in-movers the faster the transition and the less the conflict as new patterns of social organization emerge. He further suggested that the more similar the values of the in-movers to those of the old residents, the less the tension and conflict. With respect to the effects of heavy out-migration on community integration, Nelson (30) considered such migration to be one of the several factors contributing to the increase of cleavages and the decline of the "we-feeling" in Mormon Village during the period 1925-50.

Another aspect of internal social organization treated in several studies is the spatial organization of contact patterns and associational networks. The major changes reported to be taking place in essentially rural areas and within the county as a total unit seem to be quite consistent. In general, informal contacts appear to be somewhat more casual and extensive than formerly (3) and small primary locality groups are becoming less clearly defined, less important, and less self-reliant (1). However, Hepple and Bright (18) stated that face-to-face contact still is an important medium of communication in Shelby County, Missouri. In addition, Mayo and Bobbitt (28) in their resurvey of Wake County, North Carolina, found that although some new groups had emerged and some had ceased to exist, about two-thirds of the locality groups found 25 years before still persisted.

There was general affirmation that the functioning networks of social contacts tend to embrace increasingly larger geographic areas. A number of observers reported that the focus of social organization had changed from the local neighborhood to the village, that the village had become the chief area of "meaningful togetherness" (17), and that the village was increasingly the social and institutional center of rural life (5, 22). One intensive study of a neighborhood (31) predicted its disappearance as a separate social entity because its economic and institutional resources were too limited to support a population at the standard of living demanded by modern American civilization.

With reference to level and type of participation in organizational life by fringe residents, the studies yielded relatively little information. Beegle and Schroeder (8) reported less participation in all voluntary organizations by fringe residents than by persons in the city. Kurtz and Smith in their study of Lansing (25) concluded that former residents of the central city maintain social relationships in the city, and that farmers,

long-time residents, and those with rural backgrounds participate in the fringe area organizations to a much greater extent
than do nonfarmers, short-time residents, and residents without
rural backgrounds.

Turning attention from areas of increasing population to
areas of sparse and declining population, a few conclusions regarding changes in social organization in these latter areas may
be noted. Studies dealing with these kinds of change have been
centered in the great plains areas of Montana (1, 23) and North
Dakota (4).

Anderson (4) concluded that social participation of farmers
in group and community activities increased as population declined, but Alexander and Kraenzel (1) reported that institutional
participation declined as population was reduced and remained
sparsely distributed. Further, Anderson concluded that as population declined, competition of urban centers increased. The
distance factor also affected levels of participation centered in
any given locus. Alexander and Kraenzel (1) noted that the
farther individuals lived from village centers, the less frequently they participated in organizations.

Under conditions of a sparse and declining population the
general tendency of social organization to be centered at points
of population concentration, already noted in the general studies
of county social organization, is even more in evidence. Larger
areas of support are necessary for needed services. New forms
of social organization emphasizing formal and legal structures
are already emerging in these areas (24).

This leads to another general social organizational change
pointed out by a number of studies—the shift from more general
to more specialized and from more informal to more formal
types of association. Hay and John (17) reported that specialized
organizations in Bradford County, Pennsylvania, had increased
in number and in relative importance. Similar observations in
Missouri and Indiana were reported by Hepple and Bright (18),
and by Jehlik and Losey (21), respectively. Related conclusions,
but from a slightly different approach, were reached about types
of neighboring by Hay and John (17) and about the sources of
services by Alexander and Kraenzel (1). Neighboring on a locality basis was found to have declined whereas such contacts
based on shared special interests had increased (17). Services
were found to be provided increasingly by special interest organizations and agencies rather than by broader, more informal
social groupings (1). Hepple and Bright also reported that the
number of special groups had increased and that social

participation was greatest in those activities geared to specialized interests (18).

In the midst of such an increase in the importance and number of specialized groups and agencies, the emergence of mechanisms for intergroup and interagency contact would seem to be a logical development. Little observation of these phenomena was reported, however. Alexander and Kraenzel (1) reported that a "natural pattern" of relationships between organized secular agencies had developed, but they stressed that these contacts were not extensive and tended to be routine, passive, and superficial.

Values, Attitudes and Beliefs. As earlier indicated, relatively few researchers dealt extensively with the impact of change on value and belief systems of local populations. Some studies did concern themselves to a limited degree with the similarities or dissimilarities in sentiments and life styles and the degrees of satisfaction with different kinds of residence location. The findings reported were frequently inconsistent. To cite specific examples, one study (25) characterized the fringe as an area in which divergent life styles are to be found side by side; another (34) described the fringe as marginal in reference to both urban and rural norms; while still another (33) concluded that similar attitudes and sentiments were held by farm and nonfarm residents in the fringe.

Convergences of findings were not altogether lacking, however. Several studies that investigated the satisfaction of fringe dwellers with their residence location reported that most fringe residents evaluate this situation favorably (8, 25, 27). Further, one study (27) reported that fringe residents tended to extend their favorable reactions to their specific location to a favorable evaluation of fringe areas in general.

The associations between satisfaction and several other traits of fringe residents were also investigated. Martin (27) reported that satisfaction with and adjustment to fringe residence was greater among persons conditioned by nonurban residence than those not so conditioned, among farmers and farm managers than laborers or workers, among males than females, and among middle-aged people than young adults or elderly people. Martin also concluded that distance from the central city is not a major factor in the evaluations placed on fringe residence by their residents, that adequate living facilities with modern conveniences are associated with the degree of satisfaction among fringe residents, and that urban background is negatively associated with satisfaction, though not at a level of statistical significance.

Institutions. Investigations into institutional changes and shifts were not numerous during the decade, and pertinent conclusions are consequently sparse. In only one case did a conclusion pertain generally to various institutions. This was A. H. Anderson's contention (4) that consolidation of institutional systems lags behind the rate of population decline. Other observations generally pertained to only one institutional system.

With reference to education, three studies noted the continuation of school consolidation. Economic considerations were reported to be basic to this process (1), which was found to have developed rapidly in Indiana (21) and to be occurring, though reluctantly, in Missouri (18).

Churches were found to have declined in number, especially in open country areas (18), to have become increasingly centered in villages (21), and in many instances to have reduced their programs (18).

The number, function, and complexity of local units of government were found to have increased greatly; more than 300 units were reported operating in one county (21).

Observations on trade area size indicated a tendency toward stabilization (22). Although propinquity still functions as a force in the maintenance of rural trade centers, a greater overlap in trade areas than formerly was found (31). Changes in the number of businesses do not seem to follow closely population and agricultural changes. The same number of businesses were found in 1950 as in 1940 in a Nebraska trade area (5) where other substantial changes had occurred.

Economic Base. The economic base of community life received scant attention in the studies focussed on change. Some light was shed upon the relationship between population, market, and levels of goods and services by Anderson (4) who reported that in low-income rural areas the level of living rises as farm population declines. Harden (16) dealing briefly with the relation between population size and provision of goods and services, indicated that changes in the two were not directly proportionate. The size of the service areas varied greatly, even among communities of the same size. In addition, Harden found that distance from a city may not be as important to economic development as previously thought if the community is well organized, especially with respect to transportation and communication.

Evidence indicated that little change had taken place between

1940 and 1950, at least in Nebraska trade areas (5), in the proportions of farmers' trade given to towns and villages.

Values and intangible attitudes and skills were accorded recognition as partial determinants of economic growth and productivity. In one subsistence area (31), values were recognized as major deterrents to the improvement of economic levels. In another area where considerable community-level cooperation and little individual-monetary-success orientation had been apparent, the introduction of wage work and of ethnic groups with diverse values resulted in tension, conflict, and a disintegration of the previous system (14).

Propositions re Internal-External Relationships

Whether a particular relationship should be categorized as part of the internal structure of a community or as an internal-external linkage obviously depends upon how the community is defined. If, for example, a county is defined as a community, then the relationships between open-country farmers and villagers would properly be considered as part of the internal organization. On the other hand, if the village is "the community," such relationships would be considered as belonging to an internal-external relational system.

We have already noted two widely reported trends that could be placed in either of these categories: (a) the declining importance of rural neighborhoods as functional social units; and (b) the development of larger, urban-centered networks of social relations organized around specialized interests. These trends mark the development of new areal systems supplanting old locality ties, but their full significance remains yet to be explored. In any case, the evidence of increasing centralization of social and trade contacts in larger towns is both strong and consistent. Hay and John (17) reported that in Bradford County, Pennsylvania, intermediate-sized towns had greatly increased the diversity of their services to farmers and were emerging as farmers' "community centers." In Walworth County (22) it was noted that purely social and informal contacts were still sought by rural families in smaller localities, but that trade contacts had shifted increasingly to larger centers. Anderson and Miller (5) reported the increasing involvement of farm people in town institutions, and Kraenzel (23) found that the hubs of social organizations in the Great Plains had shifted from hamlets or the open country to larger towns and cities.

Throughout this shift to larger units of organization, the county seat community, regardless of size, seemed to hold its own as a focus of social contact. Three studies (1, 3, 24) reported an increase in importance of the county seat community in the pattern of social organization. Kraenzel (24) concluded that this was the one small village community which seemed likely to remain a center of social organization even though located in an area of declining and sparse population.

What is reported above about the internal relationships among locality groups within counties is also observed in the shifting relationship of rural parts of fringe areas with their respective urban sectors. Indeed, one study (5) went so far as to suggest that the country area surrounding the village might be the rural counterpart of the fringe in the metropolitan pattern. Whether or not urban centers and their fringe areas are single functional units, as W. A. Anderson maintained (6), the broad trends to more complex interrelationships and increasing interdependencies that have been observed in rural localities are even more evident in metropolitan fringe areas.

As yet there is no clear agreement as to the patterns of fringe area development and change. Some researchers appear to subscribe to the view that fringe area development occurs in accordance with principles applicable to all, or at least most, cases; others question the existence of uniform patterns. Among the authors in the studies reviewed, Martin (27) and Pratt (32) belong to the first group in positing the existence of relatively uniform patterns of development. Martin sees the operation of two general principles—the gradient principle and the differentiation principle. He holds that changes in satellite rural areas conform to the gradient principle and believes that rural sectors of satellite areas become increasingly differentiated into clearly defined subareas as they increasingly come under metropolitan influence.

Pratt's conclusions, based upon observations of a rural sector of the Flint, Michigan, metropolitan area, support the differentiation aspect of Martin's thesis. He traced the changes in Linden, a rural, village-centered community, as it became integrated with the Flint metropolitan community. Linden lost its unity, splitting into two specialized sectors, each with a function linked to the general metropolitan area rather than to the old community. The old types of cohesion were replaced by new forms. He concluded that there were four elements in a general theory of metropolitan community development: (a) redistribution of population and functions among segments of the total area; (b) absorption of all segments and their inhabitants into a single comprehensive organization; (c) specialization of activity in each segment of the total area; and (d) reorganization within each previously relatively free and stable community as it changes to subcommunity status.

The assertion that fringe area development follows a relatively uniform pattern which may be explained in terms of a few principles was implicitly challenged by Hatt in his discussion of Queen and Carpenter's study (34). Hatt suggested that ". . . the relationship between any particular city and its hinterland may be quite different from that of another functionally differentiated city and that, therefore, the rural-urban fringes of the two may indeed be quite separate phenomena."[10] Although none of the studies reviewed specifically tested the thesis of uniform change processes in fringe areas, Fuguitt (15), in his study of urban influences upon part-time farming, found that quite different consequences could be observed in contiguous rural areas. He noted that size of farming operation was an important mediating variable in the adjustment of farming areas to urban influences.

Turning to the influence of the encompassing, over-all social system—sometimes referred to as "mass society"—upon the local community, Nelson points to the breakdown in isolation of the rural community and notes an increase in both its dependence upon the outside world and its interdependence with nearby towns (30). W. A. Anderson (6) also noted that the rural community is increasingly subjected to new forces from the outside world. A few references are made to the mediating influences of certain organizations. Alexander and Kraenzel (1) observe that organizational influences have become important to local community life. More specifically, Jehlik and Losey (21) emphasize that greater influence is exerted by regional, national, or other extralocal organizations downward through their hierarchies than by local groups upward to the higher echelons of organization. In one study, these outside forces are reported to be overcoming the local structure of isolated and small neighborhood communities. Pearsall (31) noted that, in the Southern Appalachian area, changes over which the people have little or no control are increasing in number, frequency, and intensity. She feels that the isolated, mountain neighborhood will not likely survive such pressures very long.

On the other hand, both Pearsall and Vidich and Bensman (36) point out that resistance to these outside pressures constitutes, at least for a time, a main raison d'etre for such small systems. Pearsall sees adjustment to the outside world being thwarted by the power of the local family system and the cultural world it imparts to its members. Vidich and Bensman observe that opposition to local leaders comes not so much from local persons as from the grinding weight of mass society's trends. They assert that the romanticism of jousting with these major currents of social change seems to be the spirit which, regardless of the stresses and strains, keeps the local society functioning.

Propositions re Leadership and Decision Making

No attempt has been made, of course, to survey studies of leadership and decision making; here the concern is with the findings from the selected studies relevant to the impact of change. The major focus of attention in these studies, as within the total field of leadership, is the evolving situation and the roles of participants within that context. The conclusions are again sparse and often inconsistent.

As to whether there are general leaders for most issues or special leaders for different types of issues, a study in North Carolina concludes that decision making within small open country communities is not a specialized function. The same individuals or groups make big and little decisions and decisions that relate to different aspects of community life (13). The persistence of the generalized leader in contemporary small communities is also documented by Vidich and Bensman (36). On the other hand Jehlik and Losey (21) concluded that the "specialized leader" has replaced the all-around local leader in Henry County, Indiana.

From still another point of view, Miller (29) has demonstrated that there are regional variations in the consistency of community decision makers, at least with reference to the processes involved in building hospitals. In the Northeast the formal social structure was employed less and informal influence more in arriving at decisions than was found to be the case in the Southeast.

The decision-making process itself has been a focus of interest. Miller (29) demonstrated that this, too, varied between regions in certain major ways. For example, more time was devoted in the Northeast to appealing to the community, but these appeals were less successful than the procedure followed in the Southeast, which involved more attention to official action by persons in authoritative positions.

Hoffer and Freeman (19) undertook to determine the

community status of those persons who initiated, opposed, and legitimized eight community action processes. They found action was initiated most frequently by newcomers, next by combinations of newcomers and old-timers, and least frequently by outsiders. Opposition seemed to come mainly from old-timers, whereas legitimation was accomplished primarily by old-timers and newcomers together.

SUBSTANTIVE CONTRIBUTIONS TO THE SOLUTION OF COMMUNITY ADJUSTMENT PROBLEMS

About half of the community studies but only one of the fringe area studies reviewed made explicit reference to the practical applicability of their findings, but few developed this theme to any appreciable degree. Many simply contained statements to the effect that policy makers should give consideration to their findings. An additional five or six community studies and half of the fringe area studies contained information judged to be of specific potential utility in dealing with various community problems even though the authors did not discuss applications. The practical value of the findings of the remaining studies was not readily apparent except as general background information. Pertinent ideas of clear utility to those concerned with community adjustment problems were indeed few, disparate, and supported too frequently by little or no evidence. Most of the major contributions may be discussed under three headings: (a) community action efforts; (b) problems of areas with declining or sparsely settled populations; and (c) problems of areas with population increase.

Community Action Efforts. As has already been noted, this review has not included studies dealing with conscious efforts to improve communities. However, some of the studies reviewed dealt in some measure with action efforts as one facet of change and adjustment to change. Vogt (37) for instance, concludes that in some circumstances community survival may depend upon a conscious effort to change the basic values of the community. As to how this is to be done or how the other aspects of change are to be accomplished most effectively, little is said in any of the studies.

We are beginning to realize somewhat more clearly what it means to assert that efforts to change must be adapted to varying local situations. Freeman and Mayo (13) have dealt with one aspect of induced change in one kind of local situation. They found that in a small open-country community, marked by neighborliness and equalitarian values and by diffuse personal and institutional roles, there was a relatively clear pattern of leadership in dealing with all community issues. According to these authors the "real" leaders can be identified rather quickly by observing only a few instances of innovative effort.

In somewhat larger communities, patterns of action are considerably more complex. Miller (29), in his studies of the efforts of a number of communities to build hospitals, found regional variations in the leadership structure. In the Southeast, he suggests, those interested in effective action should pay more attention to the structure of authority and official position, whereas in the Northeast relatively more attention should be given to the less apparent networks of informal influence. In the Northeast more diversified appeals would be required to accomplish action goals.

Determinants of success or failure for community projects have received some attention within the relatively narrow range of studies surveyed. However, as yet little is known about the effects of this or that particular factor. The studies have simply pointed to areas where future research might yield significant results.

Harden (16) concluded that neither community size nor distance from major centers is determinative of success in community efforts. Hoffer and Freeman (19) point to the importance of what they term "legitimation"—the approval of those groups with social power to stop the planned or hoped for action—in the success of a project. They stipulate the necessity of either gaining the support of these groups or overcoming them with appropriate publicity.

Problems of Distance, Sparsity, and Decline of Population. Six studies had one or more statements or implications for policy regarding the amelioration of conditions in communities with sparse or declining populations. By implication, all seemed to support the forthright contentions of Doerflinger and Marshall (12) that in such areas more research is needed to assess the consequences of alternative policies, that there is a need for a balanced development of economic resources, that high school education must adapt itself to the fact that most students will later live outside the area, and that out-migration by itself will not solve the adjustment problems of these areas. Other suggestions for adjustment to these conditions may be grouped into four categories: (a) those relating particularly to the integration of the more densely settled with the sparsely settled areas of the great plains; (b) those having to do with the spatial and functional reorganization of facilities within a given area; (c) those having to do with the emphasis upon the county as a basic unit; and (d) those related to participation and formal organization.

Kraenzel (23, 24) urges a radical reorganization of the community and settlement patterns in the Great Plains, where great differences in problems and resources for social organization exist between the more densely populated areas (the Sutland) and the sparsely populated areas (the Yonland). He points to the need to recognize and deal separately with the distinctive problems of the Sutland and Yonland, while at the same time joining the areas through deliberately created social organization. Certain services need to be organized to serve both Sutland and Yonland, while other services require local units in the Yonland integrated through Sutland headquarters. Social organization within each area is not enough; a pattern of relationships must be set up so that the two areas are linked together in supportive fashion.

With reference to the internal reorganization of spatial and functional relationships, Hay and John (17) proposed the coordination of activities of rural communities. A somewhat comparable point was made by Doerflinger and Marshall (12), who suggested that each rural community need not provide an entirely full line of services and may find it helpful to specialize, permitting people to get some services in one place and other services in another. Anderson (4), in his study of four counties in North Dakota, stressed two requirements for the maximization of benefits coming from improved man-land ratios in open-country areas of declining population. Community institutions and service agents must broaden their base of service and support; and isolated, open-country farm residents should gradually but systematically relocate upon the most advantageous all-weather road or in a village or town.

Several students recommended increased use of the county as the basic community. Hay and John (17) did so by implication in their comment that trade centers are increasingly the hub of organized activities for rural communities. Kraenzel (24) commented that the county as a political and service unit may come closer to being a community than any other area or grouping within its boundaries. Doerflinger and Marshall (12) stated that the limitations to what can be done on a purely local basis suggest the need to plan for services and development on a county-wide basis. Alexander and Kraenzel (1) extended this thesis in proposing that the cooperation of counties or parts of counties could lead to a more effective provision of public services.

Various problems of maintaining the vitality of formal organization were considered. In some cases conflicting views were apparent. Kraenzel (24) suggested that the definiteness of formal structure was needed to maintain a continuity of participation in the face of the handicaps that distance imposes. On the other hand, Hay and John (17) expressed the feeling that less specialized organizations operating on a neighborhood base might be important to participation. However, Hay and John recognized the difficulties of organizing heterogeneous groups, particularly when farm and nonfarm elements are involved, and of maintaining face-to-face contacts among members of such organizations. Kraenzel (24) concluded that in extensive areas of low population density a paid official seemed to be essential to the functioning of a program and the survival of an organization.

Problems of an Increasing Population—the Fringe. Problems of fringe areas are quite diverse (34), but relatively little in the way of suggestions or applied principles could be gleaned from the studies surveyed. Only four had any relatively specific suggestions. Whitney (38), in his study of Smithfield, Rhode Island, concluded that living costs for local residents inevitably were increased as urban-level services and conveniences were provided and he expressed the hope that greater understanding of this "economic reality" might promote the integration of local areas into larger, legally defined metropolitan cities with broader tax bases and less duplication in municipal officers.

Frequent problems in areas with increasing population are those of maintaining or developing cohesion and of handling conflicts. W. A. Anderson (7) suggested that city boundaries be expanded as fringe areas developed. If this were done, he felt there would be less disparity in interests and more avoidance of conflict. Pratt (32) noted the changes that took place in the integrative functions of different institutions within a rural village as it moved from independent status to a position within a metropolitan complex. If his observations are applicable to other locales, one might expect the community integrative functions of businesses to decline and those of government and education to increase as villages come under metropolitan influence.

The survival of the rural group as an entity within the environs of a growing metropolis also received some attention.

Schaffer's conclusions (35) are that such groups can survive and achieve continuity and stability by instituting changes in family, church, and voluntary groups so that they become more urban in character.

SUMMARY AND EVALUATION

It would be gratifying to be able to conclude from our review of recent community studies that the earlier deficiencies of the field cited by Hollingshead in the passage quoted at the beginning of this chapter have been largely corrected. Unfortunately, candor forces the concession that his harsh summary evaluation of the scientific quality of the field in the late 1940's is still valid today. But if our recent progress has been somewhat short of spectacular, at least there appears to be a growing recognition of what must be done if future community research is to be of greater scientific merit than that of the past. Clearly sociologists must arrive at some agreement as to the generic meaning of "community"; or alternatively, each researcher must define his specific concept with sufficient clarity to permit classification. If a generic concept is to be acceptable, its defining qualities must of necessity be limited. In this respect, Jonassen's suggestion that community refer to "all groups whose relations are spatially contingent, rather than to a specific form of spatial group" is worthy of consideration.[11]

It is obvious, however, that relatively few generalizations are likely to apply to all of the great variety of groups that meet this criterion, and the need for typologies of specific community forms is manifest. Certainly this is not a fresh insight. Attempts to provide such typologies can be traced back fifty years and possibly more, and anyone seeking to meet the still unfilled need would do well to ponder why these earlier attempts have met with so little acceptance.

The recent attempts to develop theoretical constructs of social systems in terms of precise elements may ultimately provide a basis for more adequate community typologies. None of these systems, however, has yet been subjected to adequate tests of research utility. Meanwhile, several alternative empirical approaches to the development of community typologies are in process of development. Jonassen's use of "commuscale profiles"[12] and his more recent efforts to identify basic community factors through factor analysis of social variables[13] appear to hold considerable promise, at least in the United

States where such data are readily available. Hillery's inductive approach based upon intensive analysis of published community studies may also prove fruitful.[14] Another approach is to be noted in the efforts of Sutton and Kolaja to identify community social systems from observing and analyzing specific community actions.[15]

The clear conceptualization of "community" and the delineation of community types are necessary to the task of achieving an integration of community research, but they are not sufficient in themselves. There is the further need to secure agreement on other analytical concepts. This is not peculiar to the field of community study, of course, nor would it appear that the field requires any large number of unique concepts. There is, however, the problem raised by Reiss of determining "whether a phenomenon is or is not communal or possesses communal properties" which must be solved if a "community system" is to be distinguished from other social systems operating within the community context.[16] Indicative of our failure to make these necessary distinctions is the lack of suitable concepts to denote various types of systems with respect to their community orientation. We recognize that there are systems that operate within the community but do not involve the total community, while other systems are truly "communal" in the sense of being organized to serve the collective welfare; still others operate partly within the community, but are not confined to it, and generally have their headquarters elsewhere.[17] The changing patterns of social participation of community residents in these and other types of organizational systems are important trends in community life, yet we still do not possess an adequate conceptual framework for analyzing them.

Indispensable as it may be to the integration of community research, the provision of a conceptual framework is only one step toward the development of scientific knowledge about communities. It is a common assumption that research sociologists are eagerly awaiting new conceptual tools which they can apply in the field, but experience suggests that they frequently neglect those already available. How many community studies, for example, have sought to utilize the conceptual framework for the study of communities as social groups proposed by Hiller twenty years ago?[18] Perhaps it is inadequate, but there is little evidence that its adequacy was ever subjected to any empirical test. The same can be said of a number of other conceptual schemes that have been offered for consideration in recent years.

It should also be realized that conceptual systems merely

provide the framework for stating scientific problems; they do not provide the problems. Although conceptualizations may have been inadequate, the sterility of community research endeavors must be charged in equally large measure to the manner in which researchers have used the concepts at their disposal. More as a matter of habit than of necessity, community phenomena have been examined as objects to be described rather than as variables to be analyzed. Theoretical problems are statements of relationships, and when research is not formulated in specific relational terms it is vain to expect a theoretical contribution to be derived from it. A commendable example of the way in which specific hypotheses may be logically derived from theoretical considerations is Martin's study, The Rural-Urban Fringe: A Study of Adjustment to Residence Location (26).

The formulation of theoretical propositions should help the integration of community research by providing foci upon which various researchers might converge. One of the major difficulties in achieving any integration at the present time is the vast range of research problems to which attention has been directed. Unless special efforts are made to insure comparability, researchers will rarely define their problems identically. Even when they do deal with the same problem, they frequently employ radically different conceptual frameworks whose elements are not easily translated from one system to another.

The relative fruitfulness of the major farming area studies to which we have previously referred commends the expenditure of greater efforts on the coordination of research than has hitherto been exercised.[19] The development of regional projects in experiment station research has been a healthy move toward securing needed coordination. Such projects, however, have typically been more concerned with standardization of concepts and methods to be applied to common problems of description or analysis than with devising specific hypotheses to be independently tested in a variety of relevant situations. The same was true of the major farming area studies, in that coordination was at the level of conceptualization and specification of phenomena to be studied, with no clear formulation of theoretical problems. While it was undoubtedly assumed that substantive generalizations could be inductively derived after completion of the studies, this expectation—and consequently the full potential value of the research—was never realized. That regional research projects have thus far been more productive of empirical than theoretical generalizations can probably be attributed to this same tendency to postpone the formulation of theoretical propositions until after the research has been completed.

Thus far, we have not spoken of the "practical" or "applied" aspects of community research. Although the interest in community studies in this country arose from attempts to improve living conditions, the general trend has been away from the "ameliorative approach." In part this reflects the greater prestige of "basic" science and possibly the conscious or unconscious desire of rural sociologists to achieve higher status in the eyes of their professional colleagues. But it also stems from the recognition that effective rules of action rest upon sound knowledge. Consequently, the acquisition of such knowledge assumes a higher priority. The logic of this order of priority is undoubtedly sound, but the manifest failure to produce a coherent body of scientific knowledge about community change has effectively forestalled the development of a complementary set of validated principles which may be drawn upon in dealing with specific community problems.

Coordination of effort would appear to be a paramount need in the area of applied research. The number and variety of community social problems is tremendous, and studies of them have been largely haphazard. It is useless to retreat into the comfortable rationalization that we are scientists and not reformers or politicians and hence should not be expected to solve community problems. It is also erroneous to assume that all community research that is not "applied" is ipso facto "basic." Some unfortunately, is neither. And it must be remembered that community attempts to solve their problems are social actions. Their observation is a legitimate scientific endeavor and the prediction of their consequences a worthy scientific goal. There seems to be no intrinsic reason why social problems cannot be formulated in terms of sociological problems of theoretical import.

Whether we should study community problems and attempts to solve them is a value-judgment, but that we have only rarely done so is a statement of fact. As a consequence of this fact we have very little scientific basis for either predicting as social scientists or advising as community consultants. Furthermore, there is little likelihood that we will appreciably enlarge our stock of "applied principles" until our research is put on a more systematic basis. Otherwise we may expect our so-called principles of "community action" or "community development" to remain a hodgepodge of tired homilies (e.g., "Members of a community should be encouraged to participate in the community development program") and vapid banalities (e.g., "Leadership should be flexible").[20]

If our evaluation of the theoretical contribution and practical utility of research on community change must be largely negative, it does not follow that our outlook is necessarily pessimistic. The rational solution of problems is always contingent upon their recognition, and an inability to recognize inadequacies is scarcely a major fault in our field. We do not see any intrinsic reasons why the problems which we, and many others before us, have delineated cannot be solved. At the same time, the results of forty years of floundering convince us that our "free enterprise" approach to community research is not only inefficient but unproductive.

The difficulties of abstracting an integrated body of theoretical or utilitarian generalizations from the studies we have reviewed are not likely to be overcome by expanding the sample, changing the problem focus, or even by assigning more competent persons to the task. They stem in considerable measure from the failure to coordinate, or at least concentrate and integrate, more of our research efforts in this wide-ranging field. We are not unmindful that a number of related questions must be satisfactorily dealt with before a cooperative effort can be made: What should be coordinated? By what means? And by whom? We do suggest that a first step might be the positing of propositions of expected relationships among systematic elements under specified conditions. Some of these expectations already exist in the form of empirical findings such as those we have reported; others must be deductively derived. The derivation and organization of some such pattern of propositions would not only constitute a move toward the development of systematic theory in the area of community, but should provide research problem delineations which would lead to cumulative work.

FOOTNOTES

[1] August B. Hollingshead, "Community Research: Development and Present Condition," Amer. Sociol. Rev., 13:145, 1948.

[2] The following criteria were adopted in selecting studies for this review: (1) the date of publication should be no earlier than 1950 and no later than 1961; (2) the community or fringe area should be in the United States; (3) the study should be concerned with social or cultural change even though change might not be the major focus of interest; and (4) the study should not be concerned primarily with "community development." The application of these criteria resulted in the selection of thirty-eight studies which probably do not exhaust the universe defined by these criteria, but do, we feel, adequately represent the universe.

Previous critiques of community research may be found in Carl C. Taylor, "Techniques of Community Study and Analysis as Applied to Modern Civilized Societies," in Ralph Linton, ed., The Science of Man in the World Crisis, Columbia Univ. Press, New York, 1945, 416-41; Hollingshead, op. cit., 136-46; Julian H. Steward, "Area Research: Theory and Practice," Bul. 63, Soc. Sci. Res. Coun., New York, 1950; and Albert J. Reiss, Jr., "A Review and Evaluation of Research on Community," a working memorandum prepared for the Committee on Social Behavior for the Soc. Sci. Res. Coun., mimeo., 1954.

Statements of substantive findings from earlier rural community research have been presented by Douglas Ensminger, "Rural Neighborhoods and Communities," in Carl C. Taylor, et. al., Rural Life in the United States, Knopf, 1949, Chap. 4; Howard W. Beers, "The Rural Community," in Joseph B. Gittler, ed., Review of Sociology, Wiley & Sons, 1957, 186-220; and Edmund deS. Brunner, The Growth of a Science: A Half Century of Rural Sociological Research in the United States, Harpers, 1956, 11-41. In this regard, see also such recent texts as Irwin T. Sanders, The Community, Ronald Press, 1958; Lowry Nelson, Charles E. Ramsey, and Coolie Verner, Community Structure and Change, Macmillan, 1960; and John H. Kolb, Emerging Rural Communities, Univ. of Wis. Press, Madison, 1959. All standard textbooks in rural sociology also contain certain summaries of substantive findings from rural community research.

[3] George A. Hillery, Jr., "Definitions of Community: Areas of Agreement," Rural Soc., 20:111-23, 1955.

[4] Reiss, op. cit., p. 23.

[5] Lists of references under "Community" were consulted in the following: Indexes of the Amer. Sociol. Rev. and Rural Soc.; the International Index to periodicals, Agricultural Index, and Public Affairs Inf. Serv. Bul.

[6] Richard A. Kurtz and Joanne B. Eicher, "Fringe and Suburb: A Confusion of Concepts," Social Forces, 37:32-37, 1958.

[7] Kurtz and Smith (25) provided the major exception in their employment of two social characteristics—occupational structure and governmental structure—among their five fringe area criteria.

[8] Reiss, op. cit., p. 106.

[9] This statement appeared in Taylor's Foreword to Jehlik and Losey's study of Henry County, Indiana (21), and similar ones are in other studies of the series.

[10] Paul K. Hatt, "Discussion," Rural Soc., 18:117-18, 1953.

[11] Christen T. Jonassen, "Community Typology," in Marvin B. Sussman, ed., Community Structure and Analysis, Crowell, 1959, p. 20.

[12] Ibid., pp. 33-36.

[13] ——, "Functional Unities in Eighty-eight Community Systems," Amer. Sociol. Rev., 26:399-407, 1961.

[14] George A. Hillery, Jr., "A Critique of Selected Community Concepts," Social Forces, 37:237-42, 1959.

[15] Willis A. Sutton, Jr., and Jiri Kolaja, "Elements of Community Action," Social Forces, 38:325-31, 1960.

[16] Reiss, op. cit., p. 79.

[17] Roland L. Warren has recently suggested a reorientation of community theory to take account of the shifting relational structure of

contemporary communities in his article "Toward a Reformulation of Community Theory," Human Organization, 15:2, 8-11, 1956. In addition to noting the failure of current community models to take into account the relationships of local groups to regional, state, and national organizations, he has also presented a tentative classification of such relationships in another article, "Toward a Typology of Extra-Community Controls Limiting Local Community Autonomy," Social Forces, 34:338-41, 1956. As the title of the latter article indicates, this conceptualization is exploratory rather than definitive.

[18] E. T. Hiller, "The Community as a Social Group," Amer. Sociol. Rev., 6:189-202, 1941.

[19] There have, of course, been other coordinated series of studies. The best known, to judge from frequent references, were the studies published during the early 1940's under the general title Culture of a Contemporary Rural Community: El Cerrito, New Mexico, by Olen Leonard and C. P. Loomis; Sublette, Kansas, by Earl Bell; Landaff, New Hampshire, by Kenneth MacLeish and Kimball Young; The Old Order Amish of Lancaster County, Pennsylvania, by Walter M. Kollmorgan; Irwin, Iowa, by Edward Moe and C. C. Taylor; and Harmony, Georgia, by Waller Wynne. Slightly earlier was a series of surveys of communities sponsored by the Resettlement Administration and summarized by Charles P. Loomis in his Social Relationships and Institutions in Seven New Rural Communities, USDA, FSA, 1940. Evon Vogt's study of Homestead, New Mexico (37), was a contributing project to "The Comparative Study of Values in Five Cultures" conducted under the auspices of Harvard University's Laboratory of Social Relations. Studies under the general direction of John Gillen at the University of North Carolina on the contemporary culture of the South also are to be noted. These studies resulted in books by Morton Rubin, Plantation County, Univ. of North Carolina Press, Chapel Hill, 1951; Hylan Lewis, Blackways of Kent, Univ. of North Carolina Press, Chapel Hill, 1955; and Kenneth Moreland, Millways of Kent, Univ. of North Carolina Press, Chapel Hill, 1958.

[20] The quotations are taken from a recent textbook in the field of community and are cited not in criticism of the book but as fairly typical examples of our current offerings of knowledge to both students and the interested public.

LITERATURE CITED

(1) Alexander, Frank D., and Kraenzel, Carl F.: "Rural Social Organization of Sweet Grass County, Montana," Mont. AES* Bul. 490, 1953.

(2) Almack, Ronald B., and Hepple, Lawrence M.: "Rural Social Organization in Dent County, Missouri," Mo. AES Res. Bul. 458, 1950.

*Agricultural Experiment Station.

(3) Anderson, A. H.: "A Study of Rural Communities and Organizations in Seward County, Nebraska," Nebr. AES Bul. 405, 1951.

(4) ——: "Changes in Farm Population and Rural Life in Four North Dakota Counties," N. Dak. AES Bul. 375, 1952.

(5) ——, and Miller, C. J.: "The Changing Role of the Small Town in Farm Areas," Nebr. AES Bul. 419, 1953.

(6) Anderson, W. A.: "Social Change in a Central New York Rural Community," Cornell AES Bul. 907, 1954.

(7) ——: "Social Change in an Urban Fringe Area," Cornell AES, Dept. of Rural Sociology, mimeo., Bul. 35, 1953.

(8) Beegle, J. Allan, and Schroeder, Widick: "Social Organization in the North Lansing Fringe," Mich. AES Tech. Bul. 251, 1955.

(9) Bertrand, Alvin L., and Osborne, Harold W.: "Rural Industrialization in a Louisiana Community," La. AES Bul. 524, 1959.

(10) Blizzard, Samuel W.: "Research on the Rural-Urban Fringe: A Case Study," Sociology and Social Research, 38:143-49, 1954.

(11) Doerflinger, Jon A.: "Kenosha County, Wisconsin, Study: An Overview of the Social Effects of Population Change," Rept. No. 1, Dept. of Rural Sociology, Univ. of Wis., 1961.

(12) ——, and Marshall, D. G.: "The Story of Price County, Wisconsin: Population Research in a Rural Development County," Wis. AES Res. Bul. 220, 1960.

(13) Freeman, Charles, and Mayo, Selz C.: "Decision Makers in Rural Community Action," Social Forces, 35:319-22, 1957.

(14) Fried, Jacob: "Forty Years of Change in a Hawaiian Homestead Community: Anahole," Rural Soc., 20:51-57, 1955.

(15) Fuguitt, Glenn V.: "Urban Influences and the Extent of Part-time Farming," Rural Soc., 23:392-97, 1958.

(16) Harden, Warren R.: "Social and Economic Effects of Community Size," Rural Soc., 25:204-11, 1960.

(17) Hay, Donald G., and John, M. E.: "Rural Organization of Bradford County, Pennsylvania," Pa. AES Bul. 524, 1950.

(18) Hepple, Lawrence M., and Bright, Margaret L.: "Social Changes in Shelby County, Missouri," Mo. AES Res. Bul. 456, 1950.

(19) Hoffer, Charles R., and Freeman, Walter: "Social Action Resulting from Industrial Development," Mich. AES Spec. Bul. 401, 1955.

(20) Iwanska, Alicja: "Good Fortune: Second Chance Community," Wash. AES Bul. 589, 1958.

(21) Jehlik, Paul J., and Losey, J. Edwin: "Rural Social Organ-
     ization in Henry County, Indiana," Purdue AES Bul. 568,
     1951.
(22) Kolb, John H., and Day, LeRoy J.: "Interdependence in Town
     and Country Relations in Rural Society," Wis. AES Res. Bul.
     172, 1950.
(23) Kraenzel, Carl F.: "The Rural Community and the Agricul-
     tural Program," Mont. AES Bul. 552, 1960.
(24) ———: "Sutland and Yonland Setting for Community Organ-
     ization in the Plains," Rural Soc., 18:344-58, 1953.
(25) Kurtz, Richard A., and Smith, Joel: "Social Life in the
     Rural-Urban Fringe," Rural Soc., 26:24-38, 1961.
(26) Martin, Walter T.: The Rural-Urban Fringe: A Study of
     Adjustment to Residence Location, Univ. of Oregon Press,
     Eugene, 1953.
(27) ———: "Ecological Change in Satellite Rural Areas," Amer.
     Sociol. Rev., 22:173-83, 1957.
(28) Mayo, Selz C., and Bobbitt, Robert McD.: "Rural Organiza-
     tion: A Restudy of Locality Groups in Wake County, North
     Carolina," N. C. AES Tech. Bul. 95, 1951.
(29) Miller, Paul A.: "The Process of Decision-making Within
     the Context of Community Organization," Rural Soc., 17:
     153-61, 1952.
(30) Nelson, Lowry: The Mormon Village, Univ. of Utah Press,
     Salt Lake City, 1952.
(31) Pearsall, Marion: Little Smoky Ridge: The Natural His-
     tory of a Southern Appalachian Neighborhood, Univ. of Ala.
     Press, Tuscaloosa, 1959.
(32) Pratt, Samuel: "Metropolitan Community Development and
     Change in Subcenter Economic Functions," Amer. Sociol.
     Rev., 22:434-40, 1957.
(33) Price, Paul H., and Hillery, George A., Jr.: "The Rural-
     Urban Fringe and Louisiana's Agriculture: A Case Study
     of the Baton Rouge Area," La. AES Bul. 526, 1959.
(34) Queen, Stuart A., and Carpenter, David B.: "The Sociologi-
     cal Significance of the Rural-Urban Fringe: From the Urban
     Point of View," Rural Soc., 18:101-8, 1953.
(35) Schaffer, Albert: "A Rural Community at the Urban Fringe,"
     Rural Soc., 23:277-85, 1958.
(36) Vidich, Arthur J., and Bensman, Joseph: Small Town in
     Mass Society, Princeton Univ. Press, Princeton, N.J., 1958.
(37) Vogt, Evon Z.: Modern Homesteaders: The Life of a Twen-
     tieth Century Frontier Community, Belknap Press of Har-
     vard Univ. Press, Cambridge, Mass., 1955.

(38) Whitney, Vincent H.: "Urban Impact of a Rural Township,"
Marvin B. Sussman, ed., Community Structure and Analysis,
Crowell, 1959.

PART THREE

The Perspectives

7

George M. Beal

Social Action: Instigated Social Change in Large Social Systems

TRADITIONALLY, the action and research emphasis of rural sociologists has been placed on two main areas of instigated social change: (a) social action and (b) adoption and diffusion. This chapter deals with the social action aspect of instigated social change; the following chapter deals with adoption and diffusion. By definition, and past activities, social action has been subsumed under the general framework of social change—the alteration of the systemic attributes of society and its subsystems through the development of new systems and the alteration of old ones.

Social change may result from internal system forces and processes, called endogenous change; or, it may be produced by outside system forces, in which case it has been called exogenous change.[1] Most social changes in systems result from a combination of endogenous and exogenous change. Emphasis is here placed on instigated, purposive, social action. The "instigators" of social change have often been conceptualized as change agents—those individuals or groups attempting to bring about change or giving aid to those attempting to accomplish change. Some authors appear to prefer to limit the use of the term change agents to outside system professional aids.[2] However, it can and has been applied to individuals or groups within the system and to "nonprofessionals" such as officers of organizations, lay leaders,[3] and others. The social systems or aggregates of individuals to be changed have been called target or client systems.

Instigated social action attempts to bring about social change that will maximize (it is assumed) satisfactions for a society or subsystems of a society. At a general level, instigated social action may be thought of as a purposive pattern of choice-making, goal-directed, collective behavior.[4] The collective behavior emphasis does not deny the importance of individual or family decision-making units. However, emphasis is placed on those types of decisions that man finds he must or prefers to make coordinately with larger social aggregates to better maximize his satisfactions. Man finds that he is involved with many coordinate decisions in his neighborhood, formal groups, institutions, community,[5] county, state, and nation. It is to this larger decision-making "arena"[6] that the term social action has been traditionally applied.

If decisions are made and actions carried out regarding a community center, a hospital, a united fund drive, school reorganization, government reorganization, or area development, a plurality or at least a majority of the relevant power structure must express itself coordinately in decisions and actions. Social action has thus been analyzed in terms of the actors involved, the social systems involved, and the flow or stages of social action through time.[7] Each of these three aspects will now be examined.

THE ACTORS INVOLVED

The persons involved in social action programs have been designated by some as actors or participants in social action (31).*
The degree of involvement in social action may vary from assuming a major role in policy determination to passive acceptance of the social action. The treatment of the concept of social action as a generalized concept encompassing a wide variety of social action (e.g., from a formal group action to a multicounty or larger social system action) makes it difficult to generalize many of the characteristics of the participants or actors in terms of who they are or what they do. The characteristics of the actors may vary, depending on the arena of social action or the specific functions being performed within a given social action program. It is likely that even in the social action programs with the highest degree of involvement only a minority of the people in the general social system encompassed by the action will be active at a given time.

---

*Underlined numerals within parentheses refer to literature cited at the end of this chapter.

The various studies of social participation and of those individuals who have high participation scores, may be indicative of who will be active in social action programs. There appears to be a strong relationship between social participation in ongoing groups and participation in broader social action programs that emerge. Secondly, formal groups, institutions, and agencies often play a major role in general social action programs. Thus, there is a logical linkage between formal group participation and more general social action participation.

A limited number of research studies have attempted to determine top influentials and their characteristics, in the decision-making process in the arena of community decision making (40, 16, 28, 20, 29). The methodology used and some of the imputations made from the data collected have been criticized by a number of authors. Some of the problems involved in using this methodology are discussed later in this section. It is recognized that influence patterns and the characteristics of top influentials may vary with the arena of social action and with issue or problems around which action takes place. Though not completely comparable, the methodology involved in these community studies is basically as follows. A list of influential leaders[8] is secured from organizations, agencies, and informants. Then an "expert" panel is asked to designate the degree of influence these leaders have.[9] The criterion for the choice of leaders to be rated by the experts, as stated in one study (40, p. 10) was, ". . . person participates actively either in supporting or initiating policy decisions which have the most effect on the community." From this methodology there emerge two types of influentials. As defined in one study (40, p. 10) these are: (a) the top influentials—persons from whom particular members are drawn into various systems of power relations according to the issue at stake, and (b) the key influentials—sociometric choice leaders among the top influentials. Basic questions can be raised about this methodology.[10]

While these studies have indicated the possibility of generalization about top influentials they have also demonstrated that there are many differences among communities, some of which may be regional differences.[11] D'Antonio, et al., have summarized some of the findings from studies completed in several regions of the United States (16).[12] These "communities" varied in size from approximately 22,000 to 550,000.[13] The generalization that appears to emerge from all of these studies is that business furnishes the largest percentage in the top influentials category. With the exception of Pacific City, independent

professionals were the next most frequent source of top influentials. In the case of Pacific City, government and labor provided
more of the top influentials than did the independent professions.
Independent professionals were in fourth place in Pacific City.
A number of top influentials were drawn from government in all
communities. Education and, slightly less important, religion
also provided many top influentials. Welfare and cultural
leaders, in many cases professional, were among the top influentials in all but one of the communities. Lack of comparable
methodology makes it difficult to generalize for two additional
categories. Those in the field of communication, mainly newspaper editors or publishers, were found important in those
studies that set them out as a specific category. Top influentials
from agriculture were found in the Denver and Las Cruces
studies.

When the 11 to 13 key influentials were chosen by the top influentials in the communities studied, the greatest number again
came from the business category. There were individual community differences. In general, it appears that the finance and
mercantile groups provide the greatest number of key influentials in the business category, followed by manufacturing, transportation and utilities. Professionals, both independent (lawyers
and physicians) and dependent (educators and clergymen), provided the next greatest number of key influentials in all but one
community for which there were comparable data. Government
provided key influentials in three of the eight communities. In
those studies where the category of communications was used,
one or more from this category were found in the key influential
group. In none of the studies were any of the key influentials
found in the welfare and culture or labor groups. Key influentials
from agriculture were found in only one study, the smallest community, Las Cruces. In addition, key influentials tend to name
each other and interact more often with each other than do top
influentials.[14]

Paul Miller's national study of 218 hospital projects in small
towns found that the greatest number of those most active in the
projects came from the following categories (in descending
order): self-employed businessmen, professionals, employed
managers, farm owners and operators, and civil officials. The
greatest disproportionality, when compared with the number of
each category in the community, was among the self-employed
businessmen, professionals, employed managers, and civil
officials. Farm owners and operators did not furnish their pro-
portional share and, though 57 per cent of the population in the

communities were classified as nonsupervisory employees, this category furnished only 4 per cent of the active leaders (41, p. 22).

Prepayment health plan projects followed a similar pattern, but with a lower incidence of self-employed businessmen and a higher incidence of nonmedical professionals (41, p. 35). Again, in the organization of health departments the professional category furnished the greatest number of "most active" leaders, and housewives, doctors, and self-employed businessmen followed in that order (41, p. 36).

Pellegrin and Coates studied the role of absentee-owned corporation executives in the community power structure of a southern city of 200,000. They found that top executives of these corporations were usually a decisive force in the success of community projects because they constituted the balance of power among competing interest groups of the community. They tended to participate only in those projects in which the corporation had a stake. These top executives were discriminating in the organizations to which they belonged. They belonged on the average to only two organizations, while the average for all other executives in the community was four. Most of them belonged to the two most powerful organizations in the community. Junior executives participated actively in less powerful civic organizations and much of this participation was oriented toward the reward patterns and power structure within the corporation (47).

Schulze made a study of the power structure of a Midwestern industrial community of 20,000, approximately 30 miles from a major metropolitan center. One of the principle changes noted in this center was the gradual absorption of its major industrial plants by large, absentee-owned corporations. It was found that the overt direction of the political and civic life of the community had passed almost wholly from the hands of the economic dominants of these large industrial plants into the hands of a group of middle-class business and professional men, almost none of whom occupied a position of economic dominance in the community. While it is possible that the paid managers of the major industrial plants may still exercise considerable dominance behind the scenes or through voluntary donations, the findings appear to indicate that the economic dominants from absentee-owned corporations have disassociated themselves from active involvement in the power structure (53, pp. 6-7).

The Form and Sauer study (20) of Lansing, Michigan (population 100,000), provides the opportunity to analyze in more

detail some of the characteristics of influentials, at least as delineated in Lansing. A panel of 14 people representative of mass
communication, business, labor, welfare, education, government,
and religion, were asked to submit names of influentials. The
panel members were instructed to name ". . . locally powerful
people who could get things done in the city or who could kill
local projects. In short, they were asked to identify the most
influential persons in city-wide affairs." The top 40 persons on
whom there was the most agreement were selected for personal
interviews. Thirty-six per cent of this influential group were
executives, 44 per cent were proprietors, and 20 per cent were
professionals. Every one of the top 40 influentials indicated
that he knew everyone else on the list of 40 and that the list contained the names of the most influential local citizens. Four-
fifths of the influentials had attended college. Forty-seven per
cent of them were between ages 51 and 60, an additional 31 per
cent were between 61 and 70.

The typical influential came to Lansing more than 30 years
ago. He belonged to a wide range of local, state, and national
business, and civic and welfare organizations where he initiated
and executed major policy decisions. On the average he belonged to more than 13 organizations—3.9 business organizations, 2.4 professional organizations, 2.9 civic and welfare
organizations, 0.8 service organizations, and 3.5 social organizations. He had held the top elective or appointive offices in
almost all of the organizations in which he had become actively
involved. Almost all of the influentials had belonged to a common core of organizations—the Chamber of Commerce, Rotary,
Country Club, a leading church, and the Community Chest.
However, the highest level of active organizational involvement
for the group had occurred in the past.

The role which influentials presently play is to advise and
consult informally with present officers of local organizations
and to informally help shape organizational policies. Almost 80
per cent believed that they as individuals were responsible for
determining some of the basic organizational policies. Over 90
per cent believed that business leaders as a whole were genuine-
ly effective, if not decisive, in determining the basic policies of
most community agencies. Approximately half of the influentials
believed that a small group was responsible for making most of
the important community decisions. Half of these, again, believed that the same decision makers acted in all important
issues and half believed that the decision makers changed according to the issue.

Most of the studies cited were conducted in the larger urban areas. In a study of a small Iowa town and four surrounding townships, Ryan found that there was differentiation of named leaders, depending on the problem area posed. He also found that in almost 50 per cent of the cases there was differentiation of leaders within a given problem area, depending on the role to be performed—advisor, organizer, or representative (49).

White, in his study of a rural New York community of approximately 4,000, conceptualized five analytical types of leadership (59). The major categories of leadership conceptualized were: authority-power, innovative zeal, prestige, sympathetic understanding, and social justice in decision making. Each of these concepts was translated into a descriptive statement. He found that respondent choices differentiated leaders into three "role combination choice" groups—"mono-role specialists," "dual-role specialists," and "role generalists."

Mulford (44) reports findings for three Iowa rural communities with population ranging from 900 to 4,300. He found that community members who had high formal group office authority scores were named as organizing action programs within organizations by other officers in organizations and business and civic leaders. However, these same high formal authority officers were not named as problem solvers for the entire community. The top influentials, people named most often as "community problem solvers" were most likely to be named as problem solvers having the most influence in a number of different problem areas. Lower level influentials, those mentioned less frequently as "community problem solvers," were more often named in relation to specific problem areas. Evidence was found that there is a relatively high degree of cohesion among top influentials—they named each other as "close personal friends," as people they visit frequently, as people they see everyday, and as business acquaintances.

The Mulford study indicates the importance of specifying the problem area and the scope of audience to be influenced. He found that when a common frame of reference was given (either in terms of problem areas or audiences to be influenced) to different leadership respondent groups they tend to agree on their choice of influentials. When dissimilar frames of reference are given they tend to be less in agreement and several influence structures appear to emerge.

The degree of cooperative relationships among organizations affects the degree of agreement on influentials. In those communities with a relatively high degree of cooperation among formal organizations there is greater agreement among officers, in the aggregate, on who the top influentials are.

White (59) attempted to determine the relationship between formal and informal leadership roles. Formal leadership was measured on the basis of the number of presiding offices, board offices, and committee chairmanships held. Informal leadership was measured on the basis of the number of people in a community sample naming a specific person as a leader. No significant relationship was found between formal and informal leadership. The community sample members did tend to select informal leaders from among the upper social classes, but office holding apparently was not a necessary qualification for the selection of a person as an informal leader. However, there was a highly significant relationship between the formal and informal leadership scores of those informal leaders chosen by heads of organizations.

If there is some basis for tentative generalization in these findings, they should be of value to those engaged in social action. They should be of special importance to those change agents who are attempting important community-wide action programs in relatively large communities. Insofar as there is correspondence between the community studies and the Top Leadership U.S.A. Study (30), tentative generalizations may find application to metropolitan area, county, and regional programs. The type of data provided should be of special value at the initiation and legitimation stages[15] of social action.

However, several points may be made regarding the use of these data.[16] Even among those designed as top influentials there is differential power held by individuals and cliques of individuals. Power may exist or be exercised differentially, depending on the issue at stake or the social action undertaken. In some cases there does not appear to be a real power pyramid, in other cases there appear to be several power pyramids.[17] There may be no constant and direct relationship between power as a potential for determinative action and power as determinative action, itself (40, p. 9). On less "important" social action programs, encompassing more limited goals and objectives, initiation often comes from lower levels of influence and the top of the power structure may not become involved except possibly for legitimation. While the number of top influentials who are central in the decision-making process may be small in numbers, a large number of lower level leaders, organizations, and community members may be active and important in carrying out programs.[18] Thus, different levels of influence and different social systems become relevant at different stages of social action. The top influentials often move out of the picture at the stage of project execution. The men in the understructure of power become the doers and are activated by the top influentials.[19] Many of the top influentials do not belong to, or are not active in, formal groups. However, they do maintain their lines of communication and power into the more powerful of these formal associations. In smaller, more informal social systems, I have observed that top influentials are sometimes overtly involved in the more formal group associations and play a more "public" role in the execution of important social action programs.[20]

Depending on the arena of action, the general importance of the action, and the problem area of action, different levels of influentials and different actors are involved. Paul Miller found that even within the general problem area of health the type of goal orientation of health programs activated varying occupational groups, involved actors with different age and sex characteristics, and involved different special interest groups (41, p. 162).

The above discussion of actors involved in social action has dealt mainly with characteristics of individuals at the apex of an assumed power or influence structure. The tentative generalizations seem most applicable at the initiation and legitimation[21] stages of social action.

Another conceptualization related to actors or participants in social action may have more general value for all stages of the social action process. This conceptualization assumes that social action in essence depends on efficiently finding, mobilizing, combining, and organizing resources. Within this framework the change agent seeks to employ resources to best accomplish the chosen ends. Thus, actors, individuals, and social systems may be analyzed from the point of view of actual or potential possession of needed resources. Miller[22] (41, pp. 14-18, 136-55) discusses a number of resources that were relevant in his study of health social action programs: wealth, respect, morality, success, access, obligation,[23] time, subject matter competence, organizational skills, skill with symbols, and legendary personality. Some or all of these resources may contribute to the power (authority or influence) individuals or social systems possess. However, in practice it may prove valuable to think of authority or influence as "independent" categories of resources. Other resources may be listed, such as interest, commitment, identity, conceptual ability, research ability, interpretive ability, etc.

Some change agents have found that a valuable tool for planning and action is to delineate specific next step goals or functions to be performed, then analyze the kinds of resources needed to perform those functions and finally find, motivate, and combine those resources to reach the goal. In many cases these general conceptualizations of resources appear to have more specific application at several stages in the social action process. Take for instance the resource of access. At one stage the change agent or those with whom he is working may need a person who has the resource of access to a given individual in the power structure. In another case there may be need for the resource possessed by a person or group who have access to outside system aid of some sort. In another case there may be need for rapid access to a larger number of target system members. Such a resource of access may be possessed by a newspaper editor.

In conclusion, from the point of view of the action oriented change agent, it appears that an important consideration is determining which actors have the greatest potential for contributing to various phases of social action. Though data and generalizations are far from adequate, it appears that the approaches reviewed contribute to the building of some frames of reference and tentative generalizations that have potential for research and actions.

THE SOCIAL SYSTEMS INVOLVED IN SOCIAL ACTION

Social action has as its main objective the alteration of systemic attributes of society and its subsystems through the development of new systems, the alteration of old ones, or a combination of the two. It is believed that through these alterations individuals, systems, and subsystems and interlinked systems will more nearly maximize goal attainment. From the point of view of social action these social systems are in one sense the targets for change. In another sense, they provide the resources and are the carriers of action. Social action programs that attempt to bring about purposive social change vary greatly in the scope of the systems and subsystems involved. The target system may be a local organization or institution, a community, a county, a state, a national organization or institution, etc., each with its intricately interlinked subsystems.[24] Similarly, those systems involved as sponsors or carriers of the program may vary from informal to highly institutionalized systems and vary in complexity and territoriality.

Studies have been completed that have had as part of their objectives to determine the types of social systems involved in social action programs. For instance, Paul Miller found that in securing hospitals the Chamber of Commerce, Lions, and Rotary clubs, in that order, were most often involved as sponsoring groups. Other groups often involved were Kiwanis, American Legion, Veterans of Foreign Wars, and Farm Bureau (41, p. 23). Regional differences were found between dependence on civil governing bodies and voluntary associations for sponsoring groups (41, p. 46).

In a study of three small communities in Iowa, Wakeley (57) found major differences in the cooperative systemic linkages between organizations. He also found different organizations at the center of these cooperative systemic linkages in the three communities. White (59) found a wide variation among organizations in the amount of both total informal and total formal leadership possessed by the elected and appointed leadership (officer staffs) of various groups in the community studied. Both the heads of organizations and a sample of community members were in general agreement on the amount of informal leadership possessed by the "officer staffs" of specific groups.

The wide variety of social action programs appears to make it impossible to generalize social system participation to specific social systems. One contribution of the present state of knowledge would be to suggest a general conceptual model that could enable the change agent or the research worker to analyze relevant social systems and thus determine their potential or actual resource contribution to action programs. From this line of thought there emerges the need for a conceptualization of social systems that is general enough to encompass the wide range of social systems which may be involved in social action (either as target systems or "carrier" systems) and, at the same time, determinate enough for the study of specific systems and subsystems involved within given social action programs.

One such conceptualization has been elaborated by Loomis. Though not used explicitly by many research and action people, many of the concepts used by these people can be related to the Loomis conceptualization. Loomis defines a social system as a plurality of individual actors whose relations to each other are mutually oriented through the definition and mediation of a pattern of structured and shared symbols and expectations (37, p. 15). While it is recognized that social systems are composed of actors (individuals), the patterning of relationships are the important systemic attributes. It is further recognized that in some social systems the patterned relationships are distinct, highly structured, and persistent, while in other systems they are less distinct, less structured, and more transient. However, it is argued that regardless of the system one is viewing, the elements which constitute it as a social system remain the same.[25] Loomis develops his social system analytical framework with three sets of concepts. Each set of concepts is elaborated below.[26]

1. Conditions for Social Actions. Loomis sets out the conditions for social action as: (a) territoriality, (b) size, and (c) time.

2. Master Processes. While each of the social system elements can be articulated into specialized or elemental social processes, Loomis sets forth six "comprehensive or master processes" that have special importance in understanding social systems. These include: (a) communication—the process by which information, decisions, and directives pass through the system and provide data upon which beliefs are gained and sentiments are formed or modified; (b) boundary maintenance—the process by which the social system retains its solidarity, identity, and interaction patterns; (c) systemic linkage—the process whereby the elements of at least two social systems come to be articulated so that in some ways they function as a single system;[27] (d) institutionalization—the process whereby human behavior is made predictable and patterned, social systems are given the elements of structure and the processes of function; (e) socialization—the process whereby the social and cultural heritage is transmitted; and (f) social control—the process by which deviation is counteracted.

3. Specific Social System Elements. Within this more general level of conceptualization Loomis delineates nine specific elements of social systems:

a. End or objective—those changes which members of the social system expect to accomplish through the operation of the system.

b. Facility—the means used by the system to attain its ends.

c. Norm—the rules which prescribe what is acceptable or unacceptable.

d. Status-role—that which is to be expected from an incumbent in any social position. The two-term entity, status-role, contains the concept of status, a structural element implying position, and the concept role, a functional position.

　　e. Rank—the value an actor has for the system in which the rating is accorded.

　　f. Power—the capacity to control others. As used by Loomis there are two major forms of power, authority and influence. Authority is defined as the right, as determined by the system, to control the actions of others. Influence may be regarded as control over others which is of a non-authoritative nature.[28]

　　g. Sanctions—the rewards or penalties used to attain conformity to the ends and norms of the system.

　　h. Belief (knowledge)—any proposition about the universe which is thought to be true.

　　i. Sentiment—feelings about phenomena.

Loomis and many of his associates have used this conceptualization in their studies of social systems, social change, and social action. Others, including the present author, have found it valuable. McDermott used it in his study of Rural Development in Indiana (39). To some, it may appear to be too general and abstract for "practical" use in social action. However, the level of generality attained permits it to be used in analyzing the diverse social systems involved in social action programs. At the present state of knowledge the least that can be said about this conceptualization is that a large number of people have found it a valuable tool for analyzing social systems from both the research and action points of view.

Some authors using this approach to social system analysis have chosen to set up functional categories of social systems within which more specific social systems analyses are made. For instance, I have found such functional categories (not necessarily mutually exclusive) as the following useful in analyzing community and larger general systems: institutions, both abstract and concrete (operationally, the "core" institutions are included in this category, not formal organizations attached to the core institution); formal social systems; informal social systems; locality social systems; and social strata.[29]

In summary, it appears that the wide variety of social action programs makes it impossible to generalize the role of specific social systems in social action programs. Therefore, a broad conceptual framework is suggested that may be used in analyzing relevant social systems to determine the existing or potential role they may play in specific social action programs.

STAGES OF SOCIAL ACTION

One of the concerns of those engaged in social action research and action has been with the sequences of action through
time—the social action process. In many instances references
are made to what are considered to be basic decision-making
models.[30] More than forty years ago Lindeman (35, pp. 119-37),
derived ten steps of social action. At that time he recognized
some of the same dilemmas that still plague those engaged in
this work. Three that he recognized are: the division into
steps as being arbitrary; the difficulty of conceptualizing in
pure discipline terms; and all action programs do not originate
in the manner indicated nor do they all pass through all of the
stages specified (35, pp. 120-23).

Despite these and other limitations, it is obvious that research workers and change agents engaged in social action do
approach their task with some sort of a social action model in
mind that is divided into at least heuristic stages, and that these
models possess many concepts in common (56, pp. 56-58).
These conceptualizations often reflect the specific role definition and orientation of the person conceptualizing. For instance, Lippitt et al., reflect a major concern with the relationship between the change agent and the client system (36,
pp. 129-43). Moe appears to have the same general orientation (43, pp. 8-9).

During the past decade a number of sociologists have directed their attention toward the stages or time element of
social action. In 1950 Sanders, in his book, Making Good Communities Better, listed five stages (51, pp. 27-59): an idea takes
root; get the facts; plan a program of action in light of the facts;
launch and move the program forward; and continually take your
bearings. That same year two papers by Beal were published
that dealt with organizing for social change (5). Capener also
wrote his doctoral thesis in this area (14).

In 1953 Paul Miller published Community Health Action in
which he deemed four stages of community action to be essential to his analysis: prior community situation; initiation of
action; organization of sponsorship; and community organization
methods by which resources are mobilized (41, p. 13). That
same year, Green and Mayo published an article in Social
Forces, "A Framework for Research in the Actions of Community Groups" (22). In 1954, Kaufman listed six phases of the
community action process: rise of interest; organization and
maintenance of sponsorship; determination of goals and means

for realization; gaining and maintaining participation; carrying out activities which represent goal achievement; and evaluation (32). Hoffer and Freeman used a three-fold frame of reference for analyzing social action in 1955: initiation, legitimation, and execution (24). A Washington State Clinic on Community Health Programs listed five steps in organizing: getting started, getting facts, evaluating problems, planning a program of action to solve a problem, and putting the program across (18).

In 1956, Beal and Bohlen presented for the first time in published form for general distribution their more detailed "Construct of Social Action" for use in the National Project in Agricultural Communication training workshops on communications (2). In 1958 the Construct was developed more in detail and published under the title "How Does Social Change Occur?" in A Base Book for Agricultural Adjustment in Iowa, Part III (6).

In 1957, Christopher Sower, et al., published Community Involvement and presented a "model" for community action (54, pp. 308-17). The model included five analytical components of the action process: convergence of interest; establishment of an initiating set; legitimation and sponsorship; establishment of an execution set and mobilizing of community resources; and fulfillment of "charter."[31]

In 1957, the North Central Committee on Rural Sociology appointed a subcommittee on Social Action in Rural Development. Among other responsibilities the subcommittee was charged with the responsibility of developing a research framework which would facilitate carrying out research in the field of social action and aid in the measurement of results of action programs. From 1957 to date, this subcommittee has devoted a major part of its activities to these objectives. In addition to the general contribution of subcommittee members and the subcommittee reports, the following committee members have made specific contributions to the development and application of the construct for social action: J. K. McDermott, Purdue University (39); Frank Alexander, Cornell University (1); John Holik, University of Missouri (26); Harold R. Capener, Ohio State University (11); George Beal, Iowa State University (11); and George Beal and Ross Blount, Iowa State University (7, 8, 9).

The construct of social action to be presented is based largely on the author's paper, "How Does Social Change Occur?", revised and to some degree tested by the North Central Subcommittee on Social Action. There are several reasons for considering this particular time-sequence construct of social action in detail: (a) It appears to include most of the stages of social

action used by others who have attempted to conceptualize stages
of social action. (b) In some cases it segments more general
stages used by others, thus it specifies more stages. (c) There
has been some attempt to operationalize each stage. (d) It has
been used as a model for numerous action programs. (e) It has
been used as a research model in a limited number of field
studies.[32]

This model is functional in the sense that it places emphasis
on the description of major functions that appear to be performed in most successful action programs. There are basic
assumptions associated with the development of such an action
model. The main assumptions stated (9, p. 7) in relation to this
model are: (a) In most cases there is a complex set of interrelated functions that are performed in the successful and efficient development and implementation of a social action program.
(b) These functions can be logically integrated into a flow of actions and processes from the beginning of an idea to final implementation, reorientation, or termination. (c) For the purpose of
developing an action model and conducting field research, this
flow can be separated into heuristic stages. (d) Methods can be
devised to observe, record, measure, and analyze the empirical
referents, implicit and explicit, in the model.

None of the people associated with this model regard it as
final. It is recognized that the stages as presented may need
refinement. There may be arbitrary "forcing" of some stages
which may prove unworkable or cumbersome. There may be
the need to add other stages or reorganize existing stages.
Tighter conceptualization with more emphasis on process is
needed. The development of additional principles and generalizations to be used at each stage and flowing through some or all
of the stages is needed. It is regarded as one of several models
in early stages of development and must, along with other models,
be tested, modified, or rejected in the light of action and research
experience.

One of the major problems in developing and using a model of
social action is delineation of stages related to the placement
of them on a time sequence continuum. This poses a dilemma
because some of the stages may occur out of the stated sequence,
may occur more than once, may occur simultaneously, or may
in some cases be left out. The main purpose is the development
of a model identifying the general nature of the stages in order
to indicate the part they play in the total action, the sequence
in which they usually occur, and the essentiality of their functions for efficient, successful action programs.

A second major concern expressed regarding the model is that of the level of conceptualization of the stages and the consistency of this level. In several cases the function is stated, at least partially in terms of process and the process is applied to a specific group or target system, although the process is applicable to other stages as well. For instance, note the stage of legitimation with key figures in the relevant power structure. Since the model is functional in nature, the conceptualization of processes is not dealt with explicitly in many cases.[33] However, this does not mean that precise process research cannot be done within the suggested construct. For instance, Blount (13) has dealt with the process of communication of ends, means, power, and beliefs from the change agents to specific target systems and the effects of differential understanding and internalization of these ends, means, beliefs, and power on subsequent role performance. In addition, Blount has tested hypotheses dealing with methods used by social systems and with interaction patterns, in relation to social system performance.

A caution is raised (9, p. 9) in relation to the use of a single construct in a multiphase action program. It is possible that some action programs are accomplished within the framework of a single "flow" of the social action construct—a monophasic action program. However, in most social action programs involving different target systems, including different authority levels in a bureaucracy, the "flow" of the construct may occur several times before completion of the action program.[34] In fact, in complex action programs the construct may be applied simultaneously to several different but related actions being taken at a given point in time.

It is recognized that social action may be carried on from different philosophical points of view. These points of view may be contrasted as follows: In one, the change agents may enter the social situation with a preconceived program or, as situations arise, make arbitrary decisions and implement them through the manipulation of resources they can bring under their command. On the other hand, where target system definition of ends and means and changes or alteration of ends and means are readily accepted, the change agents may integrate themselves into the process of decision making. In reality, most social action programs probably fall some place between these poles. However, it is believed that the basic model would apply to either of the polar types mentioned, though the specific approaches and objectives may vary.[35]

Space will not allow for a detailed treatment of the construct.[36]

The stages and a brief description of each stage follow.

Step 1: Analysis of the Existing Social Systems

All social action takes place within the context of existing social systems. If the change agents (persons or groups) attempting to implement social action within some generally defined social system are to operate efficiently, it seems logical that they must have an understanding of the general social system within which the social action will take place, the important subsystems within the general social system, and the extrasystem influences upon the general social system and the subsystem. The general social system's[37] boundaries will differ for different action programs; e.g., a formal organization, an institution, a community, a county, a national organization, etc. The Loomis social system scheme of analysis, previously discussed, is suggested with particular emphasis on ends, facilities (means and activities), norms, status-roles, and power in the general social system and major subsystems. In addition, the relative status-role and power among the important subsystems and key individual power figures should be known.[38]

Step 2: Convergence of Interest

Social action begins when a problem is recognized, articulated, and defined as a need by two or more people and a decision is made to act. Usually, the original convergence of interest on a problem involves only a few people.[39] Often the convergence of interest is brought about when a person or persons from outside of the general social system converge interest with some person(s) within the general system. In the process of deciding to act there must be at least some tentative definition of the problem, selection of goals to be attained, and decision on means for action, even if only for "next step" actions.[40]

Step 3: Analysis of the Prior Social Situation

In any social system, certain leadership patterns, power relations, status-roles, expectations, and beliefs and sentiments among people and groups probably have developed out of the past experience with similar problems, projects, or activities. Certain patterns of communication, cooperation, and conflict have probably emerged. Certain methods, appeals, and organizational structures worked, others failed. Thus, if planning groups understand the relevant elements of the prior situation it should provide a basis for sounder planning and action.[41]

Step 4: Delineation of Relevant Social Systems

Very few action programs involve directly all of the subsystems of the general system in which action takes place. Out of the knowledge of the general social system, the subsystems, and extrasystems, the tentative definition of the problem, and the prior social situation it should be possible to delineate the social systems most relevant to the action program under consideration.

There are many bases upon which systems may become "relevant." A central criterion to determine relevancy is whether groups are or have in their membership the people to be reached with the program—the target system(s). A second criterion is the degree to which the group may represent the needs and interests of the people of the general social system or a particular subsystem that is the target system. A third criterion relates to the legitimation process. Though certain power structure groups may not be ultimate program target systems or help carry out actions, they may have the power of program legitimation. A fourth criterion of relevancy is related to the extent to which a group might possibly be involved in planning, sponsoring, or being central in communication channels related to the program or carrying out the program. Groups in the general social system might also be relevant if it is judged that the program being planned may conflict with those groups' points of view or impinge on their programs, members, and status. Groups both inside and outside the social system may become relevant if there is a possibility of involving them in a consulting capacity.

The tentative delineation of the relevant groups allows the planners to begin to narrow down the systems so that limited resources of time and personnel may be used more effectively. As social action progresses from one stage to another, certain systems may drop out of the "relevant" classification, others may have to be added.

Step 5: Initiating Set

At this stage there is limited initiation of action. A group or groups of people are involved to perform the consulting, legitimizing, and "sounding-board" functions. On the basis of the relevant groups and power influentials delineated in Step 4, "initiating sets" are chosen to contact those individuals and

groups for their suggestions and sanction (see Step 6: Legitimation). Thus, the initiating set is a group of persons (probably
including the change agents previously involved) who are centrally interested in consulting with the key leaders of the relevant social systems. In this sense the initiating set is "organized" to perform these "sounding-board," consulting, and
legitimating functions. The reasons why there may be need for
a number of initiating sets composed of different combinations
of people or totally different people will become more apparent
in the discussion of the next step.

Step 6: "Legitimation" With Key Power Figures of Social Systems

Legitimation is used here mainly in the sense of giving sanction (authority, justification, or "license to act") for action. It
is recognized that final legitimation for any action program
rests with the majority of the people in the relevant social system. It is also recognized that in most social systems there
are certain key people who have the power of legitimation for
most action programs or for specific kinds of action programs.
There is usually a formal legitimation structure (e.g., elected
officers in positions of authority in the relevant groups) and an
informal legitimation structure (e.g., informal leaders in positions of influence who may be even more important than the
formal legitimizers). Legitimation is especially important for
action programs initiated by voluntary nonlegal authority groups.

Legitimation at this stage of the planning process consists of
consultation with the formal and informal leaders of the social
systems which are relevant. The resource of access is important at this stage. The fact that different individuals will
possess different access to individuals in the power structure
may make it necessary to form several initiating sets. With
reference to the comments made in the preceding paragraph, it
is important to note that in most cases both formal and informal
leaders should be contacted for their reactions and suggestions
on the new program. Such an approach would tend to get the
sanction of the leaders to the program as well as suggestions
for changes.

Legitimation is also important because it is at this point that
many people are initially contacted with the basic ideas of the
new program and with what the initiating group is trying to accomplish. Important expectations of and attitudes toward the
initiating group are grounded in this contact.

Step 7: Diffusion Sets

Thus far, the existence of the problem, the recognition of need, the motivation to act, and legitimation have involved only a small group of people. However, if other individuals and relevant systems are to act they must be given the opportunity to determine, or be "convinced" of, the existence of the problem, believe a need exists, and be willing to act. At this step there is a need for people who can provide the kinds of resources needed (time, communication skills, organizational skills, access to many people or groups, etc.) to plan activities which will give opportunities for the relevant social systems to express felt needs in relation to the problem.

There appear to be two different aspects of this step. First, the planning group must make major decisions relative to the program before moving to the next step. Such decisions may take into consideration the suggestions and reactions of the consultants and legitimizers in the preceding step.

A second aspect of this step is preparation to diffuse the basic ideas of the program to the target group(s). This aspect of Step 7 is related to the point mentioned directly above because content and plans to diffuse the ideas of the new program should be based on these major decisions. At this point persons are involved who can best conceptualize and diffuse the essential ideas of the new program to the relevant target systems. The people who perform this function are called the Diffusion Sets. It is obvious that there may be a need for many different combinations of people, or completely different diffusion sets, as well as different methods and means as the process is carried out with various relevant target groups.

Step 8: Definition of Need by the More General Relevant Social Systems

At this stage, the activities planned by the diffusion sets are carried out to educate or convince the relevant social systems that a problem exists and that there is need for their action—it becomes "the people's problem." It is at this stage that the activities of the diffusion set usually attempt to accomplish broad involvement of relevant individuals, groups, and publics. This process can be as simple as providing a social situation in which existing individual felt needs are channeled into a general consensus. However, in most cases this stage involves a detailed and lengthy activity before the degree and amount of felt need is developed which will lead to action. The diffusion sets

may use techniques such as basic education, surveys, capitaliz-
ing on or creating crisis situations, channeling complaints into
actions, demonstrations, building on past programs, etc.[42]

Step 9: Decision by the Target System to Act

One might question why this step has been included, for in a
real sense the decision to act may be implicit in the decision
that a problem exists and that there is a high priority need for
its solution. However, this stage is included to emphasize the
importance of getting not only tacit agreement that the problem
exists and there is need for solution, but also a commitment
from the people to act in relation to the problem. Commitment
to action can be a basically covert phenomenon which may be
found in the individual in the form of "psychological commitment" interest, feeling of need, and willingness to act relative
to the problem. Often the attempt is made in action programs
to secure overt commitment such as a pledge of money or commitment to perform specific functions. This may be based on
the action principle which states that there is greater probability
of action occurring when the commitment is made overtly before
other persons.

Step 10: Formulation of Goals

After the target system(s) members agree that there is a
need for a solution to their problem and are "committed" to action in relation to it, group objectives or goals must be set up
and formalized by the more general target system or groups to
whom this authority is delegated. This is not to imply that the
action program thus far has not had stated or at least implicit
goals and objectives. Recognizing that man is a telic being sets
the condition that man always acts in terms of ends and means.
However, it would appear that if future activities are going to be
effectively carried out, the more general relevant systems are
going to have to go through the process of developing specific
goals and objectives or, in some cases, accept the goals and objectives suggested to them. The setting of goals by the more
general relevant social systems may be accomplished in many
different ways. The ends may have been explicitly stated as a
part of the definition of need and commitment to act stages. In
that case, a restatement of the ends may be all that is needed.
In some cases, the ends may have been implicitly stated in the
previous stages and at this stage they are made explicit. In
other cases, the more general target systems, or a representative

group (formally or informally appointed) are given the responsibility of formalizing an acceptable set of objectives. Regardless
of the method used, there must be some indication of consensus
on and commitment to goals.

The setting of goals includes the proper statement of goals
and objectives at the general and specific level in terms of
short-term, intermediate, and long-term goals. Planning groups
often skip the setting up of general and specific program goals.
They move from a general definition of the need to the various
means and methods involved in specific actions.

Step 11: Decision on Means To Be Used

Once goals are set, there is the step of exploring alternative
means or methods and their consequences that might be used
to reach those goals. Then from the range of means available,
a decision has to be made on which ones will be used to attain
the goals. As in the case of the stage of goal setting, there are
many alternative methods that may be used to accomplish this
step.

In some action programs the stages from general definition
of the need through goals to decisions on means are loosely
combined. One way of getting people to consciously define a
situation as a problem and to be motivated for action is to suggest a solution or solutions, including goals and means, to the
problem—in many instances people tend to "ignore" or repress
to the subconscious level, problems for which they see no
solutions.

Step 12: Plan of Work

Within the framework of decided-upon goals and general
means, a more specific series of actions are planned formally
or informally. Decisions on organizational structure, designa-
tion of responsibilities, training, timing, planning of specific
activities, etc., are all part of this step. A formally stated plan
of work usually includes the following elements:

a. Goals to be accomplished—these usually correspond to the
group's short-term, intermediate, and long-term objectives
stated in a logically related fashion.

b. Means to be used—such a statement usually includes a
statement of the general means to be used and, in addition, a
more detailed description of specific methods and actions to be
taken.

    c. The organizational structure and the persons and groups responsible for actions to be taken.

    d. Training required to enable those responsible to accomplish the actions to which they are assigned.

    e. Additional specification of time sequence.

An important part of the plan of work is the statement of the organizational structure. Such a statement should include role descriptions, the lines of authority, and the authority and responsibility of each person or group.

Step 13: Mobilizing Resources

Within the framework of the plan of work, attention must be given to obtaining and organizing the resources to carry out the program. The fact that this step calls not only for mobilizing but for organizing should be emphasized. It is recognized that for a program to reach this point, there already has been a great deal of mobilization and organization of resources. However, this stage refers specifically to the mobilization and organization of the resources for the carrying out of the plan of work. The plan of work usually calls for the mobilization of many different kinds of resources—human, physical facilities, financial, communication, etc.

Step 14: Action Steps

When the construct is used in a monophasic framework, these steps involve the carrying out of the action steps as developed in the plan of work. When the construct of social action is applied in a multiphasic sense, most of the action steps correspond to the specific steps of the next "flow" of the construct oriented at a new target system. However, in the multiphasic use of the construct, the action steps do not always correspond to the next flow of the construct. Therefore, certain phases of action may continue on through action steps, while other actions will involve another target system and social action phase starting with another "convergence of interest."

Step 15: Evaluation

Periodic evaluations, as suggested in the footnote to Step 1 (footnote 38), should provide some assessment of each step in the process, indicating how adequately the planning group performed each respective step. Such evaluations should provide an opportunity to plan adjustments for inadequate treatment of past steps as well as suggest "next step" actions.

After a group has completed its main functions in the planning and execution process, final evaluation can provide valuable insights into the operations and achievements of the group. Such an evaluation usually gives attention to whether stated goals were satisfactorily attained and the satisfaction with goals which were accomplished. Likewise, consideration is often given to the adequacy of the means used to achieve the group's goals as well as to the adequacy of the organizational structure and group processes involved in carrying out the program. In the multiphasic use of the construct, "final evaluation" may be applied after the final completion of the total program or at the end of each complete sequence "flow" of the construct steps.

The reader is reminded of the qualifications placed on this construct in the introduction to it. Its increased validity will be determined by continued use in research and action programs. However, at this stage of development, it appears to be a valuable integrative framework in which to place actors and social systems in order to more precisely delineate the types of resources needed and roles to be performed in the time flow of social action.

SUMMARY COMMENTS ON SOCIAL ACTION

At a general level, social action may be conceptualized as the process whereby needs are determined or defined, and resources delineated, motivated, and organized toward a goal or goals. To aid in more clearly understanding the process, three main categories of concepts and related research data have been discussed: the persons involved (actors); the social systems involved; and the stages or flow of social action. Many of the concepts and empirical data available deal with specific action programs. In recognition of the great diversity in arenas of decision making and issue orientation in social action programs, an attempt was made to "push" the concept level "up" to a more general level. It is hoped that it therefore will have more general applicability. The state of knowledge about social action appears to leave much to be desired for both the research worker and the action oriented person. On the other hand, there does appear to be a rapidly growing body of knowledge that should prove to be very valuable for more precisely conceptualizing social action programs, the resources needed and potentially available, the time flow functions that need to be performed, and how the resources of actors and social systems can be combined for the efficient accomplishment of social action goals.

FOOTNOTES

[1] Parsons uses the concepts endogenous and exogenous; for instance, see Parsons (46), pp. 25-29. Loomis uses the concepts of immanent and external to describe basically the same phenomena, Loomis (37), p. 12.

[2] See Lippitt (36), p. 12.

[3] For discussion of this see Sanders (52), pp. 9-10.

[4] For additional discussion of this point and an attempt to set up a general level model for action and research see Fox and Beal (21). Also see the definition of community organization by Blackwell (12), p. 59.

[5] Much of the discussion and empirical research related to social action has been done in a frame of reference of community. The territorial and ecological ambiguities of community as well as the distinction between what are and are not community actions have been recognized as major problems by those who have written in this field. For example, see Kaufman (31). Social action is a general concept that may be applied to many systems of action, of which the community interactional system is only one.

[6] The concepts of field (34), arena (33), and situation (15) have been used by different authors to define the social system context within which social action occurs. The term arena will often be used in this chapter. The concept general social system will also be used to indicate that social system (usually with its many subsystems) which is the major arena for decisions and actions for a specific social action program. For instance, in a social action program for street improvement in a town, the legal boundary of the town would encompass the general social system in which the major portion of action would take place. Many subsystems within the town boundaries might be involved. It is also recognized that other actors or social systems from beyond the general social system, such as the state highway department, planning consultants, etc., might also be involved. But, the major arena of decision and action would probably be the general social system included within the boundaries of the town.

[7] This distinction is similar to that made by Kaufman (31), p. 11.

[8] The frame of reference set is "broad and important community problems." The questions asked are usually in terms of "persons of influence" whom "nearly everyone would accept" on "a major project" or who participate on "issues most important to the community," influential from the point of view of ability to lead others, Hunter (28). Thus, the names secured may not have specific relevance to what may be called "less important" community problems or specific issue social actions. For elaboration of this point and a suggested typology of issues, see Barth and Johnson (4).

[9] For specific methodology employed in two studies see Miller (40), p. 10 and Hunter (28), pp. 262-71.

[10]For discussion of this and other relevant points see Polsby (48).
[11]See Miller (41), p. 45.
[12]Pacific City (Pacific Northwest), Denver, San Diego, El Paso,
Tucson, Las Cruces, and Southern City (Southeast). The study of
Lansing, Michigan, (20) is in general agreement. One notable exception
was the lack of government officials in the influential group.
[13]For an extension of this type of research to the nation as a social
system, see Hunter (30).
[14]Similar findings were found in a rural community study by
Andrews (3), pp. 217-19.
[15]See the last portion of this chapter for discussion of stages in
social action.
[16]Some of these points are made by Hunter (28), pp. 60-113.
[17]See Pellegrin and Coates (47) and Schulze (53).
[18]Specifically, see Miller (41), p. 23.
[19]For additional evidence see Miller (40), p. 13.
[20]See also Andrews (3) and Kaufman (32).
[21]These and other specific "stages" of social action are discussed
in a later section of this chapter.
[22]Paul Miller also uses the concepts of resources and proficiency
(42), p. 155.
[23]Andrews (3), p. 217, in a rural community study, found the top influentials appeared to be much more sensitive to obligation networks
than were lower level influentials and lay people.
[24]For discussion of community development in this context, see
Sanders (51), p. 8.
[25]Some criticize the social system approach as being a static, non-
processual model. Loomis has attempted to link each of the elements
of social systems with two other conceptual schemata—structural-
functional categories and elemental processes—to provide a more dynamic processual model. For instance, the process of cognitive map-
ping and validation is linked to the structural-functional category of
knowing and this is linked to the systemic element of belief. For elaboration of these points and the linkage of all systemic elements, see
Loomis (37).
[26]The following discussion is based on the work of Loomis. For the
most part, it is taken directly from Loomis. However, certain modifications have been made by the author. These modifications are based
on experience using the basic model of Loomis in research, teaching,
and action. For more detailed presentation of Loomis, see (37), pp. 12-
42 and (38), pp. 1-13.
[27]See Miller for an empirical example (41), pp. 161-62.
[28]See Miller (42), pp. 158-61, for findings related to differential use
made of authority in two regions in the United States.
[29]See Beal (6).
[30]Decision-making models and research cited include those of
Dewey (17), Northrop (45), Foote and Cottrell (19), Research Clinic on
Decision-Making (50), and Wasserman and Silander (58).
[31]For similar model see Holland, et al. (27).
[32]Two members of the North Central Committee have utilized it in-
tensively in research projects, Holik (25) and Beal and Blount (10).
[33]In this regard, see comments of Holik (26), p. 168.

[34] See Holik (26) and Beal and Blount (10).

[35] For instance, under the first polar type, the change agents would probably attempt to "sell" their programs to the legitimizers. Under the second polar type, the change agents might approach the legitimizers, lay the data before them, and abide by the decisions of the legitimizers to accept, reject, or modify tentative plans. For an additional discussion of these polar types in a slightly different framework, see Barth (4), p. 11.

[36] For more detailed discussion of the construct and the stages, see Literature Cited references (6), (9), and (11). Beal and Blount have also attempted tentative delineation of "conditions to be met" for fulfillment of the functions, explicit or implicit, in each of the stages. A measurement or evaluative device is suggested (9).

[37] For additional elaboration of the idea of general social system, see Footnote 6 of this chapter.

[38] The construct under discussion includes a stage between each of the stages that are presented in this chapter. These stages are indicated as evaluation stages and have four suggested functions included: evaluation, decision on next step actions, planning next step actions, and action. These stages are placed throughout the construct to emphasize the importance of constant evaluation, decision, and planning throughout the "flow" of the construct.

[39] See Miller (41), p. 21.

[40] For a further sociological elaboration of some steps similar to those presented here, see Sower and Freeman (55) and Hoffer (23).

[41] For additional discussion, see Miller (41), p. 13.

[42] For some of the methods used in health programs, see Miller (41), pp. 28-29.

LITERATURE CITED

(1) Alexander, Frank: "Study Design for an Experimental Program in a Selected County," Rept. of Subcommittee on Social Action, N. Cen. Rural Soc. Comm., Minneapolis, 1958.

(2) American Association of Land-Grant Colleges. Beal, George M., and Bohlen, Joe M.: "The Group Process, Instructor's Guide, Communication Training Program." Natl. Project in Agr. Communication, East Lansing, Mich., 1956.

(3) Andrews, Wade H.: "Some Correlates of Rural Leadership and Social Power Among Inter-Community Leaders," unpublished Ph.D. thesis, Mich. State Univ., East Lansing, 1956.

(4) Barth, Ernest A. T., and Johnson, Stuart D.: "Community Power and a Typology of Social Issues," Social Forces, 38:29-32, 1959.

(5) Beal, George M.: "How To Get Community Acceptance and

Participation for an Activity in Tuberculosis Control," Natl. Tuberculosis Assn. meeting, Washington, D.C., Proceedings, 1950. Beal, George M.: "Organizing for Social Change," Iowa Ext. Serv., Soc. Sci. Refresher Course, 1950.

(6) ———: "How Does Social Change Occur?" Coop. Ext. Serv., RS-284, Iowa State Univ., 1962. (A reprint from: A Base Book for Agricultural Adjustment in Iowa, Part III—The Opportunities. Spec. Rept. No. 22, Coop. Ext. Serv., 1957.)

(7) ———, and Blount, Ross: "Program Projection Research," Subcommittee on Social Action, N. Cen. Rural Soc. Comm., Minneapolis, 1958.

(8) ———, and ———: "A Descriptive and Analytical Study of Program Planning." Subcommittee on Social Action, N. Cen. Rural Soc. Comm., Chicago, 1959.

(9) ———, and ———: "The Use of the Social Action Construct in Extension Program Planning: Case Study Analysis." Subcommittee on Social Action, N. Cen. Rural Soc. Comm., Chicago, 1960.

(10) ———, and ———: "The Application of the Social Action Process to Extension Program Planning," Iowa Coop. Ext. Serv. in Agr. and Home Econ. (in process), Iowa State Univ., Ames, 1963.

(11) ———, and Capener, Harold R.: "A Social Action Model," paper presented at the Rural Soc. Society meeting, Pullman, Wash., 1958.

(12) Blackwell, Gordon W.: "A Theoretical Framework for Sociological Research in Community Organization," Social Forces, 33:57-64, 1954.

(13) Blount, Roswell C.: "Group Formation and Maintenance in Extension Program Planning," M.S. thesis, Rural Sociology, Iowa State Univ., Ames, 1960. (Available from Dept. of Rural Sociology, Iowa State Univ., Ames.)

(14) Capener, Harold E.: "A Study of the Organizational Process in an Experimental Approach to Planning an Agricultural Extension Program at the Community Level," unpublished Ph.D. thesis, Cornell Univ., Ithaca, N.Y., 1950.

(15) Cottrell, Leonard S., Jr.: "The Analysis of Situational Fields in Social Psychology," Amer. Sociol. Rev., 7:370-82, 1942.

(16) D'Antonio, William V., et al.: "Institutional and Occupational Representations in Eleven Community Influence Systems," Amer. Sociol. Rev., 26:440-46, 1961.

(17) Dewey, John: How We Think, D. C. Heath and Co., 1910; Logic: The Theory of Inquiry, Henry Holt and Co., 1938.

(18) Extension Service, State College of Wash.: "How to Get Community Action," Yakima Clinic on Community Health Problems, Ext. Serv., Bul. Pullman, 1953.

(19) Foote, Nelson N., and Cottrell, Leonard S., Jr.: Identity and Interpersonal Competence, Univ. of Chicago Press, 1955.

(20) Form, William H., and Sauer, Warren L.: Community Influentials in a Middle-Sized City," The Institute for Community Development and Services, Mich. State Univ., East Lansing, 1960.

(21) Fox, Karl A.: "The Concept of Community Development." Beal, George M.: "Comments Re Karl Fox Paper." Community Development Seminar, College of Agr., Iowa State Univ., Ames, 1961, mimeo., Dept. of Econ. and Soc., Iowa State Univ., Ames.

(22) Green, James W., and Mayo, Selz C.: "A Framework for Research in the Actions of Community Groups," Social Forces, 31:320-27, 1953.

(23) Hoffer, Charles R.: "Social Action in Community Development," Rural Soc., 23:43-51, 1958.

(24) ———, and Freeman, Walter: "Social Action Resulting from Industrial Development," Spec. Bul. 401, Agr. Exp. Sta., Mich. State Univ., 1955.

(25) Holik, John S., and Lane, V. Wayne: "A Community Development Contest as a Catalytic Agent in Social Action," Rural Soc., 26:157-69, 1961.

(26) ———, and ———: "A Power Company Community Development Contest as a Catalytic Agent in Social Action," revised for presentation at the Subcommittee on Social Action meeting, N. Cen. Rural Soc. Comm., Chicago, 1959.

(27) Holland, John B., et al.: "A Theoretical Model for Health Action," Rural Soc., 22:149-55, 1957.

(28) Hunter, Floyd: Community Power Structure, Univ. North Carolina Press, Chapel Hill, 1953.

(29) ———, et al.: Community Organization: Action and Inaction, Univ. North Carolina Press, Chapel Hill, 1956.

(30) ———: Top Leadership, U.S.A., Univ. North Carolina Press, Chapel Hill, 1959.

(31) Kaufman, Harold F.: "Toward an Interactional Conception of Community," Social Forces, 38:8-17, 1959.

(32) ———, et al.: "Health Programs and Community Action," Miss. Agr. Exp. Sta., Preliminary Reports in Community Organization, No. 1, 1954.

(33) Lasswell, Harold, and Kaplan, Abraham: Power and Society, Yale Univ. Press, New Haven, Conn., 1950.

(34) Lewin, Kurt: Field Theory in Social Science, Dorwin Cartwright, ed., Harpers, 1951.

(35) Lindeman, Edvard C.: The Community, Association Press, New York, 1921.

(36) Lippitt, Ronald, et al.: The Dynamics of Planned Change, Harcourt, Brace, 1958.

(37) Loomis, Charles P.: "Toward a Theory of Systemic Social Change," Rural Sociology in a Changing Society. Proceedings of N. Cen. Rural Sociology Committee (NCR-5) Seminar. Published by the Ohio Agr. Ext. Serv., Ohio State Univ., Columbus, 1959, pp. 12-48.

(38) ———, and Beegle, J. Allan: Rural Sociology: The Strategy of Change, Prentice-Hall, 1957.

(39) McDermott, J. K.: "Public Decision-Making in Economic Development: Perry County, Indiana," Rept. of Subcommittee on Social Action, N. Cen. Rural Soc. Comm., Minneapolis, 1958.

(40) Miller, Delbert C.: "Industry and Community Power Structure: A Comparative Study of an American and an English City," Amer. Sociol. Rev., 23:9-15, 1958.

(41) Miller, Paul A.: Community Health Action, Mich. State Univ. Press, East Lansing, 1953.

(42) ———: "The Process of Decision-Making Within the Context of Community Organization," Rural Soc., 17:153-61, 1952.

(43) Moe, Edward O.: "Change and the Role of the Change Agent," Dept. of Sociology and Anthropology, mimeo., Mich. State Univ., East Lansing, 1959.

(44) Mulford, Charles L.: "Relationships of Community Problems, Organizations and Leadership," Ph.D. thesis (in process), Dept. of Econ. and Soc., Iowa State Univ., Ames.

(45) Northrop, F. S. C.: The Logic of the Sciences and the Humanities, Macmillan, 1947.

(46) Parsons, Talcott: "Some Considerations on the Theory of Social Change," Rural Soc., 26:219-39, 1961.

(47) Pellegrin, Roland J., and Coates, Charles K.: "Absentee-Owned Corporations and Community Power Structure," Amer. Jour. Soc., 51:413-19, 1956.

(48) Polsby, Nelson W.: "The Sociology of Community Power Structure: A Reassessment," Social Forces, 37:232-36, 1959.

(49) Ryan, Bryce: "Social and Ecological Patterns in the Farm Leadership of Four Iowa Townships," Iowa State Univ., Agr. Exp. Sta. Res. Bul. 306, 1942.

(50) Rural Sociological Society: The Research Clinic on Decision-Making. State College of Wash., Pullman, 1958.

(51) Sanders, Irwin T.: Making Good Communities Better, Univ. Ky. Press, Lexington, 1950.

(52) ———: "Theories of Community Development," Rural Soc., 23:1-12, 1958.

(53) Schulze, Robert O.: "The Role of Economic Dominants in Community Power Structure," Amer. Sociol. Rev., 23:3-9, 1958.

(54) Sower, Christopher, et al.: Community Involvement, The Free Press, Glencoe, Ill., 1957.

(55) ———, and Freeman, Walter: "Community Involvement in Community Development Programs," Rural Soc., 23:25-33, 1958.

(56) USDA, Federal Extension Service: "Rural Sociologists in Extension Look Ahead," Summary of a Workshop, Fed. Ext. Serv., USDA, 1959.

(57) Wakeley, Ray E.: "Changing Community Relationships in a Corn Belt County," paper presented at the annual meeting of the Rural Soc. Society, 1960, Dept. of Econ. and Soc., ditto, Iowa State Univ., Ames.

(58) Wasserman, Paul, with Silander, Fred S.: "Decision-Making: An Annotated Bibliography," Grad. School of Business and Publ. Admin., Cornell Univ., Ithaca, N.Y., 1958.

(59) White, James E.: "Theory and Method for Research in Community Leadership," Amer. Sociol. Rev., 15:50-60, 1950.

8

Joe M. Bohlen

The Adoption and Diffusion of Ideas in Agriculture

O NE OF THE MAJOR FRAMEWORKS within which rural sociologists have conceptualized and studied instigated social change is that of the adoption and diffusion of ideas. The major focus of this research has been on the individual as the decision-making unit. Adoption-diffusion research has been one of the fastest growing, and probably most widely known and accepted, areas of research in which rural sociologists have engaged. This research emphasis, like so many others in rural sociology, grew out of a practical problem situation.

Almost from the very beginning of the land-grant colleges, these institutions made efforts to take their information about agriculture and homemaking to farm people. Especially after the Hatch Act of 1887, which created Agricultural Experiment Stations, the gap between what was known in the context of scientific agriculture and what was being used by farmers widened rapidly. The adult education activities in agriculture which had existed for almost as long as the land-grant colleges were given a nationwide formal structure with the passage of the Smith-Lever Act of 1914 creating the Federal Extension Service and the Smith-Hughes Act of 1917 creating Vocational Agriculture training for adults as well as youths.

The existence of these various agencies to provide knowledge and training to farm people eventually caused certain people in these systems to become concerned about the techniques being employed to communicate ideas to farm people. As farmers continuously increased their use of commercially produced inputs in their farm operations, businesses selling products to

farmers also developed the same concerns. In the context of instigated social change, a number of different change agents, with
perhaps varying motives, realized the importance of better
understanding their client systems—farm people in the aggregate
and subcategories of farm people. The ultimate objective of this
better understanding was to better communicate, influence, and
sell ideas, practices, and products to these client systems. The
technological revolution in United States agriculture may be, in
part, attributed to the results of the combined efforts of the concerned educational and commercial change agents.

Some of the earliest work in this research area was oriented
around the study of the Extension Service and the extension
methods and tools. M. C. Wilson, C. R. Hoffer, and A. Lee
Coleman were among those who did early work on Extension
Service methods and clientele[1] (29, 30, 15, 7, 6).*

The concerns of the Federal Extension Service and the Land-
Grant College administrators who supervised the various State
Extension Services helped to encourage the researchers in the
State Agricultural Experiment Stations to consider the adoption
of farm practices as a worthwhile area of research.

Rural sociologists became involved in this work because they
were practically the only ones on Agricultural Experiment Station staffs who were trained to research the noneconomic aspects
of adoption and use of agricultural technology. The rapidly increasing development of agricultural innovations increased the
need for research-validated answers in this area of knowledge.

The early work in this research area was oriented toward the
communications aspects of adoption with emphasis on sources of
information used and factors related to adoption. Some of this
pioneering work was done by the Iowa Agricultural Experiment
Station[2] in the study of the adoption of hybrid seed corn (21, 20,
19) and by Hoffer, in Michigan, on the acceptance of farming
practices among farmers of Dutch descent (14).

Evidence of the interest and concern of rural sociologists
generated in approximately ten years of research in this area is
best exemplified by the appointment of the Ad Hoc Subcommittee
of the Rural Sociological Society to prepare a report regarding
sociological research in this particular area. This committee
composed of Lee Coleman, Charles Hoffer, Herbert Lionberger,
Harald Pedersen, Neal Gross, and Eugene Wilkening prepared a
report which was discussed at the Rural Sociological Society
meetings (26).

---

*Underlined numerals within parentheses refer to literature cited at
the end of this chapter.

This Ad Hoc Committee concerned itself primarily with the listing of the major areas of diffusion of ideas wherein additional knowledge was needed. They listed these areas of knowledge under the following headings: (a) the differential acceptance of farm practices as a function of status, role, and motivation; (b) the differential acceptance of farm practices as a function of sociocultural systems; (c) diffusion as the study of cultural change; and (d) diffusion as a problem of communication of information. The Ad Hoc Committee had this to say about the significance of the research (26, p. 13):

Most diffusion research has been concerned with the spread and acceptance of cultural traits at the inter-cultural or at the state and national level. Research on the diffusion of agricultural technological innovations has been primarily conducted at the local community level. Therefore, diffusion studies by the rural sociologist allow for the testing of theories developed by students of cultural change within relatively homogeneous cultural areas. For example, Chapin's "S" curve of cultural change and Pemberton's thesis that the normal curve represents the diffusion process and the spread of culture can be tested in the diffusion studies of the sociologists of rural life.

Two of the crucial problems in the study of the differential acceptance of agricultural practices may be stated in their broadest implications as follows: Why are some individuals more receptive to new cultural innovations than others? Why are some sociocultural systems more receptive to new cultural innovations than others? These queries suggest that possible explanatory factors for the explanation of receptivity to culture change may be found by studies focusing on individual and on sociocultural factors. We are suggesting that such factors as the individual's motivations, his perception of his role, role conflict, mobility aspirations, and his statuses may be important leads for the analysis of determinants of receptivity to cultural innovations. We also are suggesting that another level of explanation may be sought by studying the influence of such sociocultural factors as value orientations, stratification systems, and the degree of cultural isolation on the acceptance of technological innovations. The development of empirically supported theories in the diffusion of agricultural technology can make valuable contributions to theories of cultural change in general.

Finally, one of the major problem areas of diffusion research is the study of the communication of information about agricultural innovations. We have raised such problems as: What are the functional differences between diffusion media? Under what conditions are informal and formal sources of information most effective? What types of individuals respond to different kinds of diffusion media? In testing theoretically grounded hypotheses concerning these questions, research in the dissemination of information about farm practices can contribute to theories of communication. This area of study is closely associated with the problem of learning and adult education. If the problems of communication of information about farm practices are stated with reference to existing theory in learning and education, the findings should contribute greatly to our understanding of how people are influenced to acquire new knowledge and techniques.

Other evidence of the interest and concern of rural sociologists in this field of work is the fact that when the North Central Committee of Rural Sociology, sponsored by the Land-Grant Colleges and the Farm Foundation, Chicago, Illinois, was founded in 1950, one of the first subcommittees appointed by that organization was the Committee for the Study of Diffusion of Farm Practices. The interest in this field has grown and the research projects have expanded. At the present time work is going on in approximately one-fifth of the states and a number of foreign countries.

CURRENT RESEARCH IN DIFFUSION OF NEW FARM IDEAS AND PRACTICES

In a field of research where the overwhelming majority of the activity has been in the past decade, it is difficult to separate the early from the so-called current research. Many of the propositions derived from these early works remain valid in the light of contemporary research.

If one chooses to call current research that which is now going on or has been conducted since 1950, this research field may be subsumed under the rubric of five general headings: (a) the process that individuals go through in the adoption of new practices; (b) the attributes of new ideas and practices as these affect rate and extent of adoption; (c) the adoption curve; (d) the personal and social characteristics related to the rate at which individuals adopt new ideas and practices; and (e) the differential influence of the various sources of information upon adoption as these are related to the stages of adoption and the characteristics of adopters, i.e., the communication process. The discussion of current research will be presented under these headings.[3]

The Process That Individuals Go Through in the Adoption of New Practices

The adoption of a new idea or practice is not a simple unit act, but rather a complex pattern of mental activities combined with actions taken before an individual fully accepts or adopts a new idea.

There have been several proposals as to what this process is and some have been researched (27, 3). At the present time there is relatively wide acceptance of the proposition that people go through a minimum of five stages in the process of adoption of a new idea or practice. This five stage process was first reported in the publication, "How Farm People Accept New Ideas" (16) and later elaborated upon by Beal and Bohlen (1).

These stages were logically derived on an ex post facto basis from previous research. Later the model was tested empirically and found to be valid under field conditions (9, 3).

The following are the stages as they have been developed to date:

1. Awareness. This is the stage at which the individual knows of the existence of an idea or practice, but lacks details concerning its intrinsic nature and use. Awareness may begin as an involuntary act or as serendipitous behavior.

2. Information. This is the stage at which the individual becomes interested in the idea. He seeks further basic information of a general nature regarding it. He wants to know why and how it works, how much it costs, and how it compares with other ideas or practices purported to perform the same or similar functions. He is concerned with knowing the conditions of use and the resources necessary to get optimum benefits from its use.

3. Evaluation. This is the stage at which the individual takes the knowledge he has about the idea and weighs the alternatives in terms of his own use. He considers his own resources of land, labor, capital, and management ability and decides whether or not he has the necessary resources to adopt the idea. He also evaluates the idea in terms of the available alternatives and of his over-all goal structure. He considers whether or not the adoption of the idea will help him maximize his goals and objectives. If he thinks it will, in most cases, he makes the decision to give the idea or practice a physical trial.

4. Trial. At this stage the individual has the empirical experience of observing the idea in use. The trial stage is characteristically one of small scale use by the potential adopter or his observation of use under conditions which simulate those of his own situation. At this stage the individual is concerned with the specifics of application and use; the mechanics and actions relating to how to use the idea.

5. Adoption. At this stage the individual uses the idea on a full-scale basis in his operations and is satisfied with it. He is no longer trying to decide whether or not the idea is good for

him in his operations. He has accepted it as an integral part of
the particular operation into which he has incorporated it.

I do not wish to leave the impression that the adoption process
is one composed of stages through which the adopter passes in an
irrevocable manner and that he passes through each stage completely prior to entering the next succeeding stage. The process
is portrayed in stages for heuristic purposes and those not
deeply involved in the empirical research frequently conclude
that the actual process duplicates the heuristic. Such conclusions are not warranted by the data.

The first stage, awareness, is obviously a point in time for
each individual adopter. Once one has been made aware of the
existence of a specific idea or practice, he cannot have this
particular experience again.

The exact lines of demarcation between the other stages of
the process are not nearly so neatly amenable to empirical
validation. Research efforts to measure the process seem to
indicate that the information stage begins when the individual
assumes any initiative for gathering further information about
the idea or practice.

The individual is in the evaluation stage when he is attempting
to relate the general information which he has gathered to his
own individual situation in order to determine whether or not
the idea will further the attainment of his goals or ends and
whether or not he has the means—land, labor, capital, and
management ability—to accept this idea as a feasible alternative
for goal maximization. It is obvious to the most casual observ-
er that under circumstances which are part of the individuals'
ongoing daily routine, most people tend to begin evaluating as
soon as they possess any facts. In the temporal sequence of
events, therefore, an individual seeks general information, attempts to evaluate the idea on the basis of his present state of
knowledge, decides that he needs more information and reverts
to gathering further general information. Any given individual
may, in this manner, go back and forth between the information
stage and the evaluation stage many times. However, he ultimately reaches a point at which he arrives at the conclusion
that he has all the information he desires to make a decision
about the applicability of the idea to his own circumstances. At
this point he arrives at a decision to either implement the idea
on some empirical basis or to reject it.

Studies have indicated that whenever the idea or practice is
amenable to small-scale use, individuals go through what is

called the trial stage (27, 20, 3). At this stage the individual is seeking empirical evidence gathered through personal experimentation to support (or reject) the idea which he considered to be worth trying. He is verifying the usefulness of the practice in his own situation. There is evidence that a large percentage of farmers do go through a trial before adopting an idea on a full-scale basis.

The evidence indicates that many of the earliest adopters do not need to go through an actual physical trial on their own farms in order to evaluate the efficacy of an idea or a practice. There is some presumptive evidence which indicates that those individuals who have high abilities in dealing with abstractions tend to skip the trial stage and go directly from the evaluation stage to adoption (2).

The adoption stage for any individual on any given practice is that point at which he accepts an idea or practice as a part of his ongoing behavior. He has become habituated to the idea. The mental set of critical evaluation characteristic of the previous two stages has changed to one of satisfaction with the idea or practice. This does not imply that the adopter has ceased to look for a better alternative to this accepted practice, however.

I do not claim that this model is the final answer for the understanding of the adoption process. It appears to be consistent with some theories of learning (10, p. 72) and the way in which man thinks (4). Further research in this area will undoubtedly develop refinements to this model. Considering the number of empirically validated truth claims for the basic essentials of the model, it appears to be a step in the right direction.

The Attributes of New Ideas and Practices as They Affect the Rate and Extent of Adoption

All practices are actions which result from a mental process which created ideas about ways in which given operations could be performed. These ideas range in complexity from very simple ones with empirical referents which have a high degree of visibility to those of a very complicated and abstract nature.

From the point of view of a potential adopter, the complexity of any idea and the practice related to it is a direct function of the amount of mental activity required to relate this new idea and practice to the already existing experience world of the individual.

Other factors equated, the more complex any idea is, the more slowly it tends to be adopted. The complexity of ideas may be classified on a continuum from the most simple to the most complex. The following classification has been used to analyze the degree of complexity of any given practice:

A simple change in materials and equipment. This type of change would take the least amount of mental activity. It is a change wherein basic concepts have already been accepted. This level of complexity involves variations in already accepted behavior patterns. It involves a minimal amount of change in attitudes.

An improved practice. The improved practice is one in which the adopter has to deal with two or more variables simultaneously. These variations still take place within the general framework of his existing values and attitudes concerning the particular behavior complex within which he is making changes. Also, acceptance of an improved practice does not involve major changes in existing activities. An example of the adoption of an improved practice is the situation wherein a farmer changes from broadcasting fertilizer to side dressing fertilizer on his corn crop. He has to take into consideration amounts, analyses, placement, and equipment. He doesn't have to change basic values regarding the worth of commercial fertilizer to do so.

An innovation. This type of change involves not only dealing with many variables at the same time, it involves a change in values and attitudes toward the whole behavior complex. An innovation is a change which involves reorientation of individual value structure. In order to adopt an innovation, an individual must alter certain attitudes and beliefs which he held and substitute others before he can adopt an idea of this complexity.

Hybrid seed corn was an innovation. Under the open-pollinated seed corn system the individual farmers had well established patterns of attitudes and values in regard to what were legitimate sources of seed supply and the basis upon which seed should be chosen. Neighbors and friends provided seed and the seed was chosen on a phenotypic basis. Certain individual farmers who were usually known on a primary group basis were the ones who did the choosing for those who did not select their own seed. In order to adopt hybrid seed corn an individual had to realign his values in regard to the source of seed supply and the appearance of the seed, and he had to understand that hybrid seed was being selected on the basis of its genotypic characteristics rather than its phenotypic attributes. The history of the rapid adoption of other hybrids after farmers had accepted the concept of hybridization is well known. There are other characteristics of practices or products which affect the rate at which they are adopted.

The visibility of the results of the use of a practice affects adoption of a given practice in varying degrees, those people who have a low ability to mentally handle abstract ideas tend to be more reluctant to adopt practices which do not produce highly visible outcomes when used.

Other factors equated, those practices which produce results which can be readily observed are adopted more rapidly than those whose results are not as easily detected by direct sensory observation. This results from the fact that many people must be able to empirically experience results in order to determine the efficacy of a practice in their own situations. This may partially explain the observation that weed killers which destroyed weeds after they were standing above ground and growing were adopted more rapidly than were pre-emergent weed killers. Obviously if the pre-emergent killers work perfectly there are no empirical referents in the form of dead weeds.

This factor of visibility may have its impact in more subtle ways. If the visible results or outcomes from the application of an idea vary with the conditions under which it is used, the user may attribute the variations to the variability of the practice rather than to the circumstances. For example, if a given analysis of fertilizer is applied to a field low in plant nutrients the visible impact may be greater than when the same amount is applied on a field which possesses an optimum amount of plant nutrients. The user might attribute these differences to variations in the quality of the fertilizer. As fields approach the optimum in plant nutrients the impact of any given application of fertilizer becomes decreasingly less visible.

Visibility is a function of the frame of reference which an individual has toward a phenomenon. If he understands all of the criteria for measuring the results of the use of an idea, he is more likely to use the idea at its optimum level although the results of its use may not be as dramatically visible. The importance of an adequate frame of reference for making judgments cannot be overemphasized as a prerequisite of adoption.

The level at which individuals are capable of dealing with abstractions influences the extent to which they need empirical referents in order to establish a frame of reference for the use of any given practice. This will be discussed later in this chapter.

The divisibility of the product or practice is an important factor in determining the rate at which it will be adopted. This factor is apparently most important for the majority of farmers who desire to try the product on a small-scale basis in their own situations, before adopting it on a large scale. Highly divisible products can be tried out on a small scale with little capital, labor, and management investment. Also, the consequences of a failure are reduced by the small-scale trial.

The economics of the practice is certainly a factor in the rate at which a practice or idea is adopted. A number of studies have been done to measure the importance of profitability of a practice as it affects the rate at which the practice is adopted (13, 12, 11, 5). Those practices which are perceived to have a high marginal return tend to be adopted more rapidly than practices which yield low marginal returns on the investment. However, there is some evidence that large expenditures, regardless of the marginal return, will be adopted slowly by a large number of farmers because of internal capital rationing. Those practices which give their economic returns in a given crop year or in an animal life cycle will be adopted more rapidly than those practices which require a longer period of time to yield returns. This may be partially explained by the fact that many farmers are operating from capital positions which necessitate immediate returns on the production capital which they have available. It also may be related to the fact that many of the farmers are operating farms on short-term leases. Under this circumstance, practices applied to the farm will benefit the adopter only if the returns accrue in the short run.

The Adoption Curve

Almost since the beginning of adoption-diffusion research, attention has been given to the pattern of the adoption of practices over time in given areas. In the hybrid seed corn study reported by Ryan and Gross, they discuss the bell-shaped pattern of adoption and the cumulative S-curve (20). Lionberger in his book on diffusion of ideas (17) states:

Ordinarily, adoptions are very slow at first. After an initial slow start, they increase at an increasing rate until approximately half of the potential adopters have accepted the change. After this, acceptance continues, but at a decreasing rate. A curve . . . may be obtained by graphically plotting the number of persons accepting a specific change against a scale of successive years with those accepting in previous years successively added in. This gives the characteristic S or growth curve.

Researchers have shown that the adoption of many practices tends to approximate a normal distribution curve (28, 27, 24, 23, 2). This generalization is true for both the adoption of individual farm practices and for adoption scores or scales based upon the adoption of a number of practices (23).

Analyses have also been made of the pattern or distribution of people on the basis of when they first become aware of new practices and of the patterns related to when they first gave these practices a trial. These distributions also approach the normal curve (22). An example of such a set of distributions, taken from Beal and Rogers (2, p. 8) is reproduced in Figure 8.1.

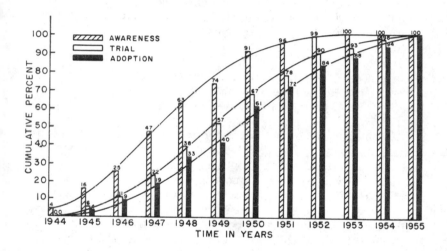

Fig. 8.1. Cumulative percentage of farm operators at the awareness, trial, and adoption stages for 2,4-D weed spray, by year.

An analysis of these awareness, trial, and adoption curves makes it possible to determine the time lag between the stages of adoption and the time intercorrelations among the stages. When several new practices are compared, a wide variation in time is found between the time of awareness and of adoption. Also, within a given practice there is a great variation in time lags from awareness to adoption which seems to be related to certain personal and social characteristics of the adopters.

Those farmers who adopt new practices relatively soon after
their introduction to the public go from awareness to adoption
much more rapidly than do those farmers who become aware at
later dates.

The data also indicate that there is a variation in the adoption
saturation time among practices. Adoption saturation is the
point at which almost all who are going to adopt a practice have
done so.

The recognition of adoption distributions has led to the categorizing of farmers on the basis of the time when they adopt
new practices. The finding that most adoption curves approximate a normal distribution has led to the use of standard deviations from the mean as a commonly accepted method of
categorizing farmers by time of adoption (23). Using this
method farmers have been categorized and given functional
names such as innovators, early adopters, early majority, majority, late majority, and laggards.

The Personal and Social Characteristics Related to the Rate at Which Individuals Adopt New Ideas and Practices

An objective of much adoption-diffusion research has been to
determine the personal and social characteristics that are related to the rate at which people have accepted a new idea or
practice after it has been introduced. In many cases the functional time of adoption categories, such as innovator, early
adopter, etc., have been used as a basis of analysis. In the past,
attempts have been made to codify the research findings to determine if there were generalizations that emerged from those
studies which dealt with the personal and social characteristics
of the several adopter categories (17, 16, 1). Different
methodology, regional and practice differences, and the fact that
studies were done at different points of time made this a difficult
task. However, there do appear to be some basic generalizations
that can be made about the personal and social characteristics of
the various adopter categories. One set of categories used and
the characteristics of these categories are as follows:

The Innovators. The innovators are the first to adopt a new
practice when it has been introduced. Statistically significant
differences have been found between this category and those who
adopt later on a number of personal and social characteristics.

They operate larger farms and have a greater amount of working capital. They tend to come from older and more established families in the community and to have higher status in the community than those who adopt later. They have more contacts both within the community and outside it. They tend not to hold formal leadership positions within the community, but to do so outside their home communities. They have a wide range of outside contacts and are active in affairs outside their home communities. Disproportionately, this group tends to seek information from land-grant colleges and other specialized expert sources of information, including technical publications and specialized mass media devices. They usually are not talked to and used as sources of information about farm practices by the farmers who live in their neighborhood and communities. There is evidence that other farmers watch them. This group may be a source of awareness of new practices for some of their neighbors.

Early Adopters. The early adopters are the next group in time to adopt a new practice when it has been introduced. In relation to those who follow them in adoption, they differ in several ways. They tend to operate larger farms than the later adopter categories. They are younger. They have a higher educational level. They have a higher socioeconomic level. They tend to participate more in the formal social activities of the community and neighborhood. Disproportionately, they tend to have official elected leadership positions in these formal organizations. They participate more in government agency programs and farmer cooperatives. They also receive more farm papers and magazines than those who follow them in adoption. They use technically qualified sources of information to a greater extent than do those who adopt later.

Early Majority. The early majority as a category tend to be slightly above average in age, education, and socioeconomic status. They receive slightly more magazines and bulletins than do those who follow and are more active in cooperatives and government agency programs. This group attends more county and local meetings where agricultural information is dispensed than those who follow them in adoption time. This group disproportionately furnishes the informal leadership in the neighborhoods and communities. When other farmers in the majority, late majority, and laggard categories mention individuals as sources of information they name disproportionately individuals who are in the early majority category.

Majority. The majority are slightly older than those who
precede them in adoption. They have about the average amount
of farming experience and participation in various organizations.
They participate more in formal organizations than those who
follow them in the adoption rate or in adoption time. They take
more farm papers and magazines than those who follow them,
but less than those who precede them in adoption. They participate more in cooperatives and government agency programs
than those who follow them, but less than those who precede
them. They receive more government bulletins than those who
follow them, but less than those who precede them.

Late Majority. The late majority are older than those who
precede them. They participate less in the formal organizations of the community (and neighborhood). They receive fewer
magazines and bulletins and they participate less in government
agency programs and farmer cooperatives.

Laggards. The laggard category contains the oldest and least
educated adopters. They participate least in the neighborhood
groups and community organizations and they receive the fewest
magazines and bulletins. This category can be distinguished
from the categories in the middle of the adoption category pattern on the basis of having the smallest farms. Neighbors and
friends, or the farm salesman and radio, are the main sources
of information used by this category.

These characteristics are more highly visible to the observ-
er and have been used in the past by extension and other government agency workers and commercial change agents as a means
of classifying the farm audiences for purposes of working with
them. There are other attributes which on the basis of the
newer research differentiate farmers on the continuum from
earliest to late adoption. Most of these have been tested in field
study and found to appear rather consistently on one end or the
other of the continuum. The following propositions seem to be
warranted:

1. The innovators and early adopters have a higher ability to
deal with abstractions than do the late adopters and laggards.

2. Innovators and early adopters are more ends oriented
while those slowest to adopt tend to be more means oriented.
The innovator tends to set economic profit maximization as his
end to achieve. Thus land, labor, and time spent on management
become means to that end. On the other hand, the late adopters
more often perceive land ownership as an end in itself. They

tend to value highly keeping on the job, not running around too much, and hard physical work—these become ends. Time spent gathering data and upon management decisions is not regarded as hard work and therefore is not valued highly by the late adopters.

3. The earlier adopters are more willing to take risks than are the later adopters. An important aspect of risk taking is willingness to borrow money or to be in debt, since internal capital rationing is often a limiting factor in new practice adoption. Earlier adopters are more prone to believe they must borrow money for their farming operation and more of them do borrow money.

4. Risk and uncertainty can be differentiated on the basis of ability to attach probability statements to future outcomes—a risk is a future outcome to which a probability statement can be attached, while no probability statements can be attached to uncertainty. Logically, knowledge would be expected to account for the difference between risk and uncertainty. Thus, it has been found that earlier adopters possess a higher practice and product knowledge than do the later adopters.

5. The innovators and early adopters tend to be more secure as individuals than the late adopters and laggards.

6. The innovators and early adopters adopt a practice much sooner after they become aware of it than do late adopters and laggards. One study indicates that the time span between awareness and adoption of a given practice was more than ten times as great for the later adopters than it was for the innovators and early adopters (2).

7. Innovators and early adopters tend to prefer different kinds of information than do the later adopters. They prefer factual and "why" information without the embellishment of details about carrying out the practice; whereas the later adopters prefer information which gives them "how" and "what" answers rather than "why" answers in relation to the new idea.

8. Innovators and early adopters make little distinction between the expertness of the source of information and its trustworthiness. Later adopters tend to distinguish between what they consider to be the most expert source of information and what they consider to be the most trustworthy source of information. In use, the later adopters tend to use the trustworthy source rather than the expert source.

9. Innovators and early adopters tend to be more cosmopolitan in their orientation and contacts. Late adopters tend to be more localistic in their orientation and contacts. Neighbors

and local friends are important as referents and reference groups for late adopters. The important referents and reference groups for innovators and early adopters tend to be individuals, informal groups, and groups beyond the community boundaries.

10. Innovators and early adopters use impersonal sources of information disproportionately and are capable of relying more on one-way communication channels in order to get information necessary to adopt new ideas. The later adopters tend to rely more on personal sources of information and two-way communication in the adoption process. Later adopter categories rely more on neighbors and friends as a source of information in all the stages of the adoption process.

11. The earlier adopters are more positively oriented toward the importance of science in agriculture. Those who adopt new practices first tend to look upon agriculture in a scientific context, whereas the later adopters are more inclined to look upon farming as an art; a traditional pattern of doing things that is passed from one generation to the next. This creates problems of communication since one who considers agriculture to be an art learned from one's father is usually reluctant to admit that there is anything essential that he does not know.

12. Those who are first to adopt new practices are also the ones who look upon farming as a profit maximizing business rather than as a way of life. The earlier adopters tend to use intrafirm analyses to determine which enterprises on their farms are yielding the greatest marginal returns, while disproportionately more of the later adopters operate on the "break even" theory.

13. Earlier adopters tend to participate disproportionately in secular and more Gesellschaft systems of the society, while later adopters participate disproportionately more in the sacred and more Gemeinschaft systems.

14. The earlier adopters also have a higher professional orientation toward farming than do the later adopters.

These personal and social characteristics have also been used as independent variables in multiple correlation analyses to explain variation in adoption scores. Considerably over 50 per cent of the variation in adoption has been accounted for by combinations of these personal and social variables, though much additional attention must be given to theoretical frameworks, concepts, and operational measures. The preliminary results indicate that social-psychological, economic, and communication behavior variables offer the greatest predictive possibilities. The following list of variables, in no way meant to be exhaustive, are indicative of the kinds of variables that have demonstrated predictive ability in one or more studies: professionalism scales, attitudes toward change, attitudes toward science, mental flexibility, ability to deal with abstractions, education, discerning ability, frame of reference, management ability, rationality, scale of farm operations, gross and net income, and the use of technically qualified sources of information.

Preliminary findings indicate the favorable potential of this type of predictive research to lead to better analyses of farming methods and practices than were possible in the past. Copp (8) and Bohlen and Beal have been using these techniques with results which appear to be favorable.

The Differential Influence of the Various Sources of Information Upon Adoption as These Are Related to the Stages of Adoption and the Characteristics of Adopters: the Communication Process

The communication aspects of diffusion of ideas and practices have two major dimensions. Individuals tend to use different sources of information at the various stages in the adoption process and the various adopter categories tend to use different sources of information at each of the stages in the adoption process. Another variable which tends to be an influence in both of these dimensions is the nature of the practice in itself. Thus, generalizations must be qualified in terms of the practices studied. There may also be unique local or regional differences in type of farming or communication channels that also affect generalizations. Individual farmers also have different communication patterns. The outline on the following page presents a general picture of the role of various sources of information at the several adoption stages.

At the <u>awareness stage</u>, mass media are mentioned more frequently than all other sources combined. At the <u>information stage</u> there is a more even distribution between the sources of information. At the <u>evaluation stage</u> friends and neighbors become the most frequently mentioned source, followed closely by commercial sources. Mass media drop to fourth in order of importance at this stage and continue there for the remaining stages. At the <u>trial stage</u> sources of information vary greatly from practice to practice. Outside sources of information appear to play a minor role at the <u>adoption stage</u>. Personal

General Rank Order of Information Sources by Stage in the Adoption Process

AWARENESS	INFORMATION	EVALUATION	TRIAL	ADOPTION
knows about practice lacks details	seek additional, more detailed information	mental trial, decision to try or reject	physical trial	full scale continued use
1. Mass media— magazines newspapers, radio, T.V.	1. Mass media	1. Neighbors and friends	1. Neighbors and friends	1. Neighbors and friends
2. Agricultural agencies; Extension, Vo-Ag., etc.	2. Commercial	2. Commercial	2. Commercial	2. Commercial
3. Neighbors— and friends, mainly other farmers	3. Neighbors and friends	3. Agricultural agencies	3. Agricultural agencies	3. Agricultural agencies
4. Commercial— dealers and salesmen	4. Agricultural agencies	4. Mass media	4. Mass media	4. Mass media

experience and satisfaction seem to be the most important factors in continued use of the practice or product at the adoption stage.

Several generalizations can be made. The more complex the idea or practice the greater the likelihood that agricultural agencies will be used as a source of information. One-way, impersonal communication plays its major role at the awareness and information stages. Personal, two-way communication is more important for the stages of evaluation, trial, and adoption.

The above analyses and generalizations are for all farmers aggregated together. Since the greatest number of farmers are in the majority and late majority category these data are "weighted" with answers from the farmers in these categories. A combination of the two models, the stages of adoption and the adopter categories, provides opportunity for more specific analysis of sources of communication. In general, it is found that the different adopter categories have significantly different communication behavior at each of the adoption stages. For instance, the most important source of information at the awareness stage for innovators is government agencies. They also use government agencies more than any other adopter category at all other stages of adoption. Laggards are highly dependent on friends and neighbors for information at all stages of the adoption process. At a more general level, it may be said that the innovators and early adopters use more impersonal sources of information while the late adopters and laggards use personal sources of information to a much greater extent.

This brief summary of research findings regarding sources of information cannot do justice to the much more specific research now under way or completed in this area. There have been a number of specific studies dealing with each of the four major categories of communication: mass media, agricultural agencies, commercial, and friends and neighbors.[4]

FUTURE RESEARCH NEEDED IN DIFFUSION OF IDEAS AND PRACTICES

The research yet to be done is that which is most needed by change agents today. As yet, researchers have begun only to open this area of research.

As examples of needed research, the following may be cited:

The adoption models which have been developed have the limitations of being overgeneralized. Much more work needs to be done to refine these models or create new ones which better explain the process that an individual goes through in adopting a new idea.

Special research emphasis needs to be given to the situational factors of the individual which affect his adoption pattern. Such factors as the enterprise pattern of his farming operation, his significant referents and reference groups, his self-image as a farmer and entrepreneur, and his values and goals must be taken into consideration. In much of the work done it has been assumed that all farmers viewed a new idea in a similar way; i.e., its complexity, its potentials, and the opportunity costs involved. This in itself must be investigated.

Concerted efforts must be made to develop better scales and other measuring devices to measure attitudinal and value patterns which are related to adoption and rate of adoption of ideas and practices.

More work is needed to find out not only who uses certain information sources, but why these sources are chosen in preference to other sources which from an objective point of view appear to be equally available and more technically competent.

Research on the adoption of new technology needs to be carried out in other cultures to determine the interrelationships, if any, which exist between the adoption of technology and the adoption of other changes. Much more needs to be known about the adoption process in those areas where the levels of literacy are low. Especially important information is in the area relating to how nonliterates structure and relate new ideas to the complex of ideas currently in use. This particular area of knowledge is scarce for literate cultures as well.

There has been little research done on the forces at play in shaping the kind and number of innovations introduced into the various phases of agriculture (and other economic production structures). Answers are needed to questions such as: What are the stimuli for inventions? What roles are played by federal and state legislation in influencing the nature and number of innovations? What is the relative impact of public versus private research on the development of new technology? What are the communication devices which come into play in determining the types and kinds of modifications made upon existing technology? What is the effect of the changing role of agriculture in the United States on the recruitment of research workers who are primarily responsible for the creation of new technology?

Since this field of research is in the embryonic stage, most of the work concerning the interaction of the sources of information and the relative communications impact of various combinations of these various sources has not been determined.

More knowledge is needed about the factors related to the time lag between mental acceptance of a practice or idea and its actual adoption and incorporation into the existing patterns of technology being employed. Most of the research to date has been done on the assumption that acceptance is followed almost immediately by implementation of the technology.

There has been little research to date attempting to determine the factors related to rejection of new ideas and replacement of adopted practices by other innovations which perform the same or similar functions.

The whole matter of the social costs and benefits of technological changes in agriculture remain to be assessed.

The methods and techniques developed by the researchers in this field need to be fitted to work on other significant problems facing agricultural people today. Research must be directed toward the adoption of ideas relating to migration, occupational choice, marital partner choice, institution and other social system change, government sponsored agricultural programs, and other aspects of political philosophy.[5]

FOOTNOTES

[1] The author is aware of the fact that some excellent research has been conducted in other countries. Bibliographies listing these reports are included as references. The availability of these reports to the general reader is a moot question.

[2] This field project was under the direction of Ray E. Wakeley, then head of Rural Sociology at Iowa State Univ. Much of the field work was carried out by J. E. Losey, later head of Rural Sociology at Purdue Univ. The data from this study were analyzed and the reports of findings were written by Ryan and Gross.

[3] The difficulty of summarizing and integrating the great amount of adoption-diffusion research is recognized. It is believed that the five major headings provide a framework for summarizing the core of the research to date. Space limitations will undoubtedly lead to overgeneralizations and omissions. The volume of research will make it impossible to footnote all publications on specific generalizations. Some of these generalizations have such a broad research validation and acceptance that it was believed unnecessary to footnote them. For those who are not acquainted with the literature in the field and wish to pursue specific aspects of the reported research in more detail, two publications are recommended; a bibliography by the subcommittee for the Study of Adoption of New Ideas and Practices (25) and a book by Lionberger (17).

[4] It is the perception of the author that the following research workers are currently carrying on unique specialized research in the following areas: mass media, Lionberger and the Missouri research group; agricultural agencies, Wilkening and the Wisconsin research group; commercial, Bohlen and Beal and the Iowa research group; and friends and neighbors, Lionberger and Coughenour and the Kentucky research group.

[5] In writing the last section on needed research, the author is grateful for the substantive help given to him by the members of the Subcommittee on Diffusion, an adjunct of The North Central Committee on Rural Sociology, NCR-5, sponsored by the Land-Grant Colleges in this region and the Farm Foundation, Chicago, Illinois. This subcommittee has the following members at this time: Joe M. Bohlen, C. Milton Coughenour, Herbert L. Lionberger, and Everett M. Rogers.

LITERATURE CITED

(1) Beal, George M., and Bohlen, Joe M.: "The Diffusion Process," Spec. Rept. 18, Iowa Agr. Ext. Serv., Ames, 1957.

(2) ———, and Rogers, Everett M.: "The Adoption of Two Farm Practices in a Central Iowa Community," Spec. Rept. 26, Iowa Agr. Exp. Sta., Ames, 1960.

(3) ———, ———, and Bohlen, Joe M.: "Validity of the Concept of Stages in the Adoption Process," Rural Soc., 22:166-68, 1957.

(4) Bohlen, Joe M., and Beal, George M.: "Sociological and

Social Psychological Factors," Chap. 20 of Capital and Credit Needs in a Changing Agriculture, Baum, E. L., Dresslin, Howard G., and Heady, Earl O., eds., Iowa State Univ. Press, Ames, 1961.

(5) Brandner, Lowell, and Straus, Murray A.: "Congruence Versus Profitability in the Diffusion of Hybrid Sorghum," Rural Soc., 24:381-83, 1959.

(6) Coleman, A. Lee: "Differential Contact with Extension Work in a New York Rural Community," Rural Soc., 16:207-16, 1951.

(7) ———: "The People's View of the Extension Service in Relation to Extension Objectives and Problems," unpublished Ph.D. thesis. Cornell Univ., Ithaca, N.Y., 1950.

(8) Copp, James H.: "Toward Generalization in Farm Practice Research," Rural Soc., 23:103-11, 1958.

(9) ———, Sill, Maurice L., and Brown, Emory J.: "The Function of Information Sources in the Farm Practice Adoption Process," Rural Soc., 23:146-57, 1958.

(10) Dewey, John: How We Think, D. C. Heath, Boston, 1910.

(11) Fliegel, Frederick C., and Kivlin, Joseph E. "Differences Among Improved Farm Practices as Related to Rates of Adoption," Pa. Agr. Exp. Sta. Bul. 691, 1962.

(12) Griliches, Zvi: "Hybrid Corn: An Exploration in the Economics of Technological Change," Econometrica, 25: 501-22, 1957.

(13) Havens, A. Eugene, and Rogers, Everett M.: "Adoption of Hybrid Corn: Profitability and the Interaction Effect," Rural Soc., 26:409-14, 1961.

(14) Hoffer, C. R.: "Acceptance of Approved Farming Practices Among Farmers of Dutch Descent," Mich. Agr. Exp. Sta. Spec. Bul. 316, 1942.

(15) ———: "Selected Social Factors Affecting Participation of Farmers in Agricultural Extension Work," Mich. Agr. Exp. Sta. Spec. Bul. 331, East Lansing, 1946.

(16) "How Farm People Accept New Ideas," N. Cen. Regional Publ. No. 1 of the Agr. Ext. Serv.; Iowa Agr. Ext. Serv., Spec. Rept. 15, Ames, 1955.

(17) Lionberger, Herbert F.: Adoption of New Ideas and Practices, Iowa State Univ. Press, Ames, 1960.

(18) ———: "Low Income Farmers in Missouri: Their Contacts With Potential Sources of Farm and Home Information," Mo. Agr. Exp. Sta. Res. Bul. 441, 1949.

(19) Ryan, Bryce: "A Study in Technological Diffusion," Rural Soc., 13:273-85, 1948.

(20) ———, and Gross, Neal: "Acceptance and Diffusion of Hybrid Corn Seed in Two Iowa Communities," Iowa Agr. Exp. Sta. Res. Bul. 372, 1950.

(21) ———, and ———: "The Diffusion of Hybrid Seed Corn in Two Iowa Communities," Rural Soc., 8:15-24, 1943.

(22) Rogers, Everett M.: "The Adoption Period," Rural Soc., 26:77-82, 1961.

(23) ———: "Categorizing the Adopters of Agricultural Practices," Rural Soc., 23:345-54, 1958.

(24) ———, and Beal, George M.: "Reference Group Influence in the Adoption of Agricultural Technology," Dept. of Econ. and Soc., Iowa State Univ., Ames, 1958.

(25) Subcommittee on Adoption of New Ideas and Practices, Subcommittee of N. Cen. Rural Soc. Comm., NCR-5: "Bibliography of Research on Social Factors in the Adoption of Farm Practices." (Bibliographical supplement to N. Cen. Reg. Publ. No. 1.) Second ed., Iowa State Univ., Ames, 1959.

(26) Subcommittee on The Diffusion and Adoption of Farm Practices, Rural Sociological Society: "Sociological Research on the Diffusion and Adoption of New Farm Practices." Ky. Agr. Exp. Sta., Lexington, 1952.

(27) Wilkening, Eugene A.: "Acceptance of Improved Farm Practices in Three Coastal Plains Counties," N. C. Agr. Exp. Sta. Tech. Bul. 98, 1952.

(28) ———: "Adoption of Improved Farm Practices as Related to Family Factors," Wis. Agr. Exp. Sta. Res. Bul. 183, 1953.

(29) Wilson, M. C.: "Distribution of Bulletins and Their Use by Farmers," USDA Ext. Serv. Cir. 78, 1928.

(30) ———: "Influence of Bulletins, News Stories, and Circular Letters Upon Farm Practices with Special Reference to Methods of Bulletin Distribution," USDA Ext. Circ. 57, 1927.

9

Robert C. Bealer
Frederick C. Fliegel

A Reconsideration of Social Change in Rural Sociology

HE CONCEPT OF SOCIAL CHANGE, as it is commonly held in sociology and particularly in rural sociology, entails a contradiction. This can be demonstrated by comparing basic assumptions regarding the concept with contemporary strategies for dealing with the topic substantively. The first part of this chapter explicates the nature of this contradiction and the necessary steps for its resolution; the second part illustrates the proposed resolution, taking concrete examples from rural sociology.

THE NEED FOR A GENERAL THEORY ORIENTATION TO SOCIAL CHANGE

The roots of the contradiction can be shown by noting two widely accepted assumptions framing the concept. First, change is considered primary or fundamental—dynamics, process, and sequence are taken to be closer to the real world than structure, statics, or constant aspects. As Edward Devereux, Jr., has succinctly put it: "Structure presupposes frozen process; but in reality, process never freezes."[1] The second assumption is that change is pervasive. Everett Rogers puts it this way: "There is one main theme which runs like a red thread through the fabric of rural society today. It is social change."[2] While the rate of transformation may vary among the many areas of human behavior, the universality of change is generally undisputed.

288

Now, if theory is to be congruent with the existential world, if theory is to accurately reflect real events, and if these are subject to constant flux, then it must focus in some degree on all events, because "change" is part and parcel of them. With this the case, it becomes impossible to have a specific, delimited subject matter area concerned with change sui generis, for the "specialty" has no way of being bounded short of embracing the entire field. One cannot then, place "change" (and theories thereto) on the same plane or in the same category with criminology, family relations, the adoption of farm practices, occupational aspiration studies, or any other specialized substantive area of the sociologists' concern. Yet this is exactly what is customarily called for, explicitly or implicitly, and it is this presumption which creates the contradiction. Put briefly, if "change" is a feature of all phenomena, then to suppose that it can be dealt with as a delimited substantive field is erroneous.

It is the central thesis of this chapter that a "general" theory orientation is necessary for adequate treatment of change. We would argue that good sociological analysis is rarely less than an examination of change and process.[3] More to the point, it is felt that the conceptualization of social change as a special area of interest, akin to medical sociology or any other specialized substantive area, is both erroneous in logic and detrimental in its consequences. These two aspects need our further attention.

We have already questioned the logicality of a separate "theory of change," given the assumptions which usually frame the concept. It can be the case, however, that in spite of formal agreement on the correctness of the assumptions of fundamentality and pervasiveness, there is, in fact, rejection of these. A protagonist could aver that the argument for a general theory orientation assumes that all changes (i.e., all events of sociological interest) are equally important and is, hence, fallacious. Under these circumstances, it could be charged that the presentation of the contradiction is a misrepresentation. It might be disputed that social change involves only those processes which are significant alterations in structure or function.[4]

According to this contention, change does not include the minor fluctuations in day-to-day or minute-by-minute interactions of persons. Nor does change (though this comes closer to the core meaning) include patterned transformations which are regular and normal, as in the family life cycle or the learning of a role. Change would be seen, for example, only in the alteration of the normal family life cycle through planned gerontocide, a sharp drop in the age at marriage, the diffusion of polygamy, or some other such occurrence. But, even granting this meaning for change, there is still a logical need for a more general orientation; it is necessary to indicate what variation of events in the existential world is "significant," what constitutes "change." With an autonomous or self-contained system this can be logically but one of two conditions: (1) a slowing down or cessation of process, or (2) a speeding up of the process of events. To be in any position to know when events are "speeded up" or "slowed down" requires information on the normal or base rate from which these deviations can be measured. It requires a knowledge of all events in a given area of interest.

Now, most social systems are not self-contained, although they are often treated this way in analyses.[5] With nonautonomous or linked systems, the source of change need not be internal. Here a totally new element can be involved in the "change," as when a change agent enters a community to set up a program or when an underdeveloped country with a characteristic subsistence type agrarian structure spurs rapid industrialization. But even this condition does not vitiate our argument. To be able to ascertain the effect of the exogenous element requires knowledge about the characteristic level of functioning of the system before the element appeared. A discrete change theory tacitly supposes one need know only limited things about the system. However, even with a more circumscribed meaning for "change," one must know "everything" about a system to be able to ascertain change in it, let alone specifying the most "crucial" elements to focus on. For this reason a theory of change is hard pressed in any attempt to be a delimited, specialized area of interest.

The argument just presented implies that sociologists should be interested in the time aspect of observation—of gathering data in a manner which acknowledges change and process as permanent conditions of the existential world. The most serious peril involved in treating change as a separate area is that the onerous and difficult task of getting valid data on process in substantive areas will not even be attempted.[6] It is our suggestion that abdication of responsibility for diachronic analysis, in effect, is exactly what occurs when change and "change theory" are made the province of a specialist rather than the concern of all sociological researchers.

Interestingly enough the early sociologists, subscribing to the two basic assumptions indicated above, attempted to develop theories from a general perspective with a strong emphasis on dynamics.[7] Herbert Spencer, Auguste Comte, Karl Marx, and

Lester Ward, among others, made conspicuous attempts at all-inclusive interpretations of social phenomena. For all these persons rejection of change as a specialized interest area resulted from their tenacious dedication to the postulates of process and change. The core datum of sociology was, quite simply, change. "Specialties," such as they might be, amounted to variations of this theme. Rejection of change as a unique area was direct, even though usually unvoiced. On the other hand, the level of abstraction used in their analyses, combined with dogmas of evolution, characteristically led to monocausal formulations of societal and group functioning. Since then the fund of sociological knowledge has increased tremendously, leading to an increasing awareness of the complexity of social phenomena. Thus, the early attempts have been generally adjudged as too abstract in level of analysis while at the same time too simple in terms of explanatory factors to satisfy current sophistication. Furthermore, these early theories were essentially deductive, and hence only empirically illustrated, rather than empirically derived or induced. As a result of all these features, the efforts of the early sociologists have been mostly rejected as inappropriate and of little utility.

Certain contemporary theorists, while apparently not concerned with process to the same degree as the early sociologists, have also come to the position that change is best not treated as a specialty interest. The primary example here is Talcott Parsons and his sociological program.[8] The basis of his denial is primarily his fervent plea for a general theory orientation for sociology.[9] There is, however, little overt support for his work in rural sociology, or for that matter, in sociology generally.[10] Although part of this response may be a rejection of Parsons' sociological conceptualizations per se, the more important aspect appears to be the tacit denial of the postulate of theory integration involved so strongly in his general theory position. This postulate calls for primary attention to the common features of disparate substantive areas rather than to their idiosyncratic aspects.[11] This postulate tends to veer sociology away from the so-called middle range theories with their characteristic recognition of discrete substantive areas. Consequently, the denial of the Parsonian position ensues in the advocacy of a discrete, independent theory of change.

This chapter contends that the rejection of the early sociologists' work and the lukewarm reception of Parsons' claims for theory integration neglect significant and helpful ideas. Although the simple deductive schemas of the early sociologists can be excluded in their substantive aspect and the complex frame of reference worked out in logical detail by Parsons may be found impractical for normal research in rural sociology, the denial of both of these specific elements in sociology should not be blinding to the kernel of sound program or metatheory in each.

In the first place, both approaches deny that change should be a unique area of specialization. The importance of this denial has already been discussed but needs reemphasis, given the patently clear lack of diachronic data, let alone analysis, in sociology. The attention to process of the early sociologists, however poorly manipulated methodologically by them, is a trait deserving emulation if change is to be placed in a proper focus. Parsons' emphasis on "general theory" appears helpful if only because we must begin with extant conditions in the profession in moving to a more adequate handling of the phenomena of change.

While arguing utility for the Parsonian general theory perspective, it should be understood that our view of this matter is a modification of current usage. Therefore, it is important to specify more completely the meaning that we give the idea. First of all, we take the perspective in a much less ambitious sense than does Parsons simply because rural sociology is an applied field with a fairly immediate accountability to society; general theory on a Parsonian scale cannot be pursued without qualifications under short-run conditions.[12] We are forced to scale down our understanding of general theory to correspond to the unyielding exigencies under which rural sociologists practice the profession of sociology. At the same time, qualification does not mean acceptance of extant conditions in rural sociology.

Since our limited conception of general theory ultimately leads toward the Parsonian ideal and since there is merit in certain of its aspects, we can profitably start from his meaning. Parsons' view of general theory poses as the most crucial features, the following: (1) the development of a "unified conceptual schema for theory and research in the social sciences,"[13] not just sociology; (2) the stipulation that such theory be "A body of logically interdependent generalized concepts of empirical reference . . . which tends, ideally, to become 'logically closed' ";[14] (3) the postulate that "any important change in our knowledge of fact in the field in question must of itself change the statement of at least one of the propositions of the theoretical system and, through the logical consequences of this change, that of other propositions to a greater or lesser degree";[15] and (4) the proviso that the empirical referent for general theory in sociology is society qua society.[16]

The first premise that all human social behavior can and should be described in terms of a common conceptual framework, is important not only for seeking standard terminology but, even more, for implying concentration of effort on the non-idiosyncratic aspects of phenomena. Rural sociologists all too frequently are arrested by the unique and the local. The latent consequence of Parson's first proposition is that it focusses attention sooner, rather than "later," on commonalities and the nonunique.

The second element's stipulation of logical congruity and empirical reference for theory underscores our claim that change cannot be handled appropriately as a discrete specialty. An adequate theory for change must recognize the generality of process, addressing the time dimension directly and characteristically.[17]

At the same time, Parsons' emphasis on codification in general theory, seen in the first and second points, needs to be narrowed in scope and rearranged in stress for our purposes. Whereas Parsons sees codification cutting across the various social science disciplines, we feel that the concrete and immediate exigencies incumbent on rural sociology restrict codification to data within the discipline. This is not totally disadvantageous. Given the strong tendency for rural sociology to be less than a tightly ordered set of observations and findings, interdisciplinary codification would seem to be premature, at least until the time when we have our own house in order. Ultimately, of course, codification should proceed across disciplines, but first there is much which can be done within our own field, not the least of which is to collate research information so that "knowledge of fact" obtained in one problem area is not totally ignored in a slightly different research context. As a result, attempts at codification, however feeble and limited, are an immediate requirement. We feel that codification should be viewed as a developmental task, proceeding in a tentative and exploratory fashion within a field until knowledge and methodological skills are developed which permit integrations of wider scope.

It also appears to us that the stress on logical consistency, in Parsons' sense, can be sterile or at least extremely difficult to promulgate in an applied context[18] and, again within the discipline, is less required than the need to sort out empirical uniformities among discrete areas of extant investigation and to systematically order them. This is not to say that conceptual clarification and unification can or should be ignored.[19]

With respect to the third and fourth elements of Parsons' view of theory, it is our suspicion that currently it is more readily possible to have theories of change in various concrete subsystems than to obtain an empirically grounded theory of change which would generalize the empirical reference to the highly abstract level of a "system of subsystems" specifiable as "society." However lamentable it might be, it is the case that most empirical research—and certainly that in rural sociology—has taken a subsystem or, at best, subsystems focal point for data collection. Of course, these materials can be made applicable to a societal level of analysis. However, without systematically building up to higher levels of generality by bridging laterally across current research areas, application at the societal level would require wide inductive leaps subject to considerable speculation, lack of verification, and possible error.[20]

In summary, what we mean by a "general theory perspective" for change is analogous in many respects to Robert Merton's "theories of the middle-range."[21] The strong reference to empirical and pragmatic considerations are the same. On the other hand, Merton's type of formulation does not seem to offer a sufficiently broad orientation to give the fundamental and pervasive aspects of process and change their due. At times this is attributable to the free license granted by middle-range theory to focus on a limited range of material, which may indeed show highly stable and patterned processes. The possible factual correctness of statics—and the implied convenience of analysis—can be too easily generalized. Even more important, as characteristically understood, "middle-range theory" emphasizes codification of research findings within substantive research areas more so than among them. A predilection toward the latter is the primary strength of a "general theory" orientation.[22] It is not that in middle-range theory there is necessarily no attempt at codification among conventional research areas— Merton's own work has shown this[23]—rather, it seems to come secondarily. Since time and talent are limited, since research efforts have to choose among goals, the matter of primary or secondary emphasis is crucially important. As Merton himself notes, "to say that both the general and the special theories are needed is to be correct and banal: the problem is one of allocating our scant resources."[24]

AN ILLUSTRATIVE APPLICATION OF A GENERAL THEORY ORIENTATION TO ADOPTION AND MOBILITY RESEARCH

The plea for a general theory orientation to social change raises at least two important questions. Why has the perspective been lacking? How can it be attained? The first question has already been touched upon in our discussion of why the perspective is required but the matter needs closer scrutiny. An answer to the second question can only be sketched in this chapter because it is a vast empirical task. To make the discussion of both questions more realistic, an illustrative application to farm practice adoption and social mobility research will be used.

For our purposes the areas selected for study are not crucial, but these happen to represent two areas of considerable current significance to rural sociologists. Both farm practice adoption and mobility research have received a large amount of research resources and both involve important social problems in that they are related to the salient American values of self-fulfillment and maximum utilization of talent. For the farmer, adoption of farm practices is usually regarded as vital in maximizing returns from farming. Slowness in adoption or failure to take on new practices is the social problem.[25] For the farmer, and more so for the larger society, research on mobility is considered important in minimizing talent loss in the movement of people from rural to urban sectors of society. The outcome sought through mobility is less equivocal than for adoption. It would appear that moving the chronic population surplus in rural areas out of agriculture is the intended concern here, although there is a backlog of sentiment and programs to "improve" rural life in order to keep the people on the land.[26] In any case, mobility research and studies of adoption incorporate both prongs of the American "farm problem"—a highly productive economic organization and a relatively overabundant farm population. Both areas are patently concerned with "change" under any definition.

Before proceeding it should be made clear that we are working with "mobility" and "adoption" ("diffusion") as these topics have been investigated by American rural sociologists, with most of the research done in the United States and of recent vintage. In the nature of the case this means that adoption is equivalent to diffusion of technological innovations and refers to the process by which a cultural item is spread within and among social systems of a society, rather than to intersocietal transfer as studied by anthropologists.[27] In similar fashion, the meaning of mobility is essentially transfer from agricultural jobs to those outside agriculture, including the intervening variables of intention to move and occupational aspirations.

Reasons for Failure To Integrate the Areas

Superficial Reasons. In attempting to account for the failure to integrate materials in the two areas, the first point that can be made is quite obvious, but no less important because of it. The two areas of research are not commonly considered to be fundamentally related.[28] Given extant research as a starting point this is understandable in a superficial sense.[29] That is, typically the subjects in the research areas are at different age levels; social mobility studies have concentrated on youth while adoption studies have covered the adult age spectrum. Furthermore, the subjects are typically in different study settings—the school providing a captive audience, the farmstead requiring voluntary cooperation.

This has to some extent dictated the kinds of research tools used and, in turn, the basic variables investigated. Paper-and-pencil tests are the conventional means of getting at underlying social-psychological variables, and are more easily employed in a mass interview situation with a captive school population. On the other hand, adoption studies have tended to stress demographic variables more heavily, because these data presumably are easier to obtain in field situations.

Correlated with differences in the kinds of variables studied in the two areas, the context for evaluating the variables has been characteristically different. In adoption studies the comparisons have tended to be internal—farmer compared with farmer. This has not been deemed particularly appropriate for mobility studies, where rural-urban contrasts have been emphasized. However, for our purposes, this difference as well as the others cited are at best matters of relative emphasis and do not represent basic incompatibilities. They do not seem to represent the fundamental reasons for the characteristic failure to relate the two areas. This has to be sought at a different level of analysis.

Structural Reasons. In one sense the structural context of the two research areas has been somewhat different. Mobility studies have a longer history and have started from a broader base; they have not been pursued exclusively in the land-grant college Agricultural Experiment Station context. The negative political implications of off-farm mobility have probably contributed to less aggressive pursuit of mobility research in the Colleges of Agriculture. In contrast, adoption research has been tremendously facilitated and expedited by the Experiment Stations. But significantly, however, both have been pursued largely from an applied or "problem" orientation in tightly administered social structures.

Now whether it need be true logically, it is true historically that a strong "problem" orientation administered through bureaucratic organization tends to drastically limit the perspective from which the problem is viewed.[30] If the subject area is identified as a "social problem," societal support of research is more directly forthcoming but commensurate pressures are engendered for immediate, clear-cut, and practicable answers. Unfortunately, the more elaborate and expansive in scope a problem gets defined by a researcher, the less immediate seems to be a solution and the less clear-cut the answer. As a consequence, the complex nature of the actual social situation is all too easily oversimplified by neglecting the notion of system.[31] This, in turn, leads to lack of examination of the connections between directly related areas, let alone facets which are in certain substantive respects different, as in the case of mobility and adoption studies.[32] In boldest terms, the "project" system of sponsored research does not readily facilitate codification.[33] The failure to codify mobility and diffusion studies recapitulates the pattern of rural sociological research more generally.

Ideological Reasons. Structural constraint against codification has a concomitant ideological component. Thus in one sense the failure to relate mobility and diffusion studies is the result of rural sociology essentially turning its back on a sociological perspective. The vantage point of society is all but lost in attempts to get at "hard" data which can be unambiguously accepted as "empirical" research, particularly by the action agencies which sponsor so much of the rural sociological research. The "problem" orientation of these agencies has generally been to the actor rather than the system. The individual per se is assumed to be more understandable, more manipulatable and, hence, presumably more assured as a unit on which to base ameliorative effort than is the group. Thus, most research in mobility and diffusion essentially takes the individual as a discrete entity at a particular point in time with little regard for the broad social milieu in which he is immersed and from whose effects he cannot escape. As a result of the acquiescence to a nominalist position,[34] there is a strong tendency to perceive different kinds of persons as representing different kinds of problem situations and so there is a failure to grasp, or even seek, the similarities among diverse roles and statuses.

The Importance of Broad Perspectives for Codification

Historical Perspective. We believe that a shift in focus making room for a much broader perspective is indicated. As a first step toward codification, we must look beyond the individual at a moment in time and place, seeing him as part of an ongoing process. We would then be able to see different kinds of individuals involved in different kinds of social problems but at the same time see the underlying similarity of historical context, i.e., the transition to an industrial-urban type of society.

In identifying such a position for American rural sociology we are not trying to promote any one particular formulation that has been concerned with the movement and direction of societal organization, or, more specifically, of the social structure of Western civilization. The Weberian concept of increasing rationalization and bureaucratization of structure,[35] Durkheim's thesis on mechanical and organic solidarity and the division of labor,[36] Toennies' polarity of Gemeinschaft-Gesellschaft and the tendency toward "maturation" in Gesellschaft,[37] among many others, point in the same direction despite diversities of emphasis and insight. Arguing the need for this perspective, it should be clear, is not a calling for "grand" theory with its speculative roots, but recognition of a "simple" fact of the existential world caught in various facets by the conceptualizations of these classical sociologists.

The processes of industrialization and urbanization are going on and need to be recognized, described, and analyzed, particularly as they relate to and have meaning for the individual.[38] In a very real sense the task of sociology, as C. Wright Mills has put it, is ". . . to understand the larger historical scene in terms of its meaning for the inner life and the external career of a variety of individuals."[39] With the exigencies imposed on the discipline (exemplified above in a modified acceptance of Parsons) the task for rural sociology is to conceptualize the particulars of the process in terms which potentially can be applied to other specialized areas. The first step in that direction is active recognition that "disparate" substantive areas are capable of fruitful joint consideration, if for no other reason than that they are part of the same historical situation.

Given the societal perspective, adoption and mobility are at the very least circumstantially connected. The pattern and degree of social mobility vitally affect the rate of adoption. This can be most simply appreciated if it is recognized that, in the mobility context, an apt way of characterizing the low-income farmer is to see him as that person who has not "chosen" (willfully or by uncontrollable circumstance) to be a commercial agriculturalist or holder of a nonfarm occupation; he has chosen to be socially nonmobile. We know such persons have much lower rates of adoption on most items than do commercial farmers.

A different way of stating this phenomenon in its causal dimension is to recognize that in a very real sense the objective outcome of adoption is social mobility. Modern technology enhances the farmer's economic position (or at least combats deterioration) and thereby facilitates social movement since one's relation to scarce goods is crucial in nearly all stratification systems and particularly so in the urban-industrial type society. This impact exists despite the fact that it is not always directly intuited as motive either by the subject or by the analyst.[40] In addition, an important relationship exists between mobility and adoption through noneconomic motives such as prestige or social honor wherein adoption of new practices connotes certain life styles and levels of "consumership."

It is quite clear on the reverse side of the adoption-mobility combination that a high level of adoption adds pressure for out-migration and impels mobility concerns, particularly for young people. With the level of living constant or increasing, no nation can increase the total population, decrease the proportion in agriculture, and not have a high level of technological innovation acceptance. But the matter goes beyond this. Lipset and Bendix have convincingly demonstrated with a mass of empirical studies that in an industrial society a sustained level of upward mobility is, if not a functional requisite, then certainly a functional concomitant of such a society.[41] With this the case, the analytical (and actual) choice situation which adheres in mobility is presented more frequently in industrial type societies, like the American case.

Thematic Perspective. This last remark exposes a logical connection between adoption and mobility which is particularly important for codification. Both areas deal with receptiveness to alternatives which are new to the person in the choice situation. This is patently the case with respect to adoption. Here adoption is not to be confused with invention—even though, as H. G. Barnett indicates,[42] the mental processes involved may be similar. In talking about innovations and new practices it must be remembered that these are only relatively new. By the same token educational and occupational alternatives, although they are not normally labeled as innovations, are new to a young person in a choice situation in much the same sense as are items of technological diffusion. As rural sociologists operating in an industrial-urban milieu, we should be interested in these alternatives precisely because they are new. We should be interested in the choice between traditional career and training alternatives and those which are not part of the rural tradition.

Unfortunately the history of the profession is not an ally here. Traditionally mobility and adoption as phenomena are cast into the mold, respectively, of "social" or "vertical" change—with emphasis on hierarchical movement of people, change in position, and percolation of ideas through strata—and "cultural" or "horizontal" change—with emphasis on material culture and its diffusion. Cast into separate sets cultural, and particularly technological, change and social change have been treated as more or less discrete. In its most extreme vein, vigorously maintaining the distinction has led to a considerable volume of naive deterministic thinking—specifically, various brands of technological determinism.[43] For analytical purposes it may in some instances be convenient to view technology as the force behind social change. In all too many instances the convenience of this thoughtway has become confused with notions of cause in a more basic sense.[44] If for no other reason than to help escape this snare does the commonality we suggest for adoption and mobility commend itself.

In summary, from the broad perspectives of (1) transition to industrial-urban social organization and (2) actors as decision makers choosing among old and new alternatives, the two research areas of mobility and adoption in rural sociology are very closely related. Similarities and interconnections have been pointed out and superficial dissimilarities hopefully dissolved, but this is only the beginning of a difficult integrative task if the two areas are really to be subsumed under more general theory, with the insights in one area feeding into the other. We have only argued the task can and should be done; we have by no means done it.[45] Rather, we have tried to present and illustrate a necessary metasociological position that can facilitate codification, a perspective which is currently alien to most rural sociologists. We have also pointed out certain structural and ideological aspects of the discipline which may vitiate efforts in this direction.

Apart from these considerations, perhaps the greatest difficulty in empirical codification lies in the fact that individual researchers often are overwhelmed by the multiplicity of variables relevant or assumed to be relevant in particular situations and by the tremendous accumulation of research and raw data. We have not yet really begun to raise questions about the transferability of particular findings to different contexts, even contexts as closely related as those involved in decisions to farm or not to farm, and decisions to adopt or not adopt a farm practice. However, if we keep before us the simple maxim that social change (and theories thereto), along with codification, is the business of everybody and not that of some specialist, we will have taken the first step toward improvement.

FOOTNOTES

[1] Edward C. Devereux, Jr., "Parsons' Sociological Theory," in The Social Theories of Talcott Parsons, Max Black, ed., Prentice-Hall, 1961, p. 53.

[2] Everett M. Rogers, Social Change in Rural Society, Appleton-Century-Crofts, 1960, p. 3.

[3] This plea is, of course, not new or idiosyncratic. See Florian Znaniecki's stress on "dynamic systems" in Cultural Sciences, Univ. of Ill. Press, Urbana, 1953. In a sense this plea also stands as a corollary to Kingsley Davis' insightful argument that good sociological analysis is never less than a "functional" analysis—because the two are synonymous when functionalism means anything at all. But more important, just as Davis sees impediments to rapid advancement for sociology through conceiving functionalism as a distinct, homogeneous phenomenon, we also feel that this is true in trying to consider change as a distinct, discrete substantive area. See the discussion below and compare Kingsley Davis, "The Myth of Functional Analysis as a Special Method in Sociology and Anthropology," Amer. Sociol. Rev., 24:757-72, 1959.

[4] For an example of this type of definition and a defense of change as a special area of interest, cf., Alvin Boskoff, "Social Change: Major Problems in the Emergence of Theoretical and Research Foci," in Modern Sociological Theory, Howard Becker and Alvin Boskoff, eds., Dryden, 1957, pp. 260-302.

[5] Spaulding has implied, though not directly stated, that the tendency toward this is a major factor in the faulty analysis found in much past and current American rural sociology. His plea for "clarity in perspective on the change which agriculture is undergoing" can only make

sense on these grounds. Cf. Irving A. Spaulding, "Change in Rural Life and the Reintegration of a Social System," Rural Soc., 24:215-25, 1959.

[6]Unfortunately discussions in the sociological literature are almost nonexistent. The methodology texts are conspicuously inattentive to the matter. Some insights are given in Morris Rosenberg and Wagner Thielens, with Paul F. Lazarsfeld, "The Panel Study," in Marie Jahoda, et al., Research Methods in Social Relations, Dryden, 1951, pp. 588-609; Nathan Goldfarb, An Introduction to Longitudinal Statistical Analysis, The Free Press, Glencoe, Ill., 1960, pp. 55-73.

[7]For a succinct and penetrating overview in this respect see C. C. Zimmerman, "Contemporary Trends in Sociology in America and Abroad," in Contemporary Sociology, Joseph S. Roucek, ed., Philosophical Library, New York, 1958, pp. 3-25, esp. pp. 3-12; or his Patterns of Social Change, Public Affairs Press, Washington, D.C., 1956.

[8]See particularly Talcott Parsons, Toward A General Theory of Action, edited with E. A. Shils, Harvard Univ. Press, Cambridge, Mass., 1951; The Social System, The Free Press, Glencoe, Ill., 1951, esp. pp. 536-55; Essays in Sociological Theory, rev. ed., The Free Press, Glencoe, Ill., 1954, esp. pp. 212-37.

[9]The logical requirement of needing to know over all the normal operation of a system in order to even identify change is also involved and lies behind Parsons' contention that before one can have a theory of "change" one must have a knowledge of "nonchange." This understanding supports Parsons' claim that he is not unconcerned with change, as his critics often contend. Cf., The Social System, op. cit., pp. 480-535.

[10]Substantiation of this point with completely unequivocal data is, of course, not possible. Judging the extent of influence or the degree of acceptance of a set of ideas at a moment in time is alone difficult enough. Trying, within this, to gauge a single person's influence and acceptance is next to impossible. As a result, the characterizations rest in large part upon our "intuitive" sizing up of American rural sociologists. Some objective evidence is available, however, for our position.

Theory integration presupposes the acceptance of theory. However, the close interconnections and mutual reciprocities that are supposed to exist between theory and research are not evidenced in the rural sociological record. Thus, two of the six major shortcomings noted by Taves and Gross ("A Critique of Rural Sociology Research, 1950," Rural Soc., 17:109-18, 1952) were "an apparent lack of theoretical orientation in the development of the research problem" and "lack of concern for orienting findings to a general theory," p. 117. For concurrence on this point note also, Robin M. Williams, Jr., "Review of Current Research in Rural Sociology," Rural Soc., 11:103-14, 1946; William H. Sewell, "Needed Research in Rural Sociology," Rural Soc., 15:115-30, 1950, and "Some Observations on Theory Testing," Rural Soc., 21:1-12, 1956, esp. pp. 1-2; Robert C. Bealer, "Variable Research in Rural Sociology: Some Suggestions for Needed Implementations," mimeo., 1959.

With respect specifically to Parsons, it strikes us as important that neither The Social System nor Toward A General Theory of Action was deemed relevant or significant enough to rural sociology to receive a book review in the journal. Again, a content analysis of Rural Sociology for the years 1951-61 showed that Parsons was cited at least once in footnotes in only 20 (5.2 per cent) of the 388 articles and research notes covered in the period. In contrast to Parsons, by the same criterion, Lowry Nelson was cited in 8 per cent of the material; T. Lynn Smith in 7 per cent; Edmund deS. Brunner in 5.4 per cent; W. A. Anderson in 5.2 per cent; C. R. Hoffer in 4.1 per cent. None of these people are normally considered as approaching the position on general theory manifested by Parsons. They tend to be oriented in the opposite direction.

The content analysis also showed that while Parsons' work is not a currently strong moving force in rural sociology, its influence may be increasing. Of the 20 articles, seven merely cited Parsons in an incidental way and all of these appeared prior to 1958. Seven articles were judged as explicitly and integrally incorporating aspects of Parsons' work. Six of that number appeared after 1957. C. P. Loomis was cited in 12.6 per cent of the articles and his theoretical position is essentially congruent with that of Parsons.

[11]This characterization does not mean that Parsons refuses to recognize substantive uniqueness. His differentiation of four systems (organism, personality, social system, and culture) within the general theory of action rests in part upon such criteria. See "An Approach to Psychological Theory in Terms of the Theory of Action," in Psychology: A Study of Science, Sigmund Koch, ed., McGraw-Hill, 1959, 3:612-709. Similarly, his willingness to find a differentiated role and function for the extant social sciences rests on recognition of substantive differences. See for example The Social System, op. cit., pp. 536-55. While the first situation is fundamentally essential to his theory and the second is, in part, a gesture to vested interests in the political arena of the social sciences, both nicely point up that relative primacy is not equatable to exclusive emphasis, but primacy there is. In this regard, an instructive case is Parsons' contribution to Toward a Unified Theory of Human Behavior, Roy Grinker, ed., Basic Books, 1956, pp. 55-69, 190-200, 325-39, et passim.

[12]We cannot, obviously, go into detail as to why this is true, but the broad outlines can be obtained by noting the theme contained in Paul Furfey, "Social Science and the Problem of Values," in Symposium on Sociological Theory, Llewellyn Gross, ed., Row, Peterson, 1959, pp. 509-30, esp. pp. 517-24; and Gideon Sjoberg, "Operationalism and Social Research," ibid., pp. 603-27, esp. pp. 609-16. It should be made clear that the decision offered here is not based on normative grounds but on an appraisal of what in fact can be effected given current, and forseeable future, conditions in American society.

[13]Parsons, T., Toward A General Theory of Action, op. cit., p. 4.

[14]———, Essays in Sociological Theory, op. cit., p. 212.

[15]———, The Structure of Social Action, 2nd ed., The Free Press, Glencoe, Ill., 1949, p. 7.

[16]———, The Social System, op. cit., pp. 18-19.

[17]Zimmerman, "Contemporary Trends," op. cit., has written quite cogently in this respect that ". . . much of contemporary sociology has abandoned the major study of social change. It has done so by making 'structure,' not the time-course of society, the major problem of sociology. According to these existentialist postulates, change is only a minor sociological preoccupation." P. 9.

[18]Devereux, op. cit., has made the observation that "Certainly he [Parsons] has done a great deal more of theorizing than any other contemporary American sociologist; and it is also probably true that he has done rather less of anything else. At a time when others have been turning more and more to empirical research, Parsons has never published a paper reporting directly on data derived from a specific empirical investigation." P. 1.

[19]Some important work has been done and is being carried on in this direction, most notably by Charles P. Loomis and associates; see particularly Social Systems, D. Van Nostrand, 1960; Modern Social Theories, D. Van Nostrand, 1961.

[20]For a case study in this respect note Parsons' article, "Some Considerations on the Theory of Social Change," Rural Soc., 26:219-39, 1961.

[21]Robert K. Merton, Social Theory and Social Structure, rev. ed., The Free Press, Glencoe, Ill., 1957, pp. 5-9.

[22]Parsons makes the case more pointed, asserting that codification, ". . . necessarily . . . involves reference to levels of generality higher than the level represented in the particular items of theory being codified." See his "General Theory in Sociology," in Sociology Today, Robert K. Merton, Leonard Broom and Leonard S. Cottrell, Jr., eds., Basic Books, 1959, pp. 3-4 (italics added).

[23]Cf., Merton, op. cit., pp. 225-80.

[24]Ibid., p. 9.

[25]The goal of understanding adoption so as to be able to increase rates of acceptance is anomalous in the context of American agriculture. It is sometimes questionable whether there is a need for implementing rates of adoption, given current productive capacity which, in turn, is directly traceable to the technological and managerial efficiency of our agriculture. There seems to be little concern over this point in rural sociology because justification of the need for increasing rates of adoption is often laid in the context of underdeveloped countries, where it would be difficult to oppose increased rates of innovation acceptance. For a questioning posture toward uninhibited adoption rates in the case of American agriculture see Frederick C. Fliegel, "Aspirations of Low-Income Farmers and Their Performance and Potential for Change," Rural Soc., 24:205-14, 1959.

[26]For a lucid and many-sided discussion of various facets of this matter see the sundry essays in Problems and Policies of American Agriculture, (Center for Agricultural and Economic Development, sponsors), Iowa State Univ. Press, Ames, 1959.

[27]Cf., Felix M. Keesing, Culture Change, Stanford Univ. Press, Stanford, Calif., 1953.

[28]Cf., Herbert F. Lionberger, Adoption of New Ideas and Practices, Iowa State Univ. Press, Ames, 1960. The compilation and analysis of some 100 research studies there is discouraging in terms of the recognition of this point and is nicely focused in Lionberger's chapter on "Research Limitations." His discussion on pp. 112-13 and 114-15 is particularly cogent. That Lionberger does at least indicate this matter as limiting is a note of encouragement.

[29]All references to empirical research, unless otherwise specifically cited, refer to generalizations drawn from our knowledge of these

areas. For bibliographic entree to diffusion and mobility, respectively, see, ibid., and the footnote references in A. O. Haller, "The Occupational Achievement Process of Farm-Reared Youth in Urban Industrial Society," Rural Soc., 25:321-33, 1950; and Lee G. Burchinal, "Differences in Educational and Occupational Aspirations of Farm, Small-Town, and City Boys," Rural Soc., 26:107-21, 1961.

[30]Sjoberg, op. cit., holds that "history" and "logicality" are essentially synonymous. The point is moot on the degree of congruity but the probability that a high correlation will continue in the immediate future seems beyond question. For a case study of the limiting quality of bureaucratic organization on research perspective see Joel Smith, Francis M. Sim, and Robert C. Bealer, "Client Structure and the Research Process," in Human Organization Research, Richard N. Adams and Jack J. Preiss, eds., Dorsey Press, Homewood, Ill., pp. 41-56.

[31]Robin Williams, out of his wide background in research, has written cogently that ". . . much of the public and private action in our day is taken without consideration of the repercussions that may arise out of the total social system within which the action takes place. And often even a systematic analysis of various isolated parts of the social structure turns out to be highly unrealistic, if not actually fallacious, by reason of this same neglect of context." American Society, rev. ed., Knopf, 1960, p. 5.

[32]There is no negative evaluation meant here for mobility or adoption studies in their own right. The failure refers to the situation between the areas and not within them. In fact, one of the reasons for selecting mobility and adoption is just that they are among the more adequately researched areas in rural sociology. Whatever the situation with these two areas, it was presumed that things would be no better, and probably worse, using other less adequately researched specialties.

[33]For a provocative discussion of this point cf. C. Arnold Anderson, "Trends in Rural Sociology," in Sociology Today, Robert K. Merton, Leonard Broom, and Leonard S. Cottrell, Jr., eds., Basic Books, 1959, pp. 360-75, esp. pp. 365-69.

[34]For a lively discussion of this matter see Charles K. Warriner, "Groups Are Real: A Reaffirmation," Amer. Sociol. Rev., 21:549-54, 1956.

[35]Max Weber, The Theory of Social and Economic Organization, translated by A. M. Henderson and Talcott Parsons, Oxford Univ. Press, New York, 1947; and From Max Weber: Essays in Sociology, translated by H. H. Gerth and C. Wright Mills, Oxford Univ. Press, New York, 1946.

[36]Emile Durkheim, The Division of Labor in Society, translated by George Simpson, The Free Press, Glencoe, Ill., 1947.

[37]Ferdinand Toennies, Community and Society, translated by C. P. Loomis, Mich. State Univ. Press, East Lansing, 1957.

[38]This perspective has been enjoined by some persons within the field. For example, see Spaulding, op. cit., and his "Perspective on Urbanization," Rural Soc., 27:1-6, 1962; and Edward Hassinger, "Social Relations Between Centralized and Local Social Systems," Rural Soc., 26:354-64, 1961.

[39]C. Wright Mills, The Sociological Imagination, Oxford Univ. Press, New York, 1959, p. 5.

[40]It might be pointed out that the area of direct impact of adoption is different from the context used in most research on mobility, particularly the "aspiration" studies. Mobility studies generally are concerned with the status of the urban occupation but not with prestige differences (or relative evaluation and position within a status or rank) in agriculture, whereas innovation impinges most directly through the processes of economic competition and resultant successes or failures in entrepreneurship.

[41]Seymour Martin Lipset and Reinhard Bendix, Social Mobility in Industrial Society, Univ. of Calif. Press, Berkeley, 1959, esp. pp. 57-64, 72-75.

[42]H. G. Barnett, Innovation: The Basis of Cultural Change, McGraw-Hill, 1953.

[43]William F. Ogburn's concept is perhaps the most notable. See Social Change, B. W. Huebsch, New York, 1922, pp. 200-280. For a more recent treatment cf. Hornell Hart, "The Hypothesis of Cultural Lag: A Present-Day View," in Francis R. Allen et al., Technology and Social Change, Appleton-Century Crofts, 1957, pp. 417-34. The criticisms of that idea have been many and trenchant. See for example Kingsley Davis, Human Society, Macmillan, 1949, pp. 626 ff.; James W. Woodard, "Critical Notes on the Culture Lag Concept," Social Forces, 12:388-98, 1933. Robin Williams makes the most telling point when he writes: "In American society . . . the culture has been characterized by a value system that made it possible for economic and technological activities to change rapidly and hence to take on special causal significance. In other societies and in other times, the role of technology in social change is definitely minor." American Society, op. cit., p. 571n.

[44]E.g., ". . . it has been empirically determined that technology has brought more 'liberal' attitudes, less ritualism and fatalism, improved acceptance rates for new agricultural practices, and many other such changes." Alvin L. Bertrand, ed., Rural Sociology, McGraw-Hill, 1958, pp. 408-9.

[45]A positive illustrative example that it can be done is given by Herbert Menzel, "Innovation, Integration, and Marginality: A Survey of Physicians," Amer. Sociol. Rev., 25:704-13, 1960. The article illustrates the coordination possible within the area of adoption research. By sorting through a considerable volume of material on the relationships between decision makers and their peers and the influence of these relationships on decisions, a series of fairly crucial hypotheses are stated and at least partially tested. This is an illustration of theory, in the form of particular propositions about relationships between variables, that can easily be transferred from one decision-making context to another. With this type of theory, and a lot of work in coding the abundance of particular information about actors and situations into usable categories, research can move forward much more efficiently and we will be a lot closer to developing a coherent body of empirical knowledge.

10

Irwin T. Sanders

Community Development Programs in Sociological Perspective

A
T LEAST FOUR searching questions are being asked about
community development today. One of these, in which
economists take much interest, concerns the relative advantages or disadvantages of community development programs
over other types of planned economic change in building up social capital in an industrializing society. A second question, of
particular interest to the political scientist, is the effect of
locally based improvement projects upon political behavior and
popular expectations. In other words, how useful is community
development as a preparation for activity in the larger governmental arena? A third question is philosophical in nature: By
what right do national leaders or those in foreign aid programs
embark upon grand schemes of social change which tear down
the traditional fabric of peasant society, alter the class system,
and modify basic value orientations?

Although most sociologists familiar with community development programs, either at home or abroad, would have their own
personal answers to these three questions, there remains a
fourth question which is primarily within their professional domain. It may be stated as follows: Assuming that responsible
leaders have answered the above three questions in favor of
community development programs, how does one go about the
task of making such programs work?

Such a question may at first seem to relate only to the tactics or techniques of practice, but the more one studies it, the
more its theoretical overtones stand out as significant. To
make community development programs work on a large scale,
in many places simultaneously, leaders and planners must have

307

a theoretical knowledge of social change. Or even to make a
single program work well in a given locality, leaders require a
knowledge of the group process. When this question, therefore,
of making community development programs work is addressed
to a sociologist, as it should be, he finds himself drawing upon
many subfields of his discipline in an effort to relate pertinent
theory to what the operator views as a practical problem.[1]

At such times, the sociologist becomes painfully aware that
much of the theory upon which he is drawing is untested so far
as social action programs are concerned. Indeed, for some
features of the program he may not find any relevant theory at
all. But the sociologist does have a conceptual approach, a
theoretical scheme, which helps him view a community development program as a system of social action and, in such terms,
systematize what is known and draw up hypotheses for further
research. Before we turn to the research needs, however, it is
important to note just what roles sociologists have played in the
past in connection with community development programs.

An early role was monitory, or that of warning people to take
account of social considerations. In this role, rural sociologists
brought to bear upon the problems of those setting up community development and similar programs what social scientists had
already learned about similar social action attempts. Two documents attempting this were Experience with Human Factors in
Agricultural Areas of the World[2] and Farmers of the World:
The Story of Agricultural Extension.[3] Then came a number of
books which sought to state for American citizens the points
they should keep in mind in promoting community improvement
in the United States, with the stress being upon learning from
social scientists in order to avoid making too many serious
mistakes.[4] Universities set up bureaus or other units through
which sociologists, often outside the agricultural extension
service, could help local community leaders study their problems.[5] Often, this was done in conjunction with colleagues from
other disciplines, but the sociological dimension remained prominent. Playing this type of adviser's role called for considerable
caution since the sociologist was trying to show the relevance to
a specific community of various social science findings which
had been derived in the study of phenomena other than community development.

This situation was improved when sociologists moved into a
second role, along with some anthropologists and others: namely, that of analyst. By this time, in the early 1950's, enough
experience had been gained with community development, quite

apart from agricultural extension, to permit sociologists to examine the case studies, reports, and individual experience to the
point that they began to set down principles of community development.[6] Many of these principles were not unique to community development, for they related to human motivation wherever practised as well as to all types of planned social change
and local efforts to improve conditions. Yet, these principles—
for which sociologists by no means had the monopoly—did give
a specific focus to the community development movement and
did provide in vivid form some of the "human factor" aspects in
cross-cultural perspective. This was a step forward since
sociologists, sometimes attached formally as consultants to
large-scale community development programs, could base much
of their advice on codified experience (not research) drawn up
by unusually perceptive people. Eventually, agencies such as
the Social Welfare Section of the United Nations and the Community Development Division of the United States International
Cooperation Administration (now the Agency for International
Development, AID) drew up formal lists of principles which
they thought had universal applicability.[7]

Some of the sociologists moved from these roles into the
administrator role. Here they took on a whole new set of problems which they did not have as sociologists per se, but they did
see to it that social science insights were used wherever possible in the programs they were administering. Other sociologists became practitioners in that their concern became one of
direct application of sociological principles, as well as helps
from other fields, to the task of making community development
effective. Their job was not to advance sociology as a discipline,
but to advance community development. To do this they often had
to champion it in the face of other interests competing for funds
or personnel or answer critics who said that it was not the best
approach to accomplish set goals within a given country.

This trend toward practice is being countered in recent times
by the interest of a few sociologists in playing their research
role, with community development as the object of their research.[8] In the light of what has already been said, it is easy to
see why this has developed last. Earlier, the big push was to
get things started in many countries. There was no time for
basic research (so the administrators thought) and there was a
limited body of data to be researched, but the sociologists co-
operated as advisers because they thought that at least some
attention to the human factor would forestall some mistakes, if
not assure an unalloyed success.

This research role has now assumed even greater importance than formerly because of the larger amounts of money and personnel being invested in community development and the human hopes that are tied in with it.[9] That is why this presentation focuses primarily upon community development efforts as systems of social action, which need to be studied by sociologists.

But first, some clarification of the concept community development is necessary.[10] In a previous statement, I have called attention to the fact that the term is sometimes used in the sense of process,[11] with the stress upon what happens to the people and their social life; on other occasions it is used in the sense of method, or a means by which agriculture can be improved or health standards raised; or, it may refer to a formalized program, such as the various national community development plans, as found in India, Pakistan, or the Philippines; and, finally, it may be viewed as a movement to which people are emotionally committed, a cause to which they are dedicated.[12] Because of its many facets, community development cannot be explained in a single, simple definition, but for the time being, it can be said to be equated with community improvement efforts or with community organization (in the sense of moving toward desired public goals). The fuller explanation of the term will now follow as we describe its ideology.

COMMUNITY DEVELOPMENT IDEOLOGY

It is in the study of its ideology that we encounter some of the unique features of community development.[13] There are at least four aspects of this ideology that deserve brief mention: the stress upon amelioration; the emphasis upon voluntarism and self-help; the tenet of working with and not for or on those benefiting from a program; and the concept of service and even self-sacrifice.

Amelioration

Without the Western social value of amelioration there would be no community development as we know it today. At least three aspects of amelioration can be identified with the application of the scientific method to various sectors of Western society from the seventeenth century on down. First of all, amelioration carries with it the idea of progress, or the belief that life on this earth can be improved. Arthur James Todd reminds us that "Both the word and the idea, progress, are relatively new. In general the thought of antiquity clung to the decadence concept rather than to that of development."[14] And John W. Bennett, in his introduction to the issue of Human Organization devoted to Planned Social Change, indicates the novelty of the concept of planned change.[15] The modern concept of progress, little known in Medieval Europe, became a part of Western tradition as man came to believe that he could master Nature in many ways, that he could determine his own fate within certain broad limits, and that he had something to say about the disposition of the resources at his command.

Second, amelioration carries with it not just the belief in the possibility of progress but also a desire for improvement, which becomes a positive social value. In this sense motivation for desirable change gets built into the institutional structure and becomes a social force. Although there are many population pockets in the United States where people do not seem anxious to improve their daily life, the real contrast between cultures with and without amelioration as a major value is evidenced as one tries to persuade villagers in non-Western societies to change their ancient ways for improved methods of agriculture, sanitation, or child care. The concept of progress itself is still strange to them, although its diffusion occurs as isolation breaks down and people begin to desire the same benefits which they see or about which they hear.

Third, amelioration also carries with it the idea that some people are socially responsible for its pursuit and are to be held accountable. In Western European countries, according to the findings recently published by a team of Europeans observing community development in the United States,[16] the European local governments are chiefly held responsible for the initiation and implementation of community improvement; in the United States, the stress is upon citizen involvement and the responsibility of the private, voluntary associations in cooperation with local, state, and national governments.

Despite these differences between Europe and the United States, amelioration in its three-fold aspect of belief in progress, desire for improvement, and fixing of responsibility for betterment is chiefly a Western phenomenon, which the Communist world has adapted in a somewhat different context to its approach to social change. Community development as exported around the world is culture-bound and not necessarily built on readily accepted cultural universals. This is evident in an excellent summarizing statement of the philosophical base common to those pursuing community development:[17]

Community development, we agree, is a process of social action. It aims at the participation of increasingly large numbers of people both at decision making and at action stages. Its concern is the "whole community." Economic development or increased productivity offers a good place to begin but this has to be related to other community needs. In the long run productivity depends on whether the level of living in all its aspects is raised. Community development calls for coordination of all efforts. The job is too big for any one agency or any special interest to do it alone. This means that good communications among agencies are essential and that skill in resolving differences and working together has to be acquired. Community development is not an end in itself but a way of working. Since the job of building better communities is not likely ever to be finished, the real goal of community development cannot be the solution of any specific problem but the development of people who can continue to take leadership responsibly and wisely.

Such a philosophy of community development is as new in the developing countries as the technology from the West, the newly rising parliamentary institutions, and the changing conception of man and nature which is a part of the revolution of rising expectations. To us it is a commonplace; to the villager in Asia, Africa, or Latin America it is as threatening as it is promising. It is much to ask, as community development does, that progress be substituted for fatalism and that a sense of personal responsibility replace that previously assigned to the gods, landlords, or a distant government.

Voluntarism and Self-help

The discussion of amelioration already has touched upon the importance of voluntarism and self-help. Even a cursory examination of community development literature prepared in the United States shows the strong emphasis in this country upon citizen involvement, which is a feature being transferred, in theory at least, to the community development programs of the non-Western societies. William G. Lyfield and Warren H. Schmidt list as one of the five major community development trends in the United States:[18] "There is a belief in the close relation of community development and democratic process. Community development programs emphasize the importance of citizens deciding for themselves how the program is to develop." W. B. Baker, active in community development work in the Canadian province of Saskatchewan, writes:[19] "The key assumption in community development is that planned change ought to come about primarily through the participation of local people in the decision to change. Community development is thus basically an educational process involving individualized experience, learning, maturation and growth. It seeks to maximize opportunities for local self-determination." Implicit in this concept of voluntarism is the belief that only as local people are involved in deciding about their own affairs will they become trained for the more difficult task of deciding, as voters, matters of national scope.

Self-help pushes the idea of voluntarism a bit further by insisting that local people should not merely decide what should be done but that they should be active participants in the implementation of the decision.[20] This is justified by many community developers on philosophical grounds but is also a matter of much interest to the practical politicians who wish to tap the tremendous labor reserves in the local communities throughout the world. If local people build their own roads, their own recreational facilities, and devise and support programs for economic improvement, then scarce financial resources can be shifted to other uses. Self-help is one relatively inexpensive way, it is argued, of increasing social capital.[21]

The Specialist as a Catalyst

Another important ideological component is the insistence on the part of many community developers that they are catalysts who are supposed to find out what the local people want and help them to achieve these goals; they are not supposed to issue orders and impose their wills, unless it be by indirect persuasion and education.[22] It is at this point that theory and practice often part company since many specialists, borrowed for community development purposes from fields such as health, agriculture, education, engineering, cannot shift from the authoritarian roles they have customarily played to the nondirective roles implied in this oft-expressed ideological overtone. Furthermore, much confusion also results when the specialist tries to be "democratic" when local people expect him as an educated person to be authoritarian, a point to be touched upon again.

Community development ideology, particularly as elaborated by many Americans, would insist therefore that the community

developer be much more interested in the processes of decision
making, personal enrichment, building up of satisfying social
relationships among the people, than in the completion of some
specific physical achievement (such as a road, a small storage
dam, etc.), particularly if such an achievement were at the expense of some of these underlying processes.

Service and Self-sacrifice

Running through the ideological statements one also finds a
strain of service and self-sacrifice. This is related to a special definition of the community, which is viewed as a collectivity to which local members supposedly have responsibility—if
not out of altruism, then out of self-interest.[23] Without the presence of a service <u>motif</u> few professional community developers
would want to live and work in the isolated areas where the
need is greatest, since their training would qualify them for
better-paying jobs in urban centers. This is also one reason
why many religiously motivated institutions and bodies have
moved into the community development field and it also explains
why some political idealists find this a satisfying area of work.

This discussion of ideology should do more than indicate
some of the unique features of community development; it should
point up needed areas of research for those wishing to place
such programs in sociological perspective. We have long known
that there is often a discrepancy between what people say they
believe and what they do; and, at the same time, we also know
that people are often ready to sacrifice for something they think
very important. Many thousands of people are involved in community development around the world, and they obviously differ
in their emotional attachment to the idea as well as in their
cognitive acceptance of its importance. Is it not time that we
sought to develop some satisfactory typology of possible belief
patterns, of differing rationales, and then sought to relate these
to the characteristics of the people involved and to their
achievements? If certain beliefs sustain, support, motivate,
and lead to successful results as measured by the stated goals
of particular programs, what are these beliefs and how can they
be made a part of the orientation of a wider proportion of community development workers? Furthermore, careful analysis
of ideological traits can reveal a widely differing set of expectations on the part of those who are professionally involved,
those who are politically responsible, as well as those who are

the supposed beneficiaries. The available literature today is full of high-sounding statements, of basic tenets, of dogma even which says that unless certain kinds of approaches are used dire results will occur. Sociologists should start examining these beliefs in an effort to discover their operational consequences, if any. This is one step required to place community development in sociological perspective.

THE SOCIAL CONTEXT OF COMMUNITY DEVELOPMENT PROGRAMS

Put in simplest sociological terms, a community development program—whether national or local—is a set of social relation-ships. These constitute an entity or unit which can be defined, described, analyzed, and reorganized. Many features, such as ideology, attach to the program and are important, but the pro-gram moves centrally into the sociological domain when viewed as a network of social relationships in all of their complexity.

But before we undertake the delineation of the program itself as a unit of social action, we must set it in its social context, without reference to which it has little meaning. No community program, however well conceived, exists in isolation; nor does it often work out the way those planning it expected it to. This is because it encounters social reality as it moves from the planning stage to actual operation.

One obvious meaning of community development is that it occurs in or to a community. The program of planned change, which is what community development is, has the community as its social context. The recognition of this moves us farther ahead in developing a sociological perspective. Nevertheless, it can be troublesome since the community as a concept is very nebulous to so many people; they do not know how to look at its recurring patterns of interaction and see how these patterns are related to their own program. To others, the community proves understandably so complex a phenomenon that those bent on action cannot hope to learn all that is to be known about a community before starting their efforts at local improvement.[24] As a guide and an illustration, we might look at five features of the community as a social context for a community development program, assuming that the problem before us at the moment is that of getting action started in a particular place even though the plans may have been drafted in a capital city one thousand miles away, or may be the sudden inspiration of some concerned local citizens. In either case, the community development literature tells us that we should be aware, first, of the <u>locus</u> (the geographical space and the distribution of its population); second, the <u>social values</u>; third, the <u>norms</u>; fourth, the <u>stage of organizational development of the community</u>; and, fifth, its <u>ties with the larger society</u>.

Locus

The community development program usually seeks to effectuate change in a relatively limited geographical space. It deals with a given population inhabiting a common area. Facts about this area and about this population have a direct bearing upon the type of program that is either needed or apt to succeed.[25] Thus far, the facts that we do have linking ecological and demographic factors to community action are relatively meager, although their significance is usually taken for granted. It may be easier, for example, to carry out a successful improvement program in a small urban neighborhood than for the city as a whole; or it may be more difficult to do so in a community so small that insufficient resources of money and specialized personnel result. In some cases, regional programs may prove far more successful than patchwork efforts by the smaller units making up the region. The social context, therefore, consists of the geographic base: its resources in the way of services, institutions, human skills, and its communication with other places which may have considerable influence on its activities. Just how large an area may be staked out and whether or not it can properly be called a "community" is not nearly so important as the understanding of the limitations as well as opportunities which the <u>locus</u> or area chosen has for the program. One of the contributions of seeing the program in this dimension is its accent on that which is tangible, physical, visible, on that which many people can quickly understand in improved traffic flow, better housing, new school buildings, better crops, or more productive pastures. The literature on community development indicates, however, that many so-called community development programs stop merely with physical, material improvement but fail to achieve some of the broader, social goals which they espouse. This is why <u>locus</u>, representing as it does the geographical community, is part of the context and not the essence of community development. Although the people taken as a population (numbers, composition, educational attainment, etc.)

are a part of the context, it is only as they are seen as interacting persons and not as mere statistics that they relate directly to community development.

Social Values

Students of community development programs often suggest that the change agents "take into account" the local values.[26] For example, such values as efficiency versus avoidance of hurry; male supremacy versus women's rights; and prestige based on professional competence versus that based on family background could all come into play. One needs to understand how the values impinge on a given relationship in order to know why some statuses are higher and others lower. One's perception of roles often derives from the value system to which one subscribes. Let us imagine that a consultant has been called in by a local group intent on community development.[27] He may find himself in a dominant, subordinate, or coordinate relationship with the person or persons who have specifically requested his services:[28]

1. The consultant is dominant when he comes into the situation as a prestige figure. He assumes—and the client assumes—that he will take the lead, do the thinking for the client. This occurs when specialized knowledge is valued.

2. The consultant is subordinate when the community is not accustomed to the use of experts and does not value specialized knowledge. Local people may be suspicious of outsiders, downgrading anything from outside. Those calling him in may wish to use him to serve their own ends and have a predetermined role which they hope he will play, perhaps for a fee.

3. The consultant is in a coordinate status to the extent that others are willing to accept him and work with him as an equal. If teamwork is not a value, but respect for authority is deeply engrained, he finds a coordinate status hard to achieve. As a coordinate he seeks to work himself out of a job and leave the client in command of the situation, better able to go forward on his own.

In other words, values—which are intangible at best—can be made more specific when related not only to goals and means, soon to be discussed, but also to each of the relationships which are basic to the program system. Community or national values help, therefore, in explaining and predicting the status hierarchy found within the action system, since superordination is customarily permitted to or expected of those whose status embodies more of the sought-after values. It is only in such terms

that Americans can see the rationale behind the efforts of an
official of the Agency for International Development seeking to
recruit thirteen anthropologists or rural sociologists for community development assignments in Southeast Asia, who said:
"Even though these specialists are in short supply, we can take
only men. Women would not be accepted." Whether he was
right or wrong, may be debated, but he was reflecting his interpretation of the value systems of these countries.

Norms

These, like values, are part of the cultural envelope surrounding community action programs. They constitute the "blueprints
for behavior." Some ways of behaving are permitted, some are
not. Local people, or even whole nations, have worked out ways
they prefer to use in dealing with some basic life problem.
Community organizers are accustomed to hear when they suggest some proposal: "That may work elsewhere, but it would
never succeed in this community." Or, some behavior might be
considered appropriate for some people, such as a high official,
but not deemed appropriate for those of lesser standing. A
community development program, therefore, operates in the
midst of a number of local do's and don'ts. It may generate
some of its own norms of behavior within the program, but its
members—whether operators of the program or beneficiaries
of it—are enmeshed in the folkways of the larger social setting.
Inevitably, a successful community development program reinforces some norms while threatening others since its purpose
is to usher in social change. We need to know with much greater precision than we now do, just how and why norms are modified and the extent to which they can be flaunted by those seeking
to introduce new behavior patterns in the economy, the family,
and in local government.

Stage of Organizational Development of the Community

As economic specialization grows, new forms of social organization spring up as well—cooperatives, reading associations,
veterans organizations—in fact, a whole host of groups and institutions which cater to newly felt social needs. Community
development programs must fit into or at least take account of
the kind of social structure existent at the time. As a matter

of fact, some students of developing countries or the less developed regions of an industrial society make use of a number of continua, which help compare different communities with respect to political involvement, economic complexity, religious divisions, urbanization, and the like. One part of this organization pattern is the leadership structure, which keeps the community going from day to day by the exercise of responsibility, decision making, and the social control which they consider necessary.

Another feature of the organization development is the class structure which has emerged or is emerging, for in some parts of the world this is the feature which has most relevance to efforts to introduce new farm and home practices and educational skills.

These points suggest the need for further research on the connection between the community development program and the basic social structure which surrounds it.[29] Can democratic procedures in such a program work effectively in an authoritarian social structure? If so, under what circumstances and with what emphasis? What is the desired relation between specific types of community leaders to the program itself? We can state some glib hypotheses about such matters but, upon closer examination, find these hypotheses usually reflect our Western orientation and are not necessarily based on a careful sifting of evidence already available in scattered reports.

Local Ties With the Larger Society

As already indicated, the social context includes more than the local community—though it be the geographical focus. Outside agencies and organizations frequently are the official sponsors of local programs.[30] In a developing country, the new forces being generated in the urban centers have a way of quickly finding their way, perhaps in transmuted form, to the rural areas. Villages and even towns that heretofore have been almost entirely bypassed by government services are now being given much attention by health teams, teachers, farm specialists, recruiting officers from the armed forces, and political rivals for the newly established parliaments. Where the spirit of change is in the air, even in the remote areas, community development programs have an asset, although this may be offset by an impatience at the slowness of progress or at the fact that government largesse is not what the local people expect or desire.

Under some circumstances, the emphasis upon the national nature of the program is effective, whereas in other circumstances strong appeal to local loyalties is much the better tactic. At what stage, one would like to know, in political or social development does the national government become a boon to a program rather than a burden, and how closely is this tied in with rising nationalism?

Somehow or other, if community development programs are to be conducted rationally and effectively, we will need to know more about the interaction between the programs and the features of the social context which have been mentioned here.

A DEVELOPMENT PROGRAM AS A SYSTEM OF SOCIAL ACTION

The social context has been presented in greatly abbreviated form to indicate an awareness of the complexity of variables that surround and intervene in any efforts to modify community life. The main burden of this chapter, however, is to look in a much more detailed way at a development program itself as a system of social action. If we do not understand what it is and how it operates, then we do not know at what points it makes useful contact with its social environment. The crux of the problem then becomes: How does one analyze such a program sociologically? In some ways it is unfortunate that such an effort to systematize and characterize squeezes much of the excitement and drama out of the effort to purify village wells in India, to teach Andean peasants to read, to instruct African mothers how to provide proper nutrition to their children, and to persuade Philippine villagers to construct a farm-to-market road. Now is the time, however, to look for and test whatever is generic to the community development experience, to develop what theory is possible, and to build practice upon this theory. We are concerned here with the contributions which sociologists can make to this theory.

We view a community development program in sociological perspective if we analyze it with reference to at least three features, although we recognize that the list of pertinent features could be greatly expanded. The three to be stressed here are: the program as a network of social relationships, as an organized set of goals and means, and as a series of operations or problems to be solved if the program is to be viable.

The Program as a Network of Social Relationships

This network can be viewed chronologically in terms of how it developed from the ideas and involvement of just a few people to the inclusion of many people or it can be taken as "a going concern" and looked at in its totality at a given point in time. The growth of a program, though frequently tied in with the enthusiasm and initiative of a single individual or a small group, is a complex process. Much attention has been given recently to the concept of stages of development, although some of the description of stages fails to take into account the fact that the growth involves the construction of a social network.[31] We need much more research to establish, particularly in non-Western societies, how such programs come into existence.

First, we have to differentiate between the national programs and the local programs. The national programs, based perhaps on successful local experience with this approach, follow a formula that characterizes most governmental efforts. Some official is persuaded that a community development program would be a good thing for the country. He sets about involving other officials, either those under or over him or those in coordinate positions in appropriate ministries or burcaus. Committees are set up and out of their deliberations a structure is devised and appropriations sought. This structure can be viewed at different levels. There is the line or bureaucratic set of relationships which appears on the table of organization. This in itself opens up a vast area for inquiry, since there are specified relationships to be studied in great detail. One might argue, in fact, that one does not understand a national program sociologically unless all of the possible relationships have been carefully observed and are understood. A few of these generic relationships include:

The director (may be a cabinet minister) and the associate directors (with chief administrative responsibility)
The associate directors and regional directors
The regional directors and subject-matter specialists who are assigned to or employed by the program
The regional directors and the regional political officials
The district directors and the community development workers
The specialists and the community development workers
The specialists and the villagers
The community development worker and the local intelligentsia

The community development workers and local council
      representatives
The local council representatives and fellow villagers

The picture can be further complicated by placing foreign technical assistance personnel at various levels in what may, unfortunately, be very ill-defined roles.

If we turn from the national program to one which is limited
to one or, at most, a few communities, we find that it too is a
system of social relationships. Often, there is the catalyst from
outside in the form of a school teacher, a doctor, a community
organizer, or an agricultural specialist who has established rap-
port with a few local people. These people, already in relationship with fellow villagers, begin to set up specialized relationships with some of these villagers in the interest of getting the
program under way. As they need additional help, they bring in
more people to play fairly definite roles. At last, when the program is fully staffed or assignments are worked out, it goes into
operation, hopefully establishing constructive relationships between the program personnel and the particular public whose
support or cooperation is most sought. Here again, there are
specific relationships to be studied, with most of these also
being significant in a national program as well:

Person in charge of program and his chief assistants
Professional personnel (if any) and lay volunteers[32]
Committee chairmen and committee members
Program representative (may be local villager) and the target
      group (householder, mother, farmer, etc.)
Person in charge and the representatives of communication
      media
Person in charge and local officials
Professional personnel (if any) and local intelligentsia

These examples are enough to demonstrate that any community development program, whether national or local in scope,
can be broken down into its social structure, its network of
social relationships.[33] Far too often, such programs are viewed
only as a set of activities without any comprehension that these
activities flow through a social mechanism or arrangement
which has been set up for purposes of accomplishing the program.

Now that these relationships have been pointed out, it is in
order to discuss more fully just how one goes about analyzing
them. It is obvious that in such an analysis one is not talking

about the connections between two persons, such as Mr. Smith and Mr. White, but between two statuses, such as program director and assistant director, irrespective of what their names or their personalities may happen to be. We are thus dealing with generalized statuses.[34] Theoretically, relationships are possible between any two statuses involved in the program, although many of these would not be significant for the program's operation. The clerical staff in the central office may have little contact with local villagers, although both are an integral part of the total program. At the same time, the advantage of carrying out as extensive an analysis as possible is the light shed on the importance of some relationships not previously considered so significant. The informal arrangements which develop in an official bureaucracy are part of the social structure too, and their study may show that the incumbents of certain statuses are much inclined to work out such informal patterns, even bypassing some of the formal arrangements.

Therefore, an identification of all of the possible statuses in a program suggests those which are most likely to be connected in order to get the job done. Some programs have high status density in that there is great specialization of labor and many different kinds of titles. Others are not nearly so highly structured.

A social relationship, however, is more than two connected statuses; it also involves roles which those in one status are supposed to play vis-a-vis those in other statuses.[35] One of the problems in the formation of a program of community development is the clarification of just what these roles are to be: who is to do what and how? A director directs, a community organizer organizes, an official officiates, a specialist practices his specialty but such general characterization has little meaning unless specified in terms of how the director behaves toward the regional director and vice versa, or how the community organizer behaves toward the villager and vice versa. In other words, there is an interaction component to a social relationship expressed in expected roles. Role conflict ensues when people have different ideas about the behavior for one occupying a given status in a definite social situation. These points are elaborated in every introductory sociology course throughout the land, but have been only sparingly applied to the analysis of social action programs.[36]

Another clue to the roles in a relationship are the job descriptions which may be prepared for a particular status. Some roles (behavior patterns) apply to those in one type of status, whereas other roles come into play in interaction with those in other statuses. Jack D. Gray has provided a detailed job description of what each kind of worker in the Indian community development program should do.[37] Ernest E. Neal has done the same for the role of the community development advisor.[38] Care should always be taken to prepare such descriptions in terms of what people actually do as well as what they are expected to do, for the explanation of any discrepancies between the actual and expected provides useful operational insights. As a matter of fact, for almost every status that one frequently finds in social action programs one could also find in the literature statements about their roles.

A developing program, however, develops its own rules, or norms, which set limits on how these roles are to be played. The director has authority but the rules circumscribe this authority; the community organizer is supposed to persuade the peasants to accept innovation but there are limits set on methods he may use in achieving this "persuasion." There are norms, too, which often govern the extent to which community development personnel can become involved in political activity, especially at election time. One, in trying to understand any of the relationships, thus needs not only to see the prescribed roles but also to describe the emerging norms. Oftentimes the program norms correspond with the community or social norms but need not necessarily do so.

Furthermore, any social relationship is related to the value system which is relevant to that relationship. For instance, the status hierarchy—or the superordinate-subordinate position of statuses apropos each other—is related to the value system. The deference which peasants show the educated man and his assumption of superiority over them reflects the value system; the tendency of the specialist to feel superior to the newly developing cadre of community development workers is also such a reflection, as is the assumed superiority of men over women in traditional societies. For any given relationship being studied, therefore, one can inquire as to what major values seem most relevant, realizing that these may vary from relationship to relationship within the program.

Nor should it be assumed that social relationships connect only statuses filled by individuals. Groups, such as committees or divisions, enter into relationships with each other and can be viewed also in terms of status, role, norms, and values.[39] In fact, a regional development board may interact with a village council in just as real a sense as would two separate individuals.

Pushing the application still further, the total community development program itself as a system of action is in competition with or in cooperation with other systems of action such as the educational system, health organizations, and other facets of government.

The analysis called for here is painstaking, detailed, and in some ways routine. But that is the way any scientific endeavor must proceed. It goes beyond mere job description in that it places incumbents of two positions in interaction and sees both positions together. This is necessary because the behavior of the incumbent of a particular status will vary as he deals with those filling different kinds of statuses. An official as official behaves differently with his superior, his secretary, and with the other personnel for which he is responsible.

The totality of all of these relationships makes up the social structure of the program. It charts not only the hierarchical nature of the structure (who is over whom in specified situations) but it spells out the expected behavior (roles) and the limitations set on this behavior (norms). Until we begin to derive more hypotheses from empirical data about social relationships in a community development program, we are not making the kind of contribution which sociologists are able to provide.

The Program as an Organized Set of Goals and Means

While the social structure of a program is taking shape, another process is at work: namely, that of formulating a statement of goals and establishing the means toward reaching those goals.[40]

The goals may be couched in terms of general amelioration or may be related to the resolution of a specific, gnawing problem, but must be incorporated in human behavior and not simply remain a paper statement.[41] These are the ends of action which tend to give it direction; once it has direction, action begins to take form since action that is directionless is also formless. Programs with no sense of movement are inclined to be those with unclarified, confused, or contradictory ends. The ends can be related to the expectations of those who participate, whether as leaders or as rank-and-file members. Where there are many divergent expectations, there is disagreement about specific goals. If some people help in a program to beautify the community while others enlist in the same program in order to increase business profits or to meet other people in the community, then that program will have rough going unless one goal receives sufficient support to give the necessary predominating direction to that program. Divergent expectations lead to a zig-zag rather than a beeline course; the more zig-zag the course, the less the program momentum. This momentum, which can be operationally defined according to various kinds of social impact, is thus related to goal-clarification and agreement as to ends. A study of many uncompleted programs would probably show that they failed to gain the necessary momentum because there was not sufficient agreement about direction. Those who did not know where the program was going applied the brakes and brought it to a standstill.

Equally important as determination of goals is the selection of appropriate means. Planned social change, of which a community development program is an excellent example, is supposedly rational change. A major test of rationality is the logical fit between ends and means. Programs as action systems also lose momentum, or may never gain it in the first place, if those involved agree on goals but disagree on means. Within the value system of any community, mediated by class position and occupational complexes, there are accepted norms of conduct which govern community development programs as well as other systems of action. To beautify a community by eliminating a slum might be a commonly accepted goal; but to follow the means of taking over the slum property without compensating the landlord or without giving some attention to alternate housing for those displaced could lead to heated controversy among the program supporters. A consideration of means thus involves not only types of methods but the social costs of these methods. A program of action, if it is to hold together as a system, must move toward accepted goals, but the path which the action follows is a function of the means chosen. For tactical reasons due to the social terrain, the course may be curved in places, but even while going around the curve people experience a sense of movement, a feeling that they are participating in a joint endeavor toward a prearranged destination.

A third element in the statement of goals is the establishment of priorities.[42] Although a distant destination may be agreed upon, there is also the need of deciding the intermediate points along the way. This is essentially what a list of priorities does. It specifies that, before one reaches certain ends, other more limited ends must be achieved first. The establishment of priorities calls by its very nature for the examination of means—both as to appropriateness and costs, leading to

reformulation of goals or ends. This recognizes the basic principle that those responsible for any system of action face alternatives or choices. A consideration of priorities early in the
program helps one anticipate and prepare for alternatives or
choices when they arise; else they must be dealt with on the
spur of the moment, frequently with less rationality than an
earlier consideration would have provided. At the same time,
no perfect course can be charted for any system of social action,
a fact calling for a reasonable degree of program flexibility to
meet unanticipated contingencies.

As is evident, the concept of momentum has been introduced
as an operational term for use in analyzing the movement toward
the program's statement of goals, assuming therein the selection
of means and the establishment of priorities.[43] I would suggest
that, with the techniques at our disposal, we would obtain a
fairly good measure of a program's momentum through time,
basing this measurement on objective criteria such as partici-
pant interest, state of morale, or discharge of individual assignments. Momentum described in these operational terms could
then be used as a concept to help us analyze the more abstract
features of ends, means, and priorities.

The Program as a Series of Operations

To the dimensions of social structure and goals-ends we now
need to add a third dimension to round out the minimal sociological treatment of a community development program. This
is the analysis of the program in terms of the operations which
keep it viable as a social system, or system of action.

What operations are indispensable for the continuity and effectiveness of a program? Again, we will seek an answer in
minimal rather than comprehensive terms. Several indispensable operations can be grouped under staffing, coordination, motivation, and adaptation, which will be taken up in turn.

Staffing

A program comes into existence and maintains itself only so
long as it consists of sufficient people to play the required roles
called for by the program. Recruitment is the operation through
which the program as a social system ensures the requisite
personnel. As far as the professional staff are concerned, they
are often appealed to with reference to the career patterns in
which they move; as far as the lay volunteers or participating

beneficiaries are concerned, a different basis for involvement is required. Recruitment is more than a one-shot effort at filling all necessary slots; it also includes the efforts made to ensure a flow of qualified people into whatever openings may occur. This operation, therefore, is crucial not only at the beginning but at any stage of expansion of the program or of giving it new directions.

But those connected with the program, once recruited, need to experience socialization, or the operation which prepares them specifically for their constructive participation in this particular program. In some cases, it means imparting new skills, inculcating the underlying values, and providing an insight into how each individual fits into the social network that is the program.[44] In community development this operation, usually referred to as training, is discussed in a growing body of literature, but many of these documents fail to see training as part of an over-all system requirement of the program.[45] One cannot assume that even so-called "experienced people" will know just how to play their roles in effective fashion unless they go through some socialization process, which any good program should provide. There will have to be variations within this training since different people are being asked to assume different statuses. Time needs to be taken to explain to local villagers or townspeople just what their contributions can be and why it is best that they be made in certain ways—providing, of course, such people express a desire to be a part of the program. The professional person, such as a social worker or community development expert, spends so much time learning how to get along with a client that he seldom remembers that a client has to spend some time learning how to play an expected role toward the professional person.

Once recruited and trained, there must be allocation of personnel to the statuses throughout the program. Training may assist in recruiting and selection in that those who are incapable or disinterested may be dropped from the program; it also assists those responsible for the program to get a better understanding of the skills and role-playing abilities of the new personnel so that they can be more wisely placed in the program. Any soundly conceived program as part of the allocation operation has understudies (such as vice-chairmen) who assist those in important posts and who can in time advance into these posts. The hierarchy need not be rigid but every position should lead to another calling for a wider measure of influence and control.

Coordination

To staff, however, is not to organize.[46] The different positions have to be related to each other in terms of <u>allocation of power</u>, an operation which can be equated with leadership for purposes of this analysis. Some people have more responsibilities than others—are held accountable if the program fails to achieve its objectives, and therefore have greater means at their disposal to carry through their ideas and judgments. Any field of power, though continuously fluid, does strike certain balances or tend to center about certain offices more frequently than elsewhere. Leadership is the combination of the power of an office with the style in which an incumbent exercises the power of that office. Thus it involves location in the structure as well as the personality of the leader. In training, it is important that people in specific conditions be given not only a clear idea of the power inherent in their position but also in those positions with which they are related. They should also be assisted in developing a "style" for the exercise of this power, particularly if the program is cross-cultural in character.

But power becomes bottled up, is frustrated, unless there is a relatively free flow of <u>communication</u>, another operation inherent in social systems.[47] Where program structures are large, reporting by means of memoranda, staff conferences, or other forms are necessary. Coordination in a system is the mechanism to facilitate the flow of authority, through communication, from status to status in keeping with the relative position of each status. In other words, simply to inform everybody about everything does not coordinate a program; the information must be relevant to the job to be performed.

Motivation

A program that was one hundred per cent effective, would be little more than dull routine.[48] Assuming that it had been soundly conceived, correctly staffed with properly trained individuals who had been advantageously placed, it would move steadily toward its objectives. But human beings do not submit meekly to training, they do not willingly abide by bureaucratic rules, nor is a foolproof program ever conceived. Since these are the facts of program life, every good program builds in certain incentives which inspire people to work harder to achieve program goals; it also builds in penalties for failing to do the job which is expected. Some of this motivation is noncompetitive, in that people who are embued with the conviction that what they

are doing is significant do not need as many formal outside
pressures. If they enjoy the fellowship of colleagues and the
satisfaction that comes from getting approval of superiors or
their peers (though these may not always enshrine the same
goals), they work much more diligently in the common task. If
they dread the imposition of sanctions, they also conform.

But some motivation is based on competition: not merely
meeting with the approval of one's peers but at times surpassing
some of them in order to achieve personal (or program) ends.
Through competition, people move into higher ranks less numerous than those below and fewer than the aspirants for them.
Through competition, they achieve other kinds of rewards,
tangible and intangible, which make their exertion seem worthwhile.

Every program of action, therefore, contains—whether pur-
posely introduced or developed by chance—the operation of
social control, which has both its positive and negative sides.
People can be attracted as well as pressured to carry out the
duties essential to the successful furtherance of a program.
This can develop into a very complex problem, however, when
individual goals do not coincide, at least moderately well, with
program goals. This is seen most vividly in the difficulties
faced in enlisting the support of village leaders in an outside
program of community development, particularly when they
seem to sense that the new program may threaten the basis of
their existing authority.

Adaptation

Any social system, whether it be a family, a religious body,
or a community development program, has to adapt itself to
changing conditions if it is to survive. In this process, reality
testing, or evaluation, is an important operation.[49] Ways have
to be found of noting points of tension within the system, whether
due to internal or external causes, and finding ways of redirect-
ing the tension. This tension exists not only between individuals
or subunits within the program, but it also exists between intermediate and long-term goals, and in the alternatives available
(the means) toward these goals. Tension exists, too, when allocation of power is interrupted or diverted so that those expected
to exercise authority are not empowered to do so. Reference to
the previous discussion of the social context within which community programs operate will quickly suggest many external
friction points over which tension can arise and concerning
which adaptation must occur if the program as a system is to
move ahead reasonably well.

The consideration of external factors also reveals the need for an additional operation—namely, that of boundary maintenance. In the social world, there are many pressures by expanding groups to incorporate under their aegis other groups or programs, with the result that these assimilated programs lose their identity. As long, however, as program leaders keep clear where their program ends and some other social unit begins, they maintain the integrity of their program. This is not to say that at times a program should not merge or be absorbed, and go out of existence as a separate body. But if it is to persist, and most programs tend to continue until or even after their objectives have been met, it has to keep its boundaries clear, not only for the perspective of the outsider but for the sake of those who are staffing the program.

A final operation relevant to adaptation is innovation, or the significant modification within the program itself. The introduction of a new procedure, of a new organizational pattern, of new goals, of new activities may be the rational reaction to changing circumstances. The innovation may be an internal invention or it may be a borrowed trait from some other program, but it supposedly aids in the problem-solving process which calls for adaptation.

One advantage of thinking of the program of community development as a system of action is the task imposed on leaders to view various kinds of adaptations, or modifications of operations and structures, not simply in narrow terms affecting one small part of the program; it is necessary to ask what the other effects of the alteration will be throughout the program as a whole. Of course, not all effects can be predicted but many more can be delineated than are usually taken into account by those making the major decisions in behalf of the program.

Any detailed treatment of these operations or of the earlier sections dealing with goals and means, status-role sets, or social context has not been possible within the space limitations of this chapter. Nor, if more space were available, does it necessarily prove of service to prescribe too closely for an individual just how one should view the program as a sociological phenomenon. What can be demonstrated, however, is the need for anyone working with community development to move beyond the trite terminology usually connected with discussions of such programs to the more realistic view that these programs are made up of people interrelated to each other. If this is taken as the starting point, an individual can draw upon the rich sociological literature for his own terminology to describe this interaction and can make it as elementary or as complex as he desires. In view of the fact that there are very few research studies to report on in this connection—that is, specifically about community development programs—this presentation has undertaken to show at least one way in which the sociological dimension may be added and implemented. If one uses such an approach, then many findings not originally related to community development may be applied, for there is a theoretical scheme into which such findings may be fitted.

In summary, the proposition defended here is one which maintains that it is as important in community development to be concerned with how we view the phenomenon as it is to be concerned with what we do about it. Sociology provides a useful view with implications for what is done.

FOOTNOTES

[1] The most recent survey of the literature has been made by Arthur Dunham. He lists 62 items in the bibliography prepared for the International Review of Community Development, No. 4, 1959, pp. 223-33, and 142 items in the one prepared with Rameshwar Nath Paul for the Community Development Review, Vol. 4, No. 1, 1959. At least 25 per cent of all items attributed to persons (rather than agencies, etc.) were written by sociologists. Other fields well represented are social work, adult education, cultural anthropology. For an additional shorter bibliography, see I. Chiva, Rural Communities: Problems, Methods and Types of Research, Reports and Papers in the Social Sciences, UNESCO, No. 10, 1958.

[2] Carl C. Taylor (Chairman), Irwin T. Sanders, Alexander Leighton, Douglas Ensminger, Afif Tannous, and Clayton Whipple (USDA, 1951).

[3] Edmund deS. Brunner, Irwin T. Sanders, and Douglas Ensminger, eds., Columbia Univ. Press, New York, 1945.

[4] A useful though brief review of the community organization movement in the United States is found in Gordon W. Blackwell, "A Theoretical Framework for Sociological Research in Community Organization," Social Forces, 33:59-60, 1954. Wayland J. Hayes discusses the same in "Revolution—Community Style," Social Forces, 28:1-6, 1949. Also see Arthur F. Raper, "The Role of Pilot and Demonstration Projects in Community Development Work," statement at Bangkok Community Development Conference, March, 1956, mimeo.

[5] A brief review of what American universities and colleges are doing is contained in William G. Lyfield and Warren H. Schmidt, "Trends in Community Development—Some Results of a Survey," Internat. Rev. of Community Development, No. 4, 1959, pp. 33-40. Also see Community Development: Some Achievements in the United States and Europe, EPA Project 337, Organization for European Economic Co-Operation, Paris, March 1960.

[6]F. L. W. Richardson, Jr., and R. C. Sheldon, "Community Resettlement in a Depressed Coal Region III. The Problem of Community Change: From Company Town to Planned Resettlement," Applied Anthropology, 7:1-27, 1948 (3 principles stated); Joseph Di Franco, "Differences Between Extension Education and Community Development," Comparative Extension Publ. No. 5, 1958 (summarizes principles prepared by George M. Foster, John S. Badeau, Ernest F. Witte—30 in all); Arthur F. Raper, "Some Basic Principles of Community Development Work," statement at Iran Community Development Conference, Tehran, 1956, mimeo.

[7]United Nations, Bureau of Social Affairs, Social Progress through Community Development, New York, 1955. Also see Melvin M. Tumin, "Some Social Requirements for Effective Community Development," Community Development Review, No. 11, 1958, pp. 1-39; D. Spencer Hatch, Toward Freedom from Want, Oxford Univ. Press, Bombay, 1949; National Society for the Study of Education, Community Education: Principles and Practices from World-Wide Experience, 58th Yearbook, Part 1, Univ. of Chicago Press, Chicago, 1959; William J. Cousins, "Community Development—Some Notes on the Why and the How," Community Development Review, No. 7, 1957, pp. 24-30.

[8]The most thorough statement on this matter is Harold F. Kaufman and Lucy W. Cole, "Sociological and Social Psychological Research for Community Development," Internat. Rev. of Community Development, No. 4, 1959, pp. 193-211. Bardin H. Nelson in a chapter in Alvin L. Bertrand, ed., Rural Sociology: An Analysis of Contemporary Rural Life, McGraw-Hill, 1958, discusses the role of sociological research in community development, stressing the great need for methodological emphasis. He also refers to Harold F. Kaufman, et al., Toward A Delineation of Community Research, Miss. State College Soc. Sci. Res. Center, State College, 1954, and Roy C. Buck, "Practical Applications of Community Research: Some Preliminary Considerations," Rural Soc., 19:294-97, 1954.

Other useful sources include: Albert J. Reiss, Jr., "Some Logical and Methodological Problems in Community Research," Social Forces, 33:51-57, 1954; James W. Green and Selz C. Mayo, "A Framework for Research in the Actions of Community Groups," Social Forces, 31:320-27, 1953; Willis A. Sutton, Jr., and Jiri Kolaja, "Elements of Community Action," Social Forces, 38:325-31, 1960; James N. Young and Selz C. Mayo, "Manifest and Latent Participators in a Rural Community Action Program," Social Forces, 38:140-45, 1959; Robert W. Janes and Harry L. Miller, "Factors in Community Action Programs," Social Problems, 6:51-59, 1958; Roland L. Warren, "Toward a Theory of Community Development," paper prepared for the meeting of the Society for the Study of Social Problems, New York City, 1960.

[9]The Peace Corps has set up a facility for training community development workers because of the great number of requests coming from foreign countries, particularly in Latin America, for this kind of assistance.

[10]See A. T. Mosher, "Varieties of Extension Education and Community Development," Comp. Ext. Publ., No. 2, N.Y. State College of Agr. at Cornell Univ., December 1958. Also see Frank H. Sehnert, "A Functional Framework for the Action Process in Community Development,"

Dept. of Community Development, Southern Ill. Univ., 1961, preliminary draft, mimeo., for a most thorough analysis of the extant definitions and frameworks of community development. Also see Murray G. Ross, Community Organization: Theory and Principles, Harpers, 1955.

[11] See Eduard C. Lindeman, The Community, an Introduction to the Study of Community Leadership and Organization, The Association Press, New York, 1921. Section on "The Process of Community Action" reprinted in Autonomous Groups, Vol. 11-12, 1956. "The Second Report of the Illinois College Program in Community Development," Illinois College Bulletin, Jacksonville, Ill., Sept., 1953, p. 9, states: ". . . community development is primarily concerned with the human resources, the non-material social and spiritual qualities, that deepen the meaning of life and make possible the intelligent development and use of material resources. The concern of "community activists" with the realm of values and religion, as well as with the use of knowledge to give the local community its former authority is mentioned in "Leadership and Authority in the Local Community," written by the Preparatory Commission on Autonomous Groups and Mental Health, Autonomous Groups Bulletin, 7-8, 1952, pp. 7-9.

[12] Irwin T. Sanders, "Theories of Community Development," Rural Soc., 23:1-12, 1958. Selz C. Mayo states that community development may be viewed as a social movement in "An Approach to the Understanding of Rural Community Development," Social Forces, 37:95-101, 1958.

[13] Afif I. Tannous, "Assumptions and Implications of 'Community Development' in Underdeveloped Countries," Human Organization, 13:2-4, 1954.

[14] Arthur J. Todd, Theories of Social Progress: A Critical Study of the Attempts to Formulate the Conditions of Human Advance, Macmillan, 1918, p. 93.

[15] J. W. Bennett, "Introduction: Planned Change in Perspective," Human Organization, 18:2-4, 1959.

[16] A most interesting cross-cultural comparison of community development in Western Europe and the United States is found in the report of EPA Project 337 (Organization for European Economic Co-Operation) under the title Community Development: Some Achievements in the United States and Europe, Paris, 1960. Factors fostering community development in the United States are thought to be: decentralization in government and industry, strong community spirit, attitude toward government authorities, strong role of private enterprise, limited role of local government, the human factor. Under the third factor, above, the report, p. 8, states: "The result of this community spirit from pioneer days is that if something has to be done in an American community, i.e., in a village or town community, the local inhabitants prefer to do the job themselves rather than have the local authorities do it for them."

For a discussion of the strengthening of the local commune in Yugoslavia as an agent of local improvement and political action see E. Pusic, "Basic Principles of Community Development in Yugoslavia," Internat. Rev. of Community Development, No. 5, 1960, pp. 171-76.

[17] Curtis and Dorothy Mial, "Community Development—USA," Internat. Rev. of Community Development, No. 4, 1959, p. 14.

For a careful roundup of latest thinking by numerous specialists in community development see Arthur Dunham, "The Outlook for Community Development—An International Symposium," Internat. Rev. of Community Development, No. 5, 1960, pp. 33-55. In the same publication, pp. 99-106, Kenneth D. Benne treats "Ideas and Communities," bringing out the increasing interdependence in the modern world.

[18a]"Trends in Community Development—Some Results of a Survey," Internat. Rev. of Community Development, No. 4, 1959, p. 34.

[19a]"Some Observations on the Application of Community Development to the Settlements of Northern Saskatchewan" (mimeo., no date), p. 11.

[20]For a different cultural orientation, see Murray A. Straus, "Cultural Factors in the Functioning of Agricultural Extension in Ceylon," Rural Soc., 18:249-56, 1953; and Paul S. Taylor, Community Development, Technical Lecture No. 10, United Nations Command, Office of the Economic Coordinator for Korea, August 1958.

[21]See Douglas Ensminger, "Community Development and Its Contribution to National Development," Report of the Inter-Regional Conference on Community Development and Its Role in Nation Building, Seoul, Korea, May 1961, pp. 21-33.

[22]Ellery Foster distinguishes between two basic approaches: (1) programs of specialized aid planned for people by experts, and (2) programs designed to stimulate a process of planning by people themselves to help them realize their own potentialities. "Planning for Community Development Through Its People," Human Organization, 12:5, 1953.

[23]Evidence of self-help and the service motif, however generated, is found in publications such as the following: W. A. King and J. W. Fanning, Community Development in Georgia, Univ. of Ga. College of Agr. Ext. Bul. 565, Rev., June 1951; W. Phillip Shatts, Planning Better Communities in the Metropolitan St. Louis Area, Metropolitan Plan Assn., Inc., St. Louis, Mo., 2nd ed., 1955; Community Adult Education of the Extension Service, What Some Communities Have Done for Themselves: A Catalog of Community Activities, Univ. of Mich., School of Education, 1951; Teamwork Makes Better Communities in Rural Tennessee, Univ. of Tenn., Agr. Ext. Serv., 1956, mimeo.; Carolina Power and Light Company, For a Finer Carolina in '56, 1956; Donald R. Fessler, "Organizing Community Improvement Clubs," V.P.I. Agr. Ext. Serv., Bul. 211, 1954; M. B. Clinard, "The Delhi Pilot Project in Urban Community Development," Internat. Rev. of Community Development, No. 7, 1961, pp. 161-70.

[24]For a stimulating recent article on the community, see Conrad Arensberg, "The Community as Object and as Sample," American Anthropologist, 63:241-64, 1961. Also see Willis A. Sutton, Jr., and Jiri Kolaja, "The Concept of Community," Rural Soc., 25:197-203, 1960.

[25]The kind of information useful in this connection is presented in Paul W. Barkley, "The Changing Role of Some Communities in South-Central Kansas," Co-operative Ext. Serv., Kans. State Univ., Jan. 1962.

[26]The first use of the term "change target" is generally attributed to Ronald Lippitt, Jeanne Watson, and Bruce Westley, The Dynamics of Planned Change, Harcourt, Brace, 1958.

In one sense, most of the studies of the adoption of farm and home practices are studies of the change targets and the processes by which they are reached. See Santi Priya Bose: "Characteristics of Farmers Who Adopt Agricultural Practices in Indian Villages," Rural Soc., 26: 138-45, 1961.

In this consideration of local social values one must not lose sight of the values of those responsible for the program, as pointed out under the discussion of goals. Such values come to the fore in such volumes as Education for Better Living: The Role of the School in Community Literature, 1957 Yearbook on Education Around the World, Office of Education, U.S. Dept. of Health, Education and Welfare, Bul. 1956, No. 9. An explicit value is that schools should be active agents of social change, which places the relationships of school teachers to others in the community in a specialized light.

[27]A helpful statement about the nature of professional consultation with communities, based on the analysis of sixteen community records, is Daniel J. Schler, "Experimentation on Community Processes," unpublished paper presented to the Midwest Sociological Society, April 12-14, 1962.

[28]For more on this see Irwin T. Sanders, "The Contribution of the Specialist to Community Development," Jour. of Ed. Soc., 29:151-63, 1955.

Also see H. Curtis Mial, "The Role of the Consultant," dittoed paper prepared for the Eastern Area Staff Conference, The American National Red Cross, September 1958, 9 pages.

[29]Eugene A. Wilkening, in his introductory note to an issue of Rural Soc., 23:97-102, 1958, devoted to social aspects of practice adoption, states: "As sociologists we should not limit our concern to an understanding of specific technological behavior. The range of technological behavior is so wide that we will not be able to make generalizations that apply much beyond the specific type of practice in a particular sociocultural setting. What needs to be taken into account is the personality, farm, familial, educational, community, and other systems as functioning units, with goals, norms, statuses, and roles defined to show how acceptance of innovations fits into these on-going systems." (P. 100). Harold F. Kaufman is developing an interactional conception of community as indicated by his article under that title in Social Forces, 38:8-17, 1959.

[30]E. J. Niederfrank has drawn up a helpful list of associations which have a bearing on community development. He classifies them according to I. General farm organizations; II. Agricultural commodity associations or producer groups; III. Cooperative marketing and purchasing associations; IV. Public agency-sponsored organizations (here he places Extension); V. Civic and social organizations (including General Federation of Women's Clubs, Chambers of Commerce, League of Women Voters, etc.); VI. Health and welfare organizations; VII. Community development clubs and councils. "Rural Associations and Community Development," Internat. Rev. of Community Development, No. 4, 1959, pp. 179-85.

Useful analysis of the "external agent" in change is found in the writings of Roland L. Warren: "Toward a Reformulation of Community Theory," Human Organization, 15:8-11, 1956; "Group Autonomy and Community Development," Autonomous Groups, 15, 1959-60. T. R. Batten has also written on "Interaction between National Agencies and

Local Groups," Autonomous Groups, 15, 1959-60. Pertinent, but at quite a different level of analysis, are publications that set forth resources from outside the community to be called upon by leaders of various programs. See A Handbook for Improving Iowa's Communities, Institute of Public Affairs of the State Univ. of Iowa, Iowa City, 1957.

[31]For a useful review of the literature on stages in community development, see George M. Beal, "Social Action: Instigated Social Change in Large Social Systems," Chap. 7, in this volume.

Readers will see numerous resemblances between this chapter and some of the other excellent studies of social action models and community development stages. See especially: George Beal and Harold Capener, "A Social Action Model," unpublished manuscript, 1958; Mildred C. Barry, "A Theoretical Framework for Community Organization," Health Education Monographs, No. 3, 1959; Seba Eldridge, The Dynamics of Social Action, Public Affairs Press, Washington, D.C., 1952; James W. Green and Selz C. Mayo, "A Framework for Research in Action of Community Groups," Social Forces, 31:320-27, 1953; Charles R. Hoffer, "Social Action in Community Development," Rural Soc., 23:43-51, 1958; John B. Holland, Kenneth E. Tiedke, and Paul A. Miller, "Theoretical Model for Health Action," Rural Soc., 22:149-55, 1957; Harold F. Kaufman, Willis A. Sutton, Jr., Frank D. Alexander, and Allen D. Edwards, "Toward a Delineation of Community Research," Social Science Studies, Community Series No. 4, Soc. Sci. Res. Center, Miss. State College, May 1954; Christopher Sower, John Holland, Kenneth Tiedke, and Walter Freeman, Community Involvement: The Webs of Formal and Informal Ties that Make for Action, The Free Press, Glencoe, Ill., 1957.

The Near East Foundation, with extensive work in rural reconstruction since World War I, views the evolution of most programs as consisting of three stages: exploratory, the period of demonstrations, the period of integration. See "Suggested Criteria for Evaluating Certain Types of Technical Assistance Programs," Foundation mimeo., Feb. 1957, 5 pages.

[32]For a classic study in this connection see David L. Sills, The Volunteers: Means and Ends in a National Organization, The Free Press, Glencoe, Ill., 1957.

[33]The energy that has gone into the development of community councils in such states as Michigan and Wisconsin, to cite but two, is really an effort to help work out social relationships among representatives of organizations or sections of the community. In some cases the organization of a community council becomes the chief end if those responsible fail to see the council in the larger context of social action.

[34]The diverse statuses in a program are shown in the following paragraph, taken from an article by William J. Cousins:

"Whenever countries have decided to undertake Community Development on a large scale, there is the necessity of having administrators with a broad and balanced view of the various aspects of development. This means at the top, middle, and lowest levels. If these people are not available, the existing personnel must be reoriented to fit into this programme. They must be generalists who respect and are able to work closely with and coordinate the efforts of various subject-matter specialists. They must be specialists in the sense of having special ability and skills to do the job. These skills may spring from broad experience in administration, social work or social science. . . . The common characteristics of all of these Community Development Technicians will be their broad understanding of the integrated nature of the Community Development process and their sensitivity to and ability to work with people—whether they be administrators, subject specialists, or cultivators." "Community Development—Some Notes on the Why and the How," Community Development Rev., December 1957, p. 27.

Jack D. Gray lists the following as the kind of workers needed for community development: a. the village extension worker; b. technical specialists; c. trainers (pre-service and in-service); d. administrators; e. policy-making officials. "Training for Community Development," Community Development Bul., September 1956, p. 44.

[35]Skillful use of role analysis is made by James W. Green in his study of community development in Pakistan. See "Success and Failure in Technical Assistance: A Case Study," Human Organization, 20:2-10, 1961. Likewise, Willis E. Sibley examines the status and roles of teachers in "Social Structures and Planned Change: A Case Study from the Philippines," Human Organization, 19:209-11, 1960-61.

An article by Bond L. Bible, Francena L. Nolan, and Emory J. Brown on "Consensus on Role Definition of the County Extension Executive Committee Member," Rural Soc., 26:146-56, 1961, has the following summary:

"In general, most executive committee members and extension agents felt that executive committee members should assist with all areas of extension program development and functioning of the organization, i.e., local policy making, program planning, program execution, and program evaluation. However, extension agents expected committee members to assume more responsibility than the members wanted in planning and executing the program. Committee members generally wanted more responsibility than the agents defined for them in establishing administrative policies and evaluating the program. They tended to emphasize their control function rather than their planning function. In the area of committee-agent relationships committee members indicated greater dependency upon the leadership of extension agents than the latter group would like them to have." (P. 154.)

Needless to say, such analysis sheds considerable light on the problem of role repertoire in the committee member-extension agent relationship, which is a key one in this type of program.

Also see Eugene A. Wilkening, "Consensus in Role Definition of County Extension Agents Between the Agents and Local Sponsoring Committee Members," Rural Soc., 23:184-97, 1958.

[36]Roland L. Warren makes a useful distinction between the "task-oriented" and the "process-oriented" types of community development practitioners. "Toward a Theory of Community Development," paper already cited. William W. Biddle discusses the status of "community educator" in his Adult Development: Some Guidelines for Community Educators, Tenth Annual Report of the Program of Community Dynamics, Earlham College, 1957.

[37]Jack D. Gray, op. cit., (note 34), pp. 45-49.

[38]Ernest E. Neal, "The Role of the Community Development Advisor," Community Development Bul., September 1956, pp. 54-61.

[39]John S. Holik and V. Wayne Lane studied the group processes involved in community development in a Missouri community. See "A Community Development Contest as a Catalytic Agent in Social Action," Rural Soc., 26:157-69, 1961.

[40]The problem of goals is discussed in two helpful studies: Alexander Fanelli and Raymond Payne, "A Study of Organized Communities in Mississippi," Social Science Studies, Community Ser. No. 1, Soc. Sci. Res. Center, Miss. State College, June 1953; Selz C. Mayo, "Organized Rural Communities: A Series of Case Studies from Western North Carolina," N. C. State College, Agr. Exp. Sta., Progress Report Rs-20, 1954.

[41]For an interesting though brief statement of the connection between power commitment and ends (utilitarian and symbolic) see Roy C. Buck, "Some Fundamental Problems in Community Development," Mobilizing Forces for Dynamic Action in Country Life, Proceedings the American Country Life Association, 1958.

[42]For a discussion of the setting of action priorities in Ind͏ see J D. Mezirow, "Community Development as an Educational P͏ ͏ess " Internat. Rev. of Community Development, No. 5, 1960, ͏

[43]Some rural sociologists are concerning themsel͏ ͏ ͏ ͏ ͏ne study of goals and their relation to social action. See Ch͏ ͏ ͏. Ramsey, Robert A. Polson, and George E. Spencer, "Val͏ ͏ and the Adoption of Practices," Rural Soc., 24:35-47, 1959; an͏ ͏ ͏. Wilkening and Donald E. Johnson, "Goals in Farm Decisio͏ ͏ ͏ ͏g as Related to Practice Adoption," Res. Bul. 225, Univ ͏ ͏is. ͏61.

[44]The question of trai͏ ͏ people ͏ether lay or professional, for programs of commu͏ ͏ ͏evelopm ͏ might be viewed in part as filling out the needed ͏ ͏ repertoire ͏ the statuses that they will occupy. This is ill ͏ ͏ated by an ex͏ ͏nation of articles contained in such publications as Internati͏ ͏ Review of Community Development whose issue of No. 3, 1959, ͏ ͏evoted entirely to "Training Local Leaders." Ibrahim Shamim, i͏ ͏ne of the articles, discusses the approach used in Pakistan. It is ͏ ͏eresting to compare this article with James W. Green, "Success and ͏ ͏ailure in Technical Assistance," Human Organization, 20:2-10, 1͏ ͏, which also deals with Pakistan's AID Program.

[45]Ill͏ ͏rative documents are William W. Biddle, "Training of Commun͏ ͏ Educators: Earlham College Contribution to Community Development," Earlham College Bul., Fall 1958; J. Paul Leagans, "India's Experience with Training in Extension Education for Community Development," Comparative Ext. Publ. No. 15, N.Y. State College of Agr. at Cornell Univ., May 1961; United Nations, "Experiments in Training for Community Development," May 1957, mimeo.

[46]For publications dealing with coordination and leadership see Charles Freeman and Selz C. Mayo, "Decision Makers in Rural Community Action," Social Forces, 35:319-22, 1957; John M. Fenley, ed., "Thoughts on Administration in Extension and Rural Development," Comparative Ext. Publs., Mimeo. Release No. 8, April 1961; "Training Local Leaders," complete issue of Internat. Rev. of Community Development, No. 3, 1959; A. V. S. Lochhead, "Administrative Co-ordination of Community Development Programmes," reprinted in Community Development Rev., No. 4, March 1957.

[47]See J. Paul Leagans, "The Communication Process in Rural Development," Comparative Ext. Publs., Mimeo., Release No. 6, March 1961. Also see Charles L. Cleland, "Characteristics of Social Systems Within Which Selected Types of Information Are Transmitted," Rural Soc., 25:212-18, 1960; S. A. Rahim, "Diffusion and Adoption of Agricultural Practices: A Study in a Village in East Pakistan," Tech. Publ. No. 7, Comilla, Pakistan Academy for Village Development, 1961.

[48]An excellent summary of fundamental principles is found in Howard W. Beers, "Motivation for Community Development," Health Education Monographs, No. 3, 1959, pp. 2-7.

[49]For three examples of effective evaluation see: American Friends Service Committee, Social and Technical Assistance in India: An Interim Report, Philadelphia, December 31, 1956; Howard W. Beers, "Survival Capacity of Extension Work in Greek Villages," Rural Soc., 15:274-82, 1950; Howard W. Beers, "Program Evaluation in India," Rural Soc., 25:431-41, 1960.

PART FOUR

The Opportunities

II

James H. Copp

The Future of Rural
Sociology in an
Industrialized Society*

THE PRECEDING CHAPTERS have summarized the state of
affairs in rural society and the state of knowledge in several fields of rural sociology. Given this basis, what can
be said about the future of rural sociology? What are the hazards? What are the opportunities? Before undertaking a
modest exploration of these questions it may be valuable to attempt a characterization of the nature of rural sociology.

This book has demonstrated again that rural sociology does
not have a distinct subject matter. There is no division of
sociology which is not dealt with in some respect by rural
sociologists. Although there is no division of sociology which
is not involved in rural sociology, the discipline of rural
sociology is even broader in scope, including work in social
psychology, economics, and political science, wherever the
problems may lead. This lack of concern with the limits of
academic fields is a reflection of the nature of problems, which
do not stop at academic boundaries.

This, in turn, leads to a major distinguishing characteristic
of rural sociologists. Rural sociology embodies a distinct attitude or state of mind. Rural sociologists, as an occupational
group, have not avoided applied contexts for their work. Indeed,
they display a strong problem orientation, maintaining their
heritage of concern with rural social problems.[1] In other words,
the distinct flavor of rural sociology as an occupational

---

*Several of the ideas discussed in this epilogue were first presented
in M. E. John and James H. Copp, "Rural Sociology in an Industrialized
Society," a paper read at the fifty-fourth annual meeting of the American
Sociological Association in Chicago, September 3, 1959.

subculture lies in its emphasis on problem-oriented research and application. This has been regarded as one of the grave limitations of the profession, but it has also been one of the great strengths. The perspective of rural sociologists may often have been naive, but it has rarely been out of touch with the existential world.[2]

A second major distinguishing characteristic of rural sociology lies in the nature of its work site. Although the substantive nature of the work may differ little from that of sociology in general, rural sociologists perform their work in a particular situation—the rural areas. The context in which they work makes for a difference in degree—not of kind—between rural and other sociologies. The phenomena dealt with by rural sociologists have certain peculiarities, by virtue of being rural, that should be mentioned.[3]

The one most distinguishing attribute of rural areas is that they are beyond the city. Rural sociology might be characterized as the sociology of the hinterland.[4] If we may assume, and the supporting evidence is substantial, that power, innovation, and communications are concentrated primarily in the large city or metropolis, then we have the city as the active, initiating agent and the country as the passive, resisting agent in the continual elaborations taking place in civilization. Few revolutions, political or intellectual, have succeeded without the collaboration of the city. On the other hand, most reforms or innovations are accomplished over opposition disproportionately concentrated in rural areas.[5]

In other words, in rural areas the pace of life is slower, communication is more difficult, occupational interests are focussed on the local place and family, the rate of interaction is lower,[6] and legal restrictions are fewer. These conditions make for a style of life conducive to particularism, diffuseness, affectivity, localism, and tradition. This is not an argument for a "rural" type of person; rather, the argument is that the ecological conditions under which people live and make their living outside the large cities (in rural areas) lead to differences in degree between rural and metropolitan people. The country may become urbanized, but it will never become "urban."

These considerations lead to the proposition that it is the city that has been responsible for the existence and relevance of rural sociology. Only when the city has come into intense competition with rural areas for people, space, or moral loyalties has there been a strong interest in rural sociology. It is interesting to note that in the United States the number of rural sociologists in a state and the amount of activity in the field is generally directly related to the urbanization of the state.[7] Rural sociology is strongest in such states as New York, Pennsylvania, Ohio, Wisconsin, and Michigan; it is weakest in the rural states of New England, parts of the South, and many of the Great Plains and Mountain States. The strong suspicion arises that rural sociology derives its relevance from the city. These observations lend credence to the assertions that as our society becomes increasingly urbanized, rural sociologists will not become extinct as an occupational type and that rural sociology is not doomed to obsolescence.

Several chapters in this book have pointed to the changing rural-urban distribution of power in our society. This, in the long run, will have repercussions on the traditional relationship between rural sociology and the Colleges of Agriculture. The repercussions may at times appear debilitating, but in the long run they may prove to be liberating, releasing rural sociologists from preoccupations fixed by the College of Agriculture milieu.[8] These repercussions will force the rural sociologist to look farther afield for his clients, to locate new sources of funding, and to widen his scope of responsibility to the total society. Actually, all of these transitions already are well under way, and their gradualism has precluded sharp dislocations in the discipline. Let us now turn to a consideration of those areas in which rural sociology can be expected to make a significant contribution to our industrialized society.

Although the United States is regarded as a highly urbanized country, ninety-two per cent of the land is utilized for agricultural and forest purposes.[9] Spatially, more than nine-tenths of this country is hinterland and under rural forms of social organization. Knowledge and understanding of the rural portion of our country will become increasingly important as urban people look to rural areas for recreation and residence. No one is more strategically located nor better qualified to make this interpretation than the rural sociologist. Thus our first opportunity is in continuing and improving the present program of work.

A second opportunity for rural sociologists lies in the sociological analysis of the changing structure of agriculture. It is strange to note that rural sociology lacks a sociology-of-occupations tradition of research dealing with rural occupations. Such analyses will become more important in the future as the farmer becomes a more specialized and select occupational type. Again, rural sociologists are connected with one of the

last areas of enterprise changing from familistic cottage industry to rationalistic factory industry, yet they are not exploiting
their opportunities for systemic analyses of structural changes.
Rural sociology has attempted to discharge its responsibility
for the study of social change through analyses of farm practice
adoption and mechanization. Thus far, the rural sociologist's
approach to social change has been microscopic and simplistic.[10]
There is no reason why the task should not be undertaken; never
before have the theoretical tools been as adequate.

This second opportunity leads quite logically to the third: the
opportunity to aid in agricultural adjustment. Rural sociologists
will never fulfill the sanguine expectations outlined by Heady and
Ackerman,[11] but they can contribute in an ancillary capacity to
the formation of public policy and they can provide a healthy
antidote to certain naive assumptions about the fluidity of farm
manpower. Paradoxically, the need in this area may not be so
much for additional research as in codifying what is known and
translating it into forms usable by policymakers.

A fourth opportunity for rural sociology lies in what may be
one of the most serious domestic crises of the latter part of the
twentieth century. Up to now, with woefully few exceptions,
urban uses of rural land have proceeded in an unplanned,
laissez-faire manner. Residential subdivisions of low- and
high-cost housing have invaded rural areas, and industries,
shops, and retail outlets have moved into the rural areas among
the residential subdivisions. The face of rural America surrounding our large cities has changed tremendously during the
mid-century, but it is a change that has had little direction. As
a result, our suburban and fringe areas are a jumbled confusion—we have problems of water, sewerage, noxious industries,
substandard housing, inadequate institutional facilities, and out-
moded political units, all intermixed.[12] One of the great tasks
of the remainder of the century will be correcting the follies of
the unplanned, inadequately controlled expansion of the preceding years. Conceivably, the rural sociologist has something to
contribute in unsnarling and rectifying our "sub-urban" social
organization, and in evolving new forms of municipal organization.

The next opportunity, the fifth, lies in the opposite direction.
Growth does not uniformly characterize all areas in the nation;
in fact, one half of the counties in the United States lost population between 1950 and 1960. Another thirty per cent of the
counties, although they grew, grew slower than the national
average.[13] In other words, one quarter of the counties in the

United States are growing vigorously at the expense of the other three quarters. We are faced with the paradox of runaway growth and decline or relative stagnation in the central cities and rural areas of our changing society. The policy problems are great, for the people left behind in the declining communities are frequently low in income, education, and skill, and they tend to be above average in age. Rural sociologists face a tremendous challenge to their research, consultation, and social action skills in aiding communities to adjust to changing circumstances. Unfortunately, the most serious problems of decline lie in those divisions of the nation (West North Central, East South Central, West South Central, Mountain, and South Atlantic) already inadequately staffed with professional rural sociologists.

A sixth opportunity for rural sociologists lies in the city itself. For example, the city creates problems of adjustment for hinterland people who move into the population centers. Some of our greatest "rural problems" occur within the great metropolises where Appalachian mountaineers, Southern Negroes, and Puerto Ricans are being absorbed. Much of the maladjustment of all immigrant peoples coming to the city lies in the maladaptation or breakdown of a rural style of life in an urban milieu. Historically, we have rarely looked at the migrant as a displaced rural person. To the extent that rural sociologists are masters of their subject matter, they should be of great assistance in furthering the adaptation of migrants. Another example of opportunities for rural sociologists in the city lies in the study of the actual and potential consumers of goods and services produced in rural areas, whether it be food, recreation, or building lots. Urban areas also provide fruitful fields for replication and extension of generalizations developed in rural research. In addition, many of the skills developed by rural sociologists may be transferred profitably to the solution of urban problems.

Finally, a seventh opportunity for rural sociology lies outside the United States, where less developed (rural) countries are recapitulating many of the stages and problems through which this country passed. With our command of research methods and with our knowledge of the effects of industrialization on rural society we should be able to aid greatly in smoothing transformations in underdeveloped countries. Here the opportunity is twofold: application of what we know; and having a "second chance" to study changes overlooked as they took place in our own society.[14] Really, the opportunity is threefold in that the training facilities at our universities can be utilized to prepare overseas nationals as professional rural sociologists and community development leaders.

In other words, the rural sociologist, whether in his role as teacher, extension worker, community development advisor, or researcher, has a very important place in the future of our changing society. The demands are increasing rather than decreasing.[15] The seven examples of opportunities listed above are realistic extrapolations of present work and capabilities. There is work to be done; the chapters in this book exemplify the qualifications of rural sociologists for the task.

FOOTNOTES

[1] Charles J. Galpin, "The Development of the Science and Philosophy of American Rural Society," Agricultural History, 12:195-208, 1938.

[2] Cf. C. Arnold Anderson, "Trends in Rural Sociology," in Robert K. Merton, Leonard Broom, and Leonard S. Cottrell, Jr., Sociology Today, Basic Books, 1959, pp. 360-75. Though Anderson's portrait is largely accurate, it is a selective portrayal tempting a second "exercise in the sociology of knowledge."

[3] For a classic statement of rural-urban differences, see Pitirim Sorokin and Carle C. Zimmerman, Principles of Rural-Urban Sociology, Henry Holt, 1929, esp. Chaps. 2 and 13.

[4] The concepts "hinterland" and "rural" are analyzed in Lewis W. Jones, "The Hinterland Reconsidered," Amer. Sociol. Rev., 20:40-44, 1955.

[5] The above comparisons of rural and urban areas on "mental mobility" are made despite the opposite claim of Richard C. Dewey, "The Rural-Urban Continuum: Real But Relatively Unimportant," Amer. Jour. of Soc., 66:63, 1960. The interesting concept of "mental mobility" is treated by Howard Becker and Harry Elmer Barnes in Social Thought from Lore to Science, 3rd ed., Dover, New York, 1961, pp. 7-8, et passim.

[6] A comparatively recent documentation of this assertion is found in Albert J. Reiss, Jr., "Rural-Urban and Status Differences in Interpersonal Contacts," Amer. Jour. of Soc., 65:182-95, 1959.

[7] If number of members in the Rural Sociological Society in 1962 is taken as an indicator of the amount of interest and activity in the discipline in a given state, and if the percentage of the population rural in 1960 is taken as an index of rurality, there is negative Spearman rank order correlation (-.17) between membership in the Rural Sociological Society and rurality. On the other hand, for the fifty states and the District of Columbia, there is a strong positive correlation (.42) between membership and population density.

[8] Sponsorship of research always involves certain emphases and restrictions on the researcher. Experience suggests that one set of preoccupations may be substituted for another in the transition to new publics.

[9]U.S. Bureau of the Census, Statistical Abstract of the United States: 1961, 82nd ed., 1961, p. 614, Table 842.

[10]The present implicit conceptualization of social change is somewhat in conflict with the Bealer-Fliegel position. However, they personally have indicated that they do not claim to have settled the issue at the macroscopic level.

[11]Earl O. Heady and Joseph Ackerman, "Farm Adjustment Problems and Their Importance to Sociologists," Rural Soc., 24:315-25, 1959.

[12]William M. Dobriner, Class in Suburbia, Prentice-Hall, 1963, p. 22.

[13]U.S. Bureau of the Census, U.S. Census of Population: 1960, "Number of Inhabitants, United States Summary," Final Report PC (1)-1A, U.S. Govt. Print. Office, 1961, Table 25.

[14]This "second chance" also involves the opportunity to avoid repeating errors of conceptualization and procedure committed in the United States. However, as Frederick Fliegel has observed in Brazil, there seems to be a tendency to subject underdeveloped countries to underdeveloped sociology (personal communication).

[15]The number of positions for professionally trained rural sociologists has continuously increased faster than the supply. At this writing, the demand is ten to fifteen per cent greater than the supply of trained rural sociologists.

Index